Microsoft® Office User S████

Microsoft®
Excel 97
EXAM PREP™

Microsoft® Office User Specialist

Microsoft®
Excel 97
EXAM PREP™

Elizabeth Eisner Reding
Tara Lynn O'Keefe

Certification Insider™ Press
International Thomson Publishing I(T)P®

Cambridge • Albany • Bonn • Boston • Cincinnati • London • Madrid • Melbourne • Mexico City
New York • Paris • San Francisco • Singapore • Tokyo • Toronto • Washington

Microsoft Office User Specialist, Microsoft Excel 97—EXAM PREP

is published by Certification Insider™ Press and Course Technology.

Managing Editors:	Nicole Jones Pinard, Jamie Harper
Product Manager:	Jeanne Herring
Production Editor:	Nancy Shea
Developmental Editors:	Cynthia Anderson, Janice Jutras
Composition House:	GEX, Inc.
QA Manuscript Reviewers:	John McCarthy, Brian McCooey, Chris Hall, Jean-Claire Shiely, Jeff Goding
Text Designer:	Joseph Lee
Cover Designer:	Anthony Stock

© 1998 by Course Technology — I⟨T⟩P®

Course Technology is a leading expert in computer education and training and packaged this content for Certification Insider Press.

For more information contact:

Course Technology
One Main Street
Cambridge, MA 02142

International Thomson Publishing Europe
Berkshire House 168-173
High Holborn
London WC1V 7AA
England

Thomas Nelson Australia
102 Dodds Street
South Melbourne, 3205
Victoria, Australia

Nelson Canada
1120 Birchmount Road
Scarborough, Ontario
Canada M1K 5G4

International Thomson Editores
Campos Eliseos 385, Piso 7
Col. Polanco
11560 Mexico D.F. Mexico

International Thomson Publishing GmbH
Königswinterer Strasse 418
53277 Bonn
Germany

International Thomson Publishing Asia
211 Henderson Road
#05-10 Henderson Building
Singapore 0315

International Thomson Publishing Japan
Hirakawacho Kyowa Building, 3F
2-2-1 Hirakawacho
Chiyoda-ku, Tokyo 102
Japan

Disclaimer

Certification Insider Press reserves the right to revise this publication and make changes from time to time in its content without notice.

ISBN 1-57610-232-7

Printed in the United States of America

4 5 6 7 8 9 B 01 00 99 98

About the Authors

Elizabeth Eisner Reding (Gallup, NM) has authored more than twenty books specializing in Microsoft Excel, Access and PowerPoint programs. She is the founder of nerdsworth computer solutions, a company that produces computer training books, and has taught Computer Science at Santa Fe Community College, University of New Mexico at Los Alamos, and the University of New Mexico at Gallup.

Tara Lynn O'Keefe (Walnut Creek, CA) has authored two books on Microsoft Excel and one on Microsoft Office 97. She currently teaches Computer Science at Diablo Valley College in Pleasant Hill, CA. She has previously taught at Golden Gate University and Santa Rosa Junior College as well as provided corporate training in business software applications and networking.

Acknowledgments

My appreciation goes out to my husband Tim, for his undying love, support, and belief in me; to my daughters Shannon and Laura for "sharing your mom"; and to my mother, Shirlee, for a lifetime of encouragement.

—**Tara Lynn O'Keefe**

Because the production of any book is a team effort, I would like to thank the entire editorial staff at Course Technology, especially Nicole, Ann Marie, Kim, Rachel, and Brad. Also, I would like to thank Michael-bear for his support and encouragement, and Tasha and Malka for helping me meet my deadlines.

—**Elizabeth Eisner Reding**

Brief Contents

Book Contents

Excel 97

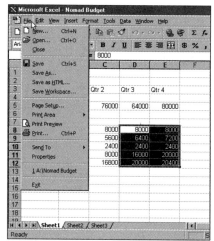

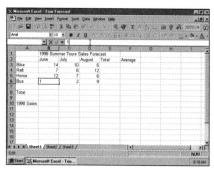

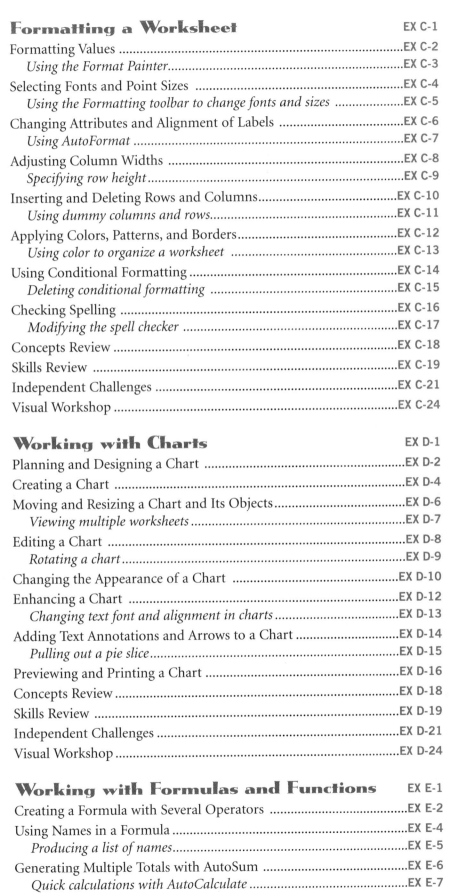
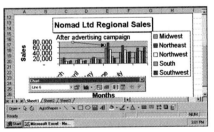

Contents

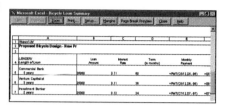

Managing Workbooks   EX F-1

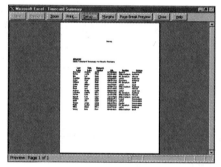

Automating Worksheet Tasks   EX G-1

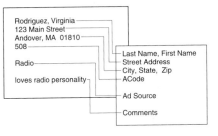

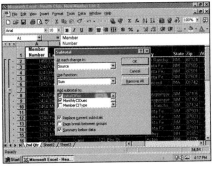

Contents

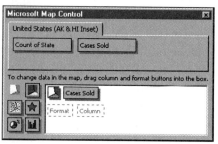

Using What-If Analysis   EX K-1

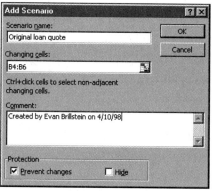

Summarizing Data with PivotTables   EX L-1

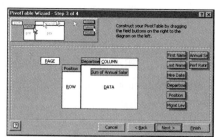

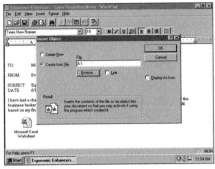

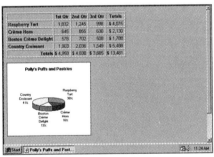

Contents

Programming with Excel

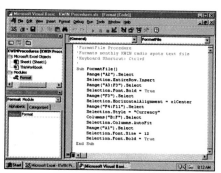

Foreword

 ## The Microsoft Office User Specialist Program

The Microsoft Office User Specialist program provides a framework for measuring end-user proficiency with Microsoft Office applications. You can become Microsoft certified at either the Proficient or the Expert level by passing a Microsoft Office User Specialist exam. For more information on the Microsoft Office User Specialist program, visit Microsoft's Web site at **www.microsoft.com/office/train_cert/**.

Why would I want to become certified?

The Microsoft Office User Specialist program provides an industry-recognized standard for measuring your mastery of Office applications. By passing one or more Microsoft Office User Specialist certification exams, you demonstrate your proficiency in a given Office application to employers, potential employers, recruiters, or staffing agencies. More and more emphasis is placed on certification as employers look for certified individuals.

How can I prepare for the Microsoft Office User Specialist exams?

The Exam Prep Series from Certification Insider Press is specifically created to prepare you for a Microsoft Office User Specialist exam. Each product in this series covers all of the required objectives of the corresponding Microsoft Office User Specialist exam. These objectives, which are determined by Microsoft, are listed on the inside front cover of this book for your information. Microsoft has approved the Exam Prep Series from Certification Insider Press as indicated by the logo on the cover. This seal of approval means that after completing any book in this series, you will be prepared to take the appropriate Microsoft Office User Specialist exam.

For the best in exam preparation, combine the Exam Prep series with the Exam Cram series. The Exam Cram Series from Certification Insider Press is also specifically created to help you pass a Microsoft Certification exam. Each product in this series is jam-packed with hundreds of test-taking tips, insight, and exam strategies that cannot be found anywhere else.

So, use the Exam Prep series to learn the necessary software skills and use the Exam Cram series to learn the latest in exam-taking strategies. Prepare to pass with Certification Insider Press today!

What is a typical test like?

The Microsoft Office User Specialist exams are based on real-world assignments and not on written tests. Using an actual document, you'll be asked to perform a series of tasks that clearly demonstrate your skills. In addition to measuring your skills, the exams also measure productivity and efficiency. All exams take less than an hour.

Where can I take a Microsoft Office User Specialist exam?

To find an ACT-Center (Approved Certification Testing Center) near you, please call IntrAtest Inc. at 1-800-933-4493.

How much does certification cost?

The estimated retail price is $50. Ask your ACT-center for more details.

Introduction

Welcome to *Microsoft Office User Specialist, Microsoft Excel 97 – EXAM PREP!* This new product from Certification Insider Press offers you a quick, visual path to Microsoft certification success. The full-color pages and step-by-step approach, along with the interactive CD-ROM, make it a perfect study guide for a Microsoft certification exam.

▶ Microsoft Certification Exams

This product has been approved by Microsoft as courseware for the Microsoft Office User Specialist program. After completing the tutorials and exercises in this book, you will be prepared to take the Proficient level Exam for Microsoft Excel 97. By passing the certification exam for a Microsoft software program, you demonstrate your proficiency in that program to employers. Microsoft Office User Specialist exams are offered at participating test centers, corporations, and employment agencies. For more information about certification, please visit Microsoft's Web site at **www.microsoft.com/office/train_cert/.**

▶ About this Product

The Exam Prep Series from Certification Insider Press is comprised of a full-color comprehensive study guide *and* an interactive CD-ROM. You can use the book by itself to prepare for the certification exam or you can take advantage of the added benefits of the CD-ROM.

▶ About the Book

What makes the book so effective at teaching software skills? It's quite simple. Each skill is presented on two facing pages, with the step-by-step instructions on the left page, and large screen illustrations on the right. You can focus on a single skill without having to turn the page. This unique design makes information extremely accessible and easy to absorb, and provides a great reference for future use.

Each lesson, or "information display," contains the following elements:

Each two-page spread focuses on a single skill.

Concise text introduces the basic principles in the lesson and integrates the brief case study.

Excel 97

Changing Attributes and Alignment of Labels

Attributes are font styling features such as bold, italics, and underlining. You can apply bold, italics, and underlining from the Formatting toolbar or from the Font tab in the Format Cells dialog box. You can also change the alignment of text in cells. Left, right, or center alignment can be applied from the Formatting toolbar, or from the Alignment tab in the Format Cells dialog box. See Table C-2 for a description of the available attribute and alignment buttons on the Formatting toolbar. Excel also has predefined worksheet formats to make formatting easier. ▰ Now that he has applied the appropriate fonts and font sizes to his worksheet labels, Evan wants to further enhance his worksheet's appearance by adding bold and underline formatting and centering some of the labels.

Steps

CourseHelp

The camera icon indicates there is a CourseHelp available with this lesson. Click the Start button, point to programs, point to CourseHelp, then click Word 97 Illustrated. Choose the CourseHelp that corresponds to this lesson.

QuickTip

Highlighting information on a worksheet can be useful, but overuse of any attribute can be distracting and make a document less readable. Be consistent by adding emphasis the same way throughout a workbook.

Time To
✔ Save

1. Press [Ctrl][Home] to select cell A1, then click the Bold button **B** on the Formatting toolbar
   The title "Advertising Expenses" appears in bold.

2. Select the range A3:J3, then click the Underline button **U** on the Formatting toolbar
   Excel underlines the column headings in the selected range.

3. Click cell A3, click the Italics button **I** on the Formatting toolbar, then click **B**
   The word "Type" appears in boldface, italic type. Notice that the Bold, Italics, and Underline buttons on the Formatting toolbar are indented. You decide you don't like the italic formatting. You remove it by clicking **I** again.

4. Click **I**
   Excel removes italics from cell A3.

5. Add bold formatting to the rest of the labels in the range B3:J3
   You want to center the title over the data.

6. Select the range A1:F1, then click the Merge and Center button ▦ on the Formatting toolbar
   The title Advertising Expenses is centered across six columns. Now you center the column headings in their cells.

7. Select the range A3:J3 then click the Center button ▤ on the Formatting toolbar
   You are satisfied with the formatting in the worksheet. Compare your screen to Figure C-8.

TABLE C-2: Attribute and Alignment buttons on the Formatting toolbar

icon	description	icon	description
B	Adds boldface	▤	Aligns left
I	Italicizes	▤	Aligns center
U	Underlines	▤	Aligns right
	Adds lines or borders	▦	Centers across columns, and combines two or more selected adjacent cells into one cell.

Quickly accessible summaries of key terms, toolbar buttons, or keyboard alternatives are connected to the lesson material. You can refer easily to this information when working on your own projects at a later time.

Hints as well as troubleshooting advice appear right where you need it – next to the step itself.

Clear, step-by-step directions, with what you type in red, explain how to complete the specific task.

Every lesson features large, full-color representations of what the screen should look like as you complete the numbered steps.

The innovative design draws your attention to the important areas of the screens.

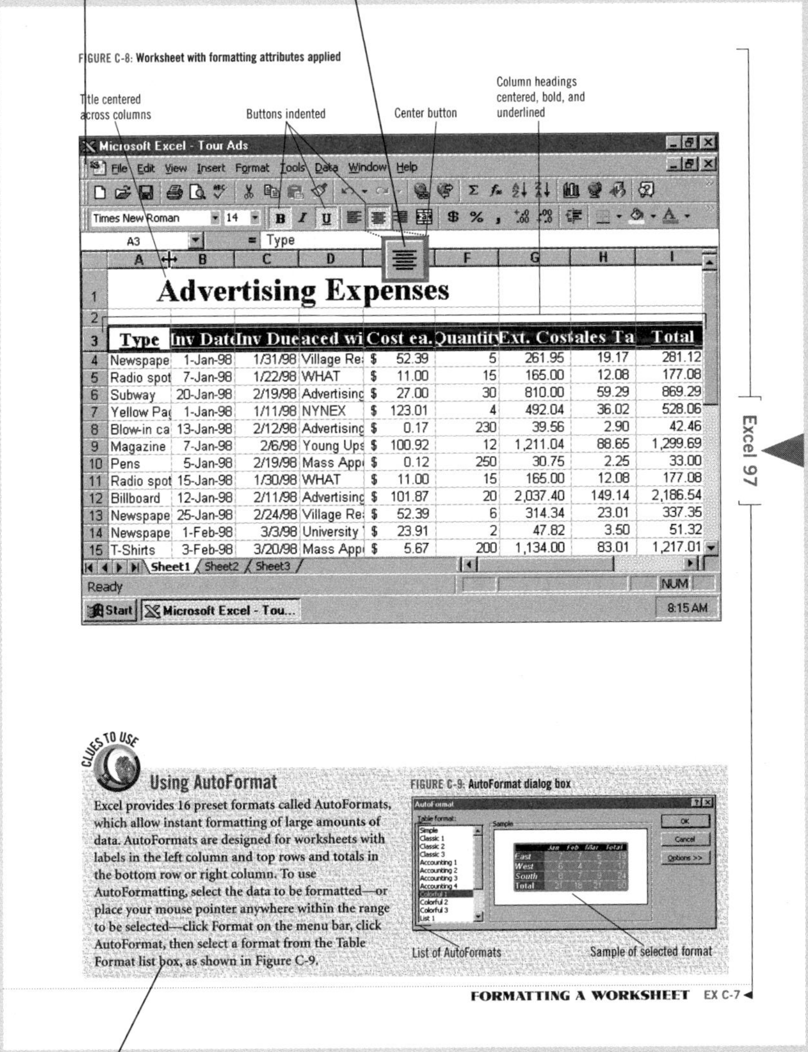

More About the Book

The two-page lesson format featured in this book provides the new user with a powerful learning experience. Additionally, this book contains the following features:

▶ **Real World Case**
The case study used throughout the book, a fictitious company called Nomad Ltd, is designed to be "real-world" in nature and introduces numerous activities that you will encounter when working with Microsoft Excel 97. A real-world case makes the problem solving process more meaningful.

▶ **Practice**
Each unit concludes with a Practice section (the blue pages) where you can quickly review what you have learned. Some of the exercises ask you to go to the Web to solve the problem, as indicated by a Web Work icon. Because Microsoft's certification exam is focused on completing documents, this section will give you the edge you need to prepare for the exam.

FIGURE C-8: Worksheet with formatting attributes applied

Title centered across columns

Buttons indented

Center button

Column headings centered, bold, and underlined

Excel 97

Advertising Expenses

Type	Inv Date	Inv Due	aced wi	Cost ea.	Quantit	Ext. Cos	Sales Ta	Total
Newspape	1-Jan-98	1/31/98	Village Re	$ 52.39	5	261.95	19.17	281.12
Radio spot	7-Jan-98	1/22/98	WHAT	$ 11.00	15	165.00	12.08	177.08
Subway	20-Jan-98	2/19/98	Advertising	$ 27.00	30	810.00	59.29	869.29
Yellow Pag	1-Jan-98	1/11/98	NYNEX	$ 123.01	4	492.04	36.02	528.06
Blow-in ca	13-Jan-98	2/12/98	Advertising	$ 0.17	230	39.56	2.90	42.46
Magazine	7-Jan-98	2/6/98	Young Ups	$ 100.92	12	1,211.04	88.65	1,299.69
Pens	5-Jan-98	2/19/98	Mass App	$ 0.12	250	30.75	2.25	33.00
Radio spot	15-Jan-98	1/30/98	WHAT	$ 11.00	15	165.00	12.08	177.08
Billboard	12-Jan-98	2/11/98	Advertising	$ 101.87	20	2,037.40	149.14	2,186.54
Newspape	25-Jan-98	2/24/98	Village Re	$ 52.39	6	314.34	23.01	337.35
Newspape	1-Feb-98	3/3/98	University	$ 23.91	2	47.82	3.50	51.32
T-Shirts	3-Feb-98	3/20/98	Mass App	$ 5.67	200	1,134.00	83.01	1,217.01

Using AutoFormat

Excel provides 16 preset formats called AutoFormats, which allow instant formatting of large amounts of data. AutoFormats are designed for worksheets with labels in the left column and top rows and totals in the bottom row or right column. To use AutoFormatting, select the data to be formatted—or place your mouse pointer anywhere within the range to be selected—click Format on the menu bar, click AutoFormat, then select a format from the Table Format list box, as shown in Figure C-9.

FIGURE C-9: AutoFormat dialog box

List of AutoFormats

Sample of selected format

FORMATTING A WORKSHEET EX C-7

Clues to Use Boxes provide concise information that either expands on the major lesson skill or describes an independent task that in some way relates to it.

About the CD-ROM

Tell me, I forget. Show me, I remember. Let me do and I know. This Chinese proverb aptly explains how the CD packaged with this book rounds out your preparation for Microsoft's certification exam. We know that people learn in three different ways – by seeing, by hearing, and by doing. This CD engages you in all three ways, using animations to present concepts, a narrator to instruct and explain, and step-by-step activities to provide hands-on practice in a safe, simulated environment.

The CD covers the basic Excel 97 skills from getting started to modifying and formatting a worksheet, and working with charts. For each topic, you first view animations and demonstrations of Excel techniques. Then you put the instruction to work by performing step-by-step examples. Along the way, every keystroke is monitored, and guidance is offered as needed.

The key features of the CD are:

Simulated Environment

The CD simulates Microsoft Excel 97, but you feel as though you're working "live." Simulation offers several benefits. You can practice skills in a safe, controlled environment so you can't get lost. Also, you don't need Excel 97 in order to use the CD. It runs under Windows 95 or Windows 3.1.

"Intelligent Technology"

This software provides the most personalized training possible. By monitoring keystrokes, the program knows when you are having trouble and provides guidance when necessary. You can also choose to have the program complete a step automatically if you get lost. The amount and level of feedback is driven by your individual needs.

Performance-Based Assessment

The CD evaluates performance of *skills*, not just knowledge of facts. Every lesson concludes with a Practice exercise in which you complete tasks with minimal guidance. The last unit in every section is a Quiz in which you must perform a series of complex tasks with no help. After you complete a Quiz, a score appears, with suggestions on what topics you should review to improve your performance.

CLUES TO USE

Licensing Agreement

By using this CD, you agree to the terms of the licensing agreement. This agreement entitles you to use the product for your own personal training. For information on licensing this CD for corporate training, please call 1-800-648-7450.

How to Use the CD

It's easy to get up and running with this software tutorial. Simply log on, view a quick introduction and a guide to navigating through the course, then advance to the Contents menu to start the course.

Starting the CD

► First, log in to the program by entering any 9-digit ID followed by your full name. The program uses the ID to establish a personal record for storing your data.

► An opening animation introduces the program.

► A short tutorial then explains how to use and navigate through the program.

► You'll advance to the Contents menu—the table of contents for the course and main launch pad for accessing the course lessons. See the Contents menu below.

► Clicking a section icon button from the Contents menu sends you to that section's menu, as shown in the figure below.

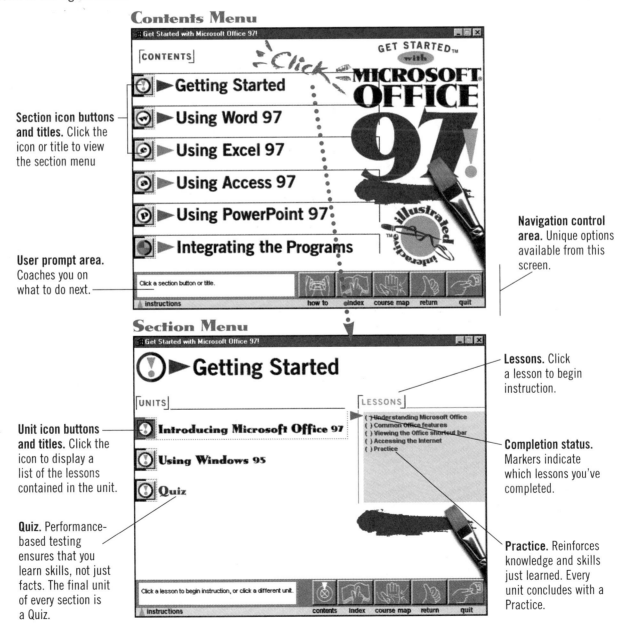

Contents Menu

Section icon buttons and titles. Click the icon or title to view the section menu

User prompt area. Coaches you on what to do next.

Navigation control area. Unique options available from this screen.

Section Menu

Unit icon buttons and titles. Click the icon to display a list of the lessons contained in the unit.

Quiz. Performance-based testing ensures that you learn skills, not just facts. The final unit of every section is a Quiz.

Lessons. Click a lesson to begin instruction.

Completion status. Markers indicate which lessons you've completed.

Practice. Reinforces knowledge and skills just learned. Every unit concludes with a Practice.

CD Instructional Strategies

The CD teaches software skills using the following three instructional strategies: presenting conceptual information, demonstrating a procedure, and instructing you to complete steps. Each lesson in the course is designed to include one or more of these three instructional treatments, which are sampled below.

Concept

First we introduce a CONCEPT...

Using animation, this concept illustrates the ease of moving cell entries in Excel.

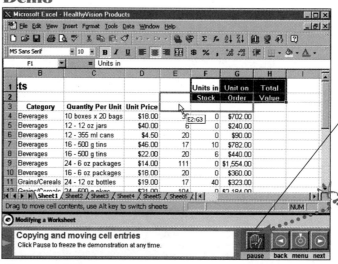

Replay button. If you missed information or didn't understand a concept, you can replay the audio and animation.

Back and Next buttons. Click these buttons to back up/advance to the previous/next screen.

Demo

then we DEMONSTRATE a procedure...

This demo shows how to use the drag-and-drop feature to move cell entries.

Play/Pause button. Start and stop the demos whenever you like.

Step by Step

then you try it STEP BY STEP.

In this step by step, you'll practice using the Copy and Paste buttons. If you make a mistake, you'll get instant feedback.

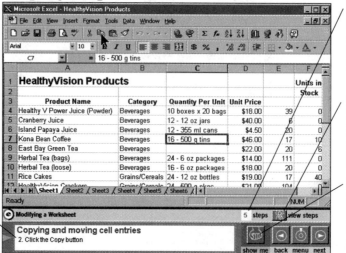

Steps counter. A quick reference to gauge how long it takes to complete the example.

View steps button. A list of all the steps in the example shows you where you are in the procedure.

Numbered steps. Step by step instructions explain how to complete the specific task.

Show me button. Having trouble performing a procedure? Ask the program to complete it for you.

Practice

This CD gives you the opportunity to practice skills. There's a Practice at the end of every unit. Audio hints provide guidance and consolidate learning. The program also provides feedback if you answer incorrectly.

Practice Scenario

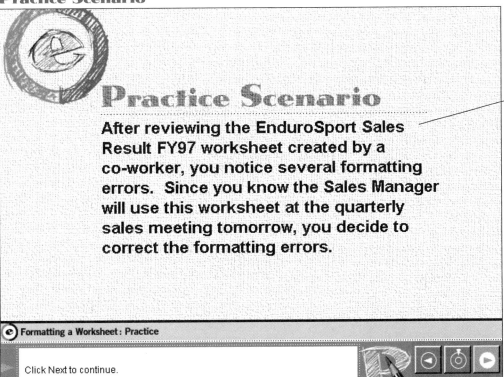

Practice Scenario

After reviewing the EnduroSport Sales Result FY97 worksheet created by a co-worker, you notice several formatting errors. Since you know the Sales Manager will use this worksheet at the quarterly sales meeting tomorrow, you decide to correct the formatting errors.

Formatting a Worksheet: Practice

Click Next to continue.

back menu next

Practice scenario. Sets up a realistic situation for completing the specified task.

Practice Step by Step

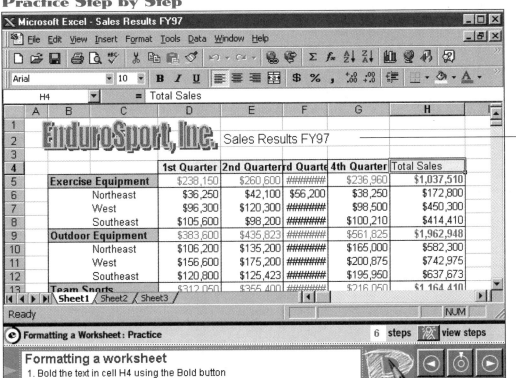

Practice session. Put skills to work and perform a series of tasks with minimal help.

Quiz

The Quiz feature on the CD tests the skills and knowledge you acquired throughout the lessons. A Quiz is provided at the end of each section and is comprised of both questions and skill-based, step-by-step tasks. Immediate feedback is provided for incorrect answers. You can view Quiz performance results and repeat the entire Quiz at any time. All results will be stored in your personal data record.

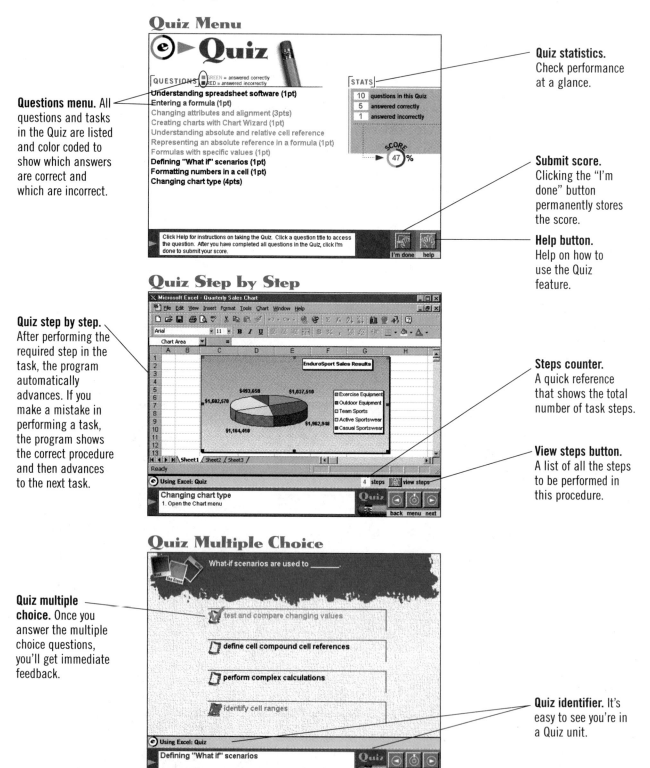

Quiz Menu

Quiz statistics. Check performance at a glance.

Questions menu. All questions and tasks in the Quiz are listed and color coded to show which answers are correct and which are incorrect.

Submit score. Clicking the "I'm done" button permanently stores the score.

Help button. Help on how to use the Quiz feature.

Quiz Step by Step

Quiz step by step. After performing the required step in the task, the program automatically advances. If you make a mistake in performing a task, the program shows the correct procedure and then advances to the next task.

Steps counter. A quick reference that shows the total number of task steps.

View steps button. A list of all the steps to be performed in this procedure.

Quiz Multiple Choice

Quiz multiple choice. Once you answer the multiple choice questions, you'll get immediate feedback.

Quiz identifier. It's easy to see you're in a Quiz unit.

How to Navigate the CD

By design, this CD is easy to navigate. A simple-to-use navigation bar lets you move through the CD to locate specific topics, monitor progress, and identify content easily.

Main Navigation Control Buttons

How to button. Help on how to use the product.

Index button. Randomly access any topic in the course and perform keyword searches.

Course map button. A graphical representation of how many units are in the course.

Return button. Sends you back to your last location in the course.

Quit button. When you exit the course, your completion status is saved for easy re-entry later.

Index

Content list. A searchable, alphabetical list of topics for each course section.

Section tabs. Available sections are easily located from the tabbed folders.

Show ALL topics. Click to show the topics listed alphabetically.

Show REVIEW topics. Click to display topics that need to be reviewed after a Quiz.

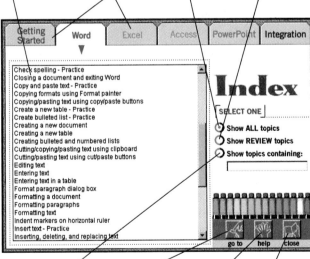

Keyword search. Look up all topics that contain the keyword.

Go to button. Sends you to the topic you selected.

Help button. Help on how to use the Index feature.

Close button. Takes you back to the menu.

CourseMap

CourseMap. The Office 97 course at a glance displayed in an easy-to-understand visual map. Completed units are highlighted.

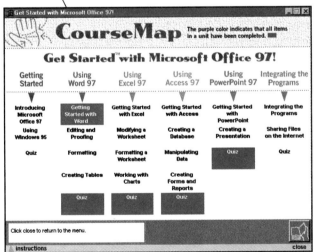

CD Contents

Getting
Started with Excel 97

Objectives

- ► Define spreadsheet software
- ► Start Excel 97
- ► View the Excel window
- ► Open and save an existing workbook
- ► Enter labels and values
- ► Preview and print a worksheet
- ► Get Help
- ► Close a workbook and exit Excel

In this unit, you will learn how to start Excel and recognize and use different elements of the Excel window and menus. You will also learn how to open existing files, enter data in a worksheet, and use the extensive online Help system. Evan Brillstein works in the Accounting Department at Nomad Ltd, an outdoor sporting gear and adventure travel company. Evan will use Excel to complete a worksheet that summarizes budget information and create a workbook to track tour sales.

Defining Spreadsheet Software

Excel is an electronic spreadsheet that runs on Windows computers. An **electronic spreadsheet** uses a computer to perform numeric calculations rapidly and accurately. See Table A-1 for common ways spreadsheets are used in business. An electronic spreadsheet is also referred to as a **worksheet**, which is the document that you produce when you use Excel. A worksheet created with Excel allows Evan to work quickly and efficiently, and to update the results accurately and easily. He will be able to produce more professional-looking documents with Excel. Figure A-1 shows a budget worksheet that Evan and his manager created using pencil and paper. Figure A-2 shows the same worksheet that they can create using Excel.

Details

Excel is better than the paper system for the following reasons:

Enter data quickly and accurately

With Excel, Evan can enter information faster and more accurately than he could using the pencil-and-paper method. For example, in the Nomad Ltd. Budget, Evan can use Excel to calculate Total Expenses and Net Income for each quarter by simply supplying the data and formulas, and Excel calculates the rest.

Recalculate easily

Fixing errors using Excel is easy, and any results based on a changed entry are recalculated automatically. If Evan receives updated Expense figures for Qtr 4, he can simply enter the new numbers and Excel will recalculate the spreadsheet.

Perform what-if analysis

One of the most powerful decision-making features of Excel is the ability to change data and then quickly recalculate changed results. Anytime you use a worksheet to answer the question "what if," you are performing a what-if analysis. For instance, if the advertising budget for May were increased to $3,000, Evan could enter the new figure into the spreadsheet and immediately find out the impact on the overall budget.

Change the appearance of information

Excel provides powerful features for enhancing a spreadsheet so that information is visually appealing and easy to understand. Evan can use boldface type and shading to add emphasis to key data in the worksheet.

Create charts

Excel makes it easy to create charts based on information in a worksheet. With Excel, charts are automatically updated as data changes. The worksheet in Figure A-2 includes a pie chart that graphically shows the distribution of Nomad Ltd. expenses for the first quarter.

Share information with other users

Because everyone at Nomad is now using Microsoft Office, it's easy for Evan to share information with his colleagues. If Evan wants to use the data from someone else's worksheet, he accesses their files through the network or by disk. For example, Evan can complete the budget for Nomad Ltd. that his manager started creating in Excel.

Create new worksheets from existing ones quickly

It's easy for Evan to take an existing Excel worksheet and quickly modify it to create a new one. When Evan is ready to create next year's budget, he can use this budget as a starting point.

FIGURE A-1: Traditional paper worksheet

Nomad Ltd

	Qtr 1	Qtr 2	Qtr 3	Qtr 4	Total
Net Sales	48,000	76,000	64,000	80,000	268,000
Expenses:					
Salary	8,000	8,000	8,000	8,000	32,000
Interest	4,800	5,600	6,400	7,200	24,000
Rent	2,400	2,400	2,400	2,400	9,600
Ads	3,600	8,000	16,000	20,000	47,600
COG	16,000	16,800	20,000	20,400	73,200
Total Exp	34,800	40,800	52,800	58,000	186,400
Net Income	13,200	35,200	11,200	22,000	81,600

FIGURE A-2: Excel worksheet

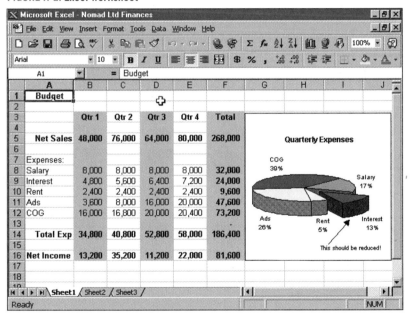

TABLE A-1: Common business spreadsheet uses

use	solution
Maintenance of values	Calculation of figures
Visual representation of values	Chart based on worksheet figures
Create consecutively numbered pages using multiple workbook sheets	Report containing workbook sheets
Organize data	Sort data in ascending or descending order
Analyze data	PivotTable or AutoFilter to create data summaries and short-lists
Create what-if data situations	Scenarios containing data outcomes using variable values

Excel 97

Starting Excel 97

To start Excel, you use the Start Button on the taskbar. Click Programs, then click the Microsoft Excel program icon. A slightly different procedure might be required for computers on a network and those that use utility programs to enhance Windows 95. If you need assistance, ask your instructor or technical support person for help. ◢ Evan's manager has started creating the Nomad Ltd budget and has asked Evan to finish it. He begins by starting Excel now.

1. Point to the **Start button** [🏁 Start] on the taskbar

The Start button is on the left side of the taskbar and is used to start, or launch, programs on your computer.

2. Click [🏁 Start]

Microsoft Excel is located in the Programs group—located at the top of the Start menu, as shown in Figure A-3.

3. Point to **Programs** on the Start menu

All the programs, or applications, found on your computer can be found in this area of the Start menu.

You can see the Microsoft Excel icon and other Microsoft programs, as shown in Figure A-4. Your desktop might look different depending on the programs installed on your computer.

4. Click the **Microsoft Excel program icon** on the Program menu

Excel opens and a blank worksheet appears. In the next lesson, you will familiarize yourself with the elements of the Excel worksheet window.

Trouble?

If you don't see the Microsoft Excel icon, look for a program group called Microsoft Office.

Trouble?

If the Office Assistant appears on your screen, simply choose to start Excel.

FIGURE A-3: **Start menu**

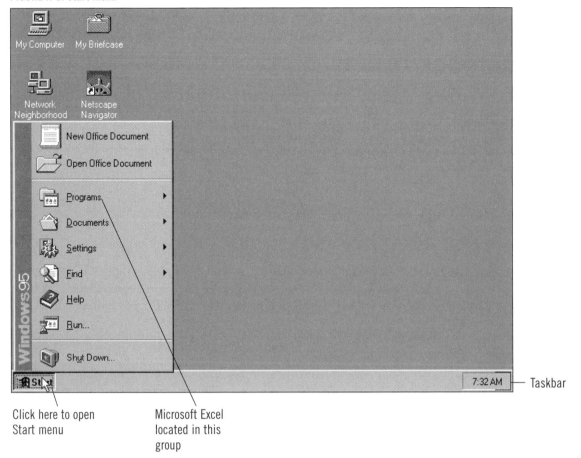

Click here to open
Start menu

Microsoft Excel
located in this
group

Taskbar

FIGURE A-4: **Programs available on your computer**

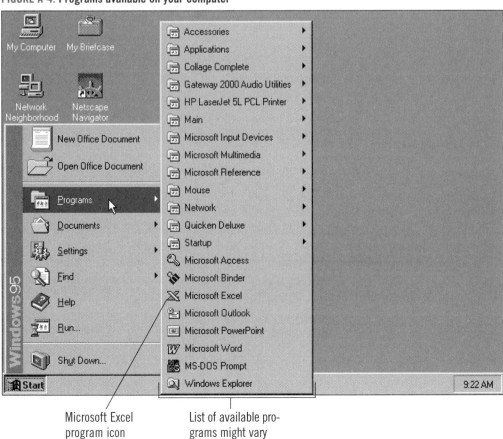

Microsoft Excel
program icon

List of available pro-
grams might vary

Viewing the Excel Window

When you start Excel, the computer displays the **worksheet window**, the area where you enter data, and the window elements that enable you to create and work with worksheets. Evan needs to familiarize himself with the Excel worksheet window and its elements before he starts working with the budget worksheet. Compare the descriptions below to Figure A-5.

Trouble?

If your worksheet does not fill the screen as shown in Figure A-5, click the Maximize button in the worksheet window.

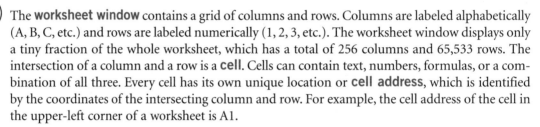

The **worksheet window** contains a grid of columns and rows. Columns are labeled alphabetically (A, B, C, etc.) and rows are labeled numerically (1, 2, 3, etc.). The worksheet window displays only a tiny fraction of the whole worksheet, which has a total of 256 columns and 65,533 rows. The intersection of a column and a row is a **cell**. Cells can contain text, numbers, formulas, or a combination of all three. Every cell has its own unique location or **cell address**, which is identified by the coordinates of the intersecting column and row. For example, the cell address of the cell in the upper-left corner of a worksheet is A1.

The **cell pointer** is a dark rectangle that highlights the cell you are working in, or the **active cell**. In Figure A-5, the cell pointer is located at A1, so A1 is the active cell. To make another cell active, click any other cell or press the arrow keys on your keyboard to move the cell pointer to another cell in the worksheet.

The **title bar** displays the program name (Microsoft Excel) and the filename of the open worksheet (in this case, Book1). The title bar also contains a control menu box, a Close button, and resizing buttons.

The **menu bar** contains menus from which you choose Excel commands. As with all Windows programs, you can choose a menu command by clicking it with the mouse or by pressing [Alt] plus the underlined letter in the menu name, referred to as the command's **shortcut key**.

The **name box** displays the active cell address. In Figure A-5, "A1" appears in the name box, indicating that A1 is the active cell.

The **formula bar** allows you to enter or edit data in the worksheet.

The **toolbars** contain buttons for the most frequently used Excel commands. The **Standard** toolbar is located just below the menu bar and contains buttons corresponding to the most frequently used Excel features. The **Formatting** toolbar contains buttons for the most common commands used for improving the worksheet's appearance. To choose a button, simply click it with the left mouse button. The face of any button has a graphic representation of its function; for instance, the Printing button has a printer on its face.

Sheet tabs below the worksheet grid enable you to keep your work in collections called **workbooks**. Each workbook contains 3 worksheets by default and can contain a maximum of 255 sheets. Sheet tabs can be given meaningful names. **Sheet tab scrolling buttons** help you move from one sheet to another.

The **status bar** is located at the bottom of the Excel window. The left side of the status bar provides a brief description of the active command or task in progress. The right side of the status bar shows the status of important keys, such as the Caps Lock key and the Num Lock key.

FIGURE A-5: **Excel worksheet window elements**

Control menu box   Name box

If you had a previous installation of
Office on your computer, your screen
may contain the Office 97 shortcut bar

Resizing buttons

Title bar

Menu bar

Standard toolbar

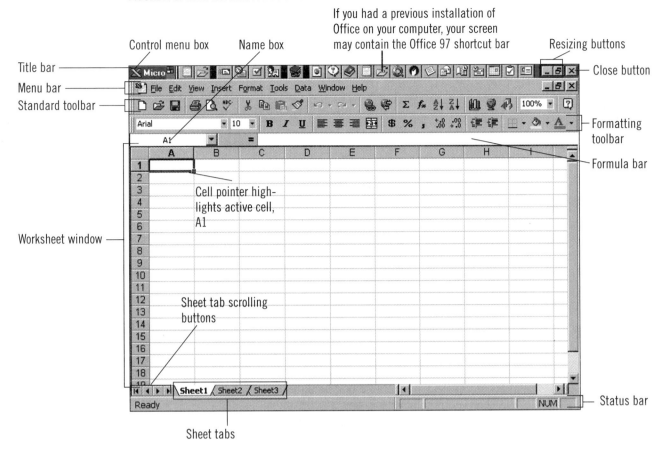

Close button

Formatting
toolbar

Formula bar

Worksheet window

Cell pointer high-
lights active cell,
A1

Sheet tab scrolling
buttons

Status bar

Sheet tabs

Opening and Saving an Existing Workbook

Sometimes it's more efficient to create a new worksheet by modifying one that already exists. This saves you from having to retype information. Throughout this book, you will be instructed to open a file from your Student Disk, use the Save As command to create a copy of the file with a new name, and then modify the new file by following the lesson steps. Saving the files with new names keeps your original Student Disk files intact in case you have to start the lesson over again or you wish to repeat an exercise. ◄──── Evan's manager has asked Evan to enter information into the Nomad Ltd budget. Follow along as Evan opens the Budget workbook, then uses the Save As command to create a copy with a new name.

Steps

Trouble?

If necessary, you can download your student files from our Web Site at http:\\course.com.

1. **Insert your Student Disk in the appropriate disk drive**

2. **Click the Open button 🖼 on the Standard toolbar**
   The Open dialog box opens. See Figure A-6.

3. **Click the Look in list arrow**
   A list of the available drives appears. Locate the drive that contains your Student Disk.

4. **Click the drive that contains your Student Disk**
   A list of the files on your Student Disk appears in the Look in list box, with the default filename placeholder in the File name text box already selected.

5. **In the File name list box click XL A-1, then click Open**
   The file XL A-1 opens. You could also double-click the filename in the File name list box to open the file. To create and save a copy of this file with a new name, you use the Save As command.

6. **Click File on the menu bar, then click Save As**
   The Save As dialog box opens.

QuickTip

You can also click 🖫 on the Standard Toolbar or use the shortcut key [Ctrl][S] to save.

7. **Make sure the Save in list box displays the drive containing your Student Disk**
   You should save all your files to your Student Disk, unless instructed otherwise.

8. **In the File name text box, double-click the current file name to select it (if necessary), then type Nomad Budget as shown in Figure A-7.**

QuickTip

Use the Save As command to create a new workbook from one that already exists; use the Save command to store any changes on your disk made to an existing file since the last time the file was saved.

9. **Click Save to save the file and close the Save As dialog box, then click OK to close the Summary Info dialog box if necessary**
   The file XL A-1 closes, and a duplicate file named Nomad Budget opens, as shown in Figure A-8. To save the workbook in the future, you can click File on the menu bar, then click Save, or click the Save button on the Standard toolbar.

FIGURE A-6: **Open dialog box**

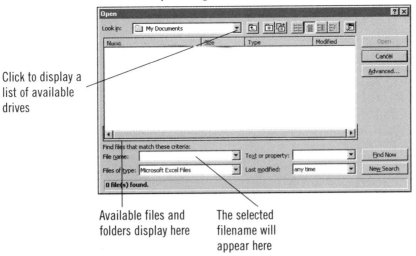

Click to display a
list of available
drives

Available files and
folders display here

The selected
filename will
appear here

FIGURE A-7: **Save As dialog box**

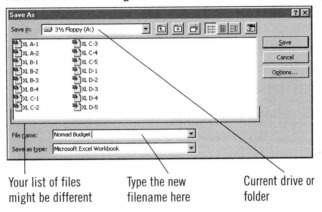

Your list of files
might be different

Type the new
filename here

Current drive or
folder

FIGURE A-8: **Nomad Budget workbook**

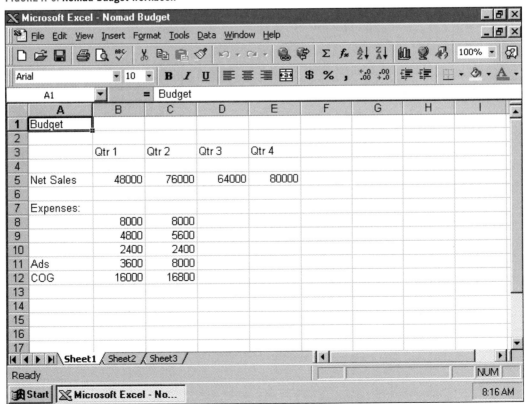

Excel 97

Entering Labels and Values

Labels are used to identify the data in the rows and columns of a worksheet. They are also used to make your worksheet readable and understandable. For these reasons, you should enter all labels in your worksheet first. Labels can contain text and numerical information not used in calculations, such as dates, times, or addresses. Labels are left-aligned by default. **Values**, which include numbers, formulas, and functions, are used in calculations. Excel recognizes an entry as a value when it is a number or begins with one of these symbols: +, -, =, @, #, or $. All values are right-aligned by default. When a cell contains both text and numbers, Excel recognizes the entry as a label. 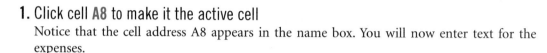 Evan needs to enter labels identifying expense categories, and the values for Qtr 3 and Qtr 4 into the Nomad budget worksheet.

1. Click cell A8 to make it the active cell
Notice that the cell address A8 appears in the name box. You will now enter text for the expenses.

Trouble?

If you notice a mistake in a cell entry after it has been confirmed, double-click the cell and use [Backspace] or [Delete] to make your corrections, then press [Enter].

2. Type Salary, as shown in Figure A-9, then click the Enter button ☑ on the formula bar
You must click ☑ to confirm your entry. You can also confirm a cell entry by pressing [Enter], pressing [Tab], or by pressing one of the arrow keys on your keyboard. If a label does not fit in a cell, Excel displays the remaining characters in the next cell to the right as long as it is empty. Otherwise, the label is **truncated**, or cut off. The contents of A8, the active cell, display in the formula bar.

3. Click cell A9, type Interest, then press [Enter] to complete the entry and move the cell pointer to cell A10; type Rent in cell A10, then press [Enter]
Now you enter the remaining expense values.

4. Drag the mouse over cells D8 through E12
Two or more selected cells is called a **range**. Since these entries cover multiple columns and rows, you can pre-select the range to make the data entry easier.

QuickTip

To enter a number, such as the year 1997, as a label so it will not be included in a calculation, type an apostrophe (') before the number.

5. Type 8000, then press [Enter]; type 6400 in cell D9, then press [Enter]; type 2400 in cell D10, then press [Enter]; type 16000 in cell D11, then press [Enter]; type 20000 in cell D12, then press [Enter]
You have entered all the values in the Qtr 3 column. The cell pointer is now in cell E8. Finish entering the expenses in column E.

6. Type the remaining values for cells E8 through E12 using Figure A-10 as a guide

7. Click the Save button 🖫 on the Standard toolbar
It is a good idea to save your work often. A good rule of thumb is to save every 15 minutes or so as you modify your worksheet, especially before making significant changes to the worksheet, or before printing.

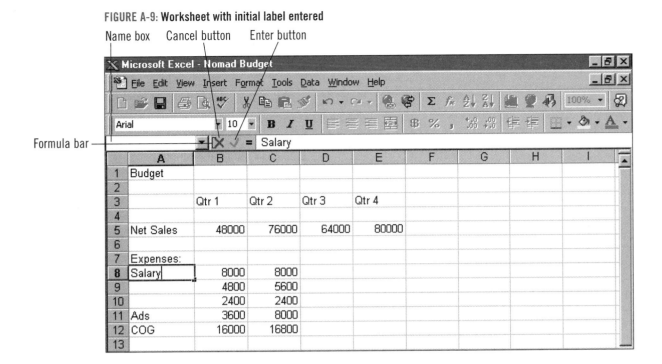

FIGURE A-9: Worksheet with initial label entered

FIGURE A-10: Worksheet with labels and values entered

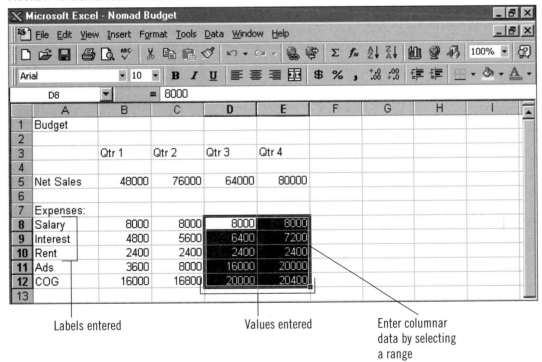

Labels entered

Values entered

Enter columnar
data by selecting
a range

Navigating the worksheet

With over a billion cells available to you, it is important to know how to move around, or navigate, the worksheet. You can use the pointer-movement keys ([↑], [↓], [←], [→]) to move a cell or two at a time, or the [Page Up] or [Page Down] to move a screenful at a time. You can also simply use your mouse pointer to click the desired cell. If the desired cell is not visible in the worksheet window, you can use the scroll bars, or the Go To command to move the location into view. To return to the top of the worksheet, cell A1, press [Ctrl][Home].

Previewing and Printing a Worksheet

When a worksheet is completed, you print it to have a paper copy to reference, file, or send to others. You can also print a worksheet that is not complete to review it or work on when you are not at a computer. Before you print a worksheet, you should first save it, as you did at the end of the previous lesson. That way, if anything happens to the file as it is being sent to the printer, you will have a clean copy saved to your disk. Then you should preview it to make sure that it will fit on the page the way you want. When you preview a worksheet, you see a copy of the worksheet exactly as it will appear on paper. Table A-2 provides printing tips. ◢◢ Evan is finished entering the labels and values into the Nomad Ltd budget as his manager asked him to. Before he submits it to her for review, he previews it and then prints a copy.

Steps 1 2 3 4

1. **Make sure the printer is on and contains paper**
   If a file is sent to print and the printer is off, an error message appears. You preview the worksheet to check its overall appearance.

2. **Click the Print Preview button 🔍 on the Standard toolbar**
   You could also click File on the menu bar, then click Print Preview. A miniature version of the worksheet appears on the screen, as shown in Figure A-11. If there was more than one page, you could click Next and Previous to move between pages. You can also enlarge the image by clicking the Zoom button. After verifying that the preview image is correct, print the worksheet.

3. **Click Print**
   The Print dialog box opens, as shown in Figure A-12.

4. **Make sure that the Active Sheet(s) radio button is selected and that 1 appears in the Number of Copies text box**
   Now you are ready to print the worksheet.

5. **Click OK**
   The Printing dialog box appears while the file is sent to the printer. Note that the dialog box contains a Cancel button that you can use to cancel the print job.

TABLE A-2: Worksheet printing tips

before you print	recommendation
Check the printer	Make sure that the printer is turned on and online, that it has paper, and that there are no error messages or warning signals
Preview the worksheet	Check the formatted image for page breaks, page setup (vertical or horizontal), and overall appearance of the worksheet
Check the printer selection	Use the Printer setup command in the Print dialog box to verify that the correct printer is selected

FIGURE A-11: Print Preview screen

Move to
another page
Enlarge the screen
image
Print the worksheet
Change print
options
Return to worksheet

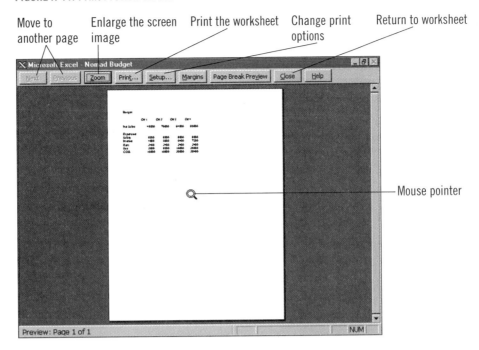

Mouse pointer

Preview: Page 1 of 1

FIGURE A-12: Print dialog box

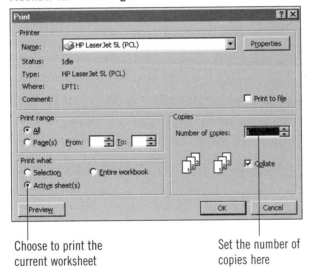

Choose to print the
current worksheet

Set the number of
copies here

Using Zoom in Print Preview

When you are in the Print Preview window, you can make the image of the page larger by clicking the Zoom button. You can also position the mouse pointer over a specific part of the worksheet page, then click to view that section of the page. While the image is zoomed in, use the scroll bars to view different sections of the page. See Figure A-13.

FIGURE A-13: Enlarging the view using Zoom

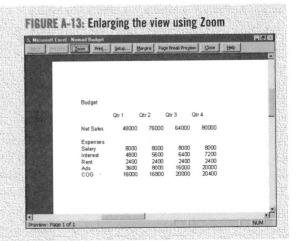

Getting Help

Excel features an extensive online Help system that gives you immediate access to definitions, explanations, and useful tips. The Office Assistant provides this information using a question and answer format. As you are working, the Office Assistant provides tips—indicated by a light bulb you can click—in response to your own working habits. Help appears in a separate balloon-shaped dialog box that you can resize and refer to as you work. You can press the F1 key at any time to get immediate help. ▸ Evan knows the manager will want to know the grand total of the expenses in the budget, and he thinks Excel can perform this type of calculation. He decides to use the animated Office Assistant to learn how to see the sum of a range using the AutoCalculate feature, located in the Status bar.

Steps 123⁴

1. **Click the Office Assistant button** 🔲 **on the Standard toolbar**
   The Office Assistant helps you find information using a question and answer format.

2. **Once the Office Assistant is displayed, click its window to activate the query box**
   You want information on calculating the sum of a range.

3. **Type How can I calculate a range?**
   See Figure A-15. Once you type a question, the Office Assistant can search for relevant topics from the help files in Excel, from which you can choose.

4. **Click Search**
   The Office Assistant displays several topics related to making quick calculations. See Figure A-16.

QuickTip

Information in Help can be printed by clicking the Options button, then clicking Print Topic.

5. **Click Quick calculations on a worksheet**
   The Quick calculations on a worksheet help window opens.

6. **Click View the total for a selected range, press [Esc] once you've read the text, then click the Close button on the dialog box title bar**
   The Help window closes and you return to your worksheet.

7. **Click the Close button in the Office Assistant window**

QuickTip

You can close the Office Assistant at any time by clicking its Close button.

Changing the Office Assistant

The default Office Assistant is Clippit, but there are eight others from which you can choose. To change the appearance of the Office Assistant, right-click the Office Assistant window, then click Choose Assistant. Click the Gallery tab, click the Back and Next buttons until you find an Assistant you want to use, then click OK. (You may need your Microsoft Office 97 CD-ROM to change Office Assistants.) Each Office Assistant makes its own unique sounds and can be animated by right-clicking its window and clicking Animate! Figure A-16 displays the Office Assistant dialog box.

FIGURE A-14: Office Assistant dialog box

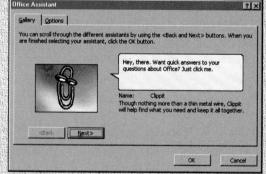

FIGURE A-15: Office Assistant

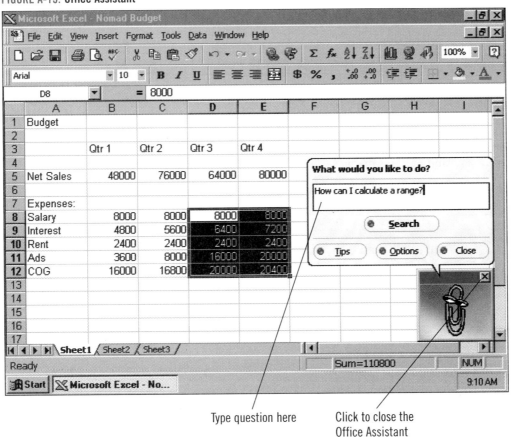

Type question here

Click to close the
Office Assistant

FIGURE A-16: Relevant Help Assistant topics

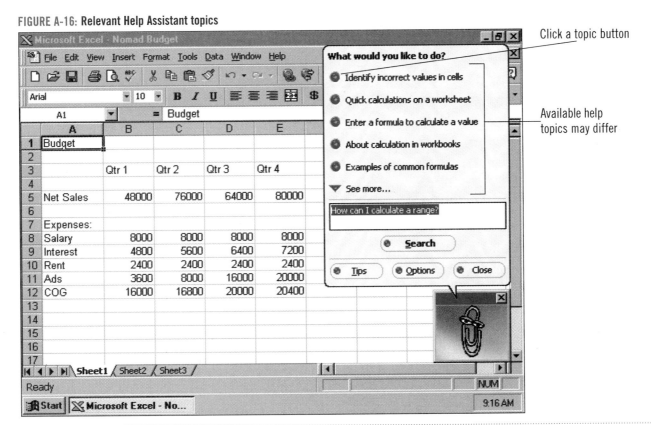

Click a topic button

Available help
topics may differ

Closing a Workbook and Exiting Excel

When you have finished working on a workbook, you need to save the file and close it. Once you have saved a file and are ready to close it, click Close on the File menu. When you have completed all your work in Excel, you need to exit the program. To exit Excel, click Exit on the File menu. ✐▬▬ Evan is done adding the information to the Budget worksheet, and he is ready to pass the printout to his manger to review, so he closes the workbook and then exits Excel.

Steps

1. Click **File** on the menu bar

The File menu opens as displayed in Figure A-17.

2. Click **Close**

You could also click the workbook Close button instead of choosing File, then Close. Excel closes the workbook and asks you to save your changes; be sure that you do. A blank worksheet window appears.

3. Click **File**, then click **Exit**

You could also click the program Close button to exit the program. Excel closes and computer memory is freed up for other computing tasks.

Trouble?

To exit Excel and close several files at once, choose Exit from the File menu. Excel will prompt you to save changes to each workbook before exiting.

FIGURE A-17: **Closing a workbook using the File menu**

Program control menu box Workbook control menu box Close command

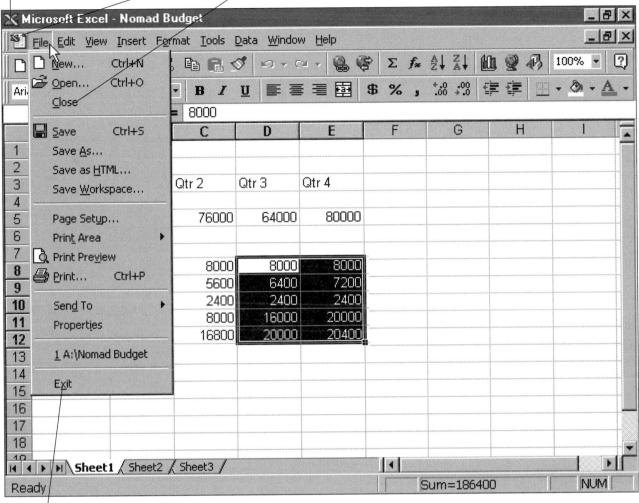

Exit command

Excel 97

Practice

▶ Concepts Review

Label each of the elements of the Excel worksheet window shown in Figure A-18.

FIGURE A-18

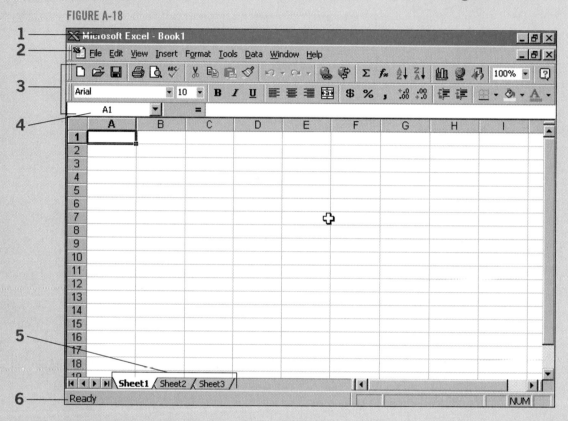

Match each of the terms with the statement that describes its function.

7. **Cell pointer**
8. **Button**
9. **Worksheet window**
10. **Name box**
11. **Cell**
12. **Workbook**

a. Area that contains a grid of columns and rows
b. The intersection of a column and row
c. Graphic symbol that depicts a task or function
d. Collection of worksheets
e. Rectangle that indicates the cell you are currently working in
f. Displays the active cell address

Select the best answer from the list of choices.

13. An electronic spreadsheet can perform all of the following tasks, *except*
    a. Display information visually
    b. Calculate data accurately
    c. Plan worksheet objectives
    d. Recalculate updated information

14. Each of the following is true about labels, *except*
    a. They are left-aligned, by default
    b. They are not used in calculations
    c. They are right-aligned, by default
    d. They can include numerical information

15. Each of the following is true about values, *except*
    a. They can include labels
    b. They are right-aligned, by default
    c. They are used in calculations
    d. They can include formulas

16. What symbol is typed before a number to make the number a label?
    a. "
    b. !
    c. '
    d. ;

17. You can get Excel Help by any of the following ways, *except*
    a. Clicking Help on the menu bar
    b. Pressing [F1]
    c. Clicking the Help button ⑦ on the Standard toolbar
    d. Minimizing the application window

18. Each key(s) can be used to confirm cell entries, *except*
    a. [Enter]
    b. [Tab]
    c. [Esc]
    d. [Shift][Enter]

19. Which button is used to preview a worksheet?
    a. ▣
    b. ▣
    c. ▣
    d. ▣

20. Which feature is used to enlarge a print preview view?
    a. Magnify
    b. Enlarge
    c. Amplify
    d. Zoom

21. Each of the following is true about the Office Assistant, *except*
    a. It provides tips based on your work habits
    b. It provides help using a question and answer format
    c. You can change the appearance of the Office Assistant
    d. It can complete certain tasks for you

► Skills Review

1. Start Excel and identify the elements in the worksheet window.

- **a.** Point to Programs in the Start menu.
- **b.** Click the Microsoft Excel program icon.
- **c.** Try to identify as many elements in the Excel worksheet window as you can without referring to the unit material.

2. Open an existing workbook.

- **a.** Open the workbook XL A-2 by clicking the Open button on the Standard toolbar.
- **b.** Save the workbook as "Country Duds" by clicking File on the menu bar, then clicking Save As.

3. Enter labels and values.

- **a.** Enter labels shown in Figure A-19.
- **b.** Enter values shown in Figure A-19.
- **c.** Save the workbook by clicking the Save button on the Standard toolbar.

FIGURE A-19

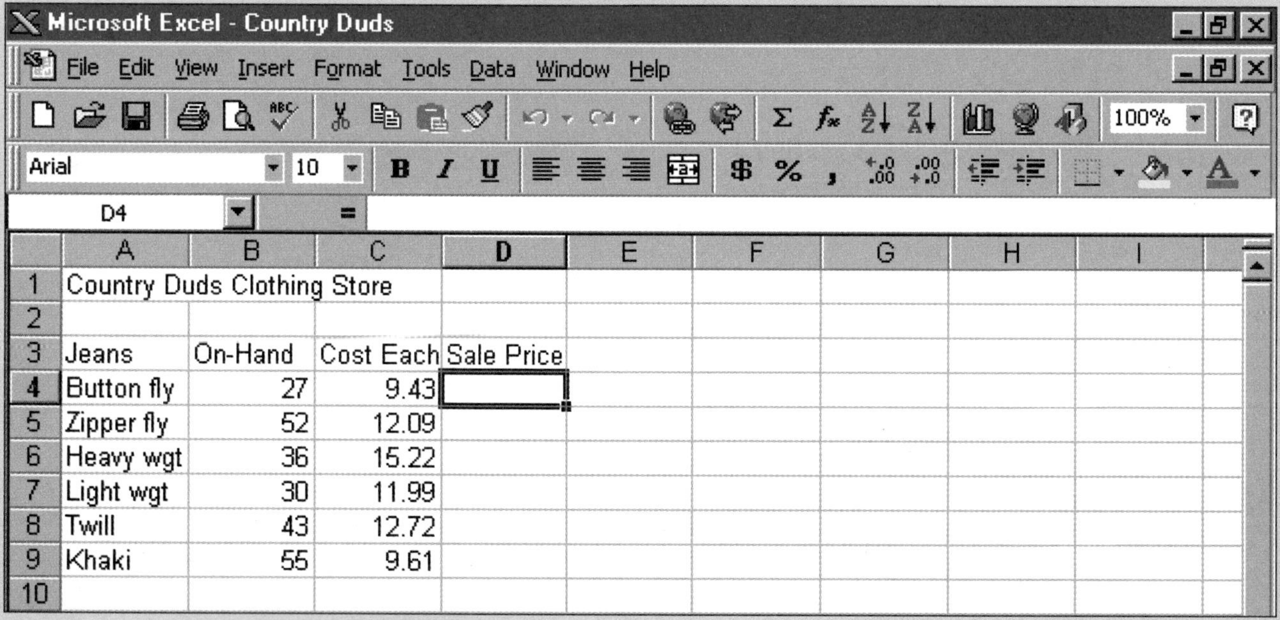
Microsoft Excel - Country Duds
File Edit View Insert Format Tools Data Window Help
100%
Arial
10
D4
=
A B C D E F G H I
1 Country Duds Clothing Store
2
3 Jeans On-Hand Cost Each Sale Price
4 Button fly 27 9.43
5 Zipper fly 52 12.09
6 Heavy wgt 36 15.22
7 Light wgt 30 11.99
8 Twill 43 12.72
9 Khaki 55 9.61
10

4. Previewing and printing a worksheet.

- **a.** Click the Print Preview button on the Standard toolbar.
- **b.** Use the Zoom button to see more of your worksheet.
- **c.** Print one copy of the worksheet.
- **d.** Hand in your printout.

5. Get Help.

- **a.** Click the Office Assistant button on the Standard toolbar if the Assistant is not displayed.
- **b.** Ask the Office Assistant for information about changing the Office Assistant character in Excel.
- **c.** Print information offered by the Office Assistant using the Print topic command on the Options menu.
- **d.** Close the Help window.
- **e.** Hand in your printout.

6. Close the workbook and exit Excel.
  a. Click File on the menu bar, then click Close.
  b. If asked if you want to save the worksheet, click No.
  c. If necessary, close any other worksheets you might have opened.
  d. Click File on the menu bar, then click Exit.

▶ Independent Challenges

1. Excel's online Help provides definitions, explanations, procedures, and other helpful information. It also provides examples and demonstrations to show you how Excel features work. Topics include elements such as the active cell, status bar, buttons, and dialog boxes, as well as detailed information about Excel commands and options.
  To complete this independent challenge:

1. Open a new workbook
2. Click the Office Assistant.
3. Type a question that will give you information about opening and saving a worksheet. (Hint: you may have to ask the Office Assistant more than one question.)
4. Print out the information and hand it in.
5. Return to your workbook when you are finished.

2. Spreadsheet software has many uses that can affect the way work is done. Some examples of how Excel can be used are discussed in the beginning of this unit. Use your own personal or business experiences to come up with five examples of how Excel could be used in a business setting.

To complete this independent challenge:

1. Open a new workbook.
2. Think of five business tasks that you could complete more efficiently by using an Excel worksheet.
3. Sketch a sample of each worksheet. See Figure A-20, a sample payroll worksheet.
4. Submit your sketches.

FIGURE A-20

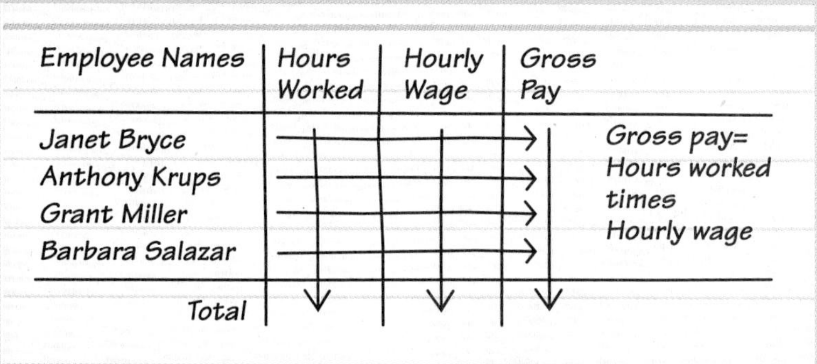

Employee Names	Hours Worked	Hourly Wage	Gross Pay	
Janet Bryce			→	Gross pay=
Anthony Krups			→	Hours worked
Grant Miller			→	times
Barbara Salazar			→	Hourly wage
Total	↓	↓	↓	

3. You are the office manager for Blossoms and Greens, a small greenhouse and garden center. Although the company is just three years old, it is expanding rapidly, and you are continually looking for ways to make your job easier. Last year you began using Excel to manage and maintain data on inventory and sales, which has greatly helped you to track this information accurately and efficiently. However, the job is still overwhelming for just one person. Fortunately, the owner of the company has just approved the hiring of an assistant for you. This person will need to learn how to use Excel. Create a short training document that your new assistant can use as a reference while becoming familiar with Excel.
To complete this independent challenge:

1. Draw a sketch of the Excel worksheet window, and label the key elements, such as toolbars, title bar, formula bar, scroll bars, etc.
2. For each labeled element, write a short description of its use.
3. List the main ways to get Help in Excel. (Hint: use the Office Assistant to learn of all the ways to get help in Excel..)
4. Identify five different ways to use spreadsheets in business.

4. Data on the World Wide Web is current and informative. It is a useful tool that can be used to gather the most up-to-date information which you can use to make smart buying decisions. Imagine that your supervisor has just told you that due to your great work, she has just found money in the budget to buy you a new computer. You can have whatever you want, but she wants you to justify the expense by creating a spreadsheet using data found on the World Wide Web to support your purchase decision.

To complete this independent challenge:

1. Open a new workbook and save it on your Student Disk as "New Computer Data."
2. Decide which features you want your ideal computer to have, and list these features.
3. Log on to the Internet and use your browser to go to the http://www.course.com. From there, click the link Student On Line Companions, then click the Microsoft Office 97 Professional Edition—Illustrated: A First Course page, then click on the Excel link for Unit A.
4. Use any of the following sites to compile your data: IBM [www.ibm.com], Gateway [www.gw2k.com], Dell [www.dell.com], or any other site you can find with related information.
5. Compile data for the components you want.
6. Make sure all components are listed and totaled. Include any tax and shipping costs the manufacturer charges.
7. Indicate on the worksheet your final purchase decision.
8. Save, print, and hand in your work.

► Visual Workshop

Create a worksheet similar to Figure A-21 using the skills you learned in this unit. Save the workbook as "Bea's Boutique" on your Student Disk. Preview, then print the worksheet.

FIGURE A-21

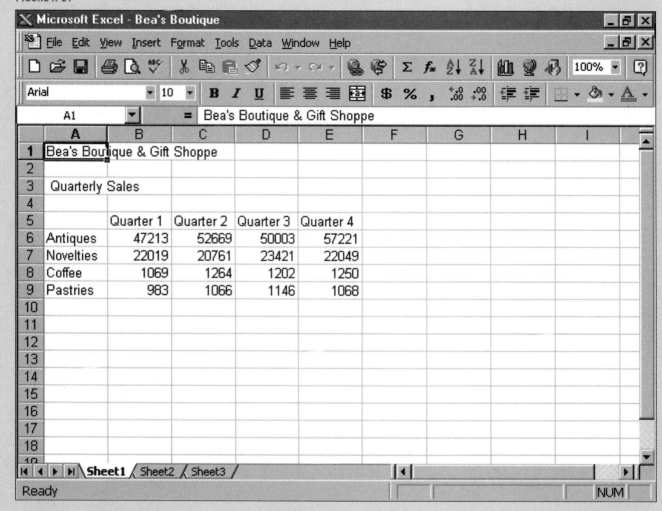

Building
and Editing Worksheets

Objectives

► **Plan, design, and create a worksheet**
► **Edit cell entries and work with ranges**
► **Enter formulas**
► **Introduce functions**
► **Copy and move cell entries**
► **Copy formulas with relative cell references**
► **Copy formulas with absolute cell references**
► **Name and move a sheet**

You will now plan and build your own worksheets. When you build a worksheet, you enter text, values, and formulas into worksheet cells. Once you create a worksheet, you can save it in a workbook file and then print it. ◄ Evan Brillstein has received a request from the Marketing Department for a forecast of this year's summer tour business, and an estimate of the average tour sales for each type of tour. Marketing hopes that the tour business will increase 20% over last year's figures. Evan needs to create a worksheet that summarizes tour sales for last year and a worksheet that forecasts the summer tour sales for this year.

Planning, Designing, and Creating a Worksheet

Before you start entering data into a worksheet, you need to know the purpose and approximate layout of the worksheet. ◄▬▬▬ Evan wants to forecast Nomad's 1998 summer tour sales. The sales goal, already identified by the Marketing Department, is to increase the 1997 summer sales by 20%. Using Figure B-1 and the planning guidelines below, work with Evan as he plans his worksheet.

Details

 Determine the purpose of the worksheet and give it a meaningful title
Evan needs to forecast summer tour sales for 1998. Evan titles the worksheet "1998 Summer Tour Sales Forecast."

 Determine your worksheet's desired results, sometimes called output
Evan needs to determine what the 1998 sales totals will be if sales increase by 20% over the 1997 sales totals, as well as the average number of tours per type.

 Collect all the information, sometimes called input, that will produce the results you want to see
Evan gathers together the sales data for the 1997 summer tour season. The season ran from June through August. The types of tours sold in these months included Bike, Raft, Horse, and Bus.

 Determine the calculations, or formulas, necessary to achieve the desired results
First, Evan needs to total the number of tours sold for each month of the 1997 summer season. Then he needs to add these totals together to determine the grand total of summer tour sales. Finally, the 1997 monthly totals and grand total must be multiplied by 1.2 to calculate a 20% increase for the 1998 summer tour season. He'll use the Paste Function to determine the average number of tours per type.

 Sketch on paper how you want the worksheet to look; that is, identify where the labels and values will go
Evan decides to put tour types in rows and the months in columns. He enters the tour sales data in his sketch and indicates where the monthly sales totals and the grand total should go. Below the totals, he writes out the formula for determining a 20% increase in sales for 1997. He also includes a label for the location of the tour averages. Evan's sketch of his worksheet is shown in Figure B-1.

 Create the worksheet
Evan enters his labels first to establish the structure of his worksheet. He then enters the values, the sales data into his worksheet. These values will be used to calculate the output Evan needs. The worksheet Evan creates is shown in Figure B-2.

FIGURE B-1: Worksheet sketch showing labels, values, and calculations

1998 Summer Tours Sales Forecast

	June	July	August	Totals	Average
Bike	14	10	6	3 month total	
Raft	7	8	12		
Horse	12	7	6		
Bus	1	2	9		
Totals	June Total	July Total	August Total	Grand Total for 1997	
1998 Sales	Total X 1.2				

FIGURE B-2: Evan's forecasting worksheet

Check title bar for correct title

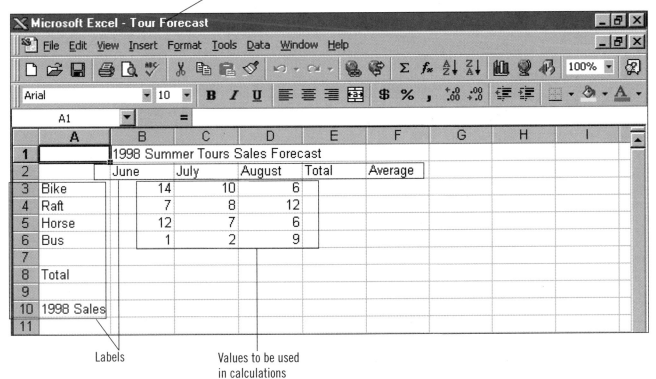

Labels

Values to be used in calculations

Editing Cell Entries and Working with Ranges

You can change the contents of any cells at any time. To edit the contents of a cell, you first select the cell you want to edit, then click the formula bar, double-click the selected cell, or press [F2]. This puts Excel into Edit mode. To make sure you are in Edit mode, check the **mode indicator** on the far left of the status bar. The mode indicator identifies the current Excel command or operation in progress. ◄═══ After planning and creating his worksheet, Evan notices that he entered the wrong value for the June bus tours and forgot to include the canoe tours. He fixes the bus tours figure, and he decides to add the canoe sales data to the raft sales figures.

1. **Start Excel, open the workbook XL B-1 from your Student Disk, then save it as Tour Forecast**

2. **Click cell B6**
   This cell contains June bus tours, which Evan needs to change to 2.

3. **Click anywhere in the formula bar**
   Excel goes into Edit mode, and the mode indicator displays "Edit." A blinking vertical line, called the **insertion point**, appears in the formula bar, and if you move the mouse pointer to the formula bar, the pointer changes to I as displayed in Figure B-3.

4. **Press [Backspace], type 2, then press [Enter] or click the Enter button ✓ on the formula bar**
   Evan now needs to add "/Canoe" to the Raft label.

5. **Click cell A4 then press [F2]**
   Excel is in Edit mode again, but this time, the insertion point is in the cell.

6. **Type /Canoe then press [Enter]**
   The label changes to Raft/Canoe.

7. **Double-click cell B4**
   Double-clicking a cell also puts Excel into Edit mode with the insertion point in the cell.

8. **Press [Delete], then type 9**
   See Figure B-4.

9. **Click ✓ to confirm the entry**

QuickTip

If you make a mistake, you can either click the Cancel button ✕ on the formula bar before accepting the cell entry, or click the Undo button ↺ on the Standard toolbar if you notice the mistake after you have accepted the cell entry. The Undo button allows you to reverse up to 16 previous actions, one at a time.

FIGURE B-3: Worksheet in Edit mode

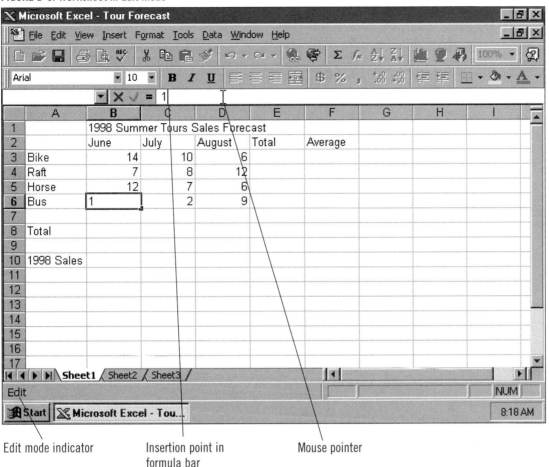

Edit mode indicator   Insertion point in   Mouse pointer
                     formula bar

FIGURE B-4: Edited worksheet

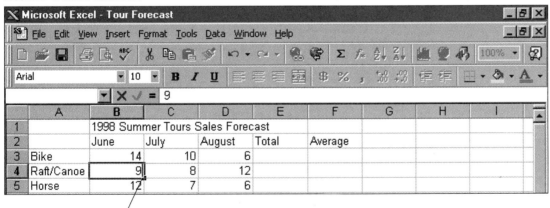

Insertion point in cell

CLUES TO USE

Using range names in a workbook

Any group of cells (two or more) is called a range. To select a range, click the first cell and drag to the last cell you want included in the range. The range address is defined by noting the first and last cells in the range. Give a meaningful name to a range by selecting cells, clicking the name box, and then typing a name. Range names—meaningful English names

that Evan uses in this worksheet—are usually easier to remember than cell addresses, they can be used in formulas, and they also help you move around the workbook quickly. Click the name box list arrow, then click the name of the range you want to go to. The cell pointer moves immediately to that range.

Excel 97

Entering Formulas

Formulas are used to perform numeric calculations such as adding, multiplying, and averaging. Formulas in an Excel worksheet start with the formula prefix—the equal sign (=). All formulas use one or more **arithmetic operators** to perform calculations. See Table B-1 for a list of Excel operators. Formulas often contain cell addresses and range names. Using a cell address or range name in a formula is called **cell referencing**. Using cell references keeps your worksheet up-to-date and accurate. If you change a value in a cell, any formula containing that cell reference will be automatically recalculated using the new value. In formulas using more than one arithmetic operator, Excel decides which operation to perform first. ◆ Evan needs to add the monthly tour totals for June, July, and August, and calculate a 20% increase in sales. He can perform these calculations using formulas.

Steps

1. Click cell **B8**

This is the cell where you want to put the calculation that will total the June sales.

2. Type = (the equal sign)

Placing an equal sign at the beginning of an entry tells Excel that a formula is about to be entered rather than a label or a value. The total June sales is equal to the sum of the values in cells B3, B4, B5, and B6.

Trouble?

If the formula instead of the result appears in the cell after you click ✓, make sure you began the formula with = (the equal sign).

3. Type **b3+b4+b5+b6**, then click the **Enter button** ✓ on the formula bar

The result of 37 appears in cell B8, and the formula appears in the formula bar. See Figure B-5. Next, you add the number of tours in July and August.

4. Click cell **C8**, type =**c3+c4+c5+c6**, then press [Tab]; in cell D8, type =**d3+d4+d5+d6**, then press [Enter]

The total tour sales for July, 27, and for August, 33, appear in cells C8 and D8 respectively.

QuickTip

It does not matter if you type the column letter in lower case or upper case when entering formulas. Excel is not case-sensitive—B3 and b3 both refer to the same cell.

5. Click cell **B10**, type =**B8*1.2**, then click ✓ on the formula bar

To calculate the 20% increase, you multiply the total by 1.2. This formula calculates the result of multiplying the total monthly tour sales for June, cell B8, by 1.2. The result of 44.4 appears in cell B10.

Now you need to calculate the 20% increase for July and August. You can use the **pointing method**, by which you specify cell references in a formula by selecting the desired cell with your mouse instead of typing its cell reference into the formula.

6. Click cell **C10**, type =, click cell **C8**, type *1.2, then press [Tab]

7. Click cell **D10**, type =, click cell **D8**, type *1.2, then click ✓

Compare your results with Figure B-6.

TABLE B-1: Excel arithmetic operators

operator	purpose	example
+	Performs addition	=A5+A7
–	Performs subtraction	=A5-10
*	Performs multiplication	=A5*A7
/	Performs division	=A5/A7

FIGURE B-5: Worksheet showing formula and result

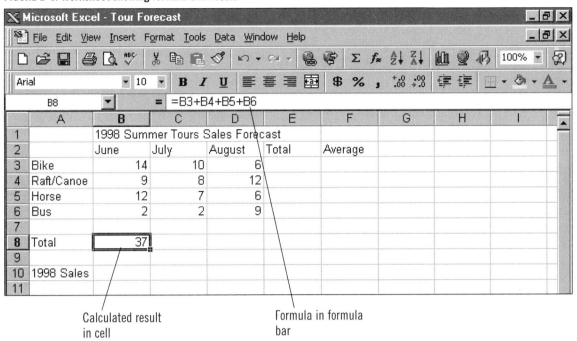

Calculated result
in cell

Formula in formula
bar

FIGURE B-6: Calculated results for 20% increase

Order of precedence in Excel formulas

A formula can include several operations. When you work with formulas that have more than one operator, the order of precedence is very important. If a formula contains two or more operators, such as 4 + .55/4000 * 25, the computer performs the calculations in a particular sequence based on these rules:

Calculated 1st   Calculation of exponents

Calculated 2nd   Multiplication and division, left to right

Calculated 3rd   Addition and subtraction, left to right

In the example 4 + .55/4000 * 25, Excel performs the arithmetic operations by first dividing 4000 into .55, then multiplying the result by 25, then adding 4. You can change the order of calculations by using parentheses. For example, in the formula (4+.55)/4000 * 25, Excel would first add 4 and .55, then divide that amount by 4000, then finally multiply it by 25. Operations inside parentheses are calculated before any other operations.

Introducing Excel Functions

Functions are predefined worksheet formulas that enable you to do complex calculations easily. Like formulas, functions always begin with the formula prefix = (the equal sign). You can enter functions manually, or you can use the Paste Function. Evan uses the SUM function to calculate the grand totals in his worksheet, and the AVERAGE function to calculate the average number of tours per type.

Steps

1. **Click cell E3**
   This is the cell where you want to display the total of all bike tours for June, July, and August. You use the AutoSum button to create the totals. AutoSum sets up the SUM function to add the values in the cells above the cell pointer. If there are no values in the cells above the cell pointer, AutoSum adds the values in the cells to the left of the cell pointer—in this case, the values in cells B3, C3, and D3.

2. **Click the AutoSum button** ∑ **on the Standard toolbar, then click the Enter button** ✓ **on the formula bar**
   The formula =SUM(B3:D3) appears in the formula bar. The information inside the parentheses is the **argument**, or the information to be used in calculating a result of the function. An argument can be a value, a range of cells, text, or another function.
   The result appears in cell E3. Next, you calculate the total of raft and canoe tours.

3. **Click cell E4, click** ∑ , **then click** ✓
   Now you calculate the three-month total of the horse tours.

4. **Click cell E5 then click** ∑
   AutoSum sets up a function to sum the two values in the cells above the active cell, which is not what you intended. You need to change the argument.

5. **Click cell B5, then drag to select the range B5:D5, then click** ✓ **to confirm the entry**
   As you drag, the argument in the SUM function changes to reflect the range being chosen, and a tip box appears telling you the size of the range you are selecting.

6. **Enter the SUM function in cells E6, E8, and E10**
   Make sure you add the values to the left of the active cell, not the values above it. See Figure B-7. Next, you calculate the average number of Bike tours using the Paste Function.

7. **Click cell F3, then click the Paste Function button** ƒ* **on the Standard toolbar**
   The Paste Function dialog box opens. See Table B-2 for frequently used functions.
   The function needed to calculate averages—named AVERAGE—is included in the Most Recently Used category.

8. **Click the function name AVERAGE in the Function category list box, click OK, then in the AVERAGE dialog box type B3:D3 in the Number 1 text box, as shown in Figure B-8**

Time To

✔ Save

9. **Click OK, then repeat steps 8 and 9 to calculate the Raft/Canoe (cell F4), Horse (cell F5), and Bus tours (cell F6) averages**
   The Time To checklist in the left margin contains Steps for routine actions. Everytime you see a Time To checklist, perform the actions listed.

FIGURE B-7: Worksheet with SUM functions entered

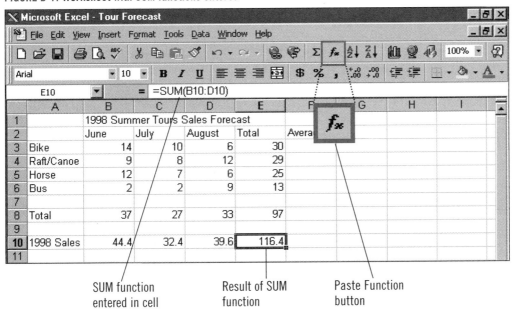

SUM function entered in cell

Result of SUM function

Paste Function button

FIGURE B-8: Using the Paste Function to create a formula

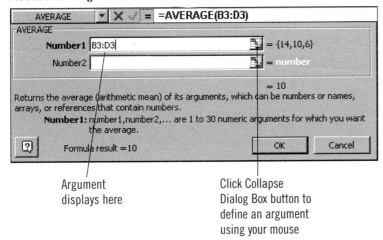

Argument displays here

Click Collapse Dialog Box button to define an argument using your mouse

TABLE B-2: Frequently Used Functions

function	description
SUM(*argument*)	Calculates the sum of the arguments
AVERAGE(*argument*)	Calculates the average of the arguments
MAX(*argument*)	Displays the largest value among the arguments
MIN(*argument*)	Displays the smallest value among the arguments
COUNT(*argument*)	Calculates the number of values in the arguments

Introducing the Paste Function

The Paste Function button *fx* is located to the right of the AutoSum button on the Standard toolbar. To use the Paste Function, click *fx*. In the Paste Function dialog box, click the category containing the function you want, then click the desired function. The function appears in the formula bar. Click OK to fill in values or cell addresses for the arguments, then click OK.

Copying and Moving Cell Entries

Using the Cut, Copy, and Paste buttons or Excel's drag-and-drop feature, you can copy or move information from one cell or range in your worksheet to another. You can also cut, copy, and paste data from one worksheet to another. Evan included the 1998 forecast for spring and fall tours sales in his Tour Info workbook. He already entered the spring report in Sheet2 and will finish entering the labels and data for the fall report. Using the Copy and Paste buttons and drag-and-drop, Evan copies information from the spring report to the fall report.

CourseHelp

The camera icon indicates there is a CourseHelp available with this lesson. Click the Start button, point to programs, point to CourseHelp, then click Excel 97 Illustrated. Choose the CourseHelp that corresponds to this lesson.

1. Click **Sheet 2** of the Tour Forecast workbook

First, you copy the labels identifying the types of tours from the Spring report to the Fall report.

2. Select the range **A4:A9**, then click the **Copy button** 📋 on the Standard toolbar

The selected range (A4:A9) is copied to the **Clipboard**, a temporary storage file that holds all the selected information you copy or cut. The Cut button ✂ removes the selected information from the worksheet and places it on the Clipboard. To copy the contents of the Clipboard to a new location, you click the new cell and then use the Paste command.

3. Click cell **A13**, then click the **Paste button** 📋 on the Standard toolbar

The contents of the Clipboard are copied into the range A13:A18. When pasting the contents of the Clipboard into the worksheet, you need to specify only the first cell of the range where you want the copied selection to go. Next, you decide to use drag-and-drop to copy the Total label.

4. Click cell **E3**, then position the pointer on any edge of the cell until the pointer changes to ↖

5. While the pointer is ↖, press and hold down [Ctrl]

The pointer changes to ↖⁺.

Trouble?

When you drag-and-drop into occupied cells, Excel asks if you want to replace the existing cells. Click OK to replace the contents with the cells you are moving.

6. While still pressing [Ctrl], press and hold the left mouse button, then drag the cell contents to cell **E12**

As you drag, an outline of the cell moves with the pointer, as shown in Figure B-9, and a tip box appears tracking the current position of the item as you move it. When you release the mouse button, the Total label appears in cell E12. You now decide to move the worksheet title over to the left. To use drag-and-drop to move data to a new cell without copying it, do not press [Ctrl] while dragging.

7. Click cell **C1**, then position the mouse on the edge of the cell until it changes to ↖, then drag the cell contents to **A1**

You now enter fall sales data into the range B13:D16.

8. Using the information shown in Figure B-10, enter the sales data for the fall tours into the range **B13:D16**

Compare your worksheet to Figure B-10.

FIGURE B-9: Using drag-and-drop to copy information

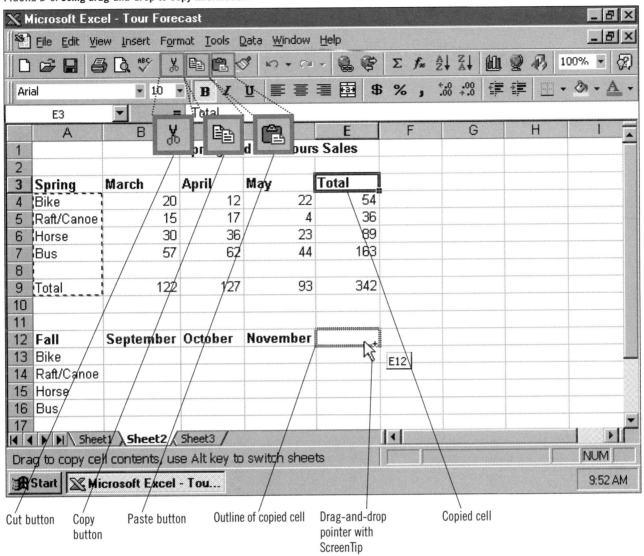

Cut button   Copy   Paste button   Outline of copied cell   Drag-and-drop   Copied cell
              button   pointer with
                                                                   ScreenTip

FIGURE B-10: Worksheet with Fall tours data entered

	September	October	November	Total
12 **Fall**				
13 Bike	17	15	18	
14 Raft/Canoe	21	8	5	
15 Horse	12	21	14	
16 Bus	25	12	18	

Copying Formulas with Relative Cell References

Copying and moving formulas allows you to reuse formulas you've already created. Copying formulas, rather than retyping them, helps to prevent typing errors. 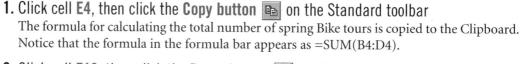 Evan wants to copy from the Spring tours report to the Fall tours report the formulas that total the tours by type and by month. He can use Copy and Paste commands and the Fill right method to copy this information.

CourseHelp

If you have trouble with the concepts in this lesson, be sure to view the CourseHelp entitled Copying Formulas.

1. Click cell E4, then click the Copy button 📋 **on the Standard toolbar**
The formula for calculating the total number of spring Bike tours is copied to the Clipboard. Notice that the formula in the formula bar appears as =SUM(B4:D4).

2. Click cell E13, then click the Paste button 📋 **on the Standard toolbar**
The formula from cell E4 is copied into cell E13, where the new result of 50 appears. Notice in the formula bar that the cell references have changed, so that the range B13:D13 appears in the formula. Formulas in Excel contain **relative cell references**. A relative cell reference tells Excel to copy the formula to a new cell, but to substitute new cell references so that the relationship of the cells to the formula in its new location remains unchanged. In this case, Excel inserted cells D13, C13, and B13, the three cell references immediately to the left of E13.

Notice that the bottom right corner of the active cell contains a small square, called the **fill handle**. Evan uses the fill handle to copy the formula in cell E13 to cells E14, E15, and E16. You can also use the fill handle to copy labels.

QuickTip

You can fill cells with sequential months, days of the week, years, and text plus a number (Quarter 1, Quarter 2, . . .) by dragging the fill handle. As you drag the fill handle, the contents of the last filled cell appears in the name box.

3. Position the pointer over the fill handle until it changes to ┼, then drag the fill handle to select the range E13:E16
See Figure B-11.

4. Release the mouse button
Once you release the mouse button, the fill handle copies the formula from the active cell (E13) and pastes it into each cell of the selected range. Again, because the formula uses relative cell references, cells E14 through E16 correctly display the totals for Raft and Canoe, Horse, and Bus tours

5. Click cell B9, click Edit on the menu bar, then click Copy
The Copy command on the Edit menu has the same effect as clicking the Copy button 📋 on the Standard toolbar.

6. Click cell B18, click Edit on the menu bar, then click Paste
See Figure B-12. The formula for calculating the September tours sales appears in the formula bar. Now you use the Fill Right command to copy the formula from cell B18 to cells C18, D18, and E18.

7. Select the range B18:E18

QuickTip

Use the Fill Series command on the Edit menu to examine all of Excel's available fill series options.

8. Click Edit on the menu bar, point to Fill, then click Right
The rest of the totals are filled in correctly. Compare your worksheet to Figure B-13.

9. Click the Save button 💾 **on the Standard toolbar**
Your worksheet is now saved.

FIGURE B-11: Selected range using the fill handle

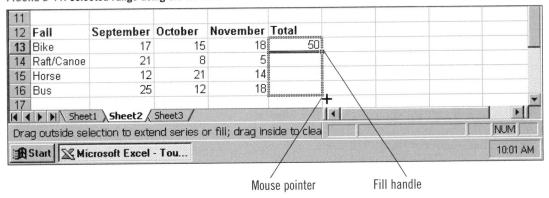

Mouse pointer   Fill handle

FIGURE B-12: Worksheet with copied formula

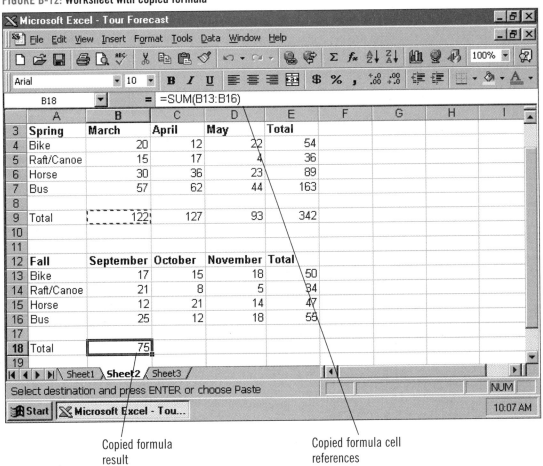

Copied formula
result

Copied formula cell
references

FIGURE B-13: Completed worksheet with all formulas copied

11					
12	**Fall**	**September**	**October**	**November**	**Total**
13	Bike	17	15	18	50
14	Raft/Canoe	21	8	5	34
15	Horse	12	21	14	47
16	Bus	25	12	18	55
17					
18	Total	75	56	55	186
19					

Copying Formulas with Absolute Cell References

Sometimes you might want a cell reference to always refer to a particular cell address. In such an instance, you would use an **absolute cell reference**. An absolute cell reference is a cell reference that always refers to a specific cell address, even if you move the formula to a new location. You identify an absolute reference by placing a dollar sign ($) before the column letter and row number of the address (for example $A$1). ✐ Marketing hopes the tour business will increase by 20% over last year's figures. Evan decides to add a column that calculates a possible increase in the number of spring tours in 1998. He wants to do a what-if analysis and recalculate the spreadsheet several times, changing the percentage that the tours might increase each time.

1. Click cell **G1**, type **Change**, and then press [→]
You can store the increase factor that will be used in the what-if analysis in cell H1.

2. Type **1.1** in cell **H1**, then press [Enter]
This represents a 10% increase in sales.

3. Click cell **F3**, type **1998?**, then press [Enter]
Now, you create a formula that references a specific address: cell H1.

4. In cell **F4**, type **=E4*H1**, then click the **Enter button** ☑ on the formula bar
The result of 59.4 appears in cell F4. Now use the fill handle to copy the formula in cell F4 to F5:F7.

5. Drag the fill handle to select the range **F4:F7**
The resulting values in the range F5:F7 are all zeros. When you look at the formula in cell F5, which is =E5*H2, you realize you need to use an absolute reference to cell H1. You can correct this error by editing cell F4 using [F4], a shortcut key, to change the relative cell reference to an absolute cell reference.

6. Click cell **F4**, press [F2] to change to Edit mode, then press [F4]
When you pressed [F2], the **range finder** outlined the equations arguments in blue and green. When you pressed [F4], dollar signs appeared, changing the H1 cell reference to an absolute reference. See Figure B-14.

7. Click the ☑ on the formula bar
Now that the formula correctly contains an absolute cell reference, use the fill handle to copy the formula in cell F4 to F5:F7.

8. Drag the fill handle to select the range **F4:F7**
Now you can complete your what-if analysis by changing the value in cell H1 from 1.1 to 1.25 to indicate a 25% increase in sales.

9. Click cell **H1**, type **1.25**, then click the ☑ on the formula bar
The values in the range F4:F7 change. Compare your worksheet to Figure B-15.

QuickTip

Before you copy or move a formula, check to see if you need to use an absolute cell reference.

CourseHelp

If you have trouble with the concepts in this lesson, be sure to view the CourseHelp entitled Copying Formulas.

FIGURE B-14: Absolute cell reference in cell F4

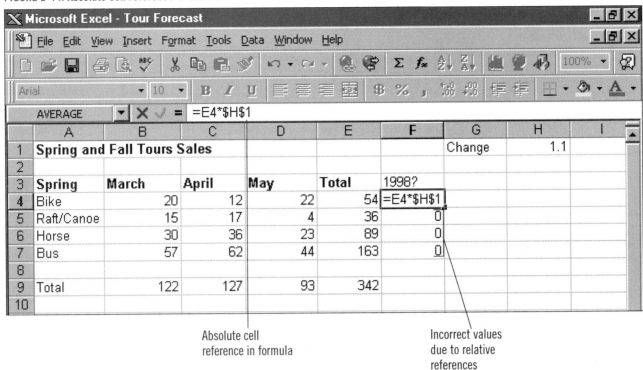

Absolute cell
reference in formula

Incorrect values
due to relative
references

FIGURE B-15: Worksheet with what-if value

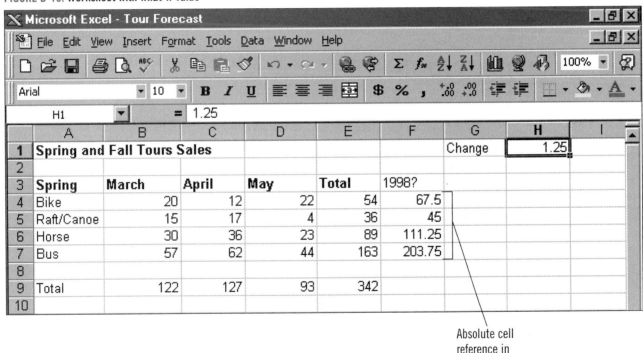

Absolute cell
reference in
formulas

Project a What-If Analysis

The ability to "plug in" values in a worksheet means you can create countless what-if analyses. A what-if analysis occurs when you insert different values into a worksheet model. This type of analysis can help you determine budgetary constraints, and can influence corporate economic decisions.

Naming and Moving a Sheet

Each workbook initially contains three worksheets. When the workbook is opened, the first worksheet is the active sheet. To move from sheet to sheet, click the desired sheet tab located at the bottom of the worksheet window. Sheet tab scrolling buttons, located to the left of the sheet tabs, allow rapid movement among the sheets. To make it easier to identify the sheets in a workbook, you can name each sheet. The name appears on the sheet tab. For instance, sheets within a single workbook could be named for individual sales people to better track performance goals. To better organize a workbook, you can easily rearrange sheets within it. Evan wants to be able to easily identify the Tour Information and the Tour Forecast sheets. He decides to name the two sheets in his workbook, then changes their order.

Steps

1. **Click the Sheet1 tab**
   Sheet1 becomes active; this is the worksheet that contains the Fall Tour Forecast information you compiled for the Marketing department. Its tab moves to the front, and the tab for Sheet2 moves to the background.

2. **Click the Sheet2 tab**
   Sheet2, containing last year's Tour Information, becomes active. Now that you have confirmed which sheet is which, rename Sheet1 so it has a name that identifies its contents.

3. **Double-click the Sheet1 tab**
   The Sheet1 text ("Sheet1") is selected. You could also click Format in the menu bar, point to Sheet, then click Rename to select the sheet name.

4. **Type Forecast, then press [Enter]**
   See Figure B-16. The new name automatically replaced the default name on the tab. Worksheet names can have up to 31 characters, including spaces and punctuation.

5. **Double-click the Sheet2 tab, then rename this sheet Information**
   You decide to rearrange the order of the sheets, so that Forecast comes after Information.

6. **Drag the Forecast sheet after the Information sheet**
   As you drag, the pointer changes to a sheet relocation indicator.
   See Figure B-17.

7. **Save and close the workbook, then exit Excel**

FIGURE B-16: Renamed sheet in workbook

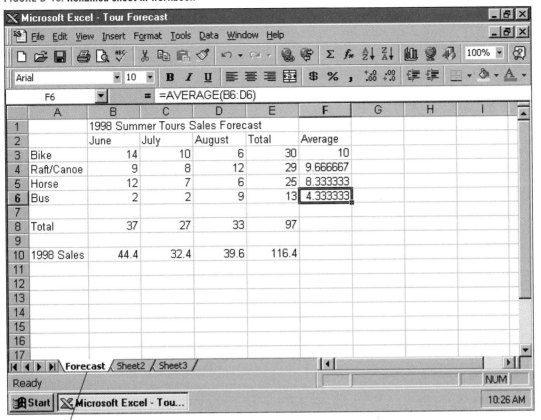

Sheet 1 renamed

FIGURE B-17: Moving Forecast after Information sheet

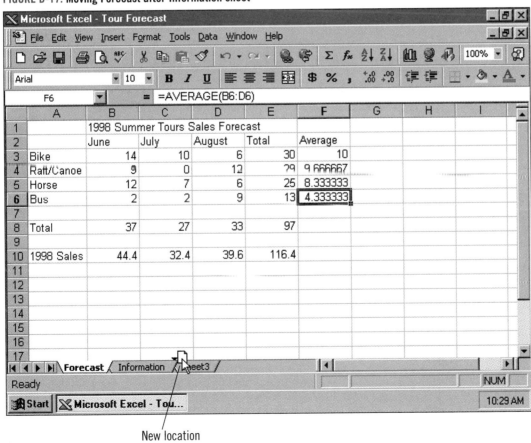

New location
indicator

Practice

► Concepts Review

Label each of the elements of the Excel worksheet window shown in Figure B-18.

FIGURE B-18

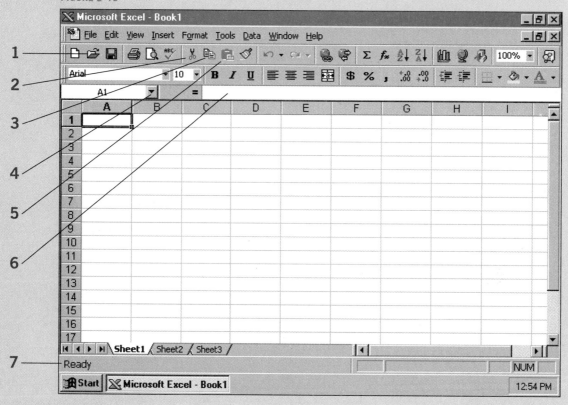

Match each of the terms with the statement that describes its function.

8. Range
9. Function
10. 📋
11. 📋
12. Formula

a. A predefined formula that provides a shortcut for commonly used calculations
b. A cell entry that performs a calculation in an Excel worksheet
c. A specified group of cells, which can include the entire worksheet
d. Used to copy cells
e. Used to paste cells

Select the best answer from the list of choices.

13. What type of cell reference changes when it is copied?
    a. Absolute
    b. Circular
    c. Looping
    d. Relative

14. Which character is used to make a reference absolute?
    a. &
    b. ^
    c. $
    d. @

▶ Skills Review

1 **Edit cell entries and work with ranges.**
   a. Open workbook XL B-2 and save it as "Mutual Funds" on your Student Disk.
   b. Change the number of Arch shares to 210.
   c. Change the price per share of RST stock to 18.45.
   d. Change the number of United shares to 100.
   e. Name the range B2:B5 "Shares".
   f. Name the range C2:C5 "Price".
   g. Save, preview, and print your worksheet.

2 **Enter formulas.**
   a. Click cell B6.
   b. Enter the formula B2+B3+B4+B5.
   c. Click cell C6.
   d. Enter the formula C2+C3+C4+C5.
   e. Save your work, then preview and print the data in the Mutual Funds worksheet.

3 **Introduce functions.**
   a. Click cell C7.
   b. Enter the MIN function for the range C2:C5.
   c. Type the label Min Price in cell A7.
   d. Save your work.
   e. Preview and print this worksheet.

4 **Copy and move cell entries.**
   a. Select the range A1:E6.
   b. Use drag-and-drop to copy the range to cell A10.
   c. Delete the range B11:C14.
   d. Save your work.
   e. Preview and print this worksheet.

5 Copy formulas with relative cell references.
  a. Click cell D2.
  b. Create a formula that multiplies B2 and C2.
  c. Copy the formula in D2 into cells D3:D5.
  d. Copy the formula in D2 into cells D11:D14.
  e. Save, preview, and print this worksheet.

6 Copy formulas with absolute cell references.
  a. Click cell G2.
  b. Type the value 1.375.
  c. Click cell E2.
  d. Create a formula containing an absolute reference that multiplies D2 and G2.
  e. Copy the formula in D2 into cells E3:E5.
  f. Copy the formula in D2 into cells E11:E14.
  g. Change the amount in cell G2 to 2.873.
  h. Save, preview, and print this worksheet.

7 Name a sheet.
  a. Name the Sheet1 tab "Funds".
  b. Move the Funds sheet so it comes after Sheet3.
  c. Save and close this worksheet.

▶ Independent Challenges

1. You are the box-office manager for Lightwell Players, a regional theater company. Your responsibilities include tracking seasonal ticket sales for the company's main stage productions and anticipating ticket sales for the next season. Lightwell Players sells four types of tickets: reserved seating, general admission, senior citizen tickets, and student tickets. The 1993–94 season included productions of *Hamlet*, *The Cherry Orchard*, *Fires in the Mirror*, *The Shadow Box*, and *Heartbreak House*.

Open a new workbook and save it as "Theater" on your Student Disk. Plan and build a worksheet that tracks the sales of each of the four ticket types for all five of the plays. Calculate the total ticket sales for each play, the total sales for each of the four ticket types, and the total sales for all tickets.

Enter your own sales data, but assume the following: the Lightwell Players sold 800 tickets during the season; reserved seating was the most popular ticket type for all of the shows except for *The Shadow Box*; no play sold more than 10 student tickets. Plan and build a second worksheet in the workbook that reflects a 5% increase in sales of all ticket types.

To complete this independent challenge:

1. Think about the results you want to see, the information you need to build into these worksheets, and what types of calculations must be performed.
2. Sketch sample worksheets on a piece of paper to indicate how the information should be laid out. What information should go in the columns? In the rows?
3. Build the worksheets by entering a title, row labels, column headings, and formulas. Use named ranges to make the worksheet easier to use, and rename the sheet tabs to easily identify the contents of each sheet. (Hint: If your columns are too narrow, position the cell pointer in the column you want to widen. To widen the column, click Format on the menu bar, click Column, click Width, choose a new column width, and then click OK.)
4. Use separate worksheets for existing ticket sales and projected sales showing the 5% increase.
5. Save your work, then preview and print the worksheets.
6. Submit your sketches and printed worksheets.

2. You have been promoted to computer lab manager at your school, and it is your responsibility to make sure there are enough computers for students during scheduled classes. Currently, you have four classrooms: three with IBM PCs and one with Macintoshes. Classes are scheduled Monday, Wednesday, and Friday in two-hour increments from 9 a.m. to 5 p.m. (the lab closes at 7 p.m.), and each room can currently accommodate 20 computers.

Open a new workbook and save it as "Lab Manager" on your Student Disk. Plan and build a worksheet that tracks the number of students who can currently use available computers per two-hour class. Create your enrollment data, but assume that current enrollment averages 85% of each room's daily capacity. Using an additional worksheet, show the impact of an enrollment increase of 25%.

To complete this independent challenge:

1. Think about how to construct these worksheets to create the desired output.
2. Sketch sample paper worksheets, to indicate how the information should be laid out.
3. Build the worksheets by entering a title, row labels, column headings, and formulas. Use named ranges to make the worksheet easier to use, and rename the sheets to identify their contents easily.
4. Use separate sheets for actual enrollment and projected changes.
5. Save your work, then preview and print the worksheets.
6. Submit your sketches and printed worksheets.

3. Nuts and Bolts is a small but growing hardware store that has hired you to organize its accounting records using Excel. The store hopes to track its inventory using Excel once its accounting records are under control. Before you were hired, one of the accounting staff started to enter expenses in a workbook, but the work was never completed. Open the workbook XL B-3 and save it as "Nuts and Bolts Finances" on your Student Disk. Include functions such as the Average, Maximum, and Minimum amounts of each of the expenses in the worksheet.

To complete this independent challenge:

1. Think about what information would be important for the accounting staff to know.
2. Use the existing worksheet to create a paper sketch of the types of functions and formulas you will use and of where they will be located. Indicate where you will have named ranges.
3. Create your sketch using the existing worksheet as a foundation. Your worksheet should use range names in its formulas and functions.
4. Rename Sheet1 "Expenses".
5. Save your work, and then preview and print the worksheet.
6. Submit your sketches and printed worksheets.

4. The immediacy of the World Wide Web allows you to find comparative data on any service or industry of interest to you. Your company is interested in investing in one of any of the most actively traded stocks in the three primary trading houses, and you have been asked to retrieve this information. To complete this independent challenge:

1. Open a new workbook and save it on your Student Disk as Stock Data.
2. Log on to the Internet and use your browser to go to the http://www.course.com. From there, click the link Student On Line Companions, then click the Microsoft Office 97 Professional Edition — Illustrated: A First Course page, then click on the Excel link for Unit B.
3. Use each of the following sites to compile your data: NASDAQ [www.nasdaq.com], the New York Stock Exchange [www.nyse.com], and the American Stock Exchange [www.amex.com].
4. Using one worksheet per exchange, locate data for the 10 most actively traded stocks.
5. Make sure all stocks are identified using their commonly known names.
6. Your company will invest a total of $100,000 and wants to make that investment in only one exchange. Still, they are asking you to research the types of stocks that could be purchased in each exchange.
7. Assume an even distribution of the original investment in the stocks, and total pertinent columns. Determine the total number of shares that will be purchased.
8. Save, print, and hand in a print of your work.

► Visual Workshop

Create a worksheet similar to Figure B-19 using the skills you learned in this unit. Save the workbook as "Annual Budget" on your Student Disk. Preview, and then print the worksheet.

FIGURE B-19

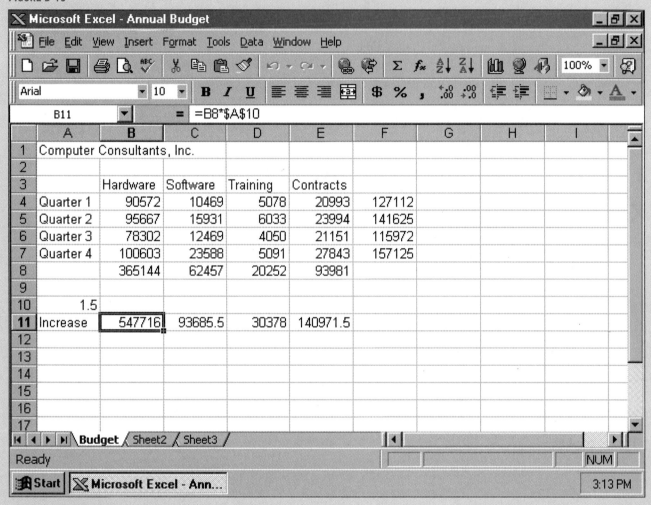

Formatting
a Worksheet

Objectives

- ► **Format values**
- ► **Select fonts and point sizes**
- ► **Change attributes and alignment of labels**
- ► **Adjust column widths**
- ► **Insert and delete rows and columns**
- ► **Apply colors, patterns, and borders**
- ► **Use conditional formatting**
- ► **Check spelling**

Now you will learn how to format a worksheet to make it easier to read and to emphasize key data. You do this by formatting cell contents, adjusting column widths, and inserting and deleting columns and rows. ✒ The marketing managers at Nomad Ltd have asked Evan Brillstein to create a worksheet that tracks tour advertising expenses. Evan has prepared a worksheet containing this information, and now he needs to use formatting techniques to make the worksheet easier to read and to call attention to important data.

Formatting Values

Formatting is how information appears in cells; it does not alter the data in any way. To format a cell, you select it, then apply the formatting you want. You can also format a range of cells. Cells and ranges can be formatted before or after data is entered. If you enter a value in a cell, and the cell appears to display the data incorrectly, you need to format the cell to display the value correctly. You might also want more than one cell to have the same format. ◄━━━ The Marketing Department has requested that Evan track tour advertising expenses. Evan developed a worksheet that tracks invoices for tour advertising. He has entered all the information and now wants to format some of the labels and values in the worksheet. Because some of the format changes he will make to labels and values might also affect column widths, Evan decided to make all his formatting changes before changing the column widths. He formats his values first.

Steps

1. **Open the worksheet XL C-1 from your Student Disk, then save it as Tour Ads**
   The tour advertising worksheet appears in Figure C-1.
   You want to format the data in the Cost ea. column so it displays with a dollar sign.

2. **Select the range E4:E32, then click the Currency Style button $ on the Formatting toolbar**
   Excel adds dollar signs and two decimal places to the Cost ea. column data. When the new format is applied, Excel automatically resizes the columns to display all the information. Columns G, H, and I contain dollar values also, but you decide to apply the comma format instead of currency.

3. **Select the range G4:I32, then click the Comma Style button , on the Formatting toolbar**
   Column J contains percentages.

4. **Select the range J4:J32, click the Percent Style button % on the Formatting toolbar, then click the Increase Decimal button ⁺.₀₀ on the Formatting toolbar to show one decimal place**
   Data in the % of Total column is now formatted in Percent style. Next, you reformat the invoice dates.

5. **Select the range B4:B31, click Format on the menu bar, then click Cells**
   The Format Cells dialog box appears with the Number tab in front and the Date format already selected. See Figure C-2. You can also use this dialog box to format ranges with currency, commas, and percentages.

6. **Select the format 4-Mar-97 in the Type list box, then click OK**
   You decide you don't need the year to appear in the Inv Due column.

7. **Select the range C4:C31, click Format on the menu bar, click Cells, click 4-Mar in the Type list box, then click OK**
   Compare your worksheet to Figure C-3.

8. **Save your work**

FIGURE C-1: Tour advertising worksheet

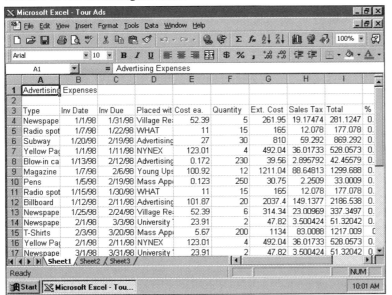

FIGURE C-2: Format Cells dialog box

Sample of
selected type

Select a type

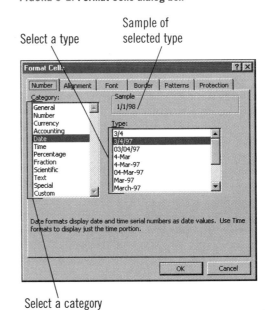

Select a category

FIGURE C-3: Worksheet with formatted values

Currency Style
button

Percent Style button   Comma Style button

Increase decimal
button

Decrease decimal
button

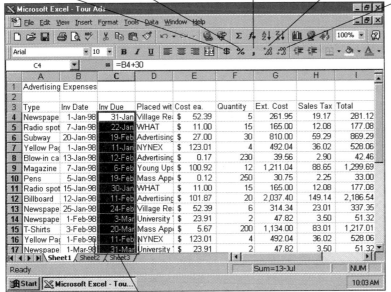

Modified date
formats

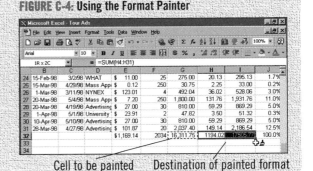

Using the Format Painter

A cell's format can be "painted" into other cells using the Format Painter button ⬧ on the Formatting toolbar. This is similar to using drag-and-drop to copy information, but instead of copying cell contents, you copy only the cell format. Select the cell containing the desired format, then click ⬧. The pointer changes to ⬧, as shown in Figure C-4. Use this pointer to select the cell or range you want to contain the painted format.

FIGURE C-4: Using the Format Painter

Cell to be painted   Destination of painted format

Selecting Fonts and Point Sizes

A **font** is the name given to a collection of characters (letters, numerals, symbols, and punctuation marks) with a specific design. The **point size** is the physical size of the text, measured in points. The default font in Excel is 10 point Arial. You can change the font, the size, or both of any entry or section in a worksheet by using the Format command on the menu bar or by using the Formatting toolbar. Table C-1 shows several fonts in different sizes. ◤━━━ Now that the data is formatted, Evan wants to change the font and size of the labels and the worksheet title so that they stand out.

1. Press **[Ctrl][Home]** to select cell A1

QuickTip

You can also open the Format Cells dialog box by right-clicking the mouse after selecting cells, then selecting Format Cells.

2. Click **Format** on the menu bar, click **Cells**, then click the **Font tab** in the Format Cells dialog box

See Figure C-5.

You decide to change the font of the title from Arial to Times New Roman, and increase the font size to 24.

Trouble?

If you don't have Times New Roman in your list of fonts, choose another font.

3. Click **Times New Roman** in the Font list box, click **24** in the Size list box, then click **OK**

The title font appears in 24 point Times New Roman, and the Formatting toolbar displays the new font and size information. Next, you make the column headings larger.

4. Select the range **A3:J3**, click **Format** on the menu bar, then click **Cells**

The Font tab should still be the front-most tab in the Format Cells dialog box.

QuickTip

The Format Cells dialog box displays a sample of the selected font. Use the Format Cells command to access the Format Cells dialog box if you're unsure of a font's appearance.

5. Click **Times New Roman** in the Font list box, click **14** in the Size list box, then click **OK**

Compare your worksheet to Figure C-6.

6. Save your work

TABLE C-1: Types of fonts

font	12 point	24 point
Arial	Excel	Excel
Helvetica	Excel	Excel
Palatino	Excel	Excel
Times	Excel	Excel

FIGURE C-5: Font tab in the Format Cells dialog box

Available fonts on your computer—yours may differ

Currently selected font

Font attribute options

Type a custom font size or select from the list

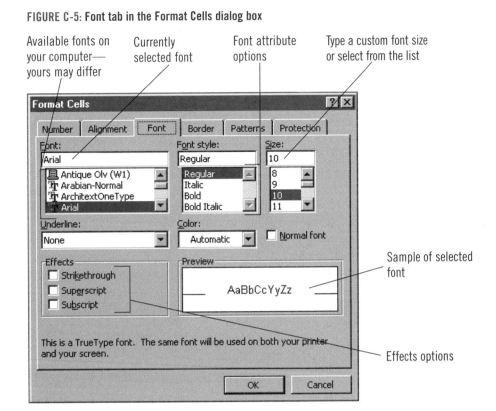

Sample of selected font

Effects options

FIGURE C-6: Worksheet with enlarged title and labels

Column headings now 14 point Times New Roman

Font and size of active cell

Title after changing to 24 point Times New Roman

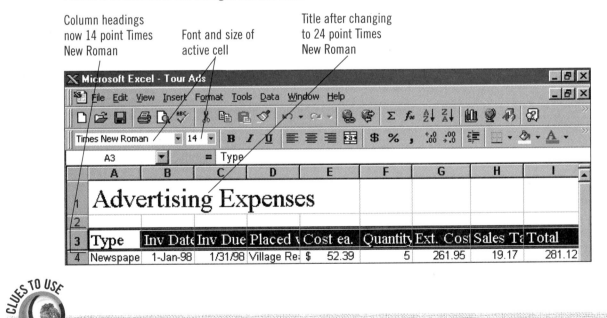

Using the Formatting toolbar to change fonts and sizes

The font and size of the active cell appear on the Formatting toolbar. Click the Font list arrow, as shown in Figure C-7, to see a list of available fonts. If you want to change the font, first select the cell, click the Font list arrow, then choose the font you want. You can change the size of selected text in the same way, by clicking the Size list arrow on the Formatting toolbar to display a list of available point sizes.

FIGURE C-7: Available fonts on the Formatting toolbar

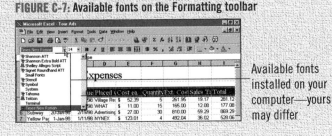

Available fonts installed on your computer—yours may differ

Changing Attributes and Alignment of Labels

Attributes are font styling features such as bold, italics, and underlining. You can apply bold, italics, and underlining from the Formatting toolbar or from the Font tab in the Format Cells dialog box. You can also change the alignment of text in cells. Left, right, or center alignment can be applied from the Formatting toolbar, or from the Alignment tab in the Format Cells dialog box. See Table C-2 for a description of the available attribute and alignment buttons on the Formatting toolbar. Excel also has predefined worksheet formats to make formatting easier. Now that he has applied the appropriate fonts and font sizes to his worksheet labels, Evan wants to further enhance his worksheet's appearance by adding bold and underline formatting and centering some of the labels.

1. Press **[Ctrl][Home]** to select cell A1, then click the **Bold button** B on the Formatting toolbar
The title "Advertising Expenses" appears in bold.

2. Select the range **A3:J3**, then click the **Underline button** U on the Formatting toolbar
Excel underlines the column headings in the selected range.

3. Click cell **A3**, click the **Italics button** I on the Formatting toolbar, then click B
The word "Type" appears in boldface, italic type. Notice that the Bold, Italics, and Underline buttons on the Formatting toolbar are indented. You decide you don't like the italic formatting. You remove it by clicking I again.

QuickTip

Highlighting information on a worksheet can be useful, but overuse of any attribute can be distracting and make a document less readable. Be consistent by adding emphasis the same way throughout a workbook.

4. Click I
Excel removes italics from cell A3.

5. Add bold formatting to the rest of the labels in the range **B3:J3**
You want to center the title over the data.

6. Select the range **A1:F1**, then click the **Merge and Center button** 🔲 on the Formatting toolbar
The title Advertising Expenses is centered across six columns. Now you center the column headings in their cells.

Time To

✔ Save

7. Select the range **A3:J3** then click the **Center button** ≣ on the Formatting toolbar
You are satisfied with the formatting in the worksheet.
Compare your screen to Figure C-8.

FIGURE C-8: Worksheet with formatting attributes applied

Title centered
across columns

Buttons indented

Center button

Column headings
centered, bold, and
underlined

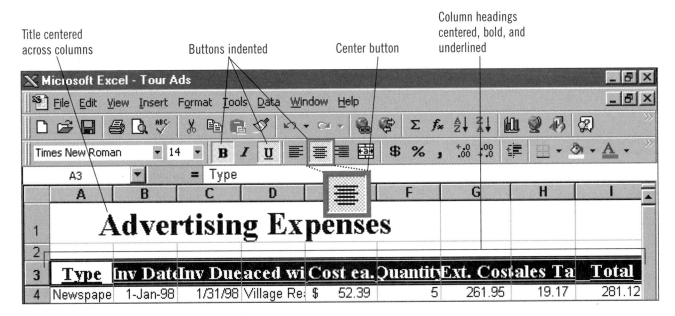

TABLE C-2: Attribute and Alignment buttons on the Formatting toolbar

icon	description	icon	description
B	Adds boldface		Aligns left
I	Italicizes		Aligns center
U	Underlines		Aligns right
	Adds lines or borders		Centers across columns, and combines two or more selected adjacent cells into one cell.

Using AutoFormat

Excel provides 16 preset formats called AutoFormats, which allow instant formatting of large amounts of data. AutoFormats are designed for worksheets with labels in the left column and top rows and totals in the bottom row or right column. To use AutoFormatting, select the data to be formatted—or place your mouse pointer anywhere within the range to be selected—click Format on the menu bar, click AutoFormat, then select a format from the Table Format list box, as shown in Figure C-9.

FIGURE C-9: AutoFormat dialog box

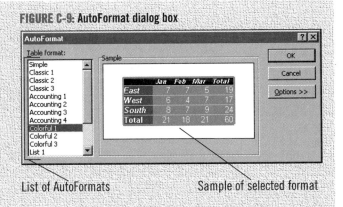

List of AutoFormats

Sample of selected format

Adjusting Column Widths

As you work with a worksheet, you might need to adjust the width of the columns to make your worksheet more usable. The default column width is 8.43 characters wide, a little less than one inch. With Excel, you can adjust the column width for one or more columns using the mouse or the Column command on the Format menu. Table C-3 describes the commands available on the Format Column menu. You can also adjust the height of rows. ◀━━ Evan notices that some of the labels in column A don't fit in the cells. He decides to adjust the widths of columns so that the labels fit in the cells.

Steps 123 4

1. **Position the pointer on the column line between columns A and B in the column header area**
   The pointer changes to ↔, as shown in Figure C-10. You make the column wider.

2. **Drag the line to the right until column A is wide enough to accommodate all of the labels for types of advertising**
   You decide to resize the columns so they automatically accommodate the widest entry in a cell.

3. **Position the pointer on the column line between columns B and C in the column header area until it changes to ↔, then double-click the left mouse button**
   The width of column B is automatically resized to fit the widest entry, in this case, the column head. This feature is called **AutoFit**.

4. **Repeat step 3 to use AutoFit to automatically resize columns C, D, and J**
   You can also use the Column Width command on the Format menu to adjust several columns to the same width.

5. **Select the range F5:I5**
   Any cells in the columns you want to resize can be selected.

6. **Click Format on the menu bar, point to Column, then click Width**
   The Column Width dialog box appears. Move the dialog box, if necessary, by dragging it by its title bar so you can see the contents of the worksheet.

7. **Type 12 in the Column Width text box, then click OK**
   The column widths change to reflect the new settings. See Figure C-11. You are satisfied and decide to save the worksheet.

8. **Save your work**

> **QuickTip**
>
> To reset columns to the default width, select the range of cells, then use the Column Standard Width command on the Format menu. Click OK in the Standard Width dialog box to accept the default width.

TABLE C-3: Format Column commands

command	description
Width	Sets the width to a specific number of characters
AutoFit Selection	Fits the widest entry
Hide	Hide(s) column(s)
Unhide	Unhide(s) column(s)
Standard Width	Resets to default widths

FIGURE C-10: Preparing to change the column width

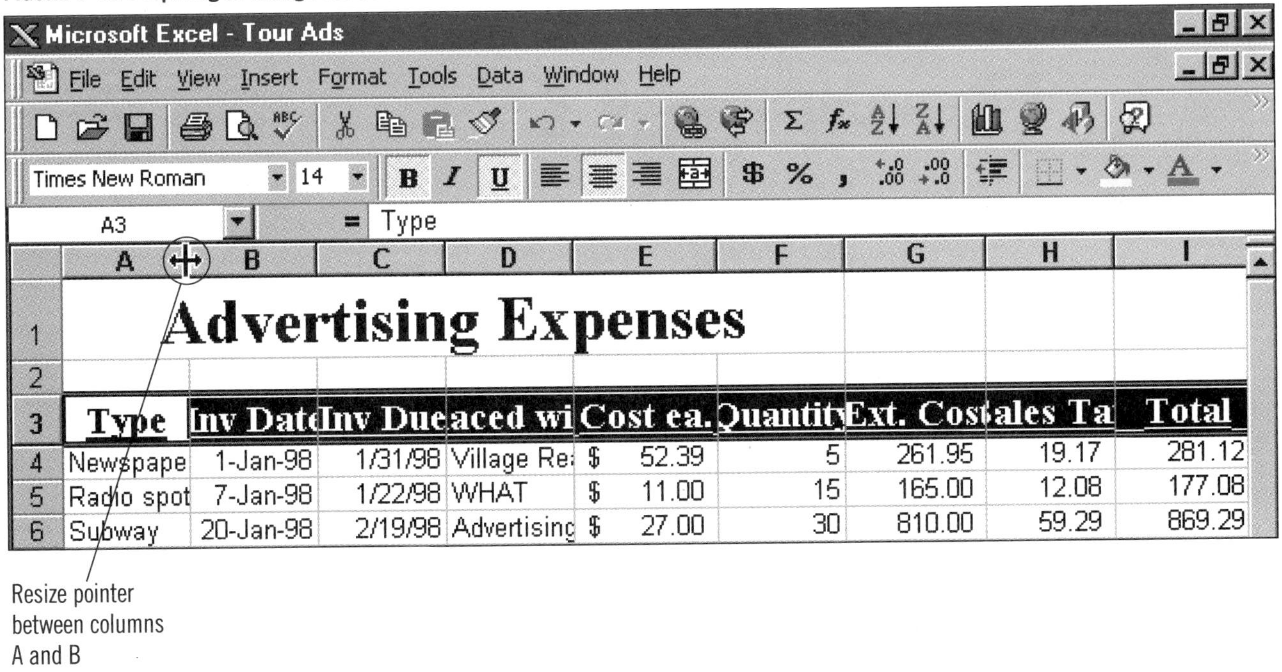

	A	B	C	D	E	F	G	H	I
1		**Advertising Expenses**							
2									
3	Type	Inv Date	Inv Due	aced wi	Cost ea.	Quantit	Ext. Cost	ales Ta	Total
4	Newspape	1-Jan-98	1/31/98	Village Re:	$ 52.39	5	261.95	19.17	281.12
5	Radio spot	7-Jan-98	1/22/98	WHAT	$ 11.00	15	165.00	12.08	177.08
6	Subway	20-Jan-98	2/19/98	Advertising	$ 27.00	30	810.00	59.29	869.29

Resize pointer
between columns
A and B

FIGURE C-11: Worksheet with column widths adjusted

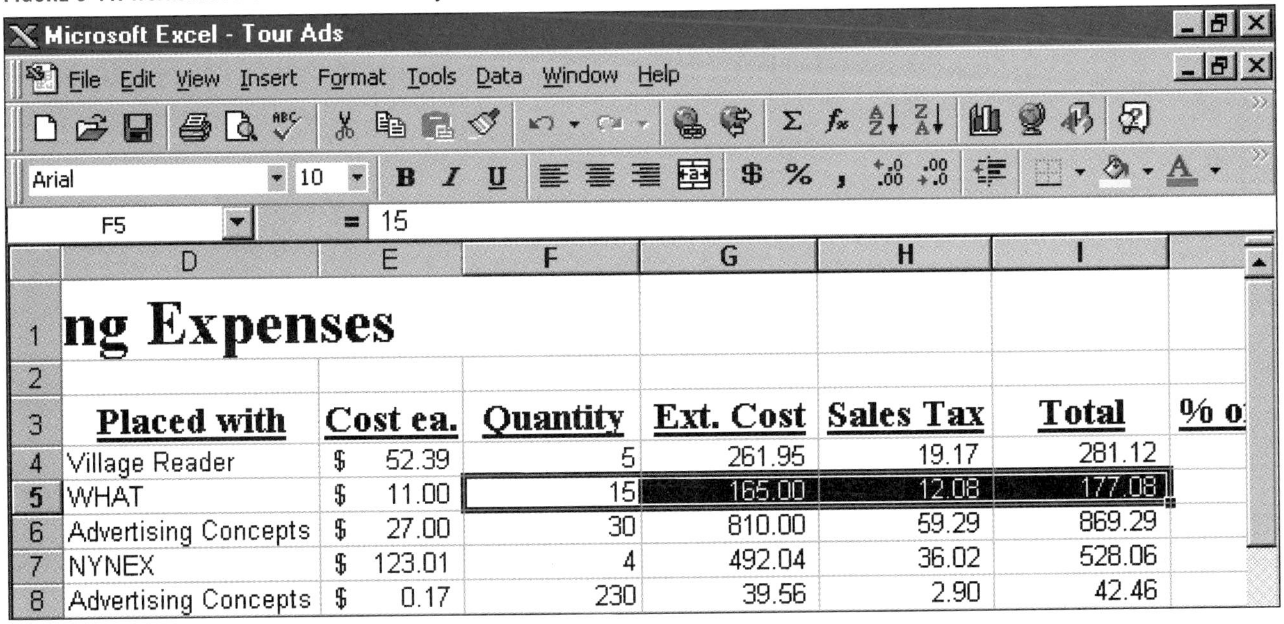

	D	E	F	G	H	I	
1	ng Expenses						
2							
3	**Placed with**	**Cost ea.**	**Quantity**	**Ext. Cost**	**Sales Tax**	**Total**	% o
4	Village Reader	$ 52.39	5	261.95	19.17	281.12	
5	WHAT	$ 11.00	15	165.00	12.08	177.08	
6	Advertising Concepts	$ 27.00	30	810.00	59.29	869.29	
7	NYNEX	$ 123.01	4	492.04	36.02	528.06	
8	Advertising Concepts	$ 0.17	230	39.56	2.90	42.46	

Specifying row height

The Row Height command on the Format menu allows you to customize row height to improve readability. Row height is calculated in points, units of measure also used for fonts—one inch equals 72 points. The row height must exceed the size of the font you are using. For example, if you are using a 12 point font, the row height must be more than 12 points. Normally, you don't need to adjust row heights manually. If you format something in a row to be a larger point size, Excel will adjust the row height to fit the largest point size in the row.

Inserting and Deleting Rows and Columns

As you modify a worksheet, you might find it necessary to insert or delete rows and columns. For example, you might need to insert rows to accommodate new inventory products or remove a column of yearly totals that are no longer current. Inserting or deleting rows or columns can help to make your worksheet more readable. Evan has already improved the appearance of his worksheet by formatting the labels and values in the worksheet. Now he decides to improve the overall appearance of the worksheet by inserting a row between the last row of data and the totals. This will help make the totals stand out more. Evan has also located a row of inaccurate data that should be deleted.

1. **Click cell A32, click Insert on the menu bar, then click Cells**
   The Insert dialog box opens. See Figure C-12. You can choose to insert a column or a row, or you can shift the data in the cells in the active column right or in the active row down. You want to insert a row to add some space between the last row of data and the totals.

2. **Click the Entire Row radio button, then click OK**
   A blank row is inserted between the title and the month labels. When you insert a new row, the contents of the worksheet shift down from the newly inserted row. When you insert a new column, the contents of the worksheet shift to the right from the point of the new column. Now delete the row containing information about hats, as this information is inaccurate.

3. **Click the row 27 selector button (the gray box containing the row number to the left of the worksheet)**
   All of row 27 is selected as shown in Figure C-13.

4. **Click Edit on the menu bar, then click Delete**
   Excel deletes row 27, and all rows below this shift up one row. You are satisfied with the appearance of the worksheet.

5. **Save your work**

QuickTip

Inserting or deleting rows or columns can also cause problems with formulas that reference cells in that area, so be sure to consider this when inserting or deleting rows or columns.

FIGURE C-12: Insert dialog box

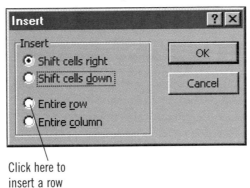

Click here to
insert a row

FIGURE C-13: Worksheet with row 27 selected

25	Pens	15-Mar-98	4/29/98	Mass Appeal, Inc.	$ 0.12	250	3
26	Yellow Pages	1-Mar-98	3/11/98	NYNEX	$ 123.01	4	49
27	Hats	20-Mar-98	5/4/98	Mass Appeal, Inc.	$ 7.20	250	1,80
28	Subway	20-Mar-98	4/19/98	Advertising Concepts	$ 27.00	30	81
29	Newspaper	1-Apr-98	5/1/98	University Voice	$ 23.91	2	4
30	Subway	10-Apr-98	5/10/98	Advertising Concepts	$ 27.00	30	81
31	Billboard	28-Mar-98	4/27/98	Advertising Concepts	$ 101.87	20	2,03
32							
33					$1,169.14	2034	16,31
34							
35							

◄ ◄ ► ► \ **Sheet1** / Sheet2 / Sheet3 /

Ready   Sum=75913.83035   NUM

Start Microsoft Excel - Tou...   8:26 AM

Row 27 selector   Inserted row
button

Excel 97

Using dummy columns and rows

You use cell references and ranges in formulas. When
you add or delete a column or row within a range used
in a formula, Excel automatically adjusts the formula to
reflect the change. However, when you add a column or
row at the end of a range used in a formula, you must
modify the formula to reflect the additional column or
row. To avoid having to edit the formula, you can
include a dummy column and dummy row within the
range you use for that formula. A dummy column is a
blank column included to the right of but within a
range. A dummy row is a blank row included at the
bottom of but within a range, as shown in Figure C-14.
Then if you add another column or row to the end of
the range, the formula will automatically be modified to
include the new data.

FIGURE C-14: Formula with dummy row

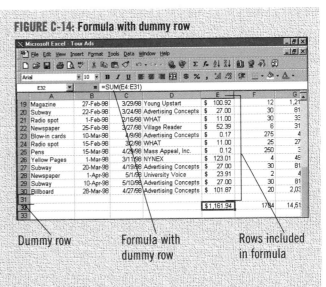

Dummy row   Formula with   Rows included
                   dummy row   in formula

Applying Colors, Patterns, and Borders

You can use colors, patterns, and borders to enhance the overall appearance of a worksheet and to improve its readability. You can add these enhancements using the Patterns tab in the Format Cells dialog box or by using the Borders and Color buttons on the Formatting toolbar. When you use the Format Cells dialog box, you can see what your enhanced text will look like in the Sample box. You can apply color to the background of a cell or range or to cell contents. If you do not have a color monitor, the colors appear in shades of gray. You can apply patterns to the background of a cell or range. And, you can apply borders to all the cells in a worksheet or only to selected cells. See Table C-4 for a list of border buttons and their functions. Evan decides to add a pattern, a border, and color to the title of the worksheet. This will give the worksheet a more professional appearance.

Steps

1. Click cell **A1**, then click the **Fill Color button list arrow** 🖫 on the Formatting toolbar
The color palette appears, as shown in Figure C-15.

2. Click **Turquoise** (fourth row, fourth color from the right)

3. Click **Format** on the menu bar, then click **Cells**
The Format Cells dialog box opens.

4. Click the **Patterns tab**, as shown in Figure C-16, if it is not already displayed
When choosing a background pattern, consider that the more cell contents contrast with the background, the more readable the contents will be. You choose the diamond pattern.

5. Click the **Pattern list arrow**, click the **thin diagonal crosshatch pattern** (third row, last pattern on the right), then click **OK**
Now you add a border.

6. Click the **Borders button list arrow** 🖫 on the Formatting toolbar, then click the **heavy bottom border** (second row, second border from the left)
Next, you change the font color.

7. Click the **Font Color button list arrow** 🄰 on the Formatting toolbar, then click **blue** (second row, third color from the right)
The text changes color, as shown in Figure C-17.

8. Preview and print the first page of the worksheet

QuickTip
Use color sparingly. Excessive use can divert the reader's attention away from the data in the worksheet.

Time To
✔ Save

TABLE C-4: Border buttons

button	description	button	description
	No border		Thin border around range
	Single underline		Left border
	Double underline		Right border
	Thick bottom, thin top border		Double bottom, single top
	Outline all in range		Thick bottom border
	Thick border around range		

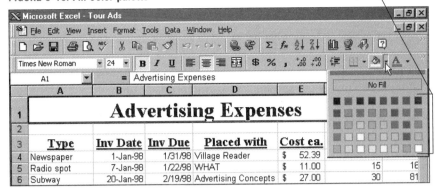

Choose from available colors

FIGURE C-15: Fill Color palette

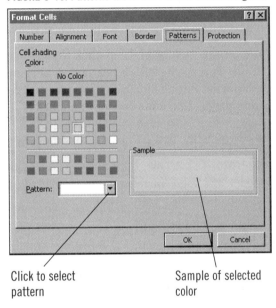

FIGURE C-16: Patterns tab in the Format Cells dialog box

Click to select pattern

Sample of selected color

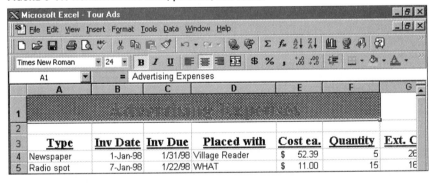

FIGURE C-17: Worksheet with color, patterns, and border

Excel 97

CLUES TO USE

Using color to organize a worksheet

You can use color to give a distinctive look to each part of a worksheet. For example, you might want to apply a light blue to all the rows containing the subway data and a light green to all the rows containing the newspaper data. Be consistent throughout a group of worksheets, and try to avoid colors that are too bright and distracting.

FORMATTING A WORKSHEET EX C-13

Using Conditional Formatting

Formatting attributes make worksheets look professional, and these same attributes can be applied depending on specific outcomes in cells. Automatically applying formatting attributes based on cell values is called **conditional formatting**. You might, for example, want advertising costs above a certain number to display in red boldface, and lower values to display in blue. Evan wants his worksheet to include conditional formatting so that extended advertising costs greater than $175 display in red boldface. He creates the conditional format in the first cell in the extended cost column.

Steps

1. Click cell **G4**

Use the scroll bars if necessary, to make column G visible.

2. Click **Format** on the menu bar, then click **Conditional Formatting**

The Conditional Formatting dialog box opens, as shown in Figure C-18. The number of input fields varies depending on which operator is selected. You can define up to 3 different conditions that let you determine outcome parameters and then assign formatting attributes to each one.

You begin by defining the first part of the condition.

3. Click the **Operator list arrow**, then click **greater than or equal to**

Next, you define the value in this condition that must be met for the formatting to be applied.

4. Click the **Value text box**, then type **175**

Once the value has been assigned, you define this condition's formatting attributes.

5. Click **Format**, click the **Color list arrow**, click **Red** (third row, first color from the left), click **Bold** in the Font Style list box, click **OK**, then click **OK** again to close the Conditional Formatting dialog box

Next, you copy the formatting to the other cells in the column.

6. Click the **Format Painter button** on the Formatting toolbar, then select the range **G5:G30**

Once the formatting is copied, you reposition the cell pointer to review the results.

7. Click cell **G4**

Compare your results to Figure C-19.

8. Press **[Ctrl][Home]** to move to cell Al

9. Save your work

FIGURE C-18: Conditional Formatting dialog box

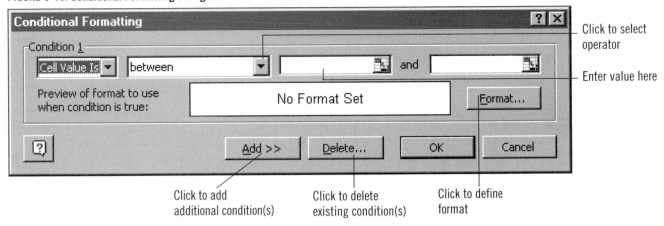

Click to select operator

Enter value here

Click to add additional condition(s)

Click to delete existing condition(s)

Click to define format

FIGURE C-19: Worksheet with conditional formatting

	B	C	D	E	F	G	H
1			Advertising Expenses				
2							
3	**Inv Date**	**Inv Due**	**Placed with**	**Cost ea.**	**Quantity**	**Ext. Cost**	**Sales T**
4	1-Jan-98	1/31/98	Village Reader	$ 52.39	5	**261.95**	19
5	7-Jan-98	1/22/98	WHAT	$ 11.00	15	165.00	12
6	20-Jan-98	2/19/98	Advertising Concepts	$ 27.00	30	810.00	59
7	1-Jan-98	1/11/98	NYNEX	$ 123.01	4	492.04	36
8	13-Jan-98	2/12/98	Advertising Concepts	$ 0.17	230	39.56	2
9	7-Jan-98	2/6/98	Young Upstart	$ 100.92	12	**1,211.04**	88
10	5-Jan-98	2/19/98	Mass Appeal, Inc.	$ 0.12	250	30.75	2
11	15-Jan-98	1/30/98	WHAT	$ 11.00	15	165.00	12
12	12-Jan-98	2/11/98	Advertising Concepts	$ 101.87	20	**2,037.40**	149
13	25-Jan-98	2/24/98	Village Reader	$ 52.39	6	314.34	23
14	1-Feb-98	3/3/98	University Voice	$ 23.91	2	47.82	3
15	3-Feb-98	3/20/98	Mass Appeal, Inc.	$ 5.67	200	**1,134.00**	83

Results of conditional formatting

Deleting conditional formatting

Because its likely that the conditions you define will change, any of the conditional formats defined can be deleted. Select the cell(s) containing conditional formatting, click Format, click Conditional Formatting, then click the Delete button. The Delete Conditional Format dialog box opens, as shown in Figure C-20. Click the checkboxes for any of the conditions you want to delete, then click OK. The previously assigned formatting is deleted—leaving the cell's contents intact.

FIGURE C-20: Delete Conditional Format dialog box

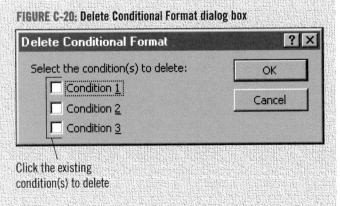

Click the existing condition(s) to delete

Checking Spelling

You may think your worksheet is complete, but if you haven't checked for spelling errors, you risk undermining the professional effect of your work. A single misspelled word can ruin your work. The spell checker in Excel is also shared by Word, PowerPoint, and Access, so any words you've added to the dictionary using those programs are also available in Excel. Evan has completed the formatting for his worksheet and is ready to check its spelling.

Steps 1 2 3 4

1. **Click the Spelling button** ABC **on the Standard toolbar**

   The Spelling dialog opens, as shown in Figure C-21, with the abbreviation Inv selected as the first misspelled word in the worksheet. The spell checker starts from the active cell and compares words in the worksheet to those in its dictionary. Any word not found in the dictionary causes the spell checker to stop. At that point, you can decide to Ignore, Change, or Add the word.

   You decide to Ignore All cases of Inv, the abbreviation of invoice.

2. **Click Ignore All, then click Ignore All again when the spell checker stops on T-Shirts**

   The spell checker found the word 'cards' misspelled. You find the correct spelling and fix the error.

3. **Scroll through the Suggestions list, click Cards, then click Change**

   The word 'Concepts' is also misspelled. Make this correction.

4. **Click Concepts in the Suggestions list, then click Change**

   When no more incorrect words are found, Excel displays the message box shown in Figure C-22.

5. **Click OK**

6. **Press [Ctrl][Home] to move to cell A1**

7. **Save your work**

8. **Preview and print the worksheet, then close the workbook and exit Excel**

FIGURE C-21: Spelling dialog box

Misspelled word

Type replacement word here or click a suggestion

Click to add word to dictionary

Click to ignore all occurrences of misspelled word

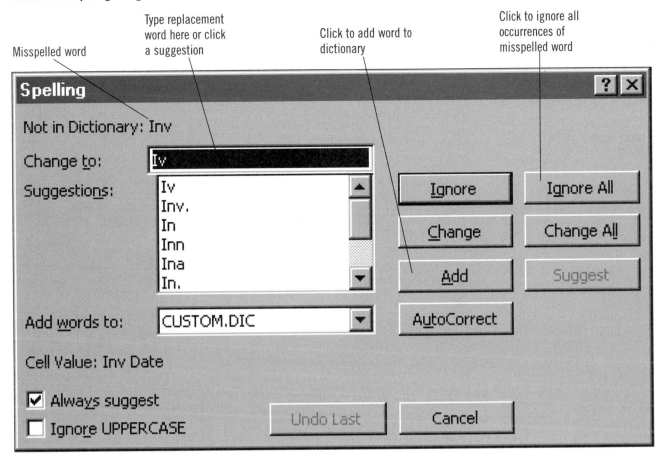

Excel 97

FIGURE C-22: Spelling completed warning box

Modifying the spell checker

Each of us use words specific to our profession or task. Because the dictionary supplied with Microsoft Office cannot possibly include all the words that each of us needs, it is possible to add words to the dictionary shared by all the components in the suite. To customize the Microsoft Office dictionary used by the spell checker, click Add when a word not in the dictionary is found. From then on, that word will no longer be considered misspelled by the spell checker.

Practice

► Concepts Review

Label each of the elements of the Excel worksheet window shown in Figure C-23.

FIGURE C-23

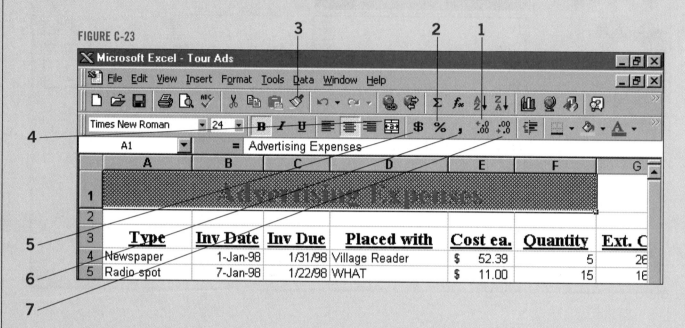

Match each of the statements to the command or button it describes.

 8. Format Cells
 9. Edit Delete
10. Insert Row/Column
11. 📋
12. 💲
13. ✓

a. Adds a new row or column
b. Erases the contents of a cell
c. Checks the spelling in a worksheet
d. Changes the point size of selected cells
e. Pastes the contents of the Clipboard in the current cell
f. Changes the format to Currency

Select the best answer from the list of choices.

14. Which button increases the number of decimal places in selected cells?

a. `,`　　　　**b.** `.00→.0`　　　　**c.** 🖌　　　　**d.** `.0→.00`

15. Each of the following operators can be used in conditional formatting, *except*

a. equal to　　　**b.** greater than　　　**c.** similar to　　　**d.** not between

16. How many conditional formats can be created in any cell?

a. 1　　　**b.** 2　　　**c.** 3　　　**d.** 4

▶ Skills Review

1. Format values.
- **a.** Open a new workbook.
- **b.** Enter the information from Table C-5 in your worksheet.
- **c.** Select the range of values in the Price and Sold columns.
- **d.** Click the Currency Style button.
- **e.** Calculate the Totals column by multiplying the price by the number sold.
- **f.** Save this workbook as Chairs on your Student Disk.

TABLE C-5

Country Oak Chairs, Inc. Quarterly Sales Sheet			
Description	**Price**	**Sold**	**Totals**
Rocker	1299	1104	
Recliner	800	1805	
Bar stool	159	1098	
Dinette	369	1254	

2. Select fonts and point sizes.
- **a.** Select the range of cells containing the column titles.
- **b.** Change the font of the column titles to Times New Roman.
- **c.** Increase the point size of the column titles to 14 point.
- **d.** Resize columns as necessary.
- **e.** Save your workbook changes.

3. Change attributes and alignment of labels.
- **a.** Select the worksheet title Country Oak Chairs, Inc.
- **b.** Click the Bold button to apply boldface to the title.
- **c.** Select the label Quarterly Sales Sheet.
- **d.** Click the Underline button to apply underlining to the label.
- **e.** Add the bold attribute to the furniture descriptions, as well as the Totals label.
- **f.** Make the Price and Sold labels italics.
- **g.** Select the range of cells containing the column titles.
- **h.** Click the Center button to center the column titles.
- **i.** Save your changes, then preview and print the workbook.

4. Adjust column widths.
- **a.** Change the width of the Price column to 11.
- **b.** Use the Format menu to resize the Description and Sold columns.
- **c.** Save your workbook changes.

5. Insert and delete rows and columns.

a. Insert a new row between rows 4 and 5.

b. Add Country Oak Chairs' newest product—a Shaker bench—in the newly inserted row. Enter "239" for the price and "360" for the number sold.

c. Use the fill handle to copy the formula in cell D4 to D5.

d. Save your changes, then preview and print the workbook.

6. Apply colors, patterns, and borders.

a. Add a border around the data entered from Table C-5.

b. Apply a light green background color to the Descriptions column.

c. Apply a light pattern to the Descriptions column.

d. Apply a dark green background to the column labels.

e. Change the color of the font in the first row of the data to light green.

f. Save your work.

g. Preview and print the worksheet, then close the workbook.

7. Use conditional formatting.

a. Open the file XL C-2 from your Student Disk.

b. Save it as "Recap" on your Student Disk.

c. Create conditional formatting that changes values to blue if they are greater than 35000, and changes values to green if they are less than 21000.

d. Use the Bold button and Center button to format the column headings and row titles.

e. Autofit the other columns as necessary.

f. Save your changes.

8. Check spelling.

a. Open the spell checker.

b. Check the spelling in the worksheet.

c. Correct any spelling errors.

d. Save your changes, then preview and print the workbook.

e. Close the workbook, then exit Excel.

▶ Independent Challenges

1. Nuts and Bolts is a small but growing hardware store that has hired you to organize its accounting records using Excel. Now that the Nuts and Bolts hardware store's accounting records are on Excel, they would like you to work on the inventory. Although more items will be added later, enough have been entered in a worksheet for you to begin your modifications.

Open the workbook XL C-3 on your Student Disk, and save it as "NB Inventory."

To complete this independent challenge:

1. Create a formula that calculates the Value of the inventory on-hand for each item.
2. Use an absolute reference to calculate the Sale Price of each item.
3. Use enhancements to make the title, column headings, and row headings more attractive.
4. Make sure all columns are wide enough to see the data.
5. Before printing, preview the file so you know what the worksheet will look like. Adjust any items as needed, check spelling, and print a copy. Save your work before closing the file.
6. Submit your final printout.

2. You recently moved to a small town and joined the Chamber of Commerce. Since the other members are not computer-literate, you volunteered to organize the member organizations in a worksheet. As part of your efforts with the Chamber of Commerce, you need to examine more closely the membership in comparison to the community. To make the existing data more professional-looking and easier to read, you've decided to use attributes and your formatting abilities.

Open the workbook XL C-4 on your Student Disk, and save it as "Community."

To complete this independent challenge:

1. Remove any blank columns.
2. Format the Annual Revenue column using the Currency format.
3. Make all columns wide enough to fit their data.
4. Use formatting enhancements, such as fonts, font sizes, and text attributes, to make the worksheet more attractive.
5. Before printing, preview the file so you know what the worksheet will look like. Adjust any items as needed, check spelling, and print a copy. Save your work before closing the file.
6. Submit your final printout.

3. Write Brothers is a Houston-based company that manufactures high-quality pens and markers. As the finance manager, one of your responsibilities is to analyze the monthly reports from your five district sales offices. Your boss, Joanne Parker, has just told you to prepare a quarterly sales report for an upcoming meeting. Because several top executives will be attending this meeting, Joanne reminds you that the report must look professional. In particular, she asks you to emphasize the company's surge in profits during the last month and to highlight the fact that the Northeastern district continues to outpace the other districts.

Plan and build a worksheet that shows the company's sales during the last three months. Make sure you include:

- The number of pens sold (units sold) and the associated revenues (total sales) for each of the five district sales offices. The five Write Brothers sales districts include: Northeastern, Midwestern, Southeastern, Southern, and Western.
- Calculations that show month-by-month totals and a three-month cumulative total.
- Calculations that show each district's share of sales (percent of units sold).
- Formatting enhancements to emphasize the recent month's sales surge and the Northeastern district's sales leadership.

To complete this independent challenge:

1. Prepare a worksheet plan that states your goal, lists the worksheet data you'll need, and identifies the formulas for the different calculations.
2. Sketch a sample worksheet on a piece of paper, indicating how the information should be organized and formatted. How will you calculate the totals? What formulas can you copy to save time and keystrokes? Do any of these formulas need to use an absolute reference? How will you show dollar amounts? What information should be shown in bold? Do you need to use more than one font? More than one point size?
3. Build the worksheet with your own sales data. Enter the titles and labels first, then enter the numbers and formulas. Save the workbook as Write Brothers on your Student Disk.
4. Make enhancements to the worksheet. Adjust the column widths as necessary. Format labels and values, and change attributes and alignment.
5. Add a column that calculates a 10% increase in sales. Use an absolute cell reference in this calculation.
6. Before printing, preview the file so you know what the worksheet will look like. Adjust any items as needed, check spelling, and print a copy. Save your work before closing the file.
7. Submit your worksheet plan, preliminary sketches, and the final printout.

4. As the manager of your company's computer lab, you've been asked to assemble data on currently available software for use in a business environment. Using the World Wide Web, you can retrieve information about current software and create an attractive worksheet for distribution to department managers. To complete this independent challenge:

1. Open a new workbook and save it on your Student Disk as Software Comparison.
2. Log on to the Internet and use your browser to go to http://www.course.com. From there, click the link Student On Line Companions, then click the Microsoft Office 97 Professional Edition—Illustrated: A First Course page, then click the Excel link for Unit C.
3. Use each of the following sites to compile your data.
   Microsoft Corporation [www.microsoft.com], and Lotus Corporation [www.lotus.com].
4. Retrieve information on word processors, spreadsheets, presentation graphics, and database programs manufactured by both companies. The software must be Windows 95 compatible.
5. Create a worksheet that includes the information in step 4 above, as well as a retail price for each component, and whether all the programs can be purchased as a suite.
6. Use formatting attributes to make this data look attractive.
7. Use conditional formatting so that individual programs that cost over $100 display in red.
8. Save, print, and hand in a print out of your work.

Visual Workshop

Create the following worksheet using the skills you learned in this unit. Open the file XL C-5 on your Student Disk, and save it as January Invoices. Create a conditional format in the Cost ea. column where entries greater than 50 are displayed in red. (Hint: The only additional font used in this exercise is Times New Roman. It is 22 points in row 1, and 14 points in row 3.)

FIGURE C-24

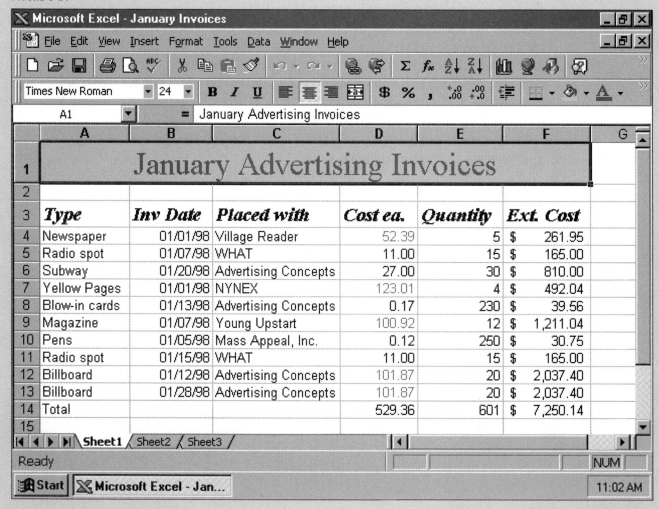

	Type	Inv Date	Placed with	Cost ea.	Quantity	Ext. Cost
4	Newspaper	01/01/98	Village Reader	52.39	5	$ 261.95
5	Radio spot	01/07/98	WHAT	11.00	15	$ 165.00
6	Subway	01/20/98	Advertising Concepts	27.00	30	$ 810.00
7	Yellow Pages	01/01/98	NYNEX	123.01	4	$ 492.04
8	Blow-in cards	01/13/98	Advertising Concepts	0.17	230	$ 39.56
9	Magazine	01/07/98	Young Upstart	100.92	12	$ 1,211.04
10	Pens	01/05/98	Mass Appeal, Inc.	0.12	250	$ 30.75
11	Radio spot	01/15/98	WHAT	11.00	15	$ 165.00
12	Billboard	01/12/98	Advertising Concepts	101.87	20	$ 2,037.40
13	Billboard	01/28/98	Advertising Concepts	101.87	20	$ 2,037.40
14	Total			529.36	601	$ 7,250.14

Working
with Charts

- ► **Plan and design a chart**
- ► **Create a chart**
- ► **Move and resize a chart and its objects**
- ► **Edit a chart**
- ► **Change the appearance of a chart**
- ► **Enhance a chart**
- ► **Add text annotations and arrows to a chart**
- ► **Preview and print a chart**

Worksheets provide an effective way to organize information, but they are not always the best format for presenting data to others. Information in a selected range or worksheet can be easily converted to the visual format of a chart. Charts quickly communicate the relationships of data in a worksheet. In this unit, you will learn how to create a chart, edit a chart and change the chart type, add text annotations and arrows to a chart, then preview and print it. ✐ Evan Brillstein needs to create a chart showing the six-month sales history of Nomad Ltd for the annual meeting. He wants to illustrate the impact of an advertising campaign that started in June.

Planning and Designing a Chart

Before creating a chart, you need to plan what you want your chart to show and how you want it to look. ✎ Evan wants to create a chart to be used at the annual meeting. The chart will show the spring and summer sales throughout the Nomad Ltd regions. In early June, the Marketing Department launched a national advertising campaign. The results of the campaign were increased sales for the summer months. Evan wants his chart to illustrate this dramatic sales increase. Evan uses the worksheet shown in Figure D-1 and the following guidelines to plan the chart:

CourseHelp

The camera icon indicates there is a CourseHelp for this lesson. Click the Start button, point to Programs, then click Excel 97 Illustrated. Choose the CourseHelp that corresponds to this lesson.

1. Determine the purpose of the chart, and identify the data relationships you want to communicate visually

You want to create a chart that shows sales throughout Nomad's regions in the spring and summer months (March through August). In particular, you want to highlight the increase in sales that occurred in the summer months as a result of the advertising campaign.

2. Determine the results you want to see, and decide which chart type is most appropriate to use; Table D-1 describes several different types of charts

Because you want to compare related data (sales in each of the regions) over a time period (the months March through August), you decide to use a column chart.

3. Identify the worksheet data you want the chart to illustrate

You are using data from the worksheet titled "Nomad Ltd Regions, Spring and Summer Sales," as shown in Figure D-1. This worksheet contains the sales data for the five regions from March through August.

4. Sketch the chart, then use your sketch to decide where the chart elements should be placed

You sketch your chart as shown in Figure D-2. You put the months on the horizontal axis (the **X-axis**) and the monthly sales figures on the vertical axis (the **Y-axis**). The **tick marks** on the Y-axis create a scale of measure for each value. Each value in a cell you select for your chart is a **data point**. In any chart, each data point is visually represented by a **data marker**, which in this case is a column. A collection of related data points is a **data series**. In this chart, there are five data series (Midwest, Northeast, Northwest, South, and Southwest), so you have included a **legend** to identify them.

FIGURE D-1: Worksheet containing sales data

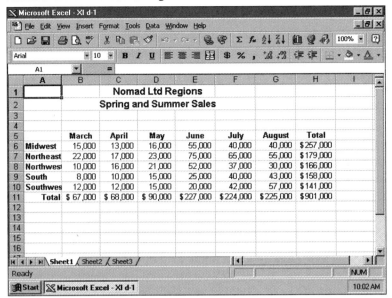

FIGURE D-2: Sketch of the column chart

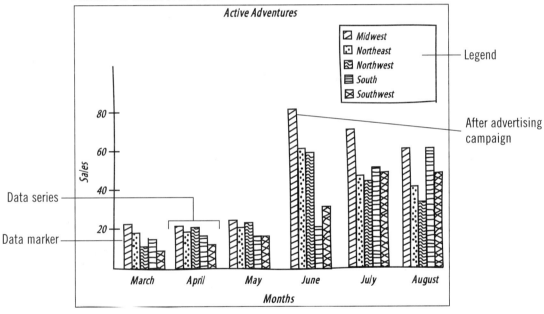

TABLE D-1: Commonly used chart types

type	button	description
Area		Shows how volume changes over time
Bar		Compares distinct, unrelated objects over time using a horizontal format; sometimes referred to as a horizontal bar chart in other spreadsheet programs
Column		Compares distinct, unrelated objects over time using a vertical format; the Excel default; sometimes referred to as a bar chart in other spreadsheet programs
Line		Compares trends over even time intervals; similar to an area chart
Pie		Compares sizes of pieces as part of a whole; can have slices pulled away from the pie, or "exploded"
XY (scatter)		Compares trends over uneven time or measurement intervals; used in scientific and engineering disciplines for trend spotting and extrapolation
Combination	none	Combines a column and line chart to compare data requiring different scales of measure

Excel 97

Creating a Chart

To create a chart in Excel, you first select the range containing the data you want to chart. Once you've selected a range, you can use Excel's Chart Wizard to lead you through the chart creation process. ▬▬▬ Using the worksheet containing the spring and summer sales data for the five regions, Evan will create a chart that shows the monthly sales of each region from March through August.

 Steps 1 2 3 4

1. Open the workbook **XL D-1** from your Student Disk, then save it as **Nomad Regions**
First, you need to select the cells you want to chart. You want to include the monthly sales figures for each of the regions, but not the totals. You also want to include the month and region labels.

QuickTip

When selecting a large, unnamed range, select the upper left-most cell in the range, press and hold [Shift], then click the lower right-most cell in the range.

2. Select the range **A5:G10**, then click the **Chart Wizard button** 📊 on the Standard toolbar
When you click 📊 the Chart Wizard opens. The first Chart Wizard dialog box lets you choose the type of chart you want to create. See Figure D-3. You can see a preview of the chart by clicking the Press and hold to view sample button.

3. Click **Next** to accept the default chart type of column
The second dialog box lets you choose the data being charted and whether the series are in rows or columns. Currently, the rows are selected as the data series. You could switch this by clicking the Columns radio button located under the Data range. Since you selected the data before clicking the Chart Wizard button, the correct range A5:G10 displays in the Data range text box. Satisfied with the selections, you accept the default choices.

4. Click **Next**
The third Chart Wizard dialog box shows a sample chart using the data you selected. Notice that the regions (the rows in the selected range) are plotted according to the months (the columns in the selected range), and that the months were added as labels for each data series. Notice also that there is a legend showing each region and its corresponding color on the chart. Here, you can choose to keep the legend, add a chart title, and add axis titles. You add a title.

5. Click the **Chart title text box**, then type **Nomad Ltd Regional Sales**
After a moment, the title appears in the Sample Chart box. See Figure D-4.

6. Click **Next**
In the last Chart Wizard dialog box, you determine the location of the chart. A chart can be displayed on the same sheet as the data, or a separate sheet in the workbook. You decide to display the chart on the current sheet.

 Trouble?

If you want to delete a chart, select it then press [Delete].

7. Click **Finish**
The column chart appears, as shown in Figure D-5. Your chart might look slightly different. Just as you had hoped, the chart shows the dramatic increase in sales between May and June. The **selection handles**, the small squares at the corners and sides of the chart borders, indicate that the chart is selected. Anytime a chart is selected (as it is now), the Chart toolbar appears. It might be floating, as shown in Figure D-5, or it might be fixed at the top or bottom of the worksheet window.

FIGURE D-3: First Chart Wizard dialog box

Chart types   Chart sub-types

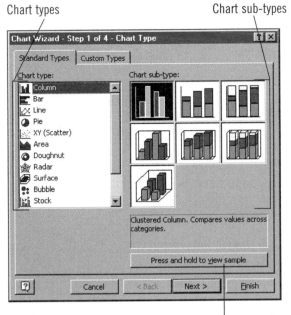

Press to view sample

FIGURE D-4: Third Chart Wizard dialog box

Sample chart   Title added   Legend

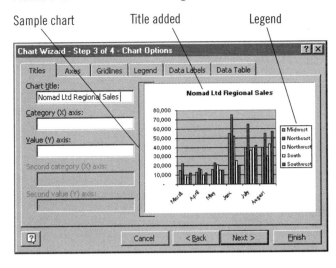

FIGURE D-5: Worksheet with column chart

Floating chart
toolbar   Title   Legend

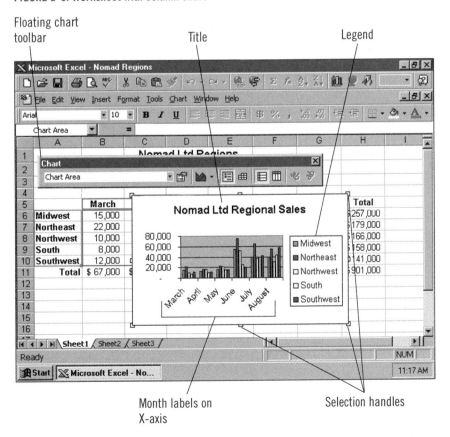

Month labels on   Selection handles
X-axis

Moving and Resizing a Chart and its Objects

Charts are graphics, or drawn **objects**, and have no specific cell or range address. You can move charts anywhere on a worksheet without affecting formulas or data in the worksheet. You can even put them on another sheet. You can also easily resize a chart to improve its appearance by dragging the selection handles. Drawn objects such as charts can contain other objects that you can move and resize. To move an object, select it then drag it or cut and copy it to a new location. To resize an object, use the selection handles. Evan wants to increase the size of the chart and position it below the worksheet data. He also wants to change the position of the legend.

Steps

Trouble?

If the Chart toolbar is in the way of the legend, move it out of your way first.

1. Make sure the chart is still selected. Scroll the worksheet until **row 28** is visible, then position the pointer over the white space around the chart
   The pointer shape indicates that you can move the chart or use a selection handle to resize it.
2. Press and hold the mouse button and drag the chart until the lower edge of the chart is in **row 28** and the left edge of the chart is in **column A**, then release the mouse button
   A dotted outline of the chart perimeter appears as the chart is being moved, the pointer changes to ✥, and the chart moves to the new location.
3. Position the pointer over one of the selection handles on the right border until it changes to ↔, then drag the right edge of the chart to the **middle of column I**
   The chart is widened. See Figure D-6.
4. Position the pointer over the top middle selection handle until it changes to ↕, then drag it to the **top of row 12**
   Now, you move the legend up so that it is slightly lower than the chart title.
5. Click the **legend** to select it, then drag it to the upper-right corner of the chart until it is slightly lower than the chart title
   Selection handles appear around the legend when you click it, and a dotted outline of the legend perimeter appears as you drag.
6. Press **[Esc]** to deselect the legend. The legend is now repositioned. See Figure D-7.
7. Save your work

FIGURE D-6: Worksheet with reposition and resized chart

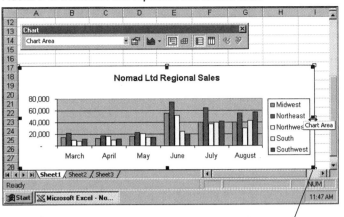

Widened to column I

FIGURE D-7: Worksheet with repositioned legend

Chart menu   Repositioned legend

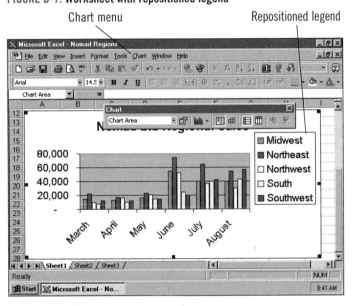

Viewing multiple worksheets

A workbook can be organized with a chart on one sheet and the data on another sheet. With this organization, you can still see the data next to the chart by opening multiple windows of the same workbook. This allows you to see portions of multiple sheets at the same time. Click Window on the menu bar, then click New Window. A new window containing the current workbook opens. To see the windows next to each other, click Window on the menu bar, click Arrange, then choose one of the options in the Arrange Windows dialog box. You can open one worksheet in one window and a different worksheet in the second window. See Figure D-8. To close one window without closing the worksheet, double-click the control menu box on the window you want to close.

FIGURE D-8: Workbook with two windows open

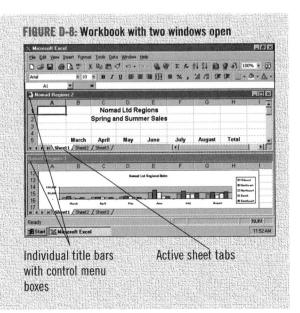

Individual title bars with control menu boxes   Active sheet tabs

Excel 97

Editing a Chart

Once you've created a chart, it's easy to modify it. You can change data values in the worksheet, and the chart will automatically be updated to reflect the new data. You can also easily change chart types using the buttons on the Chart toolbar. Table D-2 shows and describes the Chart toolbar buttons. ◄▬▬ Evan looks over his worksheet and realizes he entered the wrong data for the Northwest region in July and August. After he corrects this data, he wants to find out what percentage of total sales the month of June represents. He will convert the column chart to a pie chart to find this out.

Steps 1 2 3 4

1. Scroll the worksheet so that you can see both the chart and row 8, containing the Northwest region's sales figures, at the same time
   As you enter the correct values, watch the columns for July and August in the chart change.

2. Click cell **F8**, type **49000** to correct the July sales figure, press [→], type **45000** in cell **G8**, then press [**Enter**]
   The Northwest columns for July and August reflect the increased sales figures. See Figure D-9.

3. Select the chart by clicking anywhere within the chart border, then click the **Chart Type list arrow** 📉 ▾ on the Chart toolbar
   The chart type buttons appear, as shown in Figure D-10.

4. Click the **2-D Pie Chart button** 🥧
   The column chart changes to a pie chart showing total sales by month (the columns in the selected range). See Figure D-11. (You may need to scroll up to see the chart.) You look at the pie chart, takes some notes, and then decide to convert it back to a column chart. You now want to see if the large increase in sales would be better presented with a three-dimensional column chart.

5. Click 📉 ▾, then click the **3-D Column Chart button** 📊 to change the chart type
   A three-dimensional column chart appears. You note that the three-dimensional column format is too crowded, so you switch back to the two-dimensional format.

Time To

✔ Save

6. Click 📉 ▾, then click the **2-D Column Chart button** 📊 to change the chart type

TABLE D-2: **Chart Type buttons**

button	description	button	description
📉	Displays 2-D area chart	🏔	Displays 3-D area chart
▤	Displays 2-D bar chart	🗂	Displays 3-D bar chart
📊	Displays 2-D column chart	🏛	Displays 3-D column chart
📈	Displays 2-D line chart	✈	Displays 3-D line chart
🥧	Displays 2-D pie chart	🥟	Displays 3-D pie chart
⋰	Displays 2-D scatter chart	🐚	Displays 3-D surface chart
◕	Displays 2-D doughnut chart	🛢	Displays 3-D cylinder chart
✪	Displays radar chart	🔻	Displays 3-D cone chart

FIGURE D-9: Worksheet with new data entered for the Northwest region

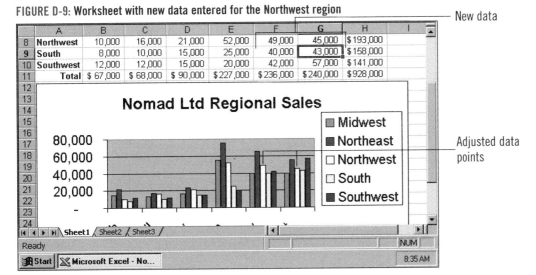

New data

Adjusted data points

FIGURE D-10: Chart Type list box

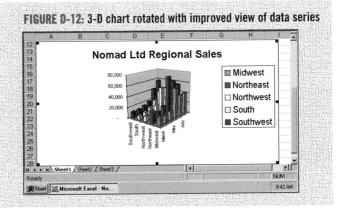

2-D Column Chart icon

2-D Pie Chart icon

FIGURE D-11: Pie chart

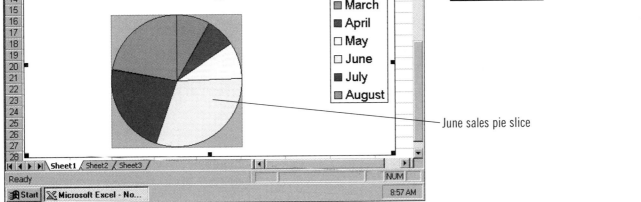

June sales pie slice

 CLUES TO USE

Rotating a chart

In a three-dimensional chart, columns or bars can sometimes be obscured by other data series within the same chart. You can rotate the chart until a better view is obtained. Double-click the chart, click the tip of one of its axes, then drag the handles until a more pleasing view of the data series appears. See Figure D-12.

FIGURE D-12: 3-D chart rotated with improved view of data series

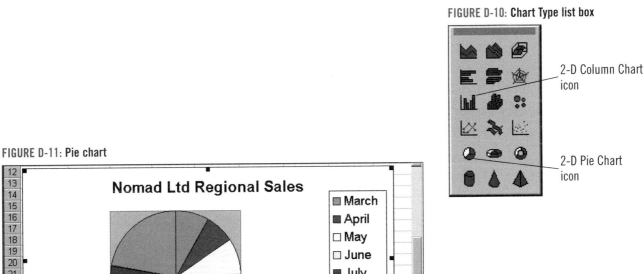

Changing the Appearance of a Chart

After you've created a chart using the Chart Wizard, you can modify its appearance by changing the colors of data series and adding or eliminating a legend and gridlines using the Chart toolbar and the Chart menu. **Gridlines** are the horizontal lines in the chart that enable the eye to follow the value on an axis. The corresponding Chart toolbar buttons are listed in Table D-3. Evan wants to make some changes in the appearance of his chart. He wants to see if the chart looks better without gridlines, and he wants to change the color of a data series.

Steps

1. Make sure the chart is still selected

You want to see how the chart looks without gridlines. Gridlines currently appear on the chart.

2. Click **Chart** on the menu bar, then click **Chart Options**

QuickTip

Experiment with different formats for your charts until you get just the right look.

3. Click the **Gridlines tab** in the Chart Options dialog box, then click the **Major Gridlines checkbox** for the Value (Y) Axis to remove the check and deselect this option

The gridlines disappear from the sample chart in the dialog box, as shown in Figure D-13. You decide that the gridlines are necessary to the chart's readability.

4. Click the **Major Gridlines checkbox** for the Value (Y) Axis, then click **OK**

The gridlines reappear. You are not happy with the color of the columns for the South data series and would like the columns to stand out more.

5. With the chart selected, double-click any column in the South data series

Handles appear on all the columns in the South data series, and the Format Data Series dialog box opens, as shown in Figure D-14. Make sure the Patterns tab is the front-most tab.

6. Click the **dark green box** (in the third row, fourth from the left), then click **OK**

All the columns in the series are dark green. Compare your finished chart to Figure D-15. You are pleased with the change.

7. Save your work

TABLE D-3: Chart enhancement buttons

button	use	button	use
	Displays formatting dialog box for the selected chart element		Charts data by row
	Selects chart type		Charts data by column
	Adds/Deletes legend		Angles selected text downward
	Creates a data table within the chart		Angles selected text upward

FIGURE D-13: **Chart Options dialog box**

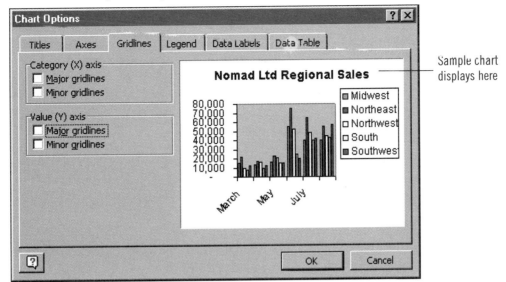

Sample chart displays here

FIGURE D-14: **Format Data Series dialog box**

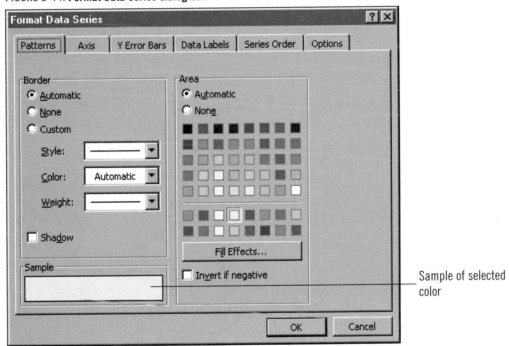

Sample of selected color

FIGURE D-15: **Chart with formatted data series**

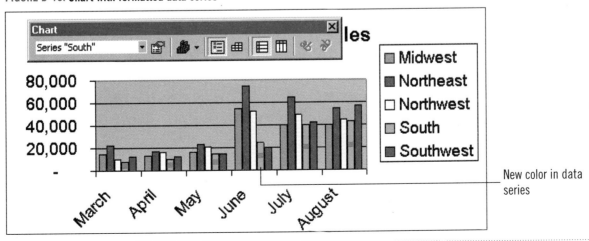

New color in data series

Enhancing a Chart

There are many ways to enhance a chart to make it easier to read and understand. You can create titles for the X-axis and Y-axis, add graphics, or add background color. You can even format the text you use in a chart. Evan wants to improve the appearance of his chart by creating titles for the X-axis and Y-axis. He also decides to add a drop shadow to the title.

1. **Make sure the chart is selected**
   You want to add descriptive text to the X-axis.

2. **Click Chart on the menu bar, click Chart Options, click the Titles tab in the Chart Options dialog box, then type Months in the Category (X) Axis text box**
   The word "Months" appears below the month labels in the sample chart, as shown in Figure D-16. You now add text to the Y-axis.

3. **Click the Value (Y) Axis text box, type Sales, then click OK**
   A selected text box containing "Sales" appears to the left of the Y-axis. Once the Chart Options dialog box is closed, you can move the axis title to a new position, by clicking on an edge of the selection and dragging it. If you wanted to edit the axis title, position the pointer over the selected text box until it becomes Ⅰ and click, then edit the text.

4. **Press [Esc] to deselect the Y-axis label**
   Next you decide to draw a rectangle with a drop shadow around the title.

5. **Click the chart title to select it**
   If necessary, you may have to move the Chart toolbar. You use the Format button on the Chart toolbar to create a drop shadow.

6. **Click the Format button 🖼 on the Chart toolbar to open the Format Chart Title dialog box, make sure the Patterns tab is active, click the Shadow checkbox, then click OK**
   A drop shadow appears around the title.

7. **Press [Esc] to deselect the chart title and view the drop shadow**
   Compare your chart to Figure D-17.

8. **Save your work**

QuickTip

The Format button 🖼 opens a dialog box with the appropriate formatting options for the selected chart element.

FIGURE D-16: Sample chart with X-axis text

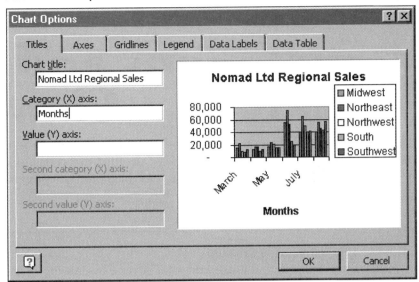

FIGURE D-17: Enhanced chart

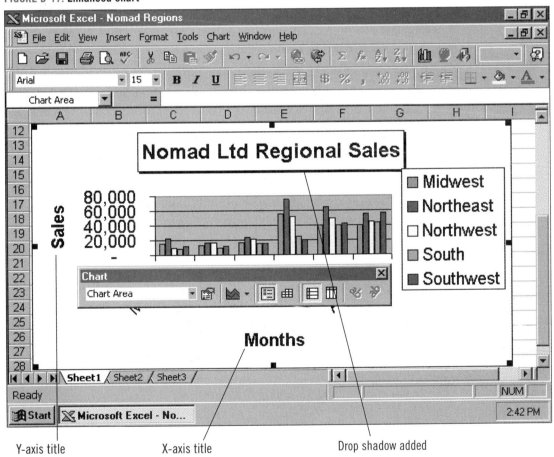

Y-axis title   X-axis title   Drop shadow added

Changing text font and alignment in charts

The font and the alignment of axis text can be modified to make it more readable or to better fit within the plot area. With a chart selected, double-click the text to be modified. The Format Axis dialog box appears. Click the Font or the Alignment tab, make the desired changes, then click OK.

Adding Text Annotations and Arrows to a Chart

You can add arrows and text annotations to highlight information in your charts. Text annotations are labels that you add to a chart to draw attention to a certain part of it. Evan wants to add a text annotation and an arrow to highlight the June sales increase.

1. Make sure the chart is selected

You want to call attention to the June sales increase by drawing an arrow that points to the top of the June data series with the annotation, "After advertising campaign." To enter the text for an annotation, you simply start typing.

2. Type After advertising campaign then click the Enter button ✔ on the formula bar

As you type, the text appears in the formula bar. After you confirm the entry, the text appears in a floating selected text box within the chart window.

3. Point to an edge of the text box, then press and hold the left mouse button

The pointer should be ✛. If the pointer changes to ⊺ or ↔, release the mouse button, click outside the text box area to deselect it, then select the text box and repeat Step 3.

4. Drag the text box above the chart, as shown in Figure D-18, then release the mouse button

You are ready to add an arrow.

5. Click the Drawing button 🖉 on the Standard toolbar

The Drawing toolbar appears.

6. Click the Arrow button ↘ on the Drawing toolbar

The pointer changes to ✛.

7. Position ✛ under the word "advertising" in the text box, click the left mouse button, drag the line to the June sales, then release the mouse button

An arrowhead appears pointing to the June sales. Compare your finished chart to Figure D-19.

8. Click the Drawing button 🖉 to close the Drawing toolbar

9. Save your work

QuickTip

You can also insert text and an arrow in the data section of a worksheet by clicking the Text Box button 🖾 on the Drawing toolbar, drawing a text box, typing the text, and then adding the arrow.

FIGURE D-18: Repositioning text annotation

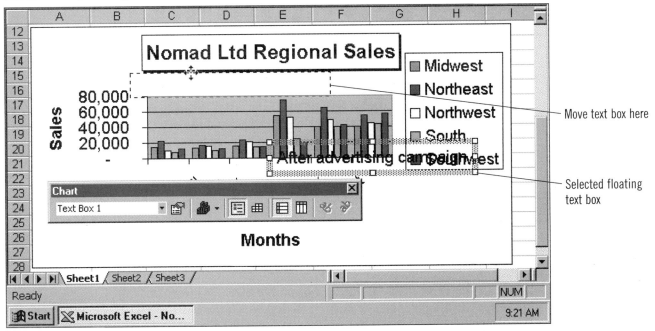

Move text box here

Selected floating text box

FIGURE D-19: Completed chart with text annotation and arrow

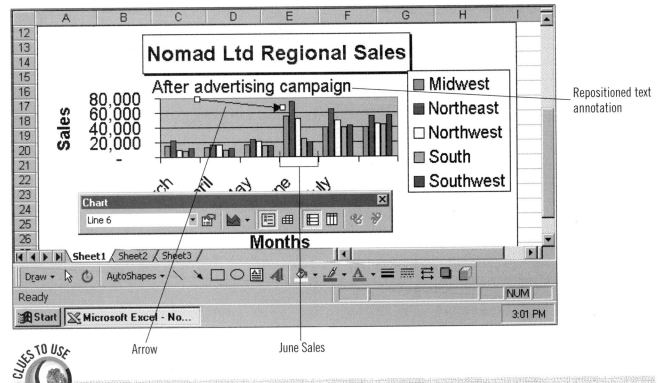

Repositioned text annotation

Arrow

June Sales

CLUES TO USE

Pulling out a pie slice

Just as an arrow can call attention to a data series, you can emphasize a pie slice by exploding it, or pulling it away from, the pie chart. Once the chart is in Edit mode, click the pie to select it, click the desired slice to select only that slice, then drag the slice away from the pie, as shown in Figure D-20.

FIGURE D-20: Exploded pie slice

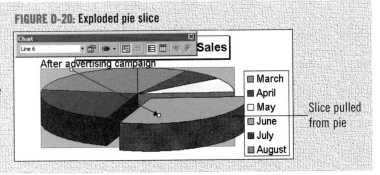

Slice pulled from pie

Previewing and Printing a Chart

After you complete a chart to your satisfaction, you will need to print it. You can print a chart by itself, or as part of the worksheet. ✎ Evan is satisfied with the chart and wants to print it for the annual meeting. He will print the worksheet and the chart together, so that the shareholders can see the actual sales numbers for each tour type.

Steps 1 2 3 4

1. **Press [Esc] twice to deselect the arrow and the chart**
   If you wanted to print only the chart without the data, you would leave the chart selected.

2. **Click the Print Preview button 🔍 on the Standard toolbar**
   The Print Preview window opens. You decide that the chart and data would look better if they were printed in **landscape** orientation—that is, with the page turned sideways. To change the orientation of the page, you must alter the page setup.

3. **Click the Setup button to display the Page Setup dialog box, then click the Page tab**

4. **Click the Landscape radio button in the Orientation section**
   See Figure D-21.
   Because each page has a left default margin of 0.75", the chart and data will print too far over to the left of the page. You change this using the Margins tab.

5. **Click the Margins tab, click the Horizontal checkbox in the Center on Page section, then click OK**
   The print preview of the worksheet appears again. The data and chart are centered on the page that has a landscape orientation, and no gridlines appear. See Figure D-22. You are satisfied with the way it looks and print it.

6. **Click Print to display the Print dialog box, then click OK**
   Your printed report should look like the image displayed in the Print Preview window.

7. **Save your work**

8. **Close the workbook and exit Excel**

FIGURE D-21: **Page tab of the Page Setup dialog box**

Landscape selected

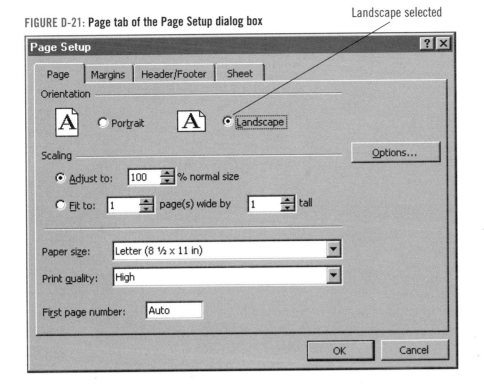

FIGURE D-22: **Chart and data ready to print**

Orientation changed
to landscape

Centered on page

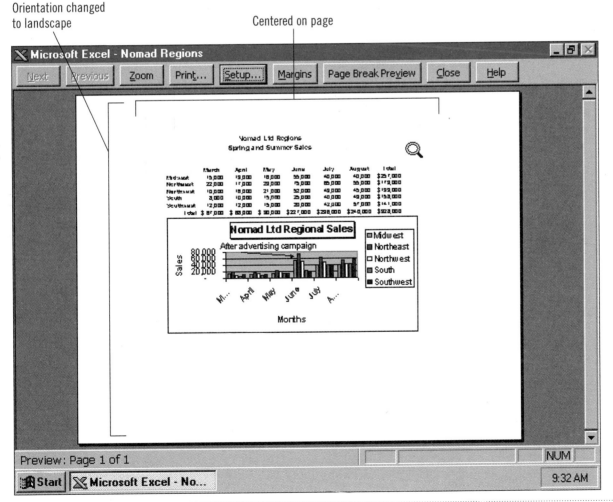

Practice

► Concepts Review

Label each of the elements of the Excel chart shown in Figure D-23.

FIGURE D-23

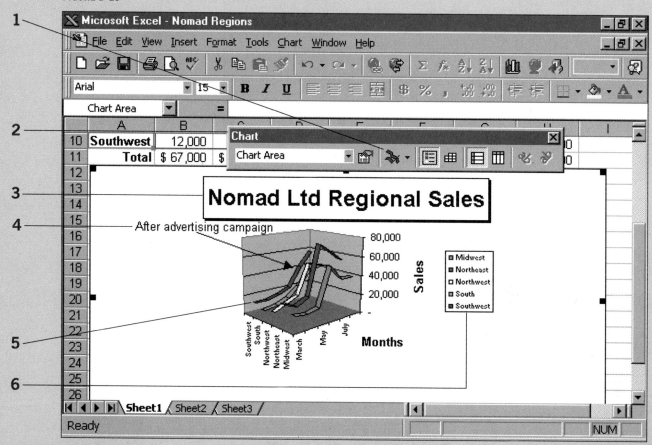

Match each of the statements with its chart type.

7. Column
8. Area
9. Pie
10. Combination
11. Line

a. Shows how volume changes over time
b. Compares data as parts of a whole
c. Displays a column and line chart using different scales of measurement
d. Compares trends over even time intervals
e. Compares data over time—the Excel default

Select the best answer from the list of choices.

12. The box that identifies patterns used for each data series is a

    a. Data point   **b.** Plot   **c.** Legend   **d.** Range

13. What is the term for a row or column on a chart?

    a. Range address   **b.** Axis title   **c.** Chart orientation   **d.** Data series

 Skills Review

1. Create a worksheet and plan a chart.

    a. Start Excel, open a new workbook, then save it as Software Used to your Student Disk.

    b. Enter the information from Table D-4 in your worksheet in range A1:E6. Resize columns and rows.

    c. Save your work.

    d. Sketch a chart for a two-dimensional column chart that shows software distribution by department.

TABLE D-4

	Excel	Word	WordPerfect	PageMaker
Accounting	10	1	9	0
Marketing	2	9	0	6
Engineering	12	5	7	1
Personnel	2	2	2	1
Production	6	3	4	0

2. Create a chart.

    a. Select the range you want to chart.

    b. Click the Chart Wizard button.

    c. Complete the Chart Wizard dialog boxes and build a two-dimensional column chart on the same sheet as the data, having a different color bar for each department and with the title "Software Distribution by Department."

    d. Save your work.

3. Move and resize a chart and its objects.

    a. Make sure the chart is still selected.

    b. Move the chart beneath the data.

    c. Drag the chart's selection handles so it fills the range A7:G22.

    d. Click the legend to select it.

    e. Make the legend longer by about ½".

    f. Change the placement of the legend to the bottom right corner of the chart area.

    g. Save your work.

4. Edit a chart.

    a. Change the value in cell B3 to 6.

    b. Click the chart to select it.

    c. Click the Chart Type list arrow on the Chart toolbar.

    d. Click the 3-D Column Chart button in the list.

    e. Rotate the chart to move the data.

    f. Save your work.

5. **Change the appearance of a chart.**
   a. Change the chart type to 2-D column chart.
   b. Make sure the chart is still selected.
   c. Turn off the displayed gridlines.
   d. Change the X- and Y-axis font to Times New Roman.
   e. Turn the gridlines back on.
   f. Save your work.

6. **Enhance a chart.**
   a. Make sure the chart is still selected, then click Chart on the menu bar, click Chart Options, then click the Titles tab.
   b. Click the Category (X) axis text box and type "Department."
   c. Click the Value (Y) axis text box, type "Types of Software," and then click OK.
   d. Change the size of the X and Y axes font and the legend font to 8 pt.
   e. Save your work.

7. **Adding a text annotation and arrows to a chart.**
   a. Select the chart.
   b. Create the text annotation "Need More Computers."
   c. Drag the text annotation about one inch above any of the Personnel bars.
   d. Change the font size of the annotation text to 8 pt.
   e. Click the Arrow button on the Drawing toolbar.
   f. Click below the text annotation, drag down any one of the Personnel bars, then release the mouse button.
   g. Open a second window so you can display the data in the new window and the chart in the original window.
   h. Close the second window.
   i. Save your work.

8. **Preview and print a chart.**
   a. Deselect the chart, then click the Print Preview button on the Standard toolbar.
   b. Center the data and chart on the page and change the paper orientation to landscape.
   c. Click Print in the Print Preview window.
   d. Save your work, close the workbook, then exit Excel.

▶ Independent Challenges

1. You are the operations manager for the Springfield Recycling Center. The Marketing Department wants you to create charts for a brochure to advertise a new curbside recycling program. The data provided contains percentages of collected recycled goods. You need to create charts that show:

- How much of each type of recycled material Springfield collected in 1995 and what percentage each type represents. The center collects paper, plastics, and glass from business and residential customers.
- The yearly increases in the total amounts of recycled materials the center has collected since its inception three years ago. Springfield has experienced a 30% annual increase in collections.

To complete this independent challenge:

1. Prepare a worksheet plan that states your goal and identifies the formulas for any calculations.
2. Sketch a sample worksheet on a piece of paper describing how you will create the charts. Which type of chart is best suited for the information you need to display? What kind of chart enhancements will be necessary? Will a 3-D effect make your chart easier to understand?
3. Open the workbook XL D-2 on your Student Disk, then save it as Recycling Center.
4. Add a column that calculates the 30% increase in annual collections based on the percentages given.
5. Create at least six different charts to show the distribution of the different types of recycled goods, as well as the distribution by customer type. Use the Chart Wizard to switch the way data is plotted (columns vs. rows and vice versa) and come up with additional charts.
6. After creating the charts, make the appropriate enhancements. Include chart titles, legends, and axes titles.
7. Before printing, preview the file so you know what the charts will look like. Adjust any items as needed.
8. Save your work. Print the charts, then print the entire worksheet. Close the file.
9. Submit your worksheet plan, preliminary sketches, and the final worksheet printouts.

2. One of your responsibilities at the Nuts and Bolts hardware store is to re-create the company's records using Excel. Another is to convince the current staff that Excel can make daily operations easier and more efficient. You've decided to create charts using the previous year's operating expenses. These charts will be used at the next monthly Accounting Department meeting.

Open the workbook XL D-3 on your Student Disk, and save it as Expense Charts.

To complete this independent challenge:

1. Decide which data in the worksheet should be charted. Sketch two sample charts. What type of charts are best suited for the information you need to display? What kind of chart enhancements will be necessary?
2. Create at least six different charts that show the distribution of expenses, either by quarter or expense type.
3. Add annotated text and arrows highlighting data.
4. In one chart, change the colors of the data series, and in another chart, use black-and-white patterns only.
5. Before printing, preview the file so you know what the charts will look like. Adjust any items as needed.
6. Print the charts. Save your work.
7. Submit your sketches and the final worksheet printouts.

3. The Chamber of Commerce is delighted with the way you've organized their membership roster using Excel. The Board of Directors wants to ask the city for additional advertising funds and has asked you to prepare charts that can be used in their presentation.

Open the workbook XL D-4 on your Student Disk, and save it as Chamber Charts. This file contains raw advertising data for the month of January.

To complete this independent challenge:

1. Calculate the annual advertising expenses based on the January summary data.
2. Use the raw data for January shown in the range A16:B24 to create charts.
3. Decide what types of charts would be best suited for this type of data. Sketch two sample charts. What kind of chart enhancements will be necessary?
4. Create at least four different charts that show the distribution of advertising expenses. Show January expenses and projected values in at least two of the charts.
5. Add annotated text and arrows highlighting important data. Change the colors of the data series if you wish.
6. Before printing, preview the file so you know what the charts will look like. Adjust any items as needed.
7. Print the charts. Save your work.
8. Submit your sketches and the final worksheet printouts.

4. Financial information has a greater impact on others if displayed in a chart. Using the World Wide Web you can find out current activity of stocks and create informative charts. Your company has asked you to chart current trading indexes by category.

To complete this independent challenge:

1. Open a new workbook and save it on your Student Disk as Trading Indexes.
2. Log on to the Internet and use your browser to go to http://www.course.com. From there, click the link Student On Line Companions, then click the Microsoft Office 97 Professional Edition - Illustrated: A First Course page, then click the Excel link for Unit D.
3. Use the following site to compile your data, NASDAQ [www.nasdaq.com].
4. Click the Index Activity button on the NASDAQ home page.
5. Locate Index Value data by category and retrieve this information.
6. Create a chart of the Index Values, by category.
7. Save, print, and hand in a print out of your work.

Excel 97

▶ Visual Workshop

Modify a worksheet using the skills you learned in this unit, using Figure D-24 for reference. Open the file XL D-5 on your Student Disk, and save it as Quarterly Advertising Budget. Create the chart, then change the data to reflect Figure D-24. Preview and print your results, and submit your printout.

FIGURE D-24

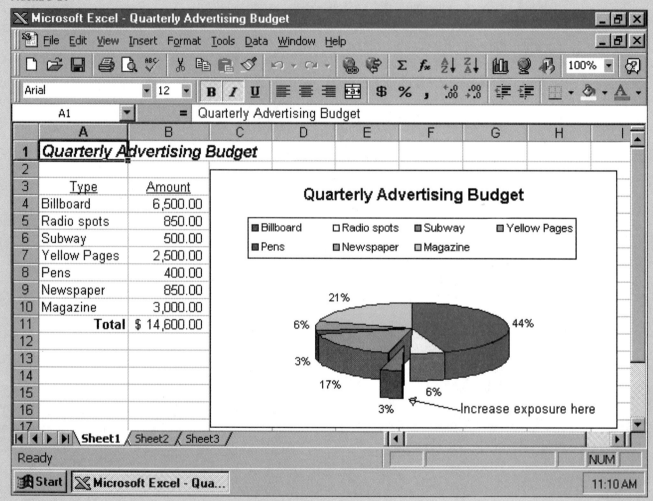

Working
with Formulas and Functions

Objectives

- ► **Create a formula with several operators**
- ► **Use names in a formula**
- ► **Generate multiple totals with AutoSum**
- ► **Use dates in calculations**
- ► **Build a conditional formula with the IF function**
- ► **Use statistical functions**
- ► **Calculate payments with the PMT function**
- ► **Display and print formula contents**

Without formulas, Excel would simply be an electronic grid with text and numbers. Used with formulas, Excel becomes a powerful data analysis software tool. As you learn how to analyze data using different types of formulas, including those that call for functions, you will discover more ways to use Excel. In this unit, you will gain a further understanding of Excel formulas and learn how to build several Excel functions. Top management at Nomad Ltd has asked Evan Brillstein to analyze various company data. To do this, Evan will create several worksheets that require the use of formulas and functions. Because management is considering raising salaries for level-two managers, Evan's first task is to create a report that compares the payroll deductions and net pay for level-two managers before and after a proposed raise.

Creating a Formula with Several Operators

You can create formulas that contain a combination of cell references (for example, Z100 and B2), operators (for example, * [multiplication] and - [subtraction]), and values (for example, 99 or 1.56). You also can create a single formula that performs several calculations. If you enter a formula with more than one operator, Excel performs the calculations in a particular sequence based on algebraic rules called **precedence**; that is, Excel performs the operation(s) within the parentheses first, then performs the other calculations. See Table E-1. Evan has been given the gross pay and payroll deductions for the first payroll period and needs to complete his analysis. He also has preformatted, with the Comma style, any cells that are to contain values. Evan begins by entering a formula for net pay that subtracts the payroll deductions from gross pay.

1. Start Excel if necessary, open the workbook titled **XL E-1**, then save it as **Pay Info for L2 Mgrs**. Next build the first part of the net pay formula in cell B11

QuickTip

If you make a mistake while building a formula, press [Esc] and begin again.

2. Click cell **B11**, then type **=B6-**
   Remember that you can type cell references in either uppercase or lowercase letters. (Excel automatically converts lowercase cell reference letters to uppercase.) You type the equal sign (=) to tell Excel that a formula follows, B6 to reference the cell containing the gross pay, and the minus sign (-) to indicate that the next entry will be subtracted from cell B6. Now, complete the formula.

Trouble?

If you receive a message box indicating "Parentheses do not match," make sure you have included both a left and a right parenthesis.

3. Type **(B7+B8+B9+B10)** then click the **Enter button** on the formula bar
   The net pay for Payroll Period 1 appears in cell B11, as shown in Figure E-1. Because Excel performs the operations within parentheses first, you can control the order of calculations on the worksheet. (In this case, Excel sums the values in cells B7 through B10 first.) After the operations within the parentheses are completed, Excel performs the operations outside the parentheses. (In this case, Excel subtracts the total of range B7:B10 from cell B6.) Next, copy the formula across row 11.

4. Copy the formula in cell **B11** into cells **C11:F11**, then return to cell **A1**
   The formula in cell B11 is copied to the range C11:F11 to complete row 11. See Figure E-2.

5. Save the workbook
   Evan is pleased with the formulas that calculate net pay totals. Next, he adds employee names to his worksheet.

TABLE E-1: Example formulas using parentheses and several operators

formula	order of precedence	calculated result
=36+(1+3)	Add 1 to 3; then add the result to 36	40
=(10-20)/10-5	Subtract 20 from 10; divide that by 10; then subtract 5	-6
=(10*2)*(10+2)	Multiply 10 by 2; add 10 to 2; then multiply the results	240

FIGURE E-1: Worksheet showing formula and result

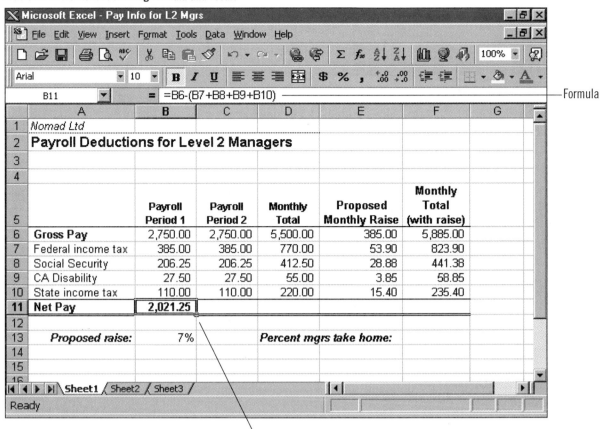

Result in cell B11

FIGURE E-2: Worksheet with copied formulas

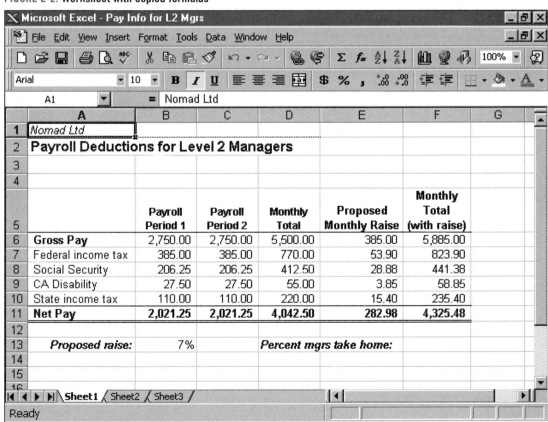

Using Names in a Formula

You can assign names to cells and ranges. Doing so reduces errors and makes a worksheet easier to follow. You also can use names in formulas. Using names in formulas facilitates formula building and provides a frame of reference for formula logic—the names make formulas easy to recognize and maintain. The formula Revenue - Cost, for example, is much easier to comprehend than the formula A2 - D3. You can produce a list of workbook names and their references at any time.　Evan wants to include a formula that calculates the percentage of monthly gross pay the managers would actually take home (net pay) if a 7% raise is granted.

1. **Click cell F6, click the name box on the formula bar to select the active cell reference, type Gross_with_Raise, then press [Enter]**
   The name assigned to cell F6, Gross_with_Raise, appears in the name box. Note that you must type underscores instead of spaces between words. Cell F6 is now named Gross_with_Raise to refer to the monthly gross pay amount that includes the 7% raise. The name box displays as much of the name as fits (Gross_with_...). Next, name the net pay cell.

2. **Click cell F11, click the name box, type Net_with_Raise, then press [Enter]**
   Now that the two cells are named, you are ready to enter the formula.

3. **Click cell F13, type =Net_with_Raise/Gross_with_Raise, then click the Enter button on the formula bar (make sure you begin the formula with an equal sign)**
   The formula bar now shows the new formula, and the result 0.735 appears in the cell. See Figure E-3. If you add names to a worksheet after all the formulas have been entered, you must click Insert on the menu bar, click Name, click Apply, click the name or names, then click OK. Now format cell F13 as a percent.

4. **Format cell F13 using the Percent Style button % on the Formatting toolbar**
   Notice that the result shown in cell F13 (74%) is rounded to the nearest whole percent as shown in Figure E-3. Save and print the completed worksheet.

5. **Return to cell A1, then save and print the worksheet**

6. **Close the workbook**

QuickTip

To delete a name, click Insert on the menu bar, point to Name, then click Define. Select the name, click Delete, then click OK.

QuickTip

You can use the Label Ranges dialog box (Insert menu, Name submenu, Label command) to specify and name cells using column and row labels in your worksheet.

FIGURE E-3: Worksheet formula that includes cell names

Formula with cell names

Cell named
Gross_with_Raise

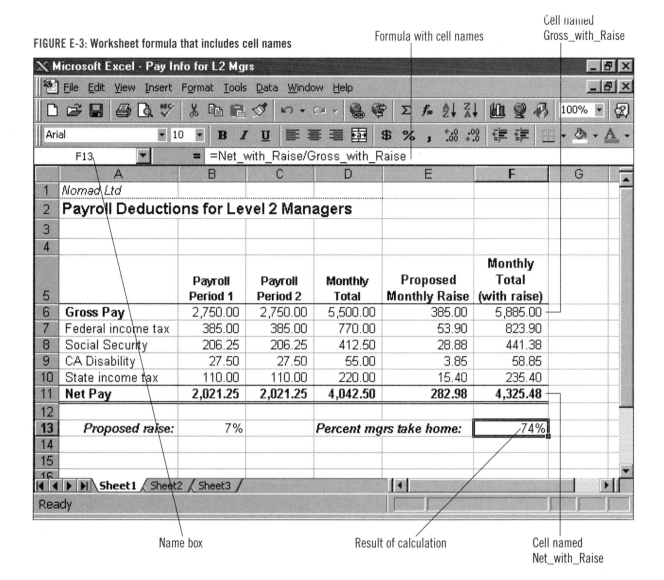

Name box

Result of calculation

Cell named
Net_with_Raise

Producing a list of names

You might want to verify the names you have in a workbook and the cells they reference. To paste a list of names in a workbook, select a blank cell that has several blank cells beside and beneath it. Click Insert on the menu bar, point to Name, then click Paste. In the Paste Name dialog box, click Paste List. Excel produces a list that includes the sheet name and the cell or range the name identifies. See Figure E-4.

FIGURE E-4: Worksheet with pasted list of names

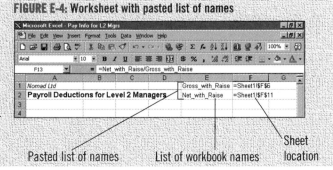

Pasted list of names

List of workbook names

Sheet location

Generating Multiple Totals with AutoSum

In most cases, the result of a function is a value derived from a calculation. Functions also can return results such as text, references, or other information about the worksheet. You enter a function, such as AVERAGE, directly into a cell; you can use the Edit Formula button; or, you can insert it with the Paste Function. You can use cell references, ranges, names, and formulas as arguments between the parentheses. As with other cell entries, you can cut, copy, and paste functions from one area of the worksheet to another and from one workbook to another. The most widely used Excel function, SUM, calculates worksheet totals and can be entered easily using the AutoSum button on the Standard toolbar. ◄━━━ Evan's manager has asked him for a report summarizing annual bicycle sales. She wants the report to compare sales of competitor's brands to sales of Nomad Ltd's bikes. Evan has entered the data for units of bicycles sold. Now he needs to complete the worksheet totals.

Steps 1 2 3 4

1. **Open the workbook titled XL E-2, then save it as Bicycle Sales**
   You need to generate multiple totals with AutoSum. You can use the [Ctrl] key to select multiple, nonadjacent ranges.

2. **Select range B5:E10, press and hold [Ctrl], then select range B12:E14**
   To select nonadjacent cells, you must press and hold [Ctrl] while selecting the additional cells. Compare your selections with Figure E-5. Now, you are is ready to total the columns in the two selected ranges.

Trouble?

If you select the wrong combination of cells, simply click on a single cell and begin again.

3. **Click the AutoSum button Σ on the Standard toolbar**
   When the selected range you want to sum (B5:E10 and B12:E14, in this example) includes a blank cell with data values above it, AutoSum enters the total in the blank cell. Next, generate annual totals in column F and grand totals in row 16.

4. **Select range B5:F16, then click Σ**
   Whenever the selected range you want to sum includes a blank cell in the bottom row or right column, AutoSum enters the total in the blank cell. In this case, Excel ignores the data values and totals only the SUM functions. Although Excel generates totals when you click the AutoSum button, it is a good idea to check the results.

5. **Click cell B16**
   The formula bar reads =SUM(B14,B10). See Figure E-6. When generating grand totals, Excel automatically references the cells containing SUM functions with a comma separator between cell references. Excel uses commas to separate multiple arguments in all functions, not just in SUM. You are ready to save and print your work.

6. **Save and print the worksheet, then close the workbook**

FIGURE E-5: Selecting nonadjacent ranges using [Ctrl]

	A	B	C	D	E	F	G	H
1	Nomad Ltd							
2	**Bicycles - Sales Summary in Units Sold**							
3								
4	*Bicycles - Other brands*	Qtr 1	Qtr 2	Qtr 3	Qtr 4	Total		
5	Mountain Climber	33	28	31	34			
6	Rock Roller	25	22	21	24			
7	Tour de Bike	23	16	20	19			
8	Youth Rock Roller	24	23	19	22			
9	Youth Tour de Bike	35	29	25	26			
10	Total							
11	*Nomad Bicycles*							
12	Mountain Master	458	379	299	356			
13	Tour Master	386	325	285	348			
14	Total							
15								
16	Grand Total							
17								
18								

Sheet1 / Sheet2 / Sheet3 /

Ready   Sum=3335

FIGURE E-6: Completed worksheet

B16 = =SUM(B14,B10)

	A	B	C	D	E	F	G	H
1	Nomad Ltd							
2	**Bicycles - Sales Summary in Units Sold**							
3								
4	*Bicycles - Other brands*	Qtr 1	Qtr 2	Qtr 3	Qtr 4	Total		
5	Mountain Climber	33	28	31	34	126		
6	Rock Roller	25	22	21	24	92		
7	Tour de Bike	23	16	20	19	78		
8	Youth Rock Roller	24	23	19	22	88		
9	Youth Tour de Bike	35	29	25	26	115		
10	Total	140	118	116	125	499		
11	*Nomad Bicycles*							
12	Mountain Master	458	379	299	356	1,492		
13	Tour Master	386	325	285	348	1,344		
14	Total	844	704	584	704	2,836		
15								
16	Grand Total	984	822	700	829	3,335		
17								
18								

Sheet1 / Sheet2 / Sheet3 /

Ready

Comma used to separate multiple arguments

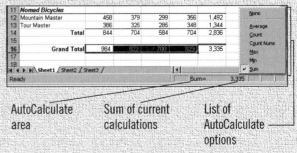

Quick calculations with AutoCalculate

To check a total quickly without entering a formula, just select the range you want to sum, and the answer appears in the status bar next to SUM=. You also can perform other quick calculations, such as averaging or finding the minimum value in a selection. To do this, right-click the AutoCalculate area in the status bar and select from the list of options. The option you select remains in effect and in the status bar until you make another selection. See Figure E-7.

FIGURE E-7: Using AutoCalculate

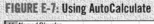

AutoCalculate area   Sum of current calculations   List of AutoCalculate options

Using Dates in Calculations

If you enter dates in a worksheet so that Excel recognizes them as dates, you can sort (arrange) the dates and perform date calculations. For example, you can calculate the number of days between your birth date and today, which is the number of days you have been alive. Commonly used date formats that Excel recognizes are listed in Table E-2. When you enter a date in any of these formats, Excel considers the entry a date function, converts the date to a serial date number, and stores that number in the cell. A date's converted serial date is the number of days to that date. The serial date of January 1, 1900; for example, is 1; the serial date of January 1, 1998 is 35431. ◄━━━━ Evan's next task is to complete the Open Accounts Receivable worksheet for Adventure Tours in the Southwest. He remembers to enter the worksheet dates in a format that Excel recognizes, so that he can take advantage of date calculation.

1. **Open the workbook titled XL E-3, then save it as Southwest Tour Receivables to the appropriate folder on your Student Disk**
   Begin by entering the current date, the date that is critical to worksheet calculations.

2. **Click cell C4, type 9/1/98, then press [Enter]**
   The date appears in cell C4 just as you typed it. You want to enter a formula that calculates the invoice due date, which is 30 days from the invoice date. The formula adds 30 days to the invoice date.

3. **Click cell F7, type =, click cell B7, type +30, then click the Enter button [✓] on the formula bar**
   Excel calculates the result by converting the 8/1/98 invoice date to a serial date number, adding 30 to it, then automatically formatting the result as a date. See Figure E-8. Because this same formula will calculate the due date for each invoice, you can copy the formula down the column using the fill handle.

QuickTip
You also can perform time calculations in Excel. For example, you can enter an employee's starting time and ending time, then calculate how many hours and minutes he or she worked. You must enter time in a format that Excel recognizes; for example, 1:35 PM (h:mm AM/PM).

4. **Copy the formula in cell F7 into cells F8:F13**
   Cell referencing causes the copied formula to contain the appropriate cell references. You are pleased at how easily Excel calculated the invoice due dates. Now you are ready to enter the formula that calculates the age of each invoice. You do this by subtracting the invoice date from the current date. Because each invoice age formula must refer to the current date, you must make cell C4, the current date cell, an absolute reference in the formula.

QuickTip
If you perform date calculations and the intended numeric result displays as a date, format the cell(s) using a number format.

5. **Click cell G7, type =, click cell C4, press [F4] to add the absolute reference symbols ($), type -, click B7, then click [✓]**
   The formula bar displays the formula $C$4-B7. The numerical result, 31, appears in cell G7 because there are 31 days between 8/1/98 and 9/1/98. Again, copy the formula down the column.

6. **Click cell G7, drag the fill handle to select range G7:G13, then press [Ctrl][Home] to deselect the range**
   The age of each invoice appears in column G, as shown in Figure E-9.

7. **Click the Save button [💾] on the Standard toolbar**

FIGURE E-8: Worksheet with formula for invoice due date

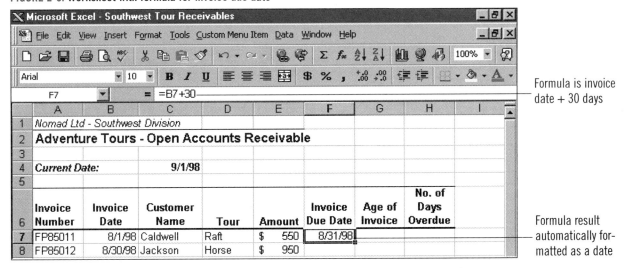

Formula is invoice date + 30 days

Formula result automatically formatted as a date

FIGURE E-9: Worksheet with copied formulas

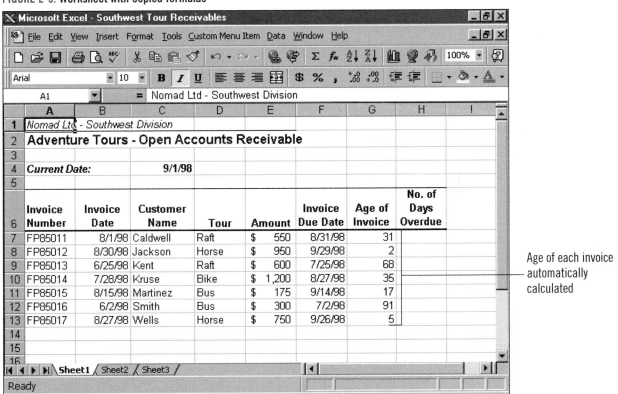

Age of each invoice automatically calculated

TABLE E-2: Commonly used date formats

format	example
M/d/yy	1/1/98
d-mmm-yy	1-Jan-98
d-mmm	1-Jan
Mmm-yy	Jan-98

Building a Conditional Formula with the IF Function

You can build a conditional formula using an IF function. A **conditional formula** is one that makes calculations based on stated conditions. For example, you can build a formula to calculate bonuses based on a person's performance rating. If a person is rated a 5 (the stated condition) on a scale of 1 to 5, with 5 being the highest rating, he or she receives 10% of his or her salary as a bonus; otherwise, there is no bonus. When the condition is a question that can be answered with a true or false response, Excel calls this stated condition a **logical test**. The IF function has three parts, separated by commas: a condition or logical test, an action to take if the logical test or condition is true, then an action to take if the logical test or condition is false. Another way of expressing this is: IF(test_cond,do_this,else_this). Translated into an Excel IF function, the formula to calculate bonuses would look something like: IF(Rating=5,Salary*0.10,0). The translation would be: If the rating equals 5, multiply the salary by 0.10 (the decimal equivalent of 10%), then place the result in the selected cell. If the rating does not equal 5, place a 0 in the cell. When entering the logical test portion of an IF statement, typically you use some combination of the comparison operators listed in Table E-3. Evan is almost finished with the worksheet. To complete it, he needs to use an IF function that calculates the number of days each invoice is overdue.

Steps

1. Click cell **H7**

The cell pointer is now positioned where the result of the function will appear. You want the formula to calculate the number of days overdue as follows: If the age of the invoice is greater than 30, calculate the days overdue (Age of Invoice - 30), and place the result in cell H7; otherwise, place a 0 (zero) in the cell. The formula will include the IF function and cell references.

2. Type **=IF(G7>30,** (make sure to type the comma)

You have entered the first part of the function, the logical test. Notice that you used the symbol for greater than (>). So far, the formula reads: If Age of Invoice is greater than 30 (in other words, if the invoice is overdue). Next, tell Excel the action to take if the invoice is over 30 days old.

3. Type **G7-30,** (make sure to type the comma)

This part of the formula, between the first and second commas, is what you want Excel to do if the logical test is true; that is, if the age of the invoice is over 30. Continuing the translation of the formula, this part means: Take the Age of Invoice value and subtract 30. Finally, tell Excel the action to take if the logical test is false (that is, if the age of the invoice is 30 days or less).

4. Type **0**, then click the **Enter button** ☑ on the formula bar (you do not have to type The) to complete the formula

The formula is complete and the result, 1 (the number of days overdue), appears in cell H7. See Figure E-10. Next, Copy the formula.

5. Copy the formula in cell H7 into cells **H8:H13**

Compare your results with Figure E-11, then save and print your work.

6. Save, then print the workbook

FIGURE E-10: Worksheet with IF function

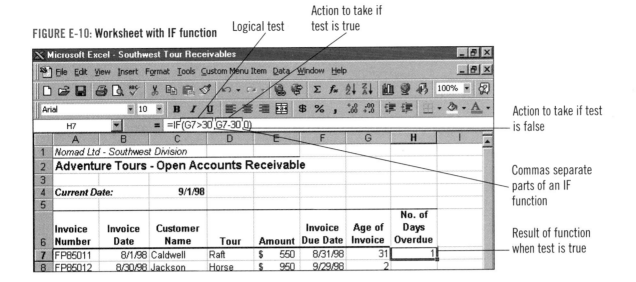

FIGURE E-11: Completed worksheet

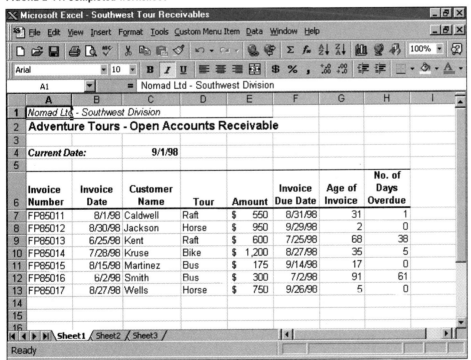

TABLE E-3: Comparison operators

operator	function
<	Less than
>	Greater than
=	Equal to
<=	Less than or equal to
>=	Greater than or equal to
<>	Not equal to

Using Statistical Functions

Excel offers several hundred worksheet functions. A small group of these functions calculates statistics such as averages, minimum values, and maximum values. See Table E-4 for a brief description of these commonly used functions. Evan's manager has asked him to present detailed information about open accounts receivable. To do this, Evan adds some statistical functions to the worksheet. He begins by using the MAX function to calculate the maximum value in a range.

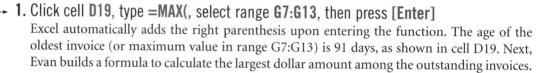

Trouble?

If you have difficulty clicking cells or ranges when you build formulas, try scrolling to reposition the worksheet area until all participating cells are visible.

1. **Click cell D19, type =MAX(, select range G7:G13, then press [Enter]**
   Excel automatically adds the right parenthesis upon entering the function. The age of the oldest invoice (or maximum value in range G7:G13) is 91 days, as shown in cell D19. Next, Evan builds a formula to calculate the largest dollar amount among the outstanding invoices.

2. **In cell D20, type =MAX(, select range E7:E13, then press [Enter]**
   Note that the largest amount owed is $1,200, as shown in cell D20. Now you can use the MIN function to find the smallest dollar amount and the age of the newest invoice.

3. **In cell D21, type =MIN(, select range E7:E13, then press [Enter]; in cell D22, type =MIN(, select range G7:G13, then press [Enter]**
   The smallest dollar amount owed is $175, as shown in cell D21, and the newest invoice is two days old. In the next step, you use a function to count the number of invoices by counting the number of entries in column A.

QuickTip

If you don't see the desired function in the Function name list, scroll to display more function names.

4. **In cell D23, type =, then click the Paste Function button ƒx on the Standard toolbar to open the Paste Function dialog box**

5. **Under Function category, click Statistical, then under Function name click COUNT**
   After selecting the function name, notice that the description of the COUNT function reads, "Counts the number of cells that contain numbers . . ." Because the invoice numbers (for example, FP85011) are considered text entries, not numerical entries, the COUNT function will not work. There is another function, COUNTA, that counts the number of cells that are not empty and therefore can be used to count the number of invoice number entries.

6. **Under Function name, click COUNTA, then click OK**
   Excel automatically opens the Formula Palette and automatically references the range that is directly above the active cell as the first argument (in this case, range D19:D22, which is not the range you want to count). See Figure E-12. You need to select the correct range of invoice numbers. Because the desired invoice numbers are not visible, you need to collapse the dialog box so that you can select the correct range.

7. **With the Value1 argument selected in the Formula Palette, click the Value1 Collapse Dialog Box button, ▦, select range A7:A13 in the worksheet, click the Redisplay Dialog Box button ▦, then click OK**
   Compare your worksheet with Figure E-13.

8. **Save, print, then close the workbook**

FIGURE E-12: Formula Palette showing COUNTA function

Edit Formula button

Click to pick a
different function

Collapse Dialog Box
button

Formula Palette

Result of the
COUNTA function

Result of the
formula

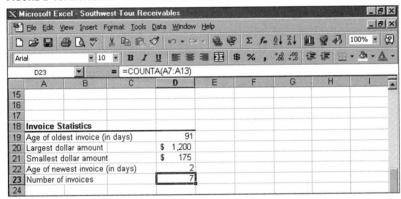

=COUNTA(D19:D22)

18	Invoice Statistics	
19	Age of oldest invoice (in days)	91
20	Largest dollar amount	$ 1,200
21	Smallest dollar amount	$ 175
22	Age of newest invoice (in days)	2
23	Number of invoices	=COUNTA(D19:D22)

Incorrect range

FIGURE E-13: Worksheet with invoice statistics

D23 = =COUNTA(A7:A13)

18	Invoice Statistics	
19	Age of oldest invoice (in days)	91
20	Largest dollar amount	$ 1,200
21	Smallest dollar amount	$ 175
22	Age of newest invoice (in days)	2
23	Number of invoices	7

TABLE E-4: Commonly used statistical functions

function	worksheet action
AVERAGE	Calculates an average value
COUNT	Counts the number of values
COUNTA	Counts the number of nonblank entries
MAX	Finds the largest value
MIN	Finds the smallest value
SUM	Calculates a total

CLUES TO USE

Using the Formula Palette to enter and edit formulas

When you use the Paste Function to build a formula, the Formula Palette displays the name and description for the function and each of its arguments, the current result of the function, and the current result of the entire formula. You also can use the Formula Palette to edit functions in formulas. To open the Formula Palette from either a blank cell or one containing a formula, click the Edit Formula button on the formula bar.

Calculating Payments with the PMT Function

PMT is a financial function that calculates the periodic payment amount for money borrowed. For example, if you want to borrow money to buy a car, the PMT function can calculate your monthly payment on the loan. Let's say you want to borrow $15,000 at 9% interest and pay the loan off in five years. Excel's PMT function can tell you that your monthly payment will be $311.38. The parts of the PMT function are: PMT(rate, nper, pv, fv, type). See Figure E-14 for an illustration of a PMT function that calculates the monthly payment in the car loan example.

For several months, the management at Nomad Ltd has been planning the development of a new mountain bike. Evan's manager has asked him to obtain quotes from three different lenders on borrowing $25,000 to begin developing the new product. He obtained loan quotes from a commercial bank, a venture capitalist, and an investment banker. Now Evan can summarize the information using Excel's PMT function.

Steps 1 2 3 4

1. **Open the workbook titled XL E-4, then save it as Bicycle Loan Summary**
   You have already entered all the data with the lender data already entered; you are ready to calculate the commercial loan monthly payment in cell E5.

2. **Click cell E5, type =PMT(C5/12,D5,B5) (make sure you type the commas); then click the Enter button** ☑ **on the formula bar**
   Note that the payment of ($543.56) in cell E5 is a negative amount. (It appears in red on a color monitor.) Excel displays the result of a PMT function as a negative value to reflect the negative cash flow the loan represents to the borrower. You must divide the annual interest by 12 because you are calculating monthly, not annual, payments. Because you want to show the monthly payment value as a positive number, you can convert the loan amount to a negative number by placing a minus sign in front of the cell reference.

   QuickTip

   It is important to be consistent about the units you use for *rate* and *nper*. If, for example, you express *nper* as the number of *monthly* payments, then you must express the interest rate as a *monthly* rate, not an annual rate.

3. **Edit cell E5 so it reads =PMT(C5/12,D5,-B5), then click** ☑
   A positive value of $543.56 now appears in cell E5. See Figure E-15. Now, copy the formula to generate the monthly payments for the other loans.

4. **Click cell E5, then drag the fill handle to select range E5:E7**
   A monthly payment of $818.47 for the venture capitalist loan appears in cell E6. A monthly payment of $1,176.84 for the investment banker loan appears in cell E7. You are surprised that the monthly payments vary so much. You will not know the entire financial picture until you take one more step and calculate the total payments and total interest for each lender.

5. **Click cell F5, type =E5*D5, then press [Tab]; in cell G5, type =F5-B5, then click** ☑

6. **Copy the formulas in cells F5:G5 into cells F6:G7**
   You can experiment with different interest rates, loan amounts, or terms for any one of the lenders; the PMT function generates a new set of values automatically. Compare your results to Figure E-16.

7. **Save the workbook, then print the worksheet**

FIGURE E-14: Example of PMT function for car loan

$$PMT(.09/12, 60, 15000) = \$311.38$$

Interest rate per period | Number of payments | Present value of loan amount | Monthly payment calculated

FIGURE E-15: PMT function calculating monthly loan payment

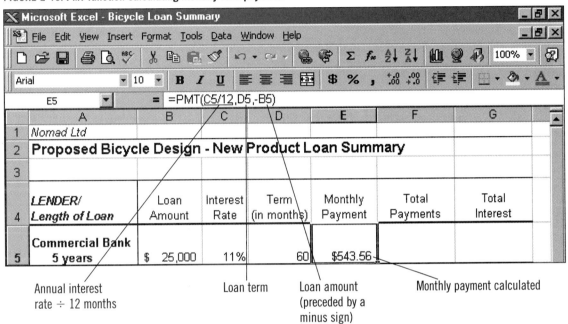

Annual interest rate ÷ 12 months | Loan term | Loan amount (preceded by a minus sign) | Monthly payment calculated

FIGURE E-16: Completed worksheet

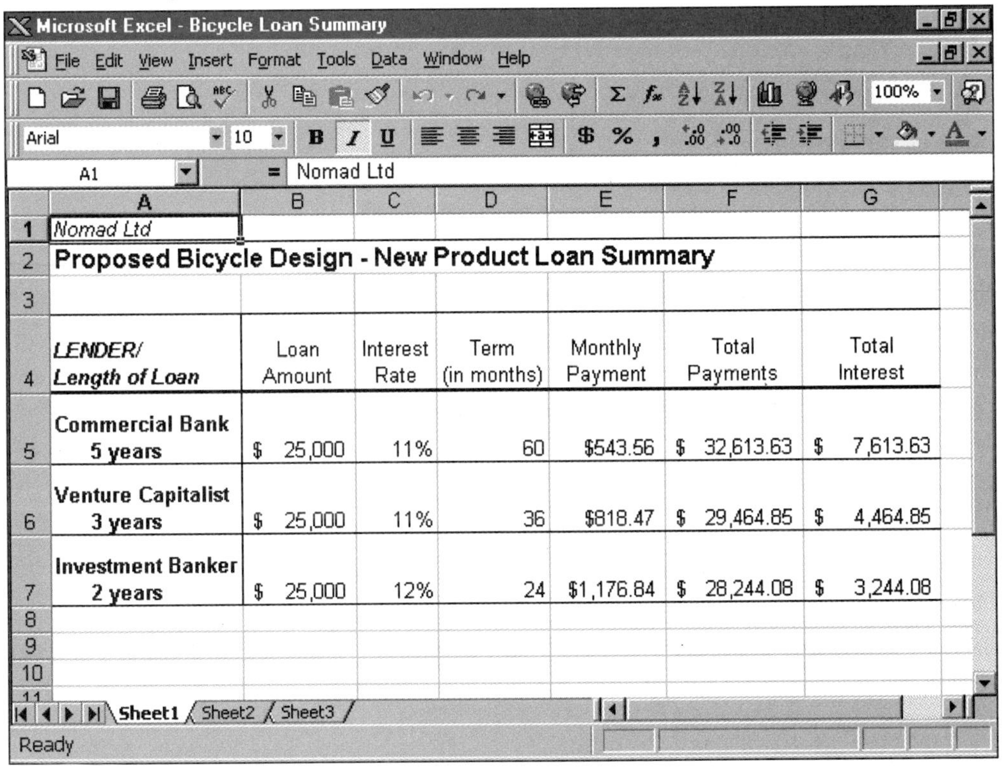

Excel 97

Displaying and Printing Formula Contents

Excel usually displays the result of formula calculations in the worksheet area and displays formula contents for the active cell in the formula bar. However, you can instruct Excel to display the formulas directly in the worksheet locations in which they were entered. You can document worksheet formulas in this way: by first displaying the formulas then printing them. These formula printouts are valuable paper-based worksheet documentation. Because formulas are often longer than their corresponding values, landscape orientation is the best choice for printing formulas. ✎ Evan is ready to produce a formula printout to submit with the worksheet.

1. **Click Tools on the menu bar, click Options, then click the View tab**
   The View tab of the Options dialog box appears, as shown in Figure E-17.

2. **Under Window options, click the Formulas check box to select it, then click OK**
   The columns have widened and retain their original formats. You need to scroll horizontally to see that the column widths adjust automatically to accommodate the formulas.

3. **Scroll horizontally to bring columns D through G into view**
   Instead of formula results appearing in the cells, Excel shows the actual formulas. See Figure E-18. In order to see how this worksheet will print, you can preview it.

4. **Click the Print Preview button 🔍 on the Standard toolbar**
   The status bar reads Preview: Page 1 of 3, indicating that the worksheet will print on three pages. You want to print it on one page and include the row number and column letter headings. You can do this by selecting several Page Setup options.

5. **Click the Setup button in the Print Preview window, then click the Page tab**
   Select the Landscape orientation and the Fit to scaling options.

6. **Under Orientation, click the Landscape option button; then under Scaling, click the Fit to option button**
   Selecting Landscape instructs Excel to print the worksheet sideways on the page. The Fit to option ensures that the document is printed on a single page. Finally, select the Sheet tab to turn on the printing of row number and column letters.

7. **Click the Sheet tab, under Print click the Row and Column Headings check box, click OK, then position the Zoom pointer 🔍 over column A and click**
   The worksheet formulas now appear on a single page, in landscape orientation, with row (number) and column (letter) headings. See Figure E-19. Notice that the contents of cell A2 are slightly hidden.

8. **Click the Print button in the Print Preview window, then click OK**
   After you retrieve the printout, you want to return the worksheet to display formula results. You can do this by pressing [Ctrl][`] (grave accent mark) to toggle between displaying formula results and displaying formula contents.

9. **Press [Ctrl][`] to re-display formula results, save and close the workbook, then exit Excel**

QuickTip

All Page Setup options—such as landscape orientation, fit to scaling, and printing row and column headings—apply to the active worksheet and are saved with the workbook.

FIGURE E-17: View tab of the Options dialog box

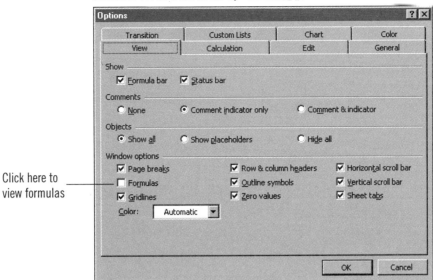

Click here to view formulas

FIGURE E-18: Worksheet with formulas visible

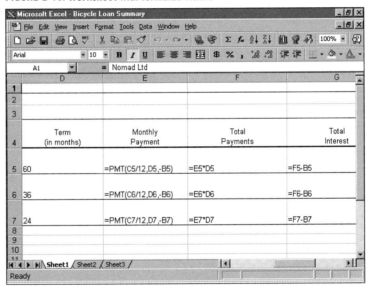

Column headings

FIGURE E-19: Print Preview window

Row headings

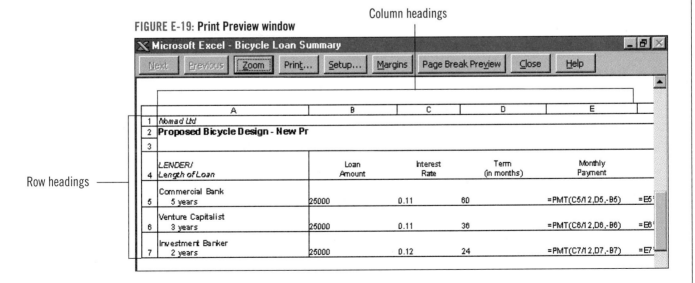

Practice

▶ Concepts Review

Label each of the elements of the Excel screen shown in Figure E-20.

FIGURE E-20

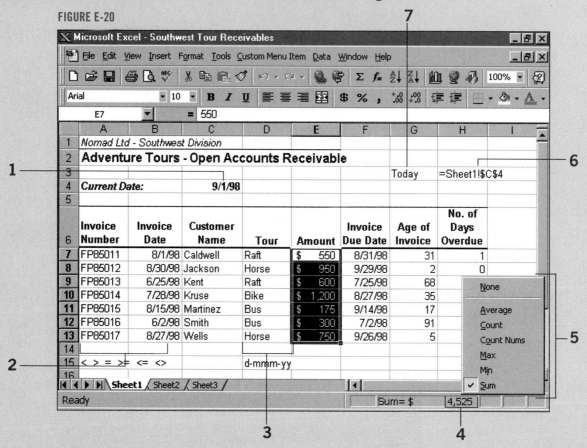

Match each of the terms with the statement that best describes its function.

8. **Parentheses**
9. **COUNTA**
10. **test_cond**
11. **COUNT**
12. **pv**

a. Part of the IF function in which the conditions are stated
b. Function used to count the number of numerical entries
c. Part of the PMT function that represents the loan amount
d. Function used to count the number of nonblank entries
e. Symbols used in formulas to control formula calculation order

Select the best answer from the list of choices.

13. **To generate a positive payment value when using the PMT function, you must**
    a. Enter the function arguments as positive values.
    b. Enter the function arguments as negative values.
    c. Enter the amount being borrowed as a negative value.
    d. Enter the interest rate divisor as a negative value.

14. **When you enter the rate and nper arguments in a PMT function**
    a. Multiply both units by 12.
    b. Be consistent in the units used.
    c. Divide both values by 12.
    d. Use monthly units instead of annual units.

15. **To express conditions such as less than or equal to, you can use a(n)**
    a. IF function.
    b. Comparison operator.
    c. AutoCalculate formula.
    d. PMT function.

► Skills Review

1. **Create a formula with several operators.**
   a. Open workbook XL E-5, and save it as "Annual Bonuses".
   b. In cell C15, enter the formula C13+(C14*7).

2. **Use names in a formula.**
   a. Name cell C13 "Dept_Bonus".
   b. Name cell C14 "Project_Bonus".
   c. In cell E4, enter the formula Dept_Bonus*D4+Project_Bonus.
   d. Copy formula in cell E4 into the range E5:E10.
   e. Format range E4:E10 with the Comma Style button.
   f. In cell F4, enter a formula that sums C4 and E4.
   g. Copy the formula in cell F4 into the range F5:F10.
   h. Return to cell A1, then save your work.

3. **Generate multiple totals with AutoSum.**
   a. Select range E11:F11.
   b. Enter the totals using AutoSum.
   c. Format range E11:F11 using the Currency Style button.
   d. Save your work, preview, then print the worksheet.

4. **Use dates in calculations.**
   a. Make the Merit Pay sheet active.
   b. In cell D6, enter the formula B6+183.
   c. Copy the formula in cell D6 into the range D7:D14.
   d. Save your work.

5. **Build a conditional formula with the IF function.**
   a. In cell F6, enter the formula IF(C6=5,E6*0.05,0).
   b. Copy the formula in cell F6 into the range F7:F14.
   c. Save your work.

6. **Use statistical functions.**
   a. In cell C19, enter a function to calculate the average of range E6:E14.
   b. In cell C20, enter a function to calculate the largest value in range F6:F14.
   c. In cell C21, enter a function to calculate the smallest value in range C6:C14.
   d. In cell C22, enter a function to calculate the number of entries in range A6:A14.
   e. Save, preview, then print this worksheet.

7. **Calculate payments with the PMT function.**
   a. Make the Loan sheet active.
   b. In cell B9, enter the formula PMT(B5/12,B6,-B4).
   c. In cell B10, enter the formula B9*B6.
   d. AutoFit column B, if necessary.
   e. In cell B11, enter the formula B10-B4.
   f. Save, then print the worksheet.

8. **Display and print formula contents.**
   a. Click Tools on the menu bar, click Options, then click the View tab, if necessary.
   b. Turn formulas on, then click OK.
   c. Adjust the column widths as necessary.
   d. Save, preview, and print this worksheet in landscape orientation with the row and column headings.
   e. Close the workbook.

► Independent Challenges

1. As the store manager of Heavenly Cones Ice Cream Parlor, you have been asked to create a worksheet that totals the monthly sales of all the stores products. Your monthly report should include the following:

- Sales totals for the current month for each product
- Sales totals for the last month for each product
- The percent change in sales from last month to this month

To document the report further, you decide to include a printout of the worksheet formulas.

To complete this independent challenge:

1. Open the workbook titled XL E-6, then save it as "Heavenly Sales" to the appropriate folder on your Student Disk.
2. Complete the headings for weeks 2 through 4. Enter the weekly totals and the current month's totals, then copy them where appropriate. Calculate the percent change in sales from last month to this month. (*Hint:* The formula in words would be (Current Month-Last Month)/Last Month.) After you enter the percent change formula for regular ice cream, copy the formula down the column.
3. Save, preview, then print the worksheet on a single page. If necessary, print in landscape orientation. If you make any page setup changes, save the worksheet again.
4. Display and print the worksheet formulas with row and column headings. Again, print the formulas on one page.
5. Close the workbook without saving the changes for displaying formulas.
6. Submit your printouts.

2. You are an auditor with a certified public accounting firm. High Rollers, a manufacturer of skating products including roller skates and skateboards, has contacted you to audit its financial records. They have asked you to assist them in preparing their year-end sales summary. Specifically, they want to add expenses and show the percent each expense category represents of annual expenses. They also want to show what percent each expense category represents of annual sales. You should include a formula calculating the difference between sales and expenses and another formula calculating expenses divided by sales. The expense categories and their respective dollar amounts are as follows: Building Lease $36,000; Equipment $235,000; Office $24,000; Salary $350,000; Taxes $315,000. Use these expense amounts to prepare the year-end sales and expenses summary for High Rollers.

To complete this independent challenge:

1. Open the workbook titled XL E-7, then save it as "High Rollers Sales".
2. Name the cell containing the formula for annual expenses "Annual_Expenses". Use the name Annual_Expenses in the first formula calculating percent of annual expenses. Copy this formula as appropriate. Make sure to include a formula that sums all the values for percent of annual expenses, which should equal 1 or 100%.

3. Enter a formula calculating what percent of annual sales each expense category represents. Use the name Annual_Sales in the formula. Enter formulas calculating annual sales minus annual expenses and expenses divided by sales using only the names Annual_Sales and Annual_Expenses. Add formulas for totals as appropriate.

4. Format the cells using the Currency, Percent, or Comma style. Widen the columns as necessary to increase readability.

5. Save, preview, then print the worksheet on a single page. If necessary, use landscape orientation. Save any page setup changes you make.

6. Display and print worksheet formulas on a single page with row and column headings.

7. Close the workbook without saving the changes for displaying formulas.

8. Submit your printouts.

3. As the owner of Build-To-Fit, a general contracting firm specializing in home-storage projects, you are facing yet another business challenge at your firm. Because jobs are taking longer than expected, you decide to take out a loan to purchase some new power tools. According to your estimates, you need a $5,000 loan to purchase the tools. You check three loan sources: the Small Business Administration (SBA), your local bank, and your parents. Each source offers you a loan on its own terms. The local bank offers you the loan at 9.5% interest over four years. The SBA will loan you the money at 9% interest, but you have to pay it off in three years. Your parents offer you an 8% loan, but they require you to pay it back in two years, when they expect to retire. To analyze all three loan options, you decide to build a tool loan summary worksheet. Using the loan terms provided, build a worksheet summarizing your options.

To complete this independent challenge:

1. Open a new workbook, then save it as "Loan Options".

2. Enter labels and worksheet data. You need headings for the loan source, loan amount, interest rate, term or number of payments, monthly payment, total payments, and total interest. Fill in the data provided for the three loan sources.

3. Enter formulas as appropriate: a PMT formula for the monthly payment; a formula calculating the total payments based on the monthly payment and term values; and a formula for total interest based on the total payments and the loan amount.

4. Format the worksheet as desired.

5. Save, preview, then print the worksheet on a single page using landscape orientation. Along with the worksheet, submit a printout of worksheet formulas showing row and column headings. Do not save the worksheet with these settings.

6. Submit your printouts.

4. You can get up-to-date information on nearly any major company on the World Wide Web (WWW). When you get ready to make a major purchase, such as a vehicle, you can search the Web to gather the latest information available on the desired product. You have decided to purchase a new vehicle, and you are excited about logging on to the Web to research your planned purchase. Your self-imposed spending limit is $30,000, including purchase price and total interest on the loan. Create a spreadsheet using vehicle information found on the WWW to support your purchase decision. To complete this independent challenge:

1. Open a new workbook, then save it as "My New Car" to the appropriate folder on your Student Disk.

2. Decide which features you want your ideal vehicle to have, and list these somewhere in your spreadsheet.

3. Log on to the Internet and use your web browser to go to http://www.course.com. From there, click the link Student Online Companions, click the link for this textbook, then click the Excel link for unit E.

4. Use any of the following sites to compile your data: Cadillac, Ford, GM, Honda, Toyota, or any other site with related information.

5. Compare at least three vehicles showing the automaker, the vehicle make and model year, the number of doors, color, and list sales price. Also compare the three vehicles based on the financing available. Specifically, calculate a loan amount (include list sales price, tax, and license fees), a monthly payment based on a five-year loan at 10.25% interest, the total of the payments, and the total interest paid. Make sure the total payments do not exceed your limit of $30,000.

6. Indicate on the worksheet your final purchase decision and the rationale behind that decision.

7. Save, print, then submit your printout.

Visual Workshop

Create the worksheet shown in Figure E-21. (Hint: Enter the items in range C9:C11 as labels by typing an apostrophe before each formula.) Save the workbook as "Mortgage Payment Calculator" to the appropriate folder on your Student Disk. Preview, print, then submit the worksheet.

FIGURE E-21

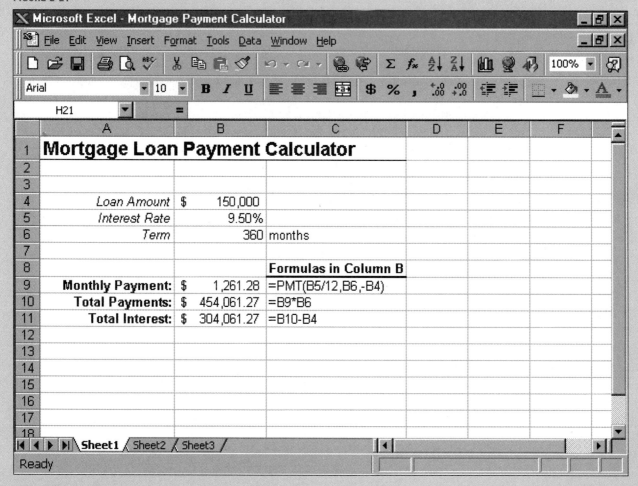

Managing
Workbooks

Objectives

► Freeze columns and rows
► Insert and delete sheets
► Reference worksheet data
► Hide and protect worksheet areas
► Specify headers and footers
► Save custom views of a worksheet
► Control page breaks and page numbering
► Set margins and alignment

In this unit, you will learn several Excel features to help you manage and print workbook data. Nomad Ltd has increased the number of its hourly workers by 50% over the past year. Evan Brillstein's manager has designed a timecard summary worksheet to track salary costs for hourly workers. She turned the management of this worksheet over to Evan. In doing so, she has alerted him that she will need several reports generated from the worksheet data.

Freezing Columns and Rows

As rows and columns fill up with data, you might need to scroll through the worksheet to add, delete, modify, and view information. Looking at information without row or column labels can be confusing. In Excel, you can temporarily freeze columns and rows, which enables you to view separate areas of your worksheets at the same time. **Panes** are the columns and rows that **freeze**, or remain in place, while you scroll through your worksheet. The freeze feature is especially useful when you're dealing with large worksheets. Sometimes, though, even freezing is not sufficient. In those cases, you can create as many as four areas, or panes, on the screen at one time and move freely within each of them. ✐ Evan has been asked to verify the hourly pay rate, total hours worked, and total pay for two janitors at Nomad Ltd, Wilbur Collins and Orson Wilks. Because the worksheet is becoming more difficult to read as its size increases, Evan decides to freeze the column and row labels. To gather the requested information, Evan needs to view simultaneously a person's last name, total number of hours, hourly pay rate, and total pay. To do this, he will freeze columns A, B, and C and rows 1 through 5.

1. Open the workbook titled **XL F-1**, save it as **Timecard Summary**, then scroll through the Monday worksheet to view the data

2. Return to cell A1, then click cell **D6**
   Position the pointer in cell A1 to reorient the worksheet, then move to cell D6 because you want to freeze columns A, B, and C. By doing so, you can still view the last name when you scroll to the right. Because you want to be able to scroll down the worksheet and read the column headings, you also freeze the labels in rows 1 through 5. When instructed to do so, Excel freezes the columns to the left and the rows above the cell pointer.

Trouble?

If you do not see a thin vertical line in the worksheet area between columns C and D and a thin horizontal black line between rows 5 and 6, click Window on the menu bar, click Unfreeze Panes, then repeat Steps 2 and 3.

3. Click **Window** on the menu bar, then click **Freeze Panes**
   Everything to the left and above the active cell is frozen. A thin line appears along the column border to the left of the active cell, and another line appears along the row above the active cell indicating that columns A through C and rows 1 through 5 are frozen.

4. Scroll to the right until columns A through C and L through P are visible
   Because columns A, B, and C are frozen, they remain on the screen; columns D through K are temporarily hidden from view. Notice that the information you are looking for in row 12 (last name, total hours, hourly pay rate, and total pay for Wilbur Collins) is readily available. You jot down Wilbur's data but still need to verify Orson Wilks's information.

5. Scroll down until row 23 is visible
   Notice that in addition to columns A through C, rows 1 through 5 remain on the screen as well. See Figure F-1. Evan jots down the information for Orson Wilks. Even though a pane is frozen, you can click in the frozen area of the worksheet and edit the contents of the cells there, if necessary.

QuickTip

When you open an existing workbook, the cell pointer is in the cell it was in when you last saved the workbook. Press [Ctrl][Home] to return to cell A1 prior to saving and closing a workbook.

6. Press **[Ctrl][Home]**
   Because the panes are frozen, the cell pointer moves to cell D6, not A1. Now that you have gathered the requested information, you are ready to unfreeze the panes.

7. Click **Window** on the menu bar, then click **Unfreeze Panes**
   The panes are unfrozen. You are satisfied with your ability to navigate and view the worksheet and are ready to save the workbook.

8. Return to cell A1, then save the workbook

FIGURE F-1: Scrolled worksheet with frozen rows and columns

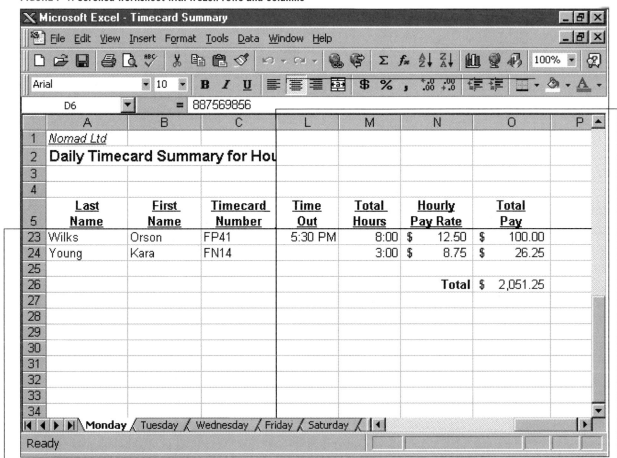

Break in row
numbers due to
frozen rows 1–5

Break in column
letters due to
frozen columns
A–C

Splitting the worksheet into multiple panes

Excel provides a way to split the worksheet area into vertical and/or horizontal panes so that you can click inside any one pane and scroll to locate desired information in that pane without any of the other panes moving. See Figure F-2. To split a worksheet area into multiple panes, drag the split box (the small box at the top of the vertical scroll bar or at the right end of the horizontal scroll bar) in the direction you want the split to appear. To remove the split, move the mouse over the split until the pointer changes to ╪, then double-click.

FIGURE F-2: Worksheet split into two horizontal panes

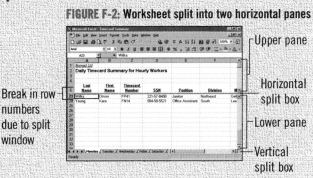

Upper pane

Horizontal
split box

Lower pane

Vertical
split box

Break in row
numbers
due to split
window

Inserting and Deleting Sheets

You can insert and delete worksheets in a workbook as needed. For example, because new workbooks open with only three sheets available (Sheet1, Sheet2, and Sheet3), you need to insert at least one more sheet if you want to have four quarterly worksheets in an annual financial budget workbook. As for other Excel features, you can do this by using commands on the menu bar or pop-up menu. ◄▬▬ Evan was in a hurry when he added the sheet tabs to the Timecard Summary workbook. He needs to insert a sheet for Thursday and delete the sheet for Sunday because hourly workers do not work on Sunday.

QuickTip

You also can copy the active worksheet by clicking Edit on the menu bar, then clicking Move or Copy Sheet. You choose the sheet the copy will precede, then select the Create a copy check box.

1. Click the **Friday sheet tab**, click **Insert** on the menu bar, then click **Worksheet**

Excel automatically inserts a new sheet tab labeled Sheet1 to the left of the selected sheet. See Figure F-3. Next, rename the inserted sheet to something more meaningful.

2. Rename the Sheet1 tab **Thursday**

Now the tabs read Monday, Tuesday, Wednesday, Thursday, Friday, and Saturday. The tabs for Sunday and Weekly Summary are not visible, but you still need to delete the Sunday worksheet.

3. Scroll until the Sunday sheet tab is visible, move the pointer over the **Sunday tab**, then click the **right mouse button**

A pop-up menu appears. See Figure F-4. The pop-up menu allows you to insert, delete, rename, move, or copy sheets, select all the sheets, or view the code in a workbook.

4. Click **Delete** on the pop-up menu

A message box warns that the selected sheet will be deleted permanently. You must acknowledge the message before proceeding.

5. Click **OK**

The Sunday sheet is deleted. Next, to check your work, you view a menu of sheets in the workbook.

QuickTip

You can scroll several tabs at once by pressing [Shift] while clicking one of the middle tab scrolling buttons.

6. Move the mouse pointer over any tab scrolling button, then **right-click**

When you right-click a tab scrolling button, Excel automatically opens a menu of the sheets in the active workbook. Compare your list with Figure F-5.

7. Click **Monday**, return to cell A1, then save the workbook

FIGURE F-3: Workbook with inserted sheet

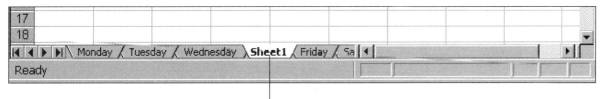

Inserted sheet

FIGURE F-4: Sheet pop-up menu

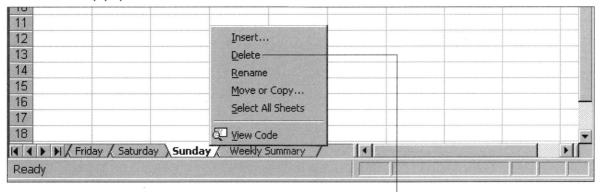

Click to delete
selected sheet

FIGURE F-5: Workbook with menu of sheets

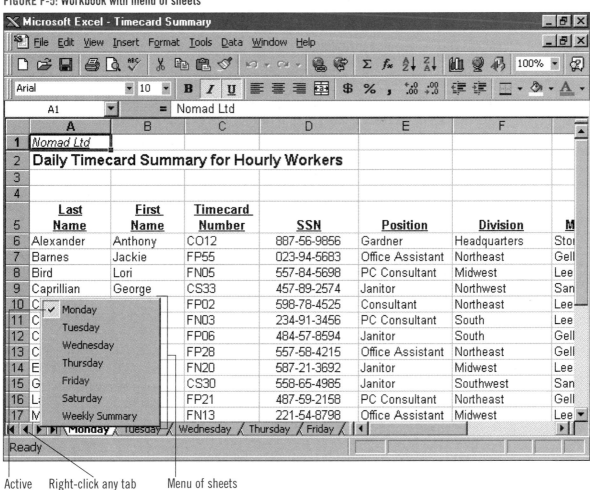

Active
sheet

Right-click any tab
scrolling button to
display menu of
sheets

Menu of sheets

Referencing Worksheet Data

You can reference data within a worksheet, between sheets, and between workbooks. For example, you can reference data within a worksheet if you want to reference a calculated total elsewhere in the sheet. Retyping the calculated result in another cell is not recommended because the data values on which the calculated total depend might change. Referencing data between sheets might be necessary if you have quarterly worksheets and an annual summary worksheet in the same workbook. Although Evan does not have timecard data for the remaining days of the week, he wants to try out the Weekly Summary sheet. He does this by creating a reference from the total pay data in the Monday sheet to the Weekly Summary sheet. First, he freezes panes to improve the view of the worksheets prior to initiating the reference between them.

1. **Click cell D6, click Window on the menu bar, click Freeze Panes, then scroll horizontally to bring columns L through O into view**
   Next, you right-click a tab scrolling button to access the pop-up menu for moving between sheets.

2. **Right-click a tab scrolling button, then click Weekly Summary**
   Because the Weekly Summary sheet will contain the reference, the cell pointer must reside there when the reference is initiated. A simple **reference** within the same sheet or between sheets is made by positioning the cell pointer in the cell to contain the reference, typing = (equal sign), positioning the cell pointer in the cell containing the contents to be referenced, and then completing the entry. You complete the entry either by pressing [Enter] or clicking the Enter button on the formula bar.

Trouble?

If you have difficulty referencing cells between sheets, press [Esc] and begin again.

3. **While in the Weekly Summary sheet, click cell C6, type =, activate the Monday sheet, click cell O6, then click the Enter button ☑ on the formula bar**
   The formula bar reads =Monday!O6. See Figure F-6. *Monday* references the Monday sheet. The ! (exclamation point) is an **external reference indicator** meaning that the cell referenced is outside the active sheet; O6 is the actual cell reference in the external sheet. The result $41.00 appears in cell C6 of the Weekly Summary sheet showing the reference to the value displayed in cell O6 of the Monday sheet. You are ready to copy the formula reference down the column.

4. **While in the Weekly Summary sheet, copy cell C6 into cells C7:C24**
   Excel copies the contents of cell C6 with its relative reference down the column. Test the reference for Anthony Alexander in cell C6 by correcting the time he clocked out for the day.

5. **Make the Monday sheet active, edit cell L6 to read 3:30 PM, then activate the Weekly Summary sheet**
   Cell C6 now shows $20.50. By changing Anthony's time-out to two hours earlier, his pay dropped from $41.00 to $20.50. This makes sense because Anthony's hours went from four to two and his hourly salary is $10.25. Additionally, the reference to Monday's total pay was automatically updated in the Weekly Summary sheet. See Figure F-7.

6. **Preview, then print the Weekly Summary sheet**

7. **Activate the Monday sheet, then unfreeze the panes**
   You are ready to save the workbook.

8. **Save the workbook**

FIGURE F-6: Worksheet showing referenced cell

Sheet referenced ⎯

External reference
indicator ⎯

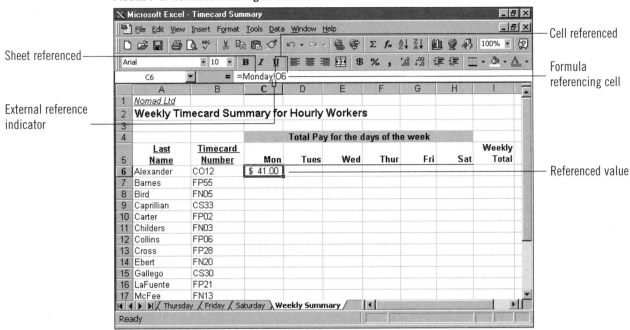

Cell referenced

Formula
referencing cell

Referenced value

FIGURE F-7: Weekly Summary worksheet with updated reference

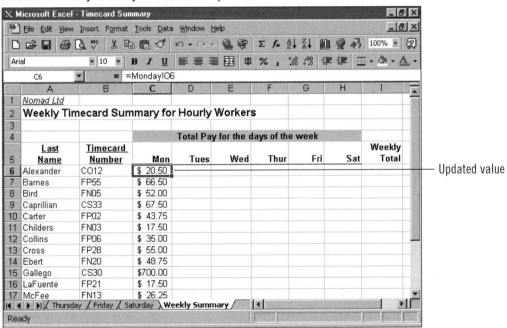

Updated value

Linking workbooks

Just as you can reference data between cells in a worksheet and between sheets, you can reference data between workbooks dynamically so that any changes made in one workbook are reflected immediately in the other workbook. This dynamic referencing is called linking. To link a single cell between workbooks, simply open both workbooks, select the cell to receive the linked data, press = (equal sign), select the cell containing the data to be linked, then press [Enter]. If you are linking more than one cell, you can copy the linked data to the Clipboard, select the upper-left cell to receive the link, click Edit on the menu bar, click Paste Special, then click Paste Link.

Hiding and Protecting Worksheet Areas

Worksheets can contain sensitive information that is not intended to be altered or even viewed by all users. In Excel, you can hide individual formulas, rows, columns, or entire sheets. In addition, you can **protect** selected cells so they cannot be changed while allowing other cells in the worksheet to be altered. See Table F-1 for a list of options you can use to hide and protect a worksheet. Cells that are protected so that their contents cannot be altered are called **locked cells**. You lock and unlock cells by clicking the Locked check box in the Format Cells dialog box. A common worksheet protection strategy is to unlock cells that will be changed, sometimes referred to as the **data entry area**, and to leave the remaining cells locked. ⬛ Because Evan will assign someone to enter the sensitive timecard information into the worksheet, he plans to hide and protect selected areas of the worksheet.

1. **Make sure the Monday sheet is active, select range I6:L25; click Format on the menu bar, click Cells, then click the Protection tab**
   You include row 25, even though it does not contain data, in the event that new data is added to the row later. Notice that the Locked box in the Protection tab is checked, as shown in Figure F-8. By default, the Locked check box is selected, which indicates that all the cells in a new workbook start out locked.

2. **Click the Locked check box to deselect it, then click OK**
   Excel stores time as a fraction of a 24-hour day. In the formula for total pay, hours must be multiplied by 24. This concept might be confusing to the data entry person, so you hide the formulas before you protect the worksheet.

3. **Select range O6:O25; click Format on the menu bar, click Cells, click the Protection tab, click the Hidden check box to select it, then click OK**
   The screen data remains the same (unhidden and unlocked) until you set the protection in the next step.

4. **Click Tools on the menu bar, point to Protection, then click Protect Sheet**
   The Protect Sheet dialog box opens. You choose not to use a password.

5. **Click OK**
   You are ready to put the new worksheet protection status to the test.

6. **Click cell O6**
   Notice that the formula bar is empty because of the hidden formula setting. Now you attempt to change the cell contents of O6, which is a locked cell.

7. **In cell O6, type T to confirm that locked cells cannot be changed, then click OK**
   When you attempt to change a locked cell, a message box reminds you of the protected cell's read-only status. See Figure F-9. Next, you attempt to make an entry in the Time In column to make sure it is unlocked.

8. **Click cell I6, type 9, and notice that Excel allows you to begin the entry; press [Esc] to cancel the entry, then save the workbook**
   Evan is satisfied that the Time In and Time Out data can be changed as needed.

QuickTip

To turn off worksheet protection, click Tools on the menu bar, point to Protection, then click Unprotect Sheet. If prompted for a password, type the password, then click OK. Keep in mind that passwords are case sensitive.

FIGURE F-8: Protection tab in Format Cells dialog box

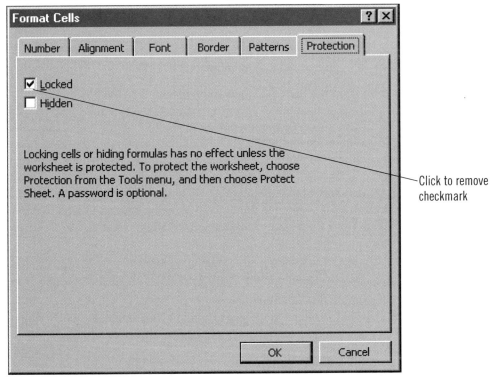

Click to remove checkmark

FIGURE F-9: Message box reminder of protected cell's read-only status

TABLE F-1: Options for hiding and protecting worksheet elements

task	menu commands
Hide/Unhide a column	Format, Column, Hide, or Unhide
Hide/Unhide a formula	Format, Cells, Protection tab, select/deselect Hidden check box
Hide/Unhide a row	Format, Row, Hide, or Unhide
Hide/Unhide a sheet	Format, Sheet, Hide, or Unhide
Protect workbook	Tools, Protection, Protect Workbook, assign optional password
Protect worksheet	Tools, Protection, Protect Sheet, assign optional password
Unlock/Relock cells	Format, Cells, Protection tab, deselect/select Locked check box

Note: Some of the hide and protect options do not take effect until protection is enabled.

Specifying Headers and Footers

A **header** is information that appears at the top of each printed page, and a **footer** is information that appears at the bottom of each printed page. You do not see headers and footers on the screen, except in the Print Preview window. By default, in Microsoft Excel 97 the header and footer are set to "none" in new worksheets. You can override the default of no headers and footers by creating your own. Excel provides a group of buttons that you can use to print specific information in your headers and footers. See Table F-2 for a description of these buttons.

Evan remembers that his manager will use the Timecard Summary sheet as part of a report to upper management. He wants to include the date and filename in the footer, and he thinks it will improve the report to make the header text larger and more descriptive.

Steps 1234

1. **With the Monday sheet active, click File on the menu bar, click Page Setup, then click the Header/Footer tab**
   The Header/Footer tab of the Page Setup dialog box opens. Notice that Excel automatically sets the header and footer to none. First, you customize the header.

2. **Click Custom Header**
   The Header dialog box opens, as shown in Figure F-10. By entering your header information in the Center section box, Excel automatically centers this information on the printout.

3. **Click the Center section box, then type Monday – 8/4**
   In the case of a long header, header text might wrap to the next line in the box but will appear on one line in the printout. Next, you change the font size and style.

4. **Drag to select the header text Monday – 8/4, then click the Font button A in the Header dialog box; in the Size box click 12, in the Font style box click Bold, click OK, then click OK to return to the Header/Footer tab**
   The new header appears in the Header box. You are ready to customize the footer.

QuickTip
You can easily turn off the header and/or footer in a worksheet by clicking the header or footer list arrow on the Header/Footer tab, scrolling to the top of the list, then choosing (none).

5. **In the Header/Footer tab, click Custom Footer**
   The Footer dialog box opens. The information you enter in the Left section box is left-aligned on the printout. The text you enter in the Right section box is right-aligned on the printout.

6. **Click the Right section box, type Workbook: and press [Spacebar], then click the File Name button 🗐 in the Footer dialog box to insert the filename code &[File], then click OK**
   You return to the Page Setup dialog box, and the revised footer appears in the Footer box. See Figure F-11.

7. **Preview, print, then save the worksheet**
   Evan is ready to submit the report to his manager.

FIGURE F-10: **Header dialog box**

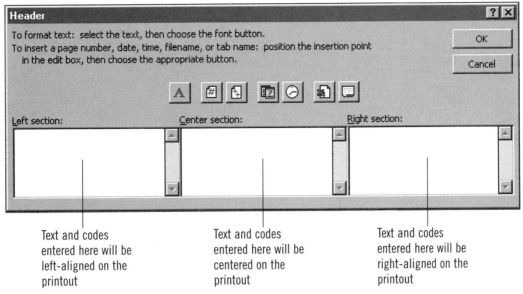

Text and codes entered here will be left-aligned on the printout

Text and codes entered here will be centered on the printout

Text and codes entered here will be right-aligned on the printout

FIGURE F-11: **Header/Footer tab with revised header and footer information**

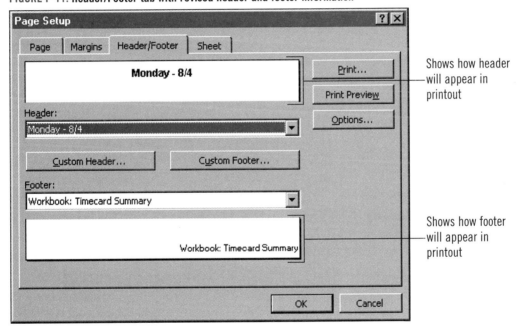

Shows how header will appear in printout

Shows how footer will appear in printout

Excel 97

TABLE F-2: **Buttons for customizing headers and footers**

button	button name	code	result
A	Font	None	Displays the Font dialog box in which you choose attributes for the header or footer
🔳	Page Number	&[Page]	Inserts current page number
🔳	Total Pages	&[Pages]	Inserts total number of printed pages
🔳	Date	&[Date]	Inserts the current date as it is stored in your computer
🔳	Time	&[Time]	Inserts the current time as it is stored in your computer
🔳	File Name	&[File]	Inserts the name of the workbook file
🔳	Sheet Name	&[Tab]	Inserts the name of the worksheet

Saving Custom Views of a Worksheet

A **view** is a set of display and/or print settings that you can name and save, then access at a later time. By using Excel's Custom Views feature, you can create several different views of a worksheet without having to save separate sheets under separate filenames. For example, if you often switch between portrait and landscape orientations when printing different parts of a worksheet, you can create two views with the appropriate print settings for each view. You define the display and/or print settings first, then name the view. 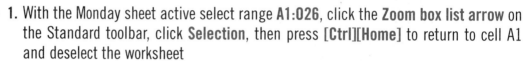 Because Evan will be generating several reports from this data, he will save the current print and display settings as a custom view. In order to better view the data to be printed, Evan decides to use the Zoom box to display the entire worksheet on one screen. The Zoom box has a default setting of 100% magnification and appears on the Standard toolbar.

1. **With the Monday sheet active select range A1:O26, click the Zoom box list arrow on the Standard toolbar, click Selection, then press [Ctrl][Home] to return to cell A1 and deselect the worksheet**
   Excel automatically adjusts the display magnification so that the data selected fit on one screen. See Figure F-12. After selecting the **Zoom box**, you also can pick a magnification percentage from the list or type the desired percentage. Now that you have set up the desired view of the data, you are ready to save the current print and display settings as a custom view.

2. **Click View, then click Custom Views**
   The Custom Views dialog box opens. Any previously defined views for the active worksheet appear in the Views box. In this case, Evan's manager had created a custom view named Generic containing default print and display settings. See Figure F-13. Next, you choose Add to create a new view.

3. **Click Add**
   The Add View dialog box opens, as shown in Figure F-14. Here, you enter a name for the view and decide whether to include print settings and hidden rows, columns and filter settings. Leave these two options checked.

4. **In the Name box, type Complete Daily Worksheet, then click OK**
   After creating a custom view of the worksheet, you return to the worksheet area. You are ready to test the two custom views. First, you turn off worksheet protection in case the views require a change to the worksheet.

5. **Click Tools on the menu bar, point to Protection, then click Unprotect Sheet**
   With the worksheet protection turned off, you are ready to show your custom views.

6. **Click View on the menu bar, then click Custom Views**
   The Custom Views dialog box opens, listing both the Complete Daily Worksheet and Generic views.

7. **Click Generic in the Views list box, click Show, then preview the worksheet**
   The Generic custom view returns the worksheet to Excel's default print and display settings. Now, you are ready to test the new custom view.

8. **Click View on the menu bar, click Custom Views, click Complete Daily Worksheet in the Views list box, click Show, then save the workbook**
   Evan is satisfied with the custom view of the worksheet he created.

FIGURE F-12: **Worksheet at 48% magnification**

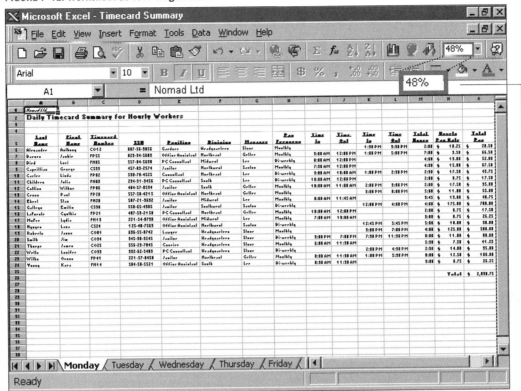

Zoom box showing
current magnification

FIGURE F-13: **Custom Views dialog box**

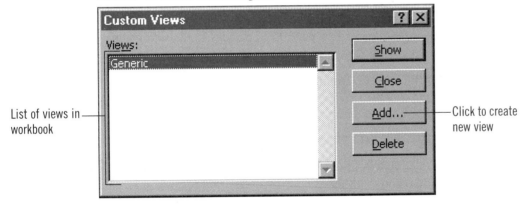

List of views in
workbook

Click to create
new view

FIGURE F-14: **Add View dialog box**

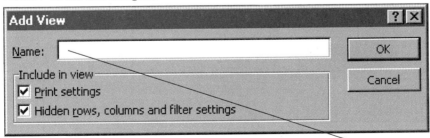

Type name of
view here

Controlling Page Breaks and Page Numbering

The vertical and horizontal dashed lines in your worksheets indicate page breaks. Excel automatically inserts a page break when your worksheet data doesn't fit on one page. These page breaks are **dynamic**, which means they adjust automatically when you insert or delete rows and columns and when you change column widths or row heights. Everything to the left of the first vertical dashed line and above the first horizontal dashed line is printed on the first page. You can override the automatic breaks by choosing the Page Break command on the Insert menu. Table F-3 describes the different types of page breaks you can use.  Evan's manager wants another report displaying no more than half the hourly workers on each page. To accomplish this, Evan must insert a manual page break. He begins by returning the screen display to 100% magnification.

1. Click the Zoom box list arrow on the Standard toolbar, then click 100%
The screen display returns to 100% magnification. Because there are 19 hourly employees, you insert the page break above the name Cynthia LaFuente.

Trouble?

If you don't see the page breaks inserted by Excel, click Tools on the menu bar, click Options, then click the View tab. Make sure the Page breaks check box is selected.

2. Click cell A16, click Insert on the menu bar, then click Page Break
A dashed line appears between rows 15 and 16 indicating a horizontal page break. See Figure F-15. Next, you preview the worksheet.

3. Preview the worksheet, then click Zoom
Notice that the status bar reads "Page 1 of 2" and that the data for the employees up through Emilio Gallego appear on the first page. Evan decides to reinstate the page number in the footer because the report now spans two pages.

4. While in the Print Preview window, click Setup, click the Header/Footer tab, click Custom Footer, click the Center section box, click the Page Number button 🔢, then click OK
Check your footer, then print the worksheet.

QuickTip

To remove a manual page break, select any cell directly below or to the right of the page break, click Insert on the menu bar, then click Remove Page Break.

5. In the Header/Footer tab, click OK, check to make sure both pages show page numbers, click Print, then click OK
Next, you save a custom view with the current display and print settings.

6. Click View on the menu bar, click Custom Views, click Add, type Half N Half, then click OK

7. Save the workbook

TABLE F-3: **Page break options**

type of page break	where to position cell pointer
Both horizontal and vertical page breaks	Select the cell below and to the right of the gridline where you want the breaks to occur
Only a horizontal page break	Select the cell in column A that is directly below the gridline where you want the page to break
Only a vertical page break	Select a cell in row 1 that is to the right of the gridline where you want the page to break

FIGURE F-15: Worksheet with horizontal page break

Dashed line indicates horizontal break after row 15

	A	B	C	D	E	F	
	X Microsoft Excel - Timecard Summary					_ 6 X	
	File Edit View Insert Format Tools Data Window Help					_ 6 X	
	A16	=	LaFuente				
1	Nomad Ltd						
2	Daily Timecard Summary for Hourly Workers						
3							
4							
5	Last Name	First Name	Timecard Number	SSN	Position	Division	M
6	Alexander	Anthony	CO12	887-56-9856	Gardner	Headquarters	Stoi
7	Barnes	Jackie	FP55	023-94-5683	Office Assistant	Northeast	Gell
8	Bird	Lori	FN05	557-84-5698	PC Consultant	Midwest	Lee
9	Caprillian	George	CS33	457-89-2574	Janitor	Northwest	San
10	Carter	Linda	FP02	598-78-4525	Consultant	Northeast	Lee
11	Childers	Julia	FN03	234-91-3456	PC Consultant	South	Lee
12	Collins	Wilbur	FP06	484-57-8594	Janitor	South	Gell
13	Cross	Paul	FP28	557-58-4215	Office Assistant	Northeast	Gell
14	Ebert	Stan	FN20	587-21-3692	Janitor	Midwest	Lee
15	Gallego	Emilio	CS30	558-65-4985	Janitor	Southwest	San
16	LaFuente	Cynthia	FP21	487-59-2158	PC Consultant	Northeast	Gell
17	McFee	Lydia	FN13	221-54-8798	Office Assistant	Midwest	Lee

Monday / Tuesday / Wednesday / Thursday / Friday /

Ready

Using Page Break Preview

By clicking View on the menu bar, then clicking Page Break Preview, or clicking Page Break Preview in the Print Preview window, you can view and change page breaks manually. Simply drag the dashed page break lines to the desired location. See Figure F-16.

FIGURE F-16: Page Break Preview window

5	Last Name	First Name	Timecard Number	SSN	Position	Division	Manager	Pay Frequenc	Time In	Time Out	Time In	Time Out
6	Alexander	Anthony	CO12	887-56-9856	Gardner	Headquarters	Stone	Monthly			1:30 PM	3:30 P
7	Barnes	Jackie	FP55	023-94-5683	Office Assistant	Northeast	Geller	Monthly	9:00 AM	######	1:00 PM	5:00 P
8	Bird	Lori	FN05	557-84-5698	PC Consultant	Midwest	Lee	Bi-weekly	8:00 AM	######		
9	Caprillian	George	CS33	457-89-2574	Janitor	Northwest	Santos	Monthly	7:30 AM	######		
10	Carter	Linda	FP02	598-78-4525	Consultant	Northeast	Lee	Bi-weekly	9:00 AM	######	1:00 PM	2:30 P
11	Childers	Julia	FN03	234-91-3456	PC Consultant	South	Lee	Bi-weekly	######	######		
12	Collins	Wilbur	FP06	484-57-8594	Janitor	South	Geller	Monthly	######	######	2:00 PM	3:00 P
13	Cross	Paul	FP28	557-58-4215	Office Assistant	Northeast	Geller	Monthly			3:00 PM	8:00 P
14	Ebert	Stan	FN20	587-21-3692	Janitor	Midwest	Lee	Monthly	8:00 AM	######		
15	Gallego	Emilio	CS30	558-65-4985	Janitor	Southwest	Santos	Bi-weekly			######	4:00 P
16	LaFuente	Cynthia	FP21	487-59-2158	PC Consultant	Northeast	Geller	Monthly	######	######		
17	McFee	Lydia	FN13	221-54-8798	Office Assistant	Midwest	Lee	Monthly	7:00 AM	######		
18	Nguyen	Lana	CS24	125-48-7569	Office Assistant	Northeast	Santos	Bi-weekly			######	5:45 P
19	Roberts	Jason	CO01	696-55-8742	Lawyer	Headquarters	Stone	Monthly			3:00 PM	7:00 P
20	Smith	Jim	CO34	345-98-3245	Janitor	Headquarters	Stone	Bi-weekly	3:00 PM	7:00 PM	7:30 PM	####
21	Thorpe	James	CO25	556-23-7845	Courier	Headquarters	Stone	Monthly	6:00 AM	######		
22	Wells	Lucifer	CO99	332-62-5489	PC Consultant	Headquarters	Stone	Bi-weekly			2:00 PM	4:30 P
23	Wilks	Orson	FP41	221-57-8458	Janitor	Northeast	Geller	Monthly	8:00 AM	######	1:00 PM	5:30 P
24	Young	Kara	FN14	584-58-5521	Office Assistant	South	Lee	Bi-weekly	8:30 AM	######		
25												
26												

Cell pointer in cell A16

Dashed page break line

Setting Margins and Alignment

You can set top, bottom, left, and right margins for a worksheet printout and determine the distance you want headers and footers to print from the edge of a page. Also, you can align data on a page by centering it horizontally and/or vertically between the margins. Evan has been asked to print selected information from the Timecard Summary. His manager wants an additional report showing last name, first name, timecard number, social security number, position, and division. First, Evan returns to the Generic custom view of the worksheet.

1. **Click View on the menu bar, click Custom Views, click Generic, then click Show**
   Excel's default print and display settings return. Notice the vertical dashed line indicating an automatic page break after column F. Now you indicate that you want to print only a selected range.

2. **Select range A1:F24, click File on the menu bar, click Print, under Print what click Selection, then click Preview**
   The Print Preview window displays only the selected cells. Next, center the data horizontally and start printing farther down the page.

3. **From the Print Preview window, click Setup, click the Margins tab, double-click the Top text box to select the 1, then type 3**
   Notice that the top margin line darkens in the Preview section of the dialog box. The Preview section reflects your activity in the Margins tab. Next, change the header so it prints 1.5" from the top edge of the page.

4. **Double-click the Header text box, then type 1.5**
   Finally, center the report horizontally on the page.

5. **In the Center on page section, click the Horizontally check box to select it**
   You have completed the changes in the Margins tab. See Figure F-17. Because all the data fits nicely on one page, you decide to set the footer to "none".

6. **Click the Header/Footer tab, click the Footer list arrow, scroll to the top of the list, then click (none)**
   Check the report to ensure that it begins farther down from the top of the page, is centered horizontally, and does not include a page number. Because the report is complete, preview and print the worksheet.

7. **Click OK to preview the worksheet, then print the worksheet**
   Compare your screen with Figure F-18. Because Evan will be switching between reports, he first prints this latest report, and then creates a custom view called Employee Info.

8. **Click View on the menu bar, click Custom Views, click Add, type Employee Info, then click OK**

9. **Save the workbook**

FIGURE F-17: Margins tab with changed settings

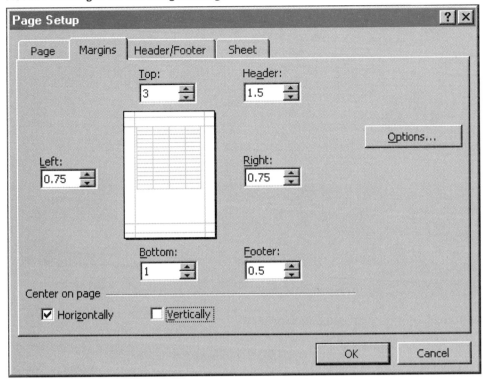

FIGURE F-18: Print Preview window showing employee information

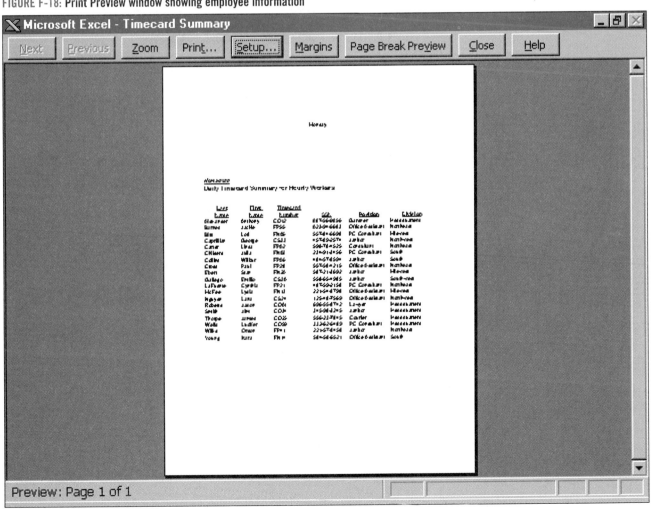

Practice

▶ Concepts Review

Label each of the elements of the Excel screen shown in Figure F-19.

FIGURE F-19

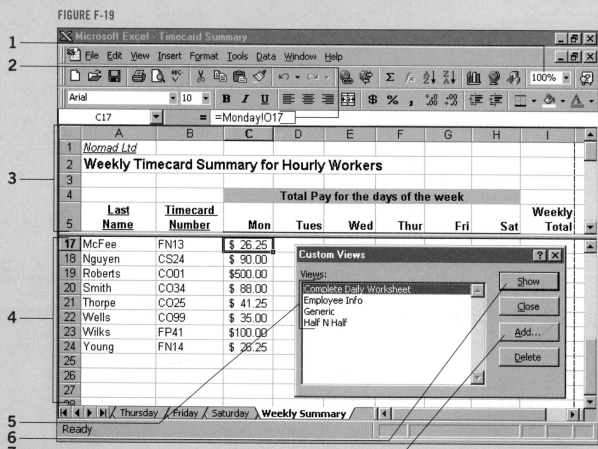

Match each of the terms with the statement that describes its function.

8. Inserts a code to print the total number of pages
9. Indicates how far down the page to start printing worksheet data
10. Indicates a page break
11. Inserts a code to print the sheet tab name in a header or footer
12. Indicates a selection to be printed

a. Dashed line
b.
c. Top margin
d.
e. Print what

Select the best answer from the list of choices.

13. You can save frequently used display and print settings by using the _____ feature.
   a. Report Manager   **b.** View menu   **c.** Custom Views   **d.** Save command

14. You freeze areas of the worksheet to_____.
   a. Freeze data and unlock formulas.
   b. Lock open windows in place.
   c. Freeze all data in place so that you can see it.
   d. Lock column and row headings in place while you scroll through the worksheet.

15. To protect a worksheet, you must first unlock those cells that _____, and then issue the Protect Sheet command.
   a. never change
   b. the user will be allowed to change
   c. have hidden formulas
   d. are locked

► Skills Review

1. **Freeze columns and rows.**
   a. Open the workbook titled XL F-2, then save it as "Quarterly Household Budget".
   b. Freeze columns A through B and rows 1 through 4 for improved viewing. (*Hint:* Click cell C4 prior to issuing the Freeze Panes command.)
   c. Scroll until columns A through B and F through H are visible.
   d. Press [Ctrl][Home] to return to cell C4.
   e. Unfreeze the panes.

2. **Insert and delete sheets.**
   a. With the 1997 sheet active, use the sheet pop-up menu to insert a new Sheet1.
   b. Activate Sheet1.
   c. Delete Sheet1.

3. **Reference worksheet data.**
   a. In the 1997 sheet, click cell C22.
   b. Type =, click cell G7, then press [Enter].
   c. In cell C23, type =, click cell G18, then press [Enter].
   d. To link data between the two worksheets, first activate the 1998 worksheet.
   e. Click cell C4.
   f. Type =.
   g. Activate the 1997 worksheet.
   h. Click cell F4, then press [Enter].
   i. In the 1998 worksheet, copy the contents of cell C4 into cells C5:C6.
   j. Preview, then print the 1998 worksheet.
   k. Save the workbook.

4. Hide and protect worksheet areas.

a. In the 1997 worksheet, select row 16.

b. Issue the Hide Row command.

c. To unlock the expense data so you can make changes, first select range C10:F17.

d. Using the Protection tab of the Format Cells dialog box, turn off the locked status.

e. Using the Tools, Protection menu options, protect the sheet.

f. To make sure the other cells are locked, click cell D4.

g. Type 3.

h. Confirm the message box warning.

i. To change the first-quarter mortgage expense to $3,400, click cell C10, then type 3400.

j. Save the workbook.

5. Specify headers and footers.

a. Activate the 1997 worksheet. Using the File, Page Setup menu options, customize the Center Section of the Header to read "Lowe Family".

b. Further customize the header by changing it to appear in 12 pt bold type.

c. Set the footer to (none).

d. Preview, then print the 1997 worksheet.

e. Save the workbook.

6. Save custom views of a worksheet.

a. In the 1997 worksheet, select the range A1:H23.

b. Using the Zoom box, set the magnification so that the entire selection appears on the screen.

c. Using the View, Custom Views menu options, add a new view called "Entire Budget".

d. Save the workbook.

7. Control page breaks and page numbering.

a. Click cell A9.

b. Using the Insert, Page Break menu options, insert a page break.

c. Customize the footer to include a page number.

d. Preview and print the worksheet.

e. Save the workbook.

8. Set margins and alignment.

a. Activate the Generic custom view.

b. Select range A1:C20.

c. Using the Print menu option, under Print what, click Selection.

d. Preview the worksheet.

e. From the Print Preview window, click Setup; using the Margins tab, change the left margin to 2", and center the worksheet vertically on the page.

f. Preview, then print the worksheet.

g. Save the workbook.

► Independent Challenges

1. You own PC Assist, a software training company. You have added several new entries to the August check register and are ready to enter September's check activity. Because the sheet for August will include much of the same information you need for September, you decide to copy it. Then you will edit the new sheet to fit your needs for September check activity. You will use sheet referencing to enter the beginning balance and beginning check number. Using your own data, you will complete five checks for the September register.

To complete this independent challenge:

1. Open the workbook entitled XL F-3, then save it as "Update to Check Register".
2. Delete Sheet2 and Sheet3, then create a worksheet for September by copying the August sheet.
3. With the September sheet active, delete the data in range A6:E24.
4. To update the balance at the beginning of the month, use sheet referencing from the last balance entry in the August sheet.
5. Generate the first check number. (*Hint:* Use a formula that references the last check number in August and adds one.)
6. Enter data for five checks.
7. Add a footer that includes your name left-aligned on the printout and the system date right-aligned on the printout. Add a header that displays the sheet name centered on the printout.
8. Save the workbook. Preview the September worksheet, then print it in landscape orientation on a single page.
9. Submit your printout.

2. You are a new employee for a computer software manufacturer. Your responsibility is to track the sales of different product lines and determine which computer operating system generates the most software sales each month. Although sales figures vary from month to month, the format in which data is entered does not. Use Table F-4 as a guide to create a worksheet tracking sales across personal computer (PC) platforms. Use your own data for the number of software packages sold in the DOS, Windows, and Macintosh columns. Create a summary report with all the sales summary information, then create three detailed reports for each software category: Games Software, Business Software, and Utilities Products.

To complete this independent challenge:

1. Create a new workbook, then save it as "Software Sales Summary".
2. Enter row and column labels, your own data, and formulas for the totals.

TABLE F-4

	DOS	Windows	Macintosh	Total
Games Software				
Space Wars 99				
Safari				
Flight School				
Total				
Business Software				
Word Processing				
Spreadsheet				
Presentation				
Graphics				
Page Layout				
Total				
Utilities Products				
Antivirus				
File recovery				
Total				

3. Create a summary report that includes the entire worksheet. Customize the header to include your name and the date. Set the footer to (none). Center the page both horizontally and vertically. Save the workbook. Preview and print the report.

4. Create three detailed report pages. Insert page breaks so that each software category is printed on a separate page. Number the report pages consecutively as follows: Games Software, page 1; Business Software, page 2; Utilities Products, page 3. Include your name and the date in the header of each page and the page number in the footer of each page. Save the workbook. Preview and print the report.

5. Submit your printouts.

3. You are a college student with two roommates. Each month you receive your long-distance telephone bill. Because no one wants to figure out who owes what, you split the bill three ways. You are sure that one of your roommates makes two-thirds of the long-distance calls. In order to make the situation more equitable, you decide to create a spreadsheet to track the long-distance phone calls each month. By doing so, you hope to determine who is responsible for each call. Create a spreadsheet with a separate area for each roommate. Track the following information for each month's long-distance calls: date of call, time of call, (AM or PM), call minutes, location called, state called, area code, phone number, and call charge. Total the charges for each roommate. Print a summary report of all three roommates' charges, and print a report for each roommate totaling his or her charges for the month.

To complete this independent challenge:

1. Create a new workbook, then save it as "Monthly Long Distance" to the appropriate folder on your Student Disk.

2. Enter column headings and row labels to track each call.

3. Use your own data, entering at least three long-distance calls for each roommate.

4. Create a report that prints all the call information for the month. Use the filename as the header. Format the header to make it stand out from the rest of the text. Enter your name and the date in the footer.

5. Create a report page for each roommate. Insert appropriate page breaks to print out a report for each roommate. Use the roommate's name as the header, formatted in 14-point italic type. Enter your name and the date in the footer. Center the reports on the page both horizontally and vertically. Save the workbook.

6. Preview, print, then submit the reports.

4. The World Wide Web can be used as a research tool to locate information on just about every topic imaginable, including careers. You have decided to conduct a job search using the Web. Currently, you are taking classes on computer programming, specializing in the C++ language and the Internet tool called Java. You plan to perform a search for jobs requiring these skills tracking the following information: position title, company name, city and state where company is located, whether experience is required, and salary. Your goal is to locate and list in a worksheet at least five jobs requiring C++ knowledge, and, in a separate worksheet, at least five jobs requiring Java knowledge.

To complete this independent challenge:

1. Open the workbook titled XL F-4, then save it as "Job Research – PC Programming".
2. Log on to the Internet and use your Web browser to go to http://www.course.com. From there, click Student Online Companions, click the link for this textbook, then click the Excel link for Unit F.
3. Use any combination of the following sites to search for and compile your data: Online Career Center, America's Job Bank, or The Monster Board.
4. Fill in information on at least five positions in each of the two above-mentioned worksheets.
5. Name the two sheets based on their content and copy sheets where appropriate.
6. Using your own judgment, customize the header, footer, margins, and alignment of each sheet.
7. Save the workbook, print both worksheets, then submit your printouts.

► Visual Workshop

Create the worksheet shown in Figure F-20. Save the workbook as "Generations of PCs". Preview, print, then submit the worksheet.

FIGURE F-20

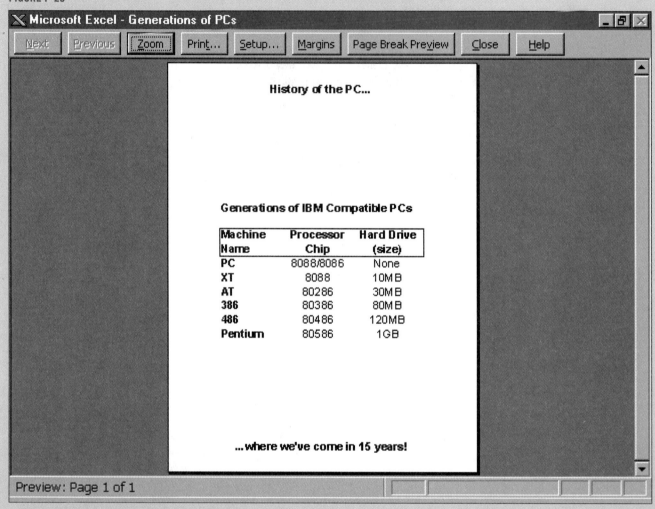

Automating
Worksheet Tasks

Objectives

► **Plan a macro**
► **Record a macro**
► **Run a macro**
► **Edit a macro**
► **Use shortcut keys with macros**
► **Use the Personal Macro Workbook**
► **Add a macro as a menu item**
► **Create a toolbar for macros**

A **macro** is a set of instructions that performs tasks in the order you specify. You create macros to automate frequently performed Excel tasks that require a series of steps. For example, if you usually type your name and date in a worksheet footer, Excel can record the keystrokes in a macro that types the text and insert the current date automatically. In this unit, you will plan and design a simple macro, then record and run the macro. Then you will edit the macro. You will also create a macro to run using shortcut keys, store a macro in the Personal Macro Workbook, add a macro option to the Tools menu, and create a new toolbar for macros. ✎ First, Evan Brillstein wants to create a macro that adds a stamp to his worksheets to identify them as originating in the accounting department.

Planning a Macro

As mentioned earlier, you create macros for tasks that you perform on a regular basis. For example, you can create a macro to enter and format text or to save and print a worksheet. To create a macro, you record the series of actions or write the instructions in a special format. Because the sequence of actions is important, you need to plan the macro carefully before you record it. Commands used to record, run, and modify macros are located on the Tools menu. Make sure to view the CourseHelp, "Using Macros," for more information before completing this lesson.

Evan wants to put a stamp on all his worksheets that identifies them as originating in the accounting department. He records a macro to automate this process. Evan plans the macro using the following guidelines:

Steps

CourseHelp

To view the CourseHelp for this lesson, click the Start button, point to Programs, point to CourseHelp, then click Microsoft Excel 97 Illustrated. Choose the Using Macros CourseHelp.

1. Assign the macro a descriptive name, and write out the steps the macro will perform
This preplanning helps eliminate careless errors. Evan decides to name the macro DeptStamp. He writes a description of the macro, as shown in Figure G-1. See Table G-1 for a list of macros Evan might create.

2. Decide how you will perform the actions you want to record
You can use the mouse, the keyboard, or a combination of the two methods. Evan decides to use a combination of the mouse and the keyboard.

3. Practice the steps you want Excel to record and write them down
Evan wrote down the sequence of actions as he performed them and he is now ready to record and test the macro.

4. Decide where to locate the description of the macro and the macro itself
Macros can be stored in an unused area of the active workbook, in a new workbook, or in the Personal Macro Workbook. Evan stores the macro in a new workbook.

TABLE G-1: Possible macros and their descriptive names

description of macro	descriptive name
Enter a frequently used proper name, such as Evan Brillstein	EvanBrillstein
Enter a frequently used company name, such as Nomad Ltd	CompanyName
Print the active worksheet on a single page, in landscape orientation	FitToLand
Turn off the header and footer in the active worksheet	HeadFootOff
Show a frequently used custom view, such as a generic view of the worksheet, setting the print and display settings back to Excel's defaults	GenericView

Macro to create stamp with the department name

Name:	DeptStamp
Description:	Adds a stamp to the top-left of worksheet identifying it as an accounting department worksheet
Steps:	1. Position the cell pointer in cell A1
	2. Type Accounting Department, then click the Enter button
	3. Click Format on the menu bar, click Cells
	4. Click Font tab, under Font style click Bold, under Underline click Single, and under Color click Red, then click OK

Viewing CourseHelp

The camera icon on the opposite page indicates there is a CourseHelp available for this lesson. CourseHelps are on-screen "movies" that bring difficult concepts to life, to help you understand the material in this book. Your instructor received a CourseHelp disk and should have installed it on the machine you are using. To start CourseHelp, click the Start button, point to Programs, point to CourseHelp, then click Microsoft Excel 97 Illustrated. In the main CourseHelp window, click the topic that corresponds to this lesson. Because CourseHelp runs in a separate window, you can start and view a movie even if you're in the middle of completing a lesson. Once the movie is finished, you can click the Word program button on the taskbar and continue with the lesson, right where you left off.

Recording a Macro

The easiest way to create a macro is to record it using Excel's Macro Recorder. You simply turn the Macro Recorder on, enter the keystrokes, select the commands you want the macro to perform, then stop the recorder. As you record the macro, each action is translated into programming code that you can later view and modify. ✒ Evan wants to create a macro that enters a department stamp in cell A1 of the active worksheet. He creates this macro by recording his actions.

1. If necessary, click the **New button** 🗋 on the Standard toolbar, then save the blank workbook as **My Excel Macros**
Now you are ready to start the macro recording process.

2. Click **Tools** on the menu bar, point to **Macro**, then click **Record New Macro**
The Record Macro dialog box opens. See Figure G-2. Notice the default name Macro1 is selected. You can either assign this name or type a new name. The first character of a macro name must be a letter; the remaining characters can be letters, numbers, or underscores; spaces are not allowed in macro names; use underscores in place of spaces. This dialog box also allows you to assign a shortcut key for running the macro and to instruct Excel where to store the macro. Enter the name of the macro, then accept the remaining dialog box settings.

3. In the Macro name box, type **DeptStamp**, then click **OK**
The dialog box closes. Excel displays the small Stop Recording toolbar containing the Stop Recording button ■, and the word "Recording" appears on the status bar. Take your time performing the steps because Excel records every keystroke, menu option, and mouse action that you make. Next, execute the steps that create the department stamp.

4. Press **[Ctrl][Home]**
The cell pointer moves to cell A1. When you begin an Excel session, macros record absolute cell references. By beginning the recording in cell A1, you ensure that the macro includes the instruction to select cell A1 as the first step.

5. In cell A1, type **Accounting Department**, then click the **Enter button** ✓ on the formula bar

6. Click **Format** on the menu bar, then click **Cells**
Now, you change the font style and attributes of the text.

7. Click the **Font tab**, in the Font style list box click **Bold**, click the **Underline list arrow** and click **Single**, then click the **Color list arrow** and click **red** (third row, first color on left)
See Figure G-3. Confirm the changes in the dialog box, then stop the macro recording.

8. Click **OK**, click the **Stop Recording button** ■ on the Stop Recording toolbar, click cell **D1** to deselect cell A1, then save the workbook
Compare your results with Figure G-4.

FIGURE G-2: Record Macro dialog box

Type macro name here —

Reflects your name and system date —

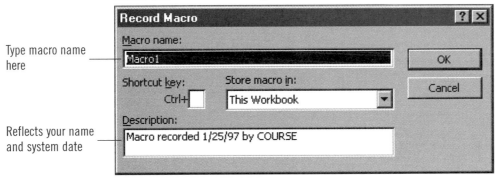

FIGURE G-3: Font tab of the Format Cells dialog box

Changes for macro —

Stop Recording button

Stop Recording toolbar

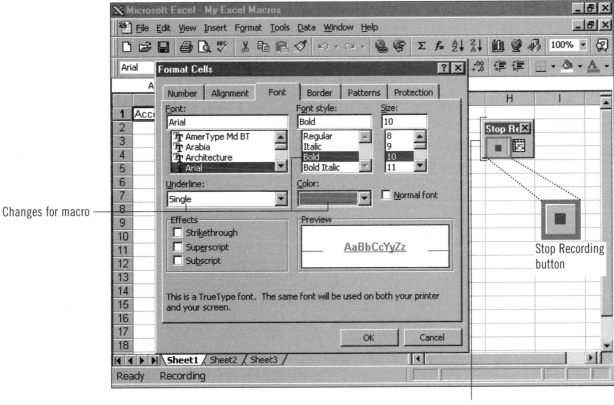

FIGURE G-4: Personalized department stamp

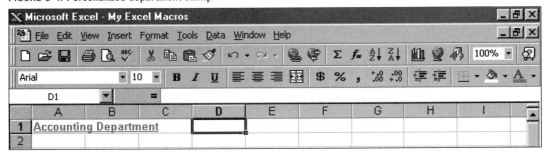

Running a Macro

Once you record a macro, you should test it to make sure that the actions performed are correct. To test a macro, you **run** or execute it. One method of running a macro is to select the macro in the Macros dialog box, then click Run. ◄ Evan clears the contents of cell A1 and then tests the DeptStamp macro. After he runs the macro from the My Excel Macros workbook, he decides to test the macro once more from a newly opened workbook.

1. **Click cell A1, click Edit on the menu bar, point to Clear, click All, then click any other cell to deselect cell A1**
   When you delete the contents of a cell, any formatting still remains in the cell. By using the Clear All option on the Edit menu, you can be sure that the cell is free of contents and formatting.

2. **Click Tools on the menu bar, point to Macro, then click Macros**
   The Macro dialog box, shown in Figure G-5, lists all the macros contained in the open workbooks.

3. **Make sure DeptStamp is selected, click Run, then deselect cell A1**
   Watch your screen as the macro quickly plays back the steps you recorded in the previous lesson. When the macro is finished, your screen should look like Figure G-6. As long as the workbook containing the macro remains open, you can run the macro from any open workbook. Now you test this.

4. **Click the New button [▯] on the Standard toolbar**
   Because the new workbook automatically fills the screen, it is difficult to be sure that the My Excel Macros workbook is still open. Use the Window menu to display a list of open workbooks before you run the macro.

5. **Click Window on the menu bar**
   A list of open workbooks displays underneath the menu options. The active workbook name (in this case, Book2) appears with a checkmark to its left. See Figure G-7. Confirming that My Excel Macros is still open, you run the macro from this new workbook.

6. **Deselect cell A1 if necessary, click Tools on the menu bar, point to Macro, click Macros, make sure 'My Excel Macros.xls'!DeptStamp is selected, click Run, then deselect cell A1**
   Cell A1 should look like Figure G-6. Notice that when multiple workbooks are open, the macro name includes the workbook name between single quotation marks, followed by an exclamation point indicating that the macro is outside the active workbook. Because you do not need to save the new workbook in which you tested the macro, you close the file without saving it.

7. **Close Book2 without saving changes, then return to the My Excel Macros workbook**

FIGURE G-5: Macro dialog box

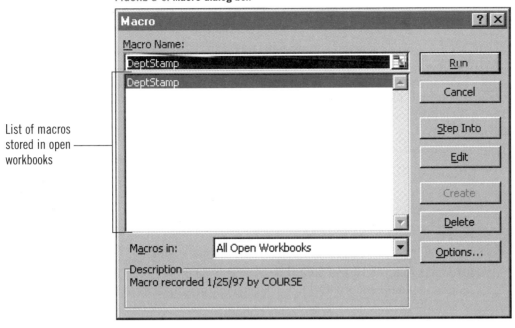

List of macros
stored in open
workbooks

FIGURE G-6: Result of running the edited DeptStamp macro

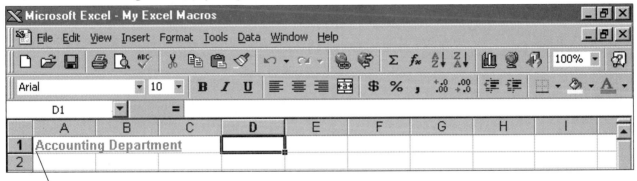

First macro
instruction positions
pointer in cell A1

FIGURE G-7: Window menu showing list of open workbooks

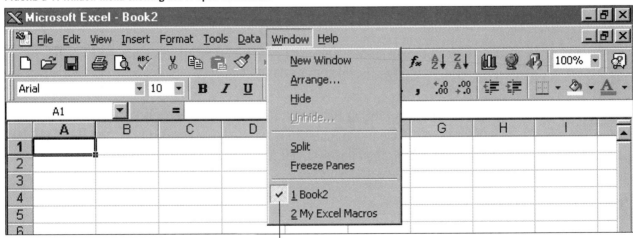

Check mark
indicates active
workbook

Editing a Macro

When you use the Macro Recorder to create a macro, the instructions are recorded automatically in Visual Basic for Applications programming language. Each macro is stored as a **module**, or program code container, attached to the workbook. Once you record a macro, you might need to change it. If you have a lot of changes to make, it might be best to re-record the macro. If you need to make only minor adjustments, you can edit the macro code, or program instructions, directly using the Visual Basic Editor. ◀━━━ Evan wants to modify his macro to change the point size of the department stamp to 12.

QuickTip

You can also start the Visual Basic Editor by clicking Tools on the menu bar, pointing to Macro, then clicking Visual Basic Editor or by pressing [Alt][F11].

1. **Make sure the My Excel Macros workbook is open, click Tools on the menu bar, point to Macro, click Macros, make sure DeptStamp is selected, then click Edit**
   The Visual Basic Editor starts showing the DeptStamp macro steps in a numbered module window (in this case, Module1). You can maximize the module window to get a better look at the macro code.

2. **Maximize the window titled My Excel Macros.xls – [Module1 (Code)], then examine the steps in the macro**
   See Figure G-8. The name of the macro and the date it was recorded appear at the top of the module window. Notice that Excel translates your keystrokes and commands into words, known as macro **code**. For example, the line .FontStyle = "Bold" was generated when you clicked Bold in the Format Cells dialog box. When you make changes in a dialog box during macro recording, Excel automatically stores all the dialog box settings in the macro code. You also see lines of code that you didn't generate directly while recording the DeptStamp macro; for example, .Name = "Arial".

3. **In the line .Size = 10, double-click 10 to select it, then type 12**
   Because Module1 is attached to the workbook and not stored as a separate file, any changes to the module are saved automatically when the workbook is saved. Next, print the change to Module1.

4. **In the Visual Basic Editor, click File on the menu bar, click Print, then click OK to print the module**
   Review the printout of Module1, then return to Excel.

5. **Click File on the menu bar, then click Close and Return to Microsoft Excel**
   You want to rerun the DeptStamp macro to view the point size edit you made using the Visual Basic Editor.

6. **Click cell A1, click Edit on the menu bar, point to Clear, click All, deselect cell A1, click Tools on the menu bar, point to Macro, click Macros, make sure DeptStamp is selected, click Run, then deselect cell A1**
   Compare your results with Figure G-9.

7. **Save the workbook**

FIGURE G-8: Visual Basic Editor showing Module1

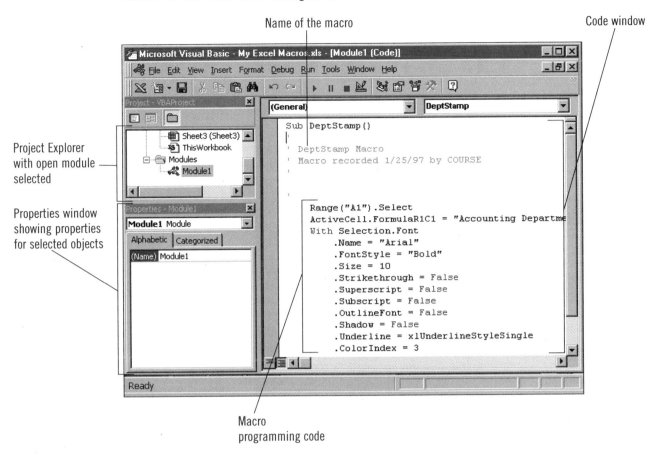

Name of the macro

Code window

Project Explorer with open module selected

Properties window showing properties for selected objects

Macro
programming code

FIGURE G-9: Result of running the edited DeptStamp macro

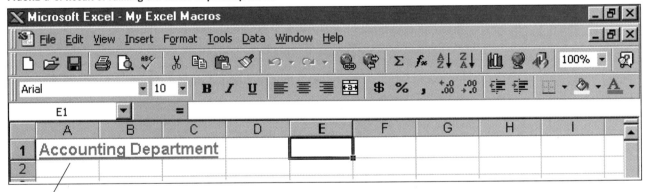

Font size enlarged
to 12pt

Adding comments to code

With practice, you will be able to interpret the lines of code within your macro. Others who use your macro, however, might want to know the function of a particular line. You can explain the code by adding comments to the macro. Comments are explanatory text added to the lines of code. When you enter a comment, you must type an apostrophe (') before the comment text. Otherwise, Excel thinks you have entered a command. On a color monitor, comments appear in green after you press [Enter]. See Figure G-8. You also can insert blank lines in the macro code to make the code more readable. To do this, type an apostrophe, then press [Enter].

Using Shortcut Keys with Macros

In addition to running a macro from the Macro dialog box, you can run a macro by assigning a shortcut key combination. Using shortcut keys to run macros reduces the number of keystrokes required to begin macro play back. You assign shortcut key combinations in the Record Macro dialog box. ~~~~~ Evan also wants to create a macro called CompanyName to enter the company name into a worksheet. He assigns a shortcut key combination to run the macro.

Steps

1. **Click cell B2**

   You will record the macro in cell B2. You want to be able to enter the company name anywhere in a worksheet. Therefore, you will not begin the macro with an instruction to position the cell pointer as you did in the DeptStamp macro.

2. **Click Tools on the menu bar, point to Macro, then click Record New Macro**

   The Record Macro dialog box opens. You notice the option Shortcut key: Ctrl+ followed by a blank box. You can type a letter (A–Z) in the Shortcut key box to assign the key combination of [Ctrl] plus a letter to run the macro. Use the key combination [Ctrl][Shift] plus a letter. Doing this avoids overriding any of Excel's previously assigned [Ctrl]+[letter] shortcut keys, such as [Ctrl]+[C] for Copy.

3. **With the default macro name selected, type CompanyName, click the Shortcut key box, press and hold [Shift], then type C**

   Compare your screen with Figure G-10. You are ready to record the CompanyName macro.

4. **Click OK to close the dialog box, then start recording the macro**

   By default, Excel records absolute cell references in macros. Beginning the macro in cell B2 causes the macro code to begin with a statement to select cell B2. Because you want to be able to run this macro in any active cell, you need to instruct Excel to record relative cell references while recording the macro. You can do this before recording the macro keystrokes by selecting the Relative Reference button 📇 on the Stop Recording toolbar.

5. **Click the Relative Reference button 📇 on the Stop Recording toolbar**

   The Relative Reference button appears indented to indicate that it is selected. See Figure G-11. This button is a toggle and retains the relative reference setting until it is clicked off.

6. **In cell B2, type Nomad Ltd, click the Enter button ✓ on the formula bar, press [Ctrl][i] to italicize the text, click the Stop Recording button ■ on the Stop Recording toolbar, then deselect cell B2**

   Nomad Ltd appears in italics in cell B2. You are ready to run the macro in cell A5 using the shortcut key combination.

7. **Click cell A5, press and hold [Ctrl][Shift], type C, deselect the cell**

   The result appears in cell A5. See Figure G-12. Because the macro played back in selected cell (A5) instead of the cell where it was recorded (B2), Evan is convinced that the macro recorded relative cell references.

8. **Save the workbook**

QuickTip

When you begin an Excel session, the Relative Reference button is toggled off, indicating that Excel is recording absolute cell references in macros. Once selected, and until it is toggled back off, the Relative Reference setting remains in effect during the current Excel session.

FIGURE G-10: Record Macro dialog box with shortcut key assigned

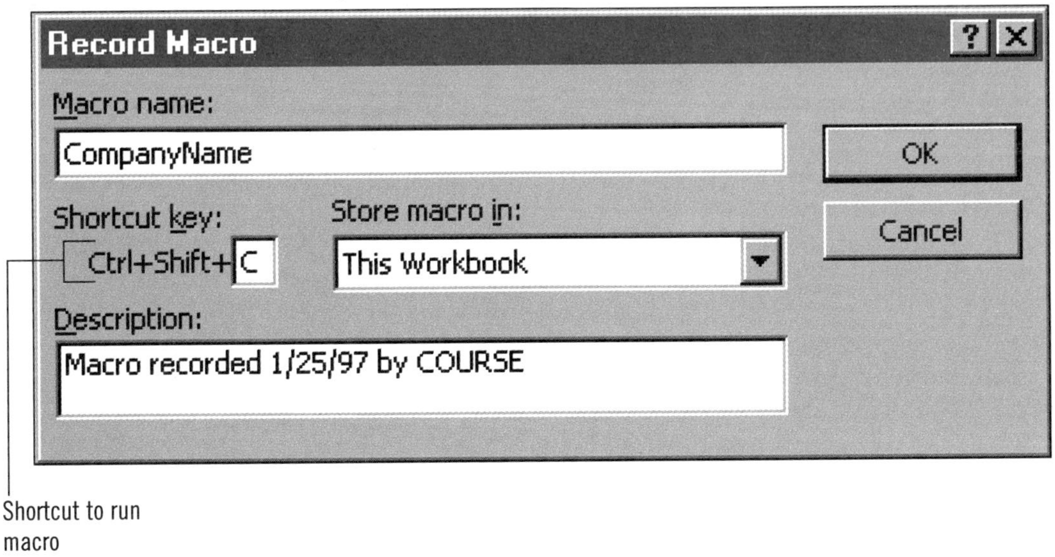

Record Macro ? X

Macro name:

CompanyName

OK

Shortcut key: Store macro in: Cancel

Ctrl+Shift+ C   This Workbook ▼

Description:

Macro recorded 1/25/97 by COURSE

Shortcut to run
macro

FIGURE G-11: Stop Recording toolbar with Relative Reference button selected

Stop Re X

Relative Reference
button instructs
Excel to record
relative references

FIGURE G-12: Result of running CompanyName macro

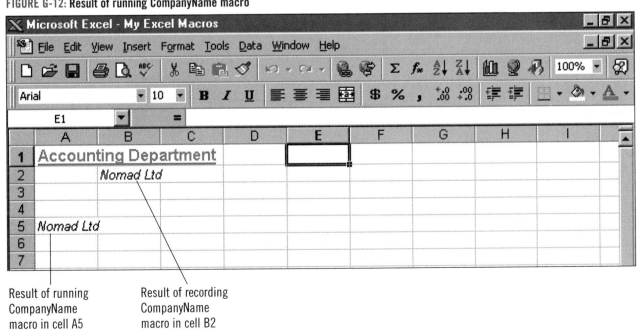

Result of running
CompanyName
macro in cell A5

Result of recording
CompanyName
macro in cell B2

Using the Personal Macro Workbook

You can store commonly used macros in a **Personal Macro Workbook**. The Personal Macro Workbook is always available, unless you specify otherwise, and gives you access to all the macros it contains, regardless of which workbooks are open. The Personal Macro Workbook file is created automatically the first time you choose to store a macro in it. Additional macros are added to the Personal Macro Workbook when you store them there. 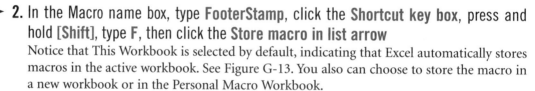 Evan often finds himself adding a footer to his worksheets identifying his department, the workbook name, the sheet name, the page number, and current date. He saves time by creating a macro that automatically inserts this footer. Because he wants this macro to be available whenever he uses Excel, Evan decides to store this macro in the Personal Macro Workbook.

Steps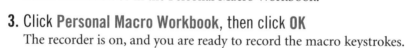

1. From any cell in the active worksheet, click **Tools** on the menu bar, point to **Macro**, then click **Record New Macro**

The Record Macro dialog box opens. Name the macro FooterStamp. You also want to assign a shortcut key.

Trouble?

If you are prompted to replace an existing macro named FooterStamp, click Yes.

2. In the Macro name box, type **FooterStamp**, click the **Shortcut key box**, press and hold [Shift], type **F**, then click the **Store macro in list arrow**

Notice that This Workbook is selected by default, indicating that Excel automatically stores macros in the active workbook. See Figure G-13. You also can choose to store the macro in a new workbook or in the Personal Macro Workbook.

QuickTip

Once created, the Personal Macro Workbook file is usually stored in the XLSTART folder under the name "Personal".

3. Click **Personal Macro Workbook**, then click **OK**

The recorder is on, and you are ready to record the macro keystrokes.

4. Click **File** on the menu bar, click **Page Setup**, click the **Header/Footer tab** (make sure to do this even if it is already active), click **Custom Footer**, in the Left section box, type **Accounting**, click the **Center section box**, click the **File Name button** 🗐, press [Spacebar], type **/**, press [Spacebar], click the **Sheet Name button** 🗐, click the **Right section box**, click the **Date button** 🗐, click **OK** to return to the Header/Footer tab

The footer stamp is set up, as shown in Figure G-14.

QuickTip

You can copy or move macros stored in other workbooks to the Personal Macro Workbook using the Visual Basic Editor.

5. Click **OK** to return to the worksheet, then click the **Stop Recording button** ■ on the Stop Recording toolbar

You want to ensure that the macro will set the footer stamp in any active worksheet. To test this, you activate Sheet2, type some sample text, run the FooterStamp macro, then preview the worksheet.

6. Activate Sheet2, in cell A1 type **Testing the FooterStamp macro**, press [Enter], press and hold [Ctrl][Shift], then type **F**

The FooterStamp macro plays back the sequence of commands. Preview the worksheet to ensure the macro worked.

7. Preview, then save the worksheet

Evan is satisfied that the FooterStamp macro works on any active worksheet. Next, Evan adds the macro as a menu item on the Tools menu.

FIGURE G-13: Record Macro dialog box showing Store macro in options

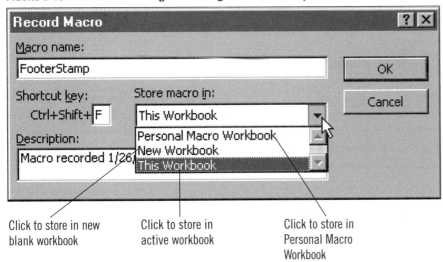

Click to store in new
blank workbook

Click to store in
active workbook

Click to store in
Personal Macro
Workbook

FIGURE G-14: Header/Footer tab showing custom footer settings

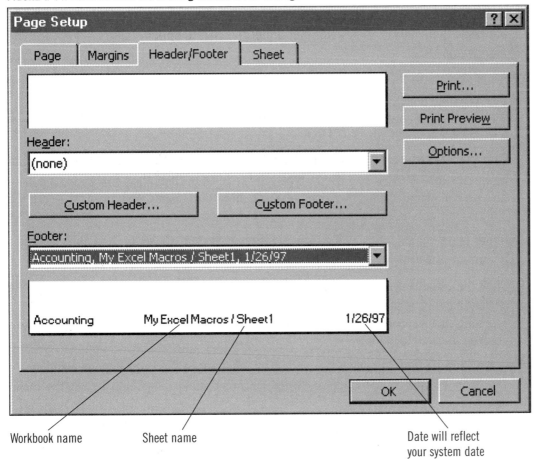

Workbook name

Sheet name

Date will reflect
your system date

CLUES TO USE

Working with the Personal Macro Workbook

Once created, the Personal Macro Workbook
automatically opens each time you start Excel. By
default, the Personal Macro Workbook is hidden as a
precautionary measure. You can add macros to the
Personal Macro Workbook when it is hidden, but you
cannot delete macros from it.

Adding a Macro as a Menu Item

The **Worksheet menu bar** is a special toolbar at the top of the Excel screen that you can customize. In addition to storing macros in the Personal Macro Workbook so that they are always available, you can add macros as items on a menu. To increase the macro's availability, Evan decides to add the FooterStamp macro as an item on the Tools menu. First, he adds a custom menu item to the Tools menu, then he assigns the macro to that menu item.

Steps

QuickTip

If you want to add a command to a menu bar, the first step is to display the toolbar containing the menu to which you want to add the command.

1. Click **Tools** on the menu bar, click **Customize**, click the **Commands tab**, then under Categories, click **Macros**
See Figure G-15.

2. Under Commands, click **Custom Menu Item**, drag the selection to Tools on the menu bar (the menu opens), then point just under the Wizard option, *but do not release the mouse button*
Compare your screen to Figure G-16.

3. Release the mouse button
Now, Custom Menu Item is the last item on the Tools menu. Next, edit the name of the menu item and assign the macro to it.

Trouble?

If you don't see 'PER-SONAL.XLS'!FooterStamp under Macro name, try repositioning the Assign Macro dialog box.

4. With the Tools menu still open, right-click **Custom Menu Item**, select the text in the Name box (**&Custom Menu Item**), type **Footer Stamp**, then click **Assign Macro**
The Assign Macro dialog box opens behind the Tools menu. You need to select the FooterStamp macro from the list.

5. Under Macro name, click **PERSONAL.XLS!FooterStamp**, click **OK**, then click **Close**
Return to the worksheet, and test the new menu item in Sheet3.

6. Click the **Sheet3 tab**, in cell A1 type **Testing macro menu item**, press **[Enter]**, then click **Tools** on the menu bar
The Tools menu appears with the new menu option at the bottom. See Figure G-17. You can now test this menu option.

7. Click **Footer Stamp**, preview the worksheet, then close the Print Preview window
The Print Preview window appears with the footer stamp. Now, you'll reset the menu options.

8. Click **Tools** on the menu bar, click **Customize**, click the **Toolbars tab**, click **Worksheet Menu Bar** to select it, click **Reset**, click **OK** to confirm, click **Close**, then click **Tools** on the menu bar to ensure the custom item has been deleted
Because you did not make any changes to your workbook, you don't need to save it. Next, you create a toolbar for macros and add macros to it.

FIGURE G-15: Commands tab of the Customize dialog box showing macro options

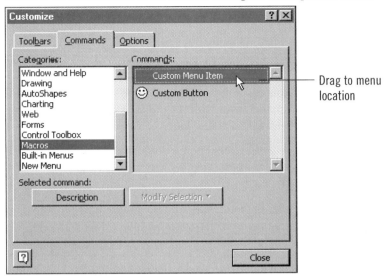

Drag to menu location

FIGURE G-16: Tools menu showing placement of Custom Menu Item

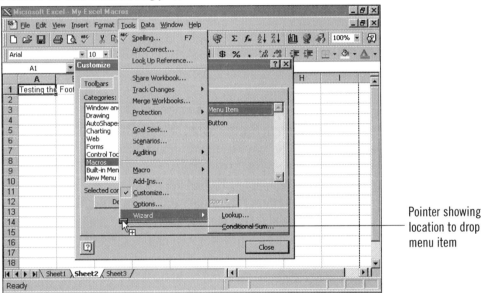

Pointer showing location to drop menu item

FIGURE G-17: Tools menu with new Footer Stamp item

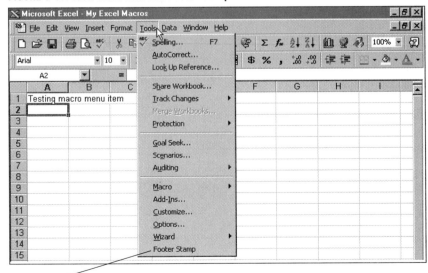

Added menu item

Creating a Toolbar for Macros

Toolbars contain buttons that allow you to access commonly used commands. You can create your own custom toolbars to organize commands so that you can find and use them quickly. Once you create a toolbar, you then add buttons to access Excel commands such as macros. Evan has decided to create a custom toolbar called Macros that will contain buttons to run two of his macros.

Steps

QuickTip

Toolbars you create or customize are available to all workbooks on your own PC. You also can ensure that a custom toolbar is available with a specific workbook by attaching the toolbar to the workbook using the Toolbar tab in the Customize dialog box.

1. **With Sheet3 active, click Tools on the menu bar, click Customize, click the Toolbars tab if necessary, then click New**
   The New Toolbar dialog box opens, as shown in Figure G-18. Under Toolbar name, a default name of Custom1 is selected. You name the toolbar Macros.

2. **Type Macros, then click OK**
   Excel adds the new toolbar named Macros to the bottom of the list and a small, empty toolbar named Macros opens. See Figure G-19. Notice that you cannot see the entire toolbar name. A toolbar starts small and automatically expands to fit the buttons assigned to it. Now you are ready to add buttons to the toolbar.

3. **If necessary, drag the Macros toolbar off the Customize dialog box and into the worksheet area; in the Customize dialog box, click the Commands tab, under Categories click Macros, then drag the ☺ Custom Button over the new Macros toolbar**
   The Macros toolbar now contains one button. Because you want the toolbar to contain two macros, you add an additional Custom Button to the toolbar.

4. **Drag the ☺ Custom Button over the Macros toolbar again**
   With the two buttons in place, you customize the buttons and assign macros to them.

5. **Right-click the leftmost ☺ on the Macros toolbar, in the Name box select &Custom Button, type Department Stamp, click Assign Macro, click DeptStamp, then click OK**
   With the first toolbar button customized, you are ready to customize the second button.

6. **With the Customize dialog box open, right-click the rightmost ☺ on the Macros toolbar, edit the name to read Company Name, click Change Button Image, click 🏃 (bottom row, third from the left) in the Macros dialog box, right-click 🏃, click Assign Macro, click Company Name to select it, click OK, then close the Customize dialog box**
   The Macros toolbar appears with the two customized macro buttons. Next, you test the buttons.

7. **Move the mouse pointer over ☺ on the Macros toolbar to display the macro name (Department Stamp), then click to run the macro; click cell B2, move the mouse pointer over 🏃 on the Macros toolbar to display the macro name (Company Name), click 🏃, then deselect the cell**
   Compare your screen with Figure G-20. Notice that the DeptStamp macro automatically replaces the contents of cell A1. Now remove the toolbar.

8. **Click Tools on the menu bar, click Customize, click the Toolbars tab if necessary, under Toolbars click Macros to select it, click Delete, click OK to confirm the deletion, then click Close**

9. **Save, then close the workbook**

Trouble?

If you are prompted to save the changes to the Personal Macro Workbook, click Yes.

FIGURE G-18: New Toolbar dialog box

Type toolbar name here

FIGURE G-19: Customize dialog box with new Macros toolbar

New Macros toolbar

Check mark indicates toolbar is in view

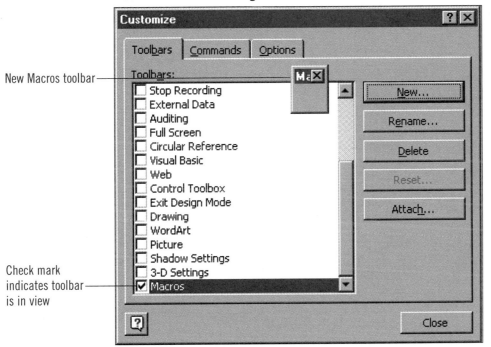

FIGURE G-20: Worksheet showing Macros toolbar with two customized buttons

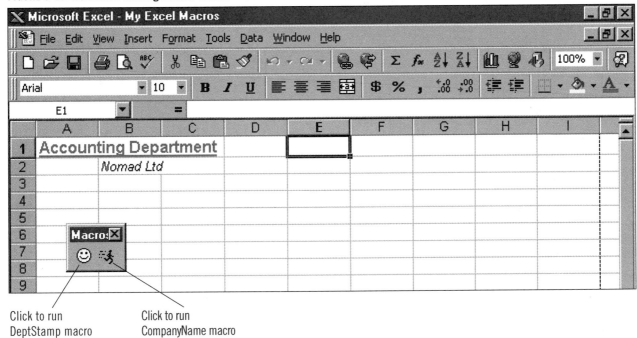

Click to run DeptStamp macro

Click to run CompanyName macro

Practice

► Concepts Review

Label each of the elements of the Excel screen shown in Figure G-21.

FIGURE G-21

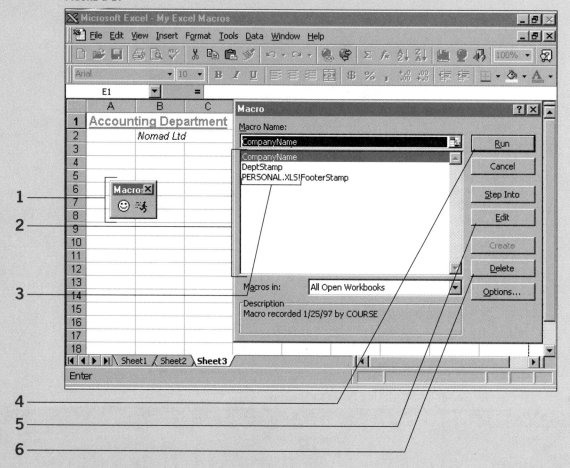

Select the best answer from the list of choices.

7. **Which of the following is the best candidate for a macro?**
    a. One-button or one-keystroke commands
    b. Often-used sequences of commands or actions
    c. Seldom-used commands or tasks
    d. Nonsequential tasks

8. **When you are recording a macro, you can execute commands by using**
    a. Only the keyboard.
    b. Only the mouse.
    c. Any combination of the keyboard and the mouse.
    d. Only menu commands.

9. **A macro is stored in**
   a. The body of a worksheet used for data.
   b. An unused area to the far right or well below the worksheet contents.
   c. A module attached to a workbook.
   d. A Custom Menu Item.

10. **Which of the following is *not* true about editing a macro?**
    a. You edit macros using the Visual Basic Editor.
    b. A macro cannot be edited and must be recorded again.
    c. You can type changes directly in the existing macro code.
    d. You can make more than one editing change in a macro.

11. **Why is it important to preplan a macro?**
    a. Macros won't be stored if they contain errors.
    b. Planning helps prevent careless errors from being introduced into the macro.
    c. It is very difficult to correct errors you make in a macro.
    d. Planning ensures that your macro will not contain errors.

12. **Macros are recorded with relative references**
    a. Only if the Relative Reference button is selected.
    b. In all cases.
    c. Only if relative references are chosen while recording the macro.
    d. Only if the Absolute Reference button is not selected.

13. **You can run macros**
    a. From the Macro dialog box.
    b. From shortcut key combinations.
    c. As items on menus.
    d. Using all of the above.

▶ Skills Review

1. **Record a macro.**
   a. Create a new workbook, then save it as "Macros".
   b. You will record a macro to enter and format your name, address, and telephone number in a worksheet. Click Tools on the menu bar, point to Macro, then click Record New Macro.
   c. In the Macro name box, type "MyAddress", click the Store macro in list arrow and click This Workbook, then click OK to begin recording.
   d. Ensure that the Relative Reference button on the Stop Recording toolbar is toggled off.
   e. Enter your personal information as follows: Type your name in cell A1; type your street address in cell A2; type your city, state, and ZIP code in cell A3; then type your telephone number in cell A4.
   f. Select range A1:D4, then format it to be 14-point Arial bold.
   g. Add a border and color of your choice to the selected range.
   h. Click the Stop Recording button on the Stop Recording toolbar.
   i. Save the workbook.

2. Run a macro.

a. Make sure range A1:D4 is selected. Using the menu commands Edit, Clear, All, clear the cell entries.

b. Click Tools on the menu bar, point to Macro, click Macros, in the list box click MyAddress, then click Run.

c. Clear the cell entries generated by running the MyAddress macro.

d. Save the workbook.

3. Edit a macro.

a. Click Tools on the menu bar, point to Macro, click Macros, click MyAddress, then click Edit.

b. Locate the line of code that defines the font size, then change the size to 18 points.

c. Edit the selected range to A1:E4 (increasing it by one column to accommodate the changed label size).

d. Add a comment line that describes this macro.

e. Print the module, then return to Excel.

f. Test the macro in Sheet1.

g. Save the workbook.

4. Use shortcut keys with macros.

a. While in Sheet1, using the Tools menu, open the Record Macro dialog box.

b. In the Macro name box, type MyName.

c. In the Shortcut key box, press and hold [Shift], then type N.

d. Click OK to begin recording.

e. Enter your full name in cell G1. Format as desired.

f. Click the Stop Recording button on the Stop Recording toolbar.

g. Clear cell G1.

h. Use the shortcut key to run the MyName macro.

i. Save the workbook.

5. Use the Personal Macro Workbook.

a. Open the Record Macro dialog box.

b. Name the macro FitToLand.

c. Choose to store the macro in the Personal Macro Workbook, then click OK. If you are prompted to replace the existing FitToLand macro, click Yes.

d. Record a macro that sets print orientation to landscape, scaled to fit on a page.

e. Stop the macro recording.

f. Activate Sheet2, and enter some test data in cell A1.

g. Run the FitToLand macro.

h. Preview Sheet2.

6. Add a macro as a menu item.

a. Click Tools on the menu bar, click Customize, click the Commands tab, under Categories click Macros, then under Commands click Custom Menu Item.

b. Drag the Custom Menu Item to the Tools menu, point to Macro, then release the mouse button.

c. Right-click Custom Menu Item on the Tools menu, then rename the item "Fit to Landscape".

d. Click Assign Macro, click PERSONAL.XLS!FitToLand, then click OK.

e. Close the Customize dialog box.

f. Activate Sheet3, then enter some test data in cell A1.

g. Run the Fit to Landscape macro from the Tools menu.

h. Preview the worksheet.

i. Using the Tools, Customize menu options, reset the toolbar titled Worksheet menu bar.

j. Save the workbook.

7. Create a toolbar for macros.

a. Makc sure the Macros workbook is activated, click Tools on the menu bar, click Customize, click the Toolbars tab, then click New.

b. Name the toolbar "My Info", then click OK.

c. Click the Commands tab, click Macros, then drag the new toolbar onto the worksheet.

d. Drag the Custom Button to the My Info toolbar.

e. Again, drag the Custom Button to the My Info toolbar.

f. Right-click the first button, rename it My Address, click Assign Macro, click MyAddress, then click OK.

g. Right-click the second button, edit the name to read My Name, click Change Button Image, click the button image of your choice; right-click the new button, click Assign Macro, change the store option to This Workbook, click MyName, then click OK.

h. Close the dialog box.

i. Clear the cell data, then test both macro buttons on the My Info toolbar.

j. Use the Toolbars tab of the Customize dialog box to delete the toolbar named My Info.

k. Save, then close the workbook.

► Independent Challenges

1. As a computer-support employee of an accounting firm, you are required to develop ways to help your fellow employees work more efficiently. Employees have asked for Excel macros that will do the following:
- Delete the current row and insert a blank row
- Delete the current column and insert a blank column
- Format a selected group of cells with a red pattern, in 12-point Times bold italic

To complete this independent challenge:

1. Plan and write the steps necessary for each macro.
2. Create a new workbook, then save it as "Excel Utility Macros".
3. Create a new toolbar called Helpers.
4. Create a macro for each employee request described above.
5. Add descriptive comment lines to each module.
6. Add each macro to the Tools menu.
7. On the Helpers toolbar, install buttons to run the macros.
8. Test each macro by using the Run command, the menu command, and the new buttons.
9. Save, then print the module for each macro.
10. Delete the new toolbar, reset the Worksheet menu bar, then submit your printouts.

2. You are an analyst in the finance department of a large bank. Every quarter, you produce a number of single-page quarterly budget worksheets. Your manager has informed you that certain worksheets need to contain a footer stamp indicating that the worksheet was produced in the finance department. The footer also should show the date, the current page number of the total pages, and the worksheet filename. You decide that the stamp should not include a header. It's tedious to add the footer stamp and to clear the existing header and footer for the numerous worksheets you produce. You will record a macro to do this.

To complete this independent challenge:

1. Plan and write the steps to create the macro.
2. Create a new workbook, then save it as "Header and Footer Stamp".
3. Create the macro described above. Make sure it adds the footer with the department name, and so forth and also clears the header.
4. Add descriptive comment lines to the macro code.
5. Add the macro to the Tools menu.
6. Create a toolbar titled Stamp, then install a button on the toolbar to run the macro.
7. Test the macro to make sure it works from the Run command, menu command, and new button.
8. Save and print the module for the macro.
9. Delete the new toolbar, reset the Worksheet menu bar, then submit your printout.

3. You are an administrative assistant to the marketing vice-president at Sweaters, Inc. A major part of your job is to create spreadsheets that project sales results in different markets. It seems that you are constantly changing the print settings so that workbooks print in landscape orientation and are scaled to fit on one page. You have decided that it is time to create a macro to streamline this process.

To complete this independent challenge:

1. Plan and write the steps necessary for the macro.
2. Create a new workbook, then save it as "Sweaters Inc Macro".
3. Create a macro that changes the page orientation to landscape and scales the worksheet to fit on a page.
4. Test the macro.
5. Save and print the module sheet.
6. Delete any toolbars you created, reset the Worksheet menu bar, then submit your printout.

4. Research conducted using the World Wide Web (WWW) usually yields vast amounts of information and can generate up-to-the-minute data in every field imaginable. Because macros are often shared among PC users, they are prone to develop viruses. Think of a virus as software that is intended to harm computers or files. Using the WWW, you can gather up-to-date information about computer viruses, particularly those known to appear as macros in Excel workbooks. You have decided to collect information on Excel macro viruses. Using a selection of Web search engines, you will gather detailed data on at least five viruses associated with Excel macros.

To complete this independent challenge:

1. Open a new workbook, then save it as "Excel Macro Viruses".
2. Log on to the Internet and use your browser to go to http://www.course.com. From there, click Student Online Companions, click the link for this textbook, then click the Excel link for Unit G.
3. Use any combination of the following sites to search for and compile your data: Yahoo!, WebCrawler, or Alta Vista.
4. Fill in information on at least five viruses known to exist in Excel macros. Possible column headings are Name of Virus, Date Discovered, Name of Macro, Who Discovered, Where Discovered, How it Gets Transmitted, Damage it Causes, and Recovery Tips.
5. Format the worksheet as desired to increase readability. (*Hint*: To word wrap text in cells, you can use the wrap text feature located in the Alignment tab of the Format Cells dialog box.)
6. Save the workbook, print the worksheet, then submit your printout.

Visual Workshop

Create the macro shown in Figure G-22. (*Hint:* Save a blank workbook as "File Utility Macros", then create a macro called SaveClose that saves a previously named workbook. Finally, include the line ActiveWorkbook.Close in the module, as shown in the figure.) Print the module. Test the macro. Submit your module printout. (The line "Macro recorded...by ..." will reflect your system date and name.)

FIGURE G-22

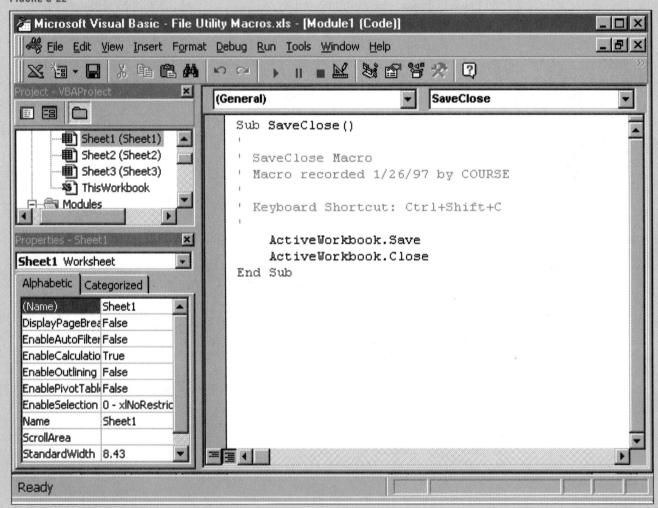

Using
Lists

Objectives

- ► Plan a list
- ► Create a list
- ► Add records with the data form
- ► Find records
- ► Delete records
- ► Sort a list by one field
- ► Sort a list by multiple fields
- ► Print a list

A **database** is an organized collection of related information. Examples of databases include a telephone book, a card catalog, and a roster of company employees. Excel refers to a database as a **list**. Using an Excel list, you can organize and manage worksheet information so that you can quickly find needed data for projects, reports, and charts. In this unit, you'll learn how to plan and create a list; add, change, find, and delete information in a list; and then sort and print a list. ◤ Nomad Ltd uses lists for analyzing new customer information. Evan's manager has asked him to build and manage a list of new customers as part of the ongoing strategy to focus the company's advertising dollars.

Planning a List

When planning a list, consider the information the list will contain and how you will work with the data now and in the future. Lists are organized into records. A **record** contains data about an object or person. Records, in turn, are divided into fields. **Fields** are columns in the list; each field describes a characteristic about the record, such as a customer's last name or street address. Each field has a **field name**, a column label that describes the field. See Table H-1 for additional planning guidelines. Also, make sure to view CourseHelp "Using Databases" before completing this lesson. ✐ At his manager's request, Evan will compile a list of new customers. Before entering the data into an Excel worksheet, he uses the following guidelines to plan the list:

Steps

1. **Identify the purpose of the list.**
   Determine the kind of information the list should contain. Evan will use the list to identify areas of the country in which new customers live.

2. **Plan the structure of the list.**
   Determine the fields that make up a record. Evan has customer cards that contain information about each new customer. A typical card is shown in Figure H-1. Each customer in the list will have a record. The fields in the record correspond to the information on the cards.

3. **Write down the names of the fields.**
   Field names can be up to 255 characters in length (the maximum column width), although shorter names are easier to see in the cells. Field names appear in the first row of a list. Evan writes down field names that describe each piece of information shown in Figure H-1.

4. **Determine any special number formatting required in the list.**
   Most lists contain both text and numbers. When planning a list, consider whether any fields require specific number formatting or prefixes. Evan notes that some Zip codes begin with zero. Because Excel automatically drops a leading zero, Evan must type an apostrophe (') when he enters a Zip code that begins with 0 (zero). The apostrophe tells Excel that the cell contains a label rather than a value. If a column contains both numbers and numbers that contain a text character, such as an apostrophe ('), you should format all the numbers as text. Otherwise, the numbers are sorted first, and the numbers that contain text characters are sorted after that; for example, 11542, 60614, 87105, '01810, '02115. To instruct Excel to sort the Zip codes properly, Evan enters all Zip codes with a leading apostrophe.

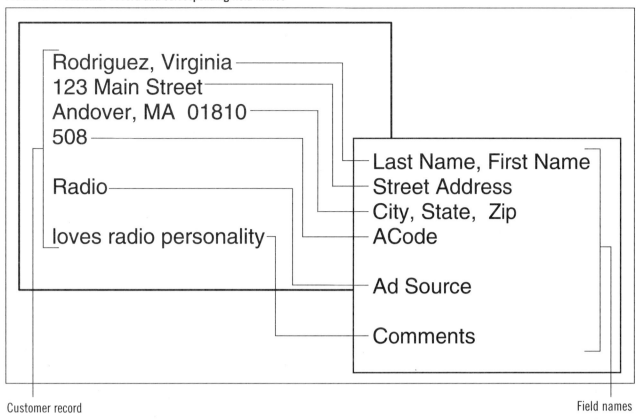

Customer record

Field names

TABLE H-1: Guidelines for planning a list

size and location guidelines	row and column content guidelines
Devote an entire worksheet to your list and list summary informationbecause some list management features can be used on only one listat a time.	Plan and design your list so that all rows have similar items in the same column.
Leave at least one blank column and one blank row between your list and list summary data. Doing this helps Excel select your list when it performs list management tasks such as sorting.	Do not insert extra spaces at the beginning of a cell because that can affect sorting and searching.
Avoid placing critical data to the left or right of the list.	Use the same format for all cells in a column.

Creating a List

Once you have planned the list structure, the sequence of fields, and any appropriate formatting, you need to create field names. Table H-2 provides guidelines for naming fields. Evan is ready to create the list using the field names he wrote down earlier.

Steps 1 2 3 4

1. **Open the workbook titled XL H-1, save it as New Customer List, then rename Sheet1 as Practice List**

   It is a good idea to devote an entire worksheet to your list.

2. **Beginning in cell A1 and moving horizontally, type each field name in a separate cell, as shown in Figure H-2**

   Always put field names in the first row of the list. Don't worry if your field names are wider than the cells; you will fix this later. Next, format the field names.

3. **Select the field headings in range A1:I1, then click the Bold button B on the Formatting toolbar; with range A1:I1 still selected, click the Borders list arrow, then click the thick bottom border (second item from left in the second row)**

   Next, enter three of the records in the customer list.

4. **Enter the information from Figure H-3 in the rows immediately below the field names, using a leading apostrophe (') for all Zip codes; do not leave any blank rows**

   If you don't type an apostrophe, Excel deletes the leading zero (0) in the Zip code. The data appears in columns organized by field name. Next, adjust the column widths so that each column is as wide as its longest entry.

5. **Select range A1:I4, click Format on the menu bar, point to Column, click AutoFit Selection, click anywhere in the worksheet to deselect the range, then save the workbook**

   Automatically resizing the column widths this way is faster than double-clicking the column divider lines between each pair of columns. Compare your screen with Figure H-4.

QuickTip

If the field name you plan to use is wider than the data in the column, you can turn on Wrap Text to stack the heading in the cell. Doing this allows you to use descriptive field names and still keep the columns from being unnecessarily wide. If you prefer a keyboard shortcut, you can press **[Alt][Enter]** to force a line break while entering field names.

TABLE H-2: Guidelines for naming fields

guideline	explanation
Use labels to name fields.	Numbers can be interpreted as parts of formulas.
Do not use duplicate field names.	Duplicate field names can cause information to be incorrectly entered and sorted.
Format the field names to stand out from the list data.	Use a font, alignment, format, pattern, border, or capitalization style for the column labels that is different from the format of your list data.
Use descriptive names.	Avoid names that might be confused with cell addresses, such as Q4.

FIGURE H-2: Field names entered and formatted in row 1

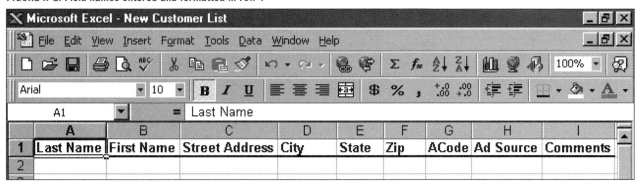

FIGURE H-3: Cards with customer information

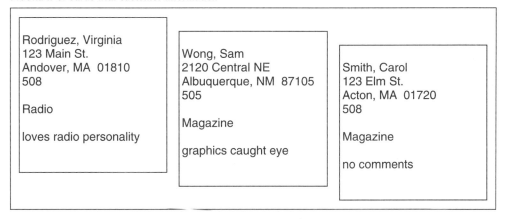

FIGURE H-4: List with three records

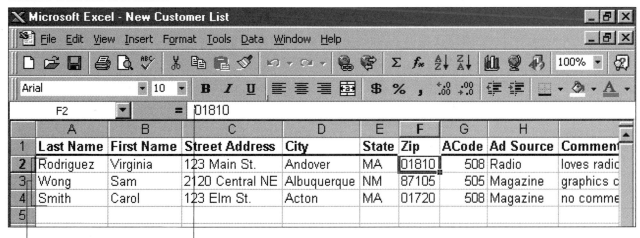

New records   Leading apostrophe

Maintaining the quality of information in a list

To protect the list information, make sure the data is entered in the correct field. Stress care and consistency to all those who enter the list data. Haphazardly entered data can yield invalid results later when it is manipulated.

Adding Records with the Data Form

You can add records to a list by typing data directly into the cells within the list range. Once the field names are created, you also can use the data form as a quick, easy method of data entry. By naming a list range in the name box, you can select the list at any time, and all new records added to the list will be included in the list range. ✎ Evan has entered all the customer records he had on his cards, but he received the names of two more customers. He decides to use Excel's data form to add the new customer information.

QuickTip

You can select the database quickly using the **[End]** key. Start in cell A1, press and hold **[Shift]**, press **[End]** [→], then press **[End]** [↓].

Trouble?

If you accidentally press [↑] or [↓] while in a data form and find yourself positioned in the wrong record, press [↑] or [↓] until you return to the desired record.

1. **Make sure the New Customer List is open, then rename Sheet2 as Working List**
   Working List contains the nearly complete customer list. Before using the data form to enter the new data, define the list range.

2. **Select range A1:I45, click the name box to select A1, type Database, then press [Enter]**
   The Database list range name appears in the name box. When you assign the name Database to the list, the commands on Excel's Data menu default to the list named "Database". Next, enter a new record using the data form.

3. **While the list is still selected, click Data on the menu bar, then click Form**
   A data form containing the first record appears, as shown in Figure H-5.

4. **Click New**
   A blank data form appears with the insertion point in the first field.

5. **Type Chavez in the Last Name box, then press [Tab] to move the insertion point to the next field**

6. **Enter the rest of the information for Jeffrey Chavez, as shown in Figure H-6**
   Press [Tab] to move the insertion point to the next field, or click in the next field's box to move the insertion point there.

7. **Click New to add Jeffrey Chavez's record and open another blank data form, enter the record for Cathy Relman as shown in Figure H-6, then click Close**
   The list records that you add with the data form are placed at the end of the list and are formatted like the previous records. Verify that the new records were added.

8. **Scroll down the worksheet to bring rows 46 and 47 into view, confirm both records, return to cell A1, then save the workbook**

FIGURE H-5: Data form showing first record in list

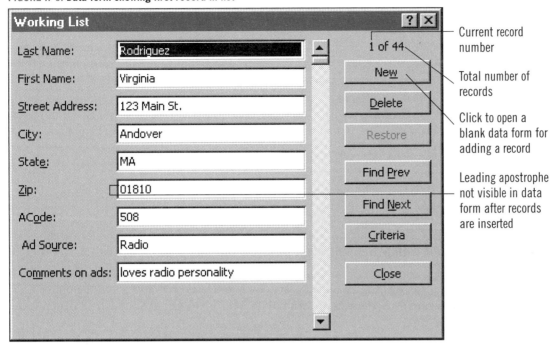

Current record number

Total number of records

Click to open a blank data form for adding a record

Leading apostrophe not visible in data form after records are inserted

FIGURE H-6: Two data forms with information for two new records

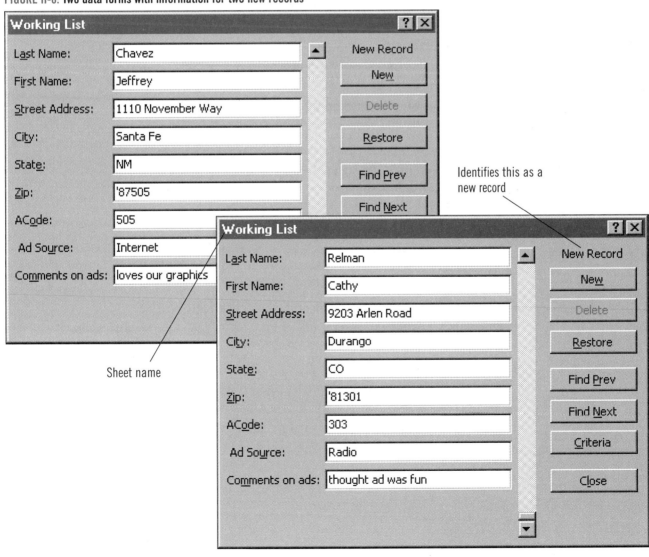

Identifies this as a new record

Sheet name

Finding Records

From time to time, you need to locate specific records in your list. You can use Excel's Find command on the Edit menu or the data form to perform searches in your list. Also, you can use the Replace command on the Edit menu to locate and replace existing entries or portions of entries with specified information. Evan's manager has asked him to list the specific Ad Source for each new customer rather than list the general ad category. She also wants to know how many of the new customers originated from the company's Internet site. Evan begins by searching for those records with the Ad Source "Internet".

Trouble?

If you receive the message, "No list found", simply select any cell within the list, then repeat Step 1.

1. From any cell within the list, click **Data** on the menu bar, click **Form**, then click **Criteria**

The data form changes so that all fields are blank and "Criteria" appears in the upper-right corner. See Figure H-7. You want to search for records whose Ad Source field contains the label "Internet".

2. Press **[Alt][U]** to move to the Ad Source box, type **Internet**, then click **Find Next**

Excel displays the first record for a customer who learned about the company through the Internet site. See Figure H-8.

3. Click **Find Next** until there are no more matching records, then click **Close**

There are six customers whose Ad Source is the Internet. Next, change the Ad Source entries that currently read "Radio" to "KWIN Radio".

QuickTip

You also can use comparison operators when performing a search using the data form. For example, you could specify >50,000 in a Salary field box to return those records whose value in the Salary field is greater than 50,000.

4. Return to cell A1, click **Edit** on the menu bar, then click **Replace**

The Replace dialog box opens with the insertion point located in the Find what box. See Figure H-9.

5. In the Find what box, type **Radio**, then click the **Replace with box**

Next, instruct Excel to search for entries containing "Radio" and replace them with "KWIN Radio".

6. In the Replace with box, type **KWIN Radio**

You are about to perform the search and replace option specified. Because you notice that there are other list entries containing the word "radio" with a lowercase "r", you choose the option "Match case" in the dialog box.

7. Click the **Match case box** to select it, then click **Find Next**

Excel moves the cell pointer to the first occurrence of "Radio". Next, instruct Excel to replace all existing entries with the information specified.

8. Click **Replace All**

The dialog box closes, and you complete the replacement and check to make sure all references to radio in the Ad Source column now read "KWIN Radio".

9. Make sure there are no entries in the Ad Source column that read "Radio", then save the workbook

FIGURE H-7: Criteria data form

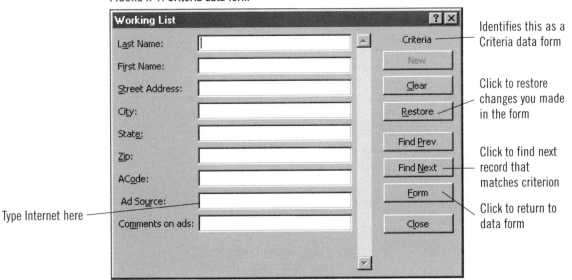

Identifies this as a
Criteria data form

Click to restore
changes you made
in the form

Click to find next
record that
matches criterion

Click to return to
data form

Type Internet here

FIGURE H-8: Finding a record using the data form

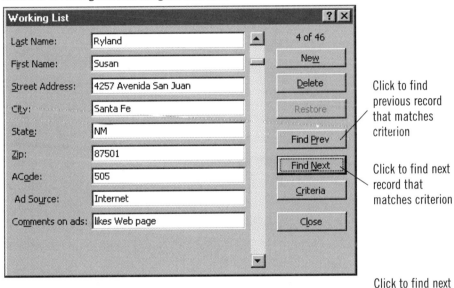

Click to find
previous record
that matches
criterion

Click to find next
record that
matches criterion

Click to find next
occurrence of item
in Find what box

FIGURE H-9: Replace dialog box

Type Radio here

Type KWIN Radio
here

Click to find exact
case matches

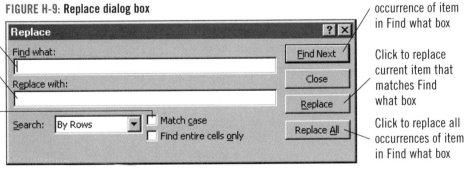

Click to replace
current item that
matches Find
what box

Click to replace all
occurrences of item
in Find what box

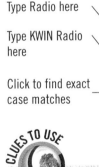

CLUES TO USE

Using wildcards to fine-tune your search

You can use special symbols called **wildcards** when defining search criteria in the data form or Find dialog box. The question mark (?) wildcard stands for any single character. For example, if you do not know whether a customer's last name is Paulsen or Paulson, you can specify Pauls?n as the search criteria to locate both options. The asterisk (*) wildcard stands for any group of characters. For example, if you specify Jan* as the search criteria in the First Name field, Excel locates all records with first names beginning with Jan (for instance, Jan, Janet, Janice, and so forth).

Deleting Records

You need to keep your list up to date by removing obsolete records. One way to remove records is to use the Delete button on the data form. You also can delete all records that meet certain criteria—that is, records that have something in common. For example, you can specify a criterion for Excel to find the next record containing Zip code 01879, then remove the record using the Delete button. If specifying one criterion does not meet your needs, you can set multiple criteria. 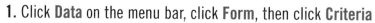 After she noticed two entries for Carolyn Smith, Evan's manager asked him to check the database for additional duplicate entries. Evan uses the data form to delete the duplicate record.

QuickTip

Besides using the data form to add, search for, and delete records, you also can use the data form to edit records. Just find the desired record and edit the data directly in the appropriate box.

QuickTip

Clicking Restore on the data form will not restore deleted record(s).

1. Click **Data** on the menu bar, click **Form**, then click **Criteria**
The Criteria data form appears. Search for records whose Last Name field contains the label "Smith" and whose First Name field contains the label "Carolyn".

2. In the **Last Name box**, type **Smith**, click the **First Name box**, type **Carolyn**, then click **Find Next**
Excel displays the first record for a customer whose name is Carolyn Smith. You decide to leave the initial entry for Carolyn Smith (record 5 of 46) and delete the second one once you confirm it is a duplicate.

3. Click **Find Next**
The duplicate record for Carolyn Smith, record number 40, appears as shown in Figure H-10. You are ready to delete the duplicate entry.

4. Click **Delete**, then click **OK** to confirm the deletion
The duplicate record for Carolyn Smith is deleted, and all the other records move up one row. The new record, Manuel Julio, is shown in the data form. Next, view the worksheet to confirm deletion of the duplicate entry.

5. Click **Close** to return to the worksheet, scroll down until rows 40–46 are visible, then read the entry in row 40
Notice that the duplicate entry for Carolyn Smith is gone and that Manuel Julio moved up a row and is now in row 41. You also notice a record for K. C. Splint in row 43, which is a duplicate entry.

6. Return to cell A1, and read the record information for K. C. Splint in row 8
After confirming another duplicate entry, you decide to delete the row.

7. Click cell **A8**, click **Edit** on the menu bar, then click **Delete**
The Delete dialog box opens as shown in Figure H-11. Choose the option to delete the entire row.

8. Click the **Entire row option button**, then click **OK**
You are pleased that the duplicate record for K. C. Splint is deleted and that the other records move up to fill in the gap.

9. Save the workbook

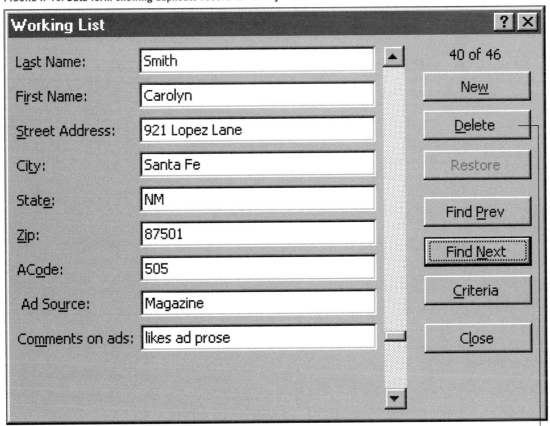

Click to delete
current record
from list

FIGURE H-11: **Delete dialog box**

Click to shift
remaining cells to
fill gap created by
deleting cells

Click to delete
current row

Click to delete
current column

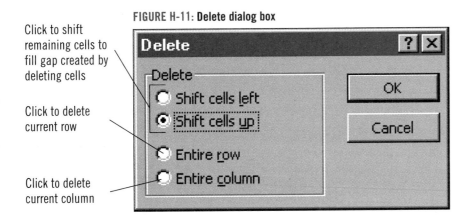

Deleting records using the data form versus deleting rows from the worksheet area

When you delete a record using the data form, you cannot undo your deletion. When you delete a record by deleting the row in which it resides inside the worksheet area, however, you can immediately restore the record by using the Undo command on the Edit menu, the Undo button, or by pressing [Ctrl][Z].

Sorting a List by One Field

Usually, you enter records in the order in which they are received, rather than in alphabetical or numerical order. When you add records to a list using the data form, the records are added to the end of the list. Using Excel's sorting feature, you can rearrange the order in which the records appear. You can use the sort buttons on the Standard toolbar to sort records by one field, or you can use the Sort command on the Data menu to perform more complicated sorts. Alternatively, you can sort an entire list or any portion of a list, or you can arrange sorted information in ascending or descending order. In ascending order, the lowest value (the beginning of the alphabet, or the earliest date) appears at the top of the list. In a field containing labels and numbers, numbers come first. In descending order, the highest value (the end of the alphabet, or the latest date) appears at the top of the list. In a field containing labels and numbers, labels come first. Table H-3 provides examples of ascending and descending sorts. Because Evan wants to be able to return the records to their original order following any sorts, he begins by creating a new field called Entry Order. Then he will perform several single field sorts on the list.

QuickTip

Before you sort records, it is a good idea to make a backup copy of your list or create a field that numbers the records so you can return them to their original order, if necessary.

QuickTip

If your sort does not perform as intended, press **[Ctrl][Z]** immediately to undo the sort and repeat the step.

1. In cell J1, enter the text and format for cell J1 as shown in Figure H-12, then AutoFit column J
   Next, fill in the entry order numbers for all records.

2. In cell J2 type **1**, press **[Enter]**, in cell J3 type **2**, press **[Enter]**, select cells **J2:J3**, drag the fill handle to cell **J45**, then return to cell A1
   With the Entry Order column complete as shown in Figure H-12, you are ready to sort the list in ascending order by last name. You must position the cell pointer within the column you want to sort prior to issuing the sort command.

3. While in cell A1, click the **Sort Ascending button** ▲↓ on the Standard toolbar
   Excel instantly rearranges the records in ascending order by last name, as shown in Figure H-13. Next, sort the list in descending order by area code.

4. Click cell **G1**, then click the **Sort Descending button** ▼↓ on the Standard toolbar
   Excel sorts the list, placing those records with higher-digit area codes at the top. Next, update the list range to include original entry order.

5. Select range A1:J45, click the **name box**, type **Database**, then press **[Enter]**
   You are now ready to return the list to original entry order.

6. Click cell J1, click the **Sort Ascending button** ▲↓ on the Standard toolbar, then save the workbook
   The list is back to its original order, and the workbook is saved.

TABLE H-3: Sort order options and examples

option	alphabetic	numeric	date	alphanumeric
Ascending	A, B, C	7, 8, 9	1/1, 2/1, 3/1	12A, 99B, DX8, QT7
Descending	C, B, A	9, 8, 7	3/1, 2/1, 1/1	QT7, DX8, 99B, 12A

FIGURE H-12: List with Entry Order field added

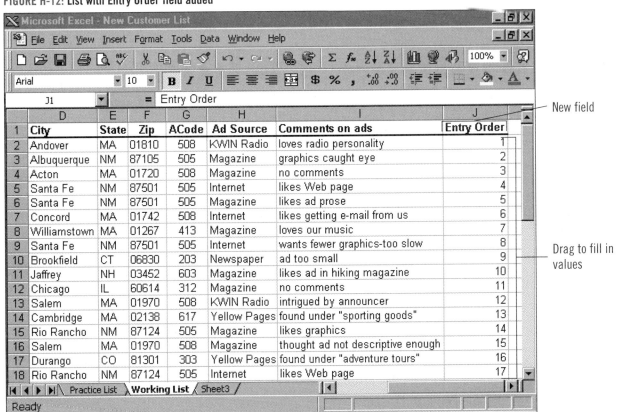

New field

Drag to fill in values

	D	E	F	G	H	I	J
1	City	State	Zip	ACode	Ad Source	Comments on ads	Entry Order
2	Andover	MA	01810	508	KWIN Radio	loves radio personality	1
3	Albuquerque	NM	87105	505	Magazine	graphics caught eye	2
4	Acton	MA	01720	508	Magazine	no comments	3
5	Santa Fe	NM	87501	505	Internet	likes Web page	4
6	Santa Fe	NM	87501	505	Magazine	likes ad prose	5
7	Concord	MA	01742	508	Internet	likes getting e-mail from us	6
8	Williamstown	MA	01267	413	Magazine	loves our music	7
9	Santa Fe	NM	87501	505	Internet	wants fewer graphics-too slow	8
10	Brookfield	CT	06830	203	Newspaper	ad too small	9
11	Jaffrey	NH	03452	603	Magazine	likes ad in hiking magazine	10
12	Chicago	IL	60614	312	Magazine	no comments	11
13	Salem	MA	01970	508	KWIN Radio	intrigued by announcer	12
14	Cambridge	MA	02138	617	Yellow Pages	found under "sporting goods"	13
15	Rio Rancho	NM	87124	505	Magazine	likes graphics	14
16	Salem	MA	01970	508	Magazine	thought ad not descriptive enough	15
17	Durango	CO	81301	303	Yellow Pages	found under "adventure tours"	16
18	Rio Rancho	NM	87124	505	Internet	likes Web page	17

FIGURE H-13: List sorted alphabetically by last name

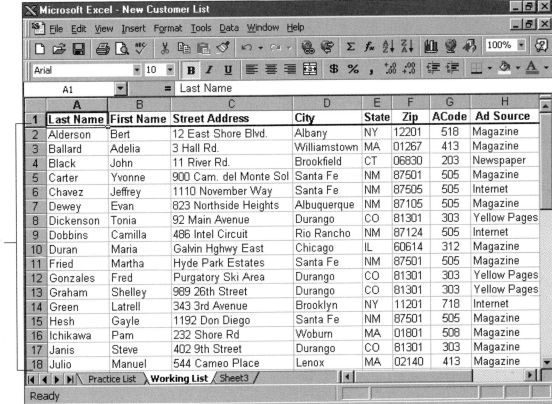

List sorted in ascending order by Last Name

	A	B	C	D	E	F	G	H
1	Last Name	First Name	Street Address	City	State	Zip	ACode	Ad Source
2	Alderson	Bert	12 East Shore Blvd.	Albany	NY	12201	518	Magazine
3	Ballard	Adelia	3 Hall Rd.	Williamstown	MA	01267	413	Magazine
4	Black	John	11 River Rd.	Brookfield	CT	06830	203	Newspaper
5	Carter	Yvonne	900 Cam. del Monte Sol	Santa Fe	NM	87501	505	Magazine
6	Chavez	Jeffrey	1110 November Way	Santa Fe	NM	87505	505	Internet
7	Dewey	Evan	823 Northside Heights	Albuquerque	NM	87105	505	Magazine
8	Dickenson	Tonia	92 Main Avenue	Durango	CO	81301	303	Yellow Pages
9	Dobbins	Camilla	486 Intel Circuit	Rio Rancho	NM	87124	505	Internet
10	Duran	Maria	Galvin Hghwy East	Chicago	IL	60614	312	Magazine
11	Fried	Martha	Hyde Park Estates	Santa Fe	NM	87501	505	Magazine
12	Gonzales	Fred	Purgatory Ski Area	Durango	CO	81301	303	Yellow Pages
13	Graham	Shelley	989 26th Street	Durango	CO	81301	303	Yellow Pages
14	Green	Latrell	343 3rd Avenue	Brooklyn	NY	11201	718	Internet
15	Hesh	Gayle	1192 Don Diego	Santa Fe	NM	87501	505	Magazine
16	Ichikawa	Pam	232 Shore Rd	Woburn	MA	01801	508	Magazine
17	Janis	Steve	402 9th Street	Durango	CO	81301	303	Magazine
18	Julio	Manuel	544 Cameo Place	Lenox	MA	02140	413	Magazine

Sorting a List by Multiple Fields

You can sort lists by as many as three fields by specifying **sort keys**, the criteria upon which the sort is based. To perform sorts on multiple fields, you must use the Sort dialog box, which you access through the Sort command on the Data menu. ◀━━━ Evan wants to sort the records alphabetically by state first, then within the state by Zip code.

QuickTip

You can specify a capitalization sort by clicking Options in the Sort dialog box, then clicking the Case sensitive box. When you choose this option, lowercase entries precede uppercase entries.

1. **Click the name box list arrow, then click Database**
   The list is selected. Because you want to sort the list by more than one field, use the Sort command on the Data menu.

2. **Click Data on the menu bar, then click Sort**
   The Sort dialog box opens, as shown in Figure H-14. You want to sort the list by state and then by Zip code.

3. **Click the Sort by list arrow, click State, then click the Ascending option button, if necessary**
   The list will be sorted alphabetically in ascending order (A–Z) by the State field. Next, define a second sort field for the Zip code.

4. **Click the top Then by list arrow, click Zip, then click the Descending option button**
   You also could sort by a third key by selecting a field in the bottom Then by list box.

5. **Click OK to execute the sort, press [Ctrl][Home], then scroll through the list to see the result of the sort**
   The list is sorted alphabetically by state in ascending order, then within each state by Zip code in descending order. Compare your results with Figure H-15. Notice that Massachusetts, New Mexico, and New York have multiple Zip codes.

6. **Return to cell A1, then save the workbook**

FIGURE H-14: **Sort dialog box**

Fields on which the sort will be based

First sort field

Second sort field

Third sort field

Indicates field name labels will not be included in sort

FIGURE H-15: **List sorted by multiple fields**

Microsoft Excel - New Customer List

File   Edit   View   Insert   Format   Tools   Data   Window   Help

A1   =   Last Name

	A	B	C	D	E	F	G	H
1	**Last Name**	**First Name**	**Street Address**	**City**	**State**	**Zip**	**ACode**	**Ad Source**
2	Dickenson	Tonia	92 Main Avenue	Durango	CO	81301	303	Yellow Pages
3	Gonzales	Fred	Purgatory Ski Area	Durango	CO	81301	303	Yellow Pages
4	Graham	Shelley	989 26th Street	Durango	CO	81301	303	Yellow Pages
5	Janis	Steve	402 9th Street	Durango	CO	81301	303	Magazine
6	Nelson	Michael	229 Route 55	Durango	CO	81301	303	Yellow Pages
7	Relman	Cathy	9203 Arlen Road	Durango	CO	81301	303	KWIN Radio
8	Black	John	11 River Rd.	Brookfield	CT	06830	203	Newspaper
9	Owen	Scott	72 Yankee Way	Brookfield	CT	06830	203	Newspaper
10	Duran	Maria	Galvin Hghwy East	Chicago	IL	60614	312	Magazine
11	Roberts	Bob	56 Water St.	Chicago	IL	60614	312	Magazine
12	Wallace	Salvatore	100 Westside Avenue	Chicago	IL	60614	312	Magazine
13	Ballard	Adelia	3 Hall Rd.	Williamstown	MA	01267	413	Magazine
14	Smith	Carol	123 Elm St.	Acton	MA	01720	508	Magazine
15	Kane	Peter	67 Main St.	Concord	MA	01742	508	Internet
16	Spencer	Robin	293 Serenity Drive	Concord	MA	01742	508	KWIN Radio
17	Ichikawa	Pam	232 Shore Rd	Woburn	MA	01801	508	Magazine
18	Paxton	Gail	100 Main Street	Woburn	MA	01801	508	Magazine

Practice List \ Working List \ Sheet3 /

Ready

First sort by state

Second sort by Zip code within state

Specifying a custom sort order

You can identify a custom sort order for the field selected in the Sort by box. To do this, click Options in the Sort dialog box, click the First key sort order list arrow, then click the desired custom order.

Commonly used custom sort orders are days of the week (Mon, Tues, Wed, and so forth) and months (Jan, Feb, Mar, and so forth), where alphabetic sorts do not sort these items properly.

Printing a List

If a list is small enough to fit on one page, you can print it as you would any other Excel worksheet. However, if you have more columns than can fit on a portrait-oriented page, try setting the page orientation to landscape. Because lists often have more rows than can fit on a page, you can define the first row of the list (containing the field names) as the **print title**. Most lists do not have any descriptive information above the field names on the worksheet. To augment the information contained in the field names, you can use headers and footers to add identifying text, such as the list title or report date. If you want to exclude any fields from your list report, you can hide the desired columns from view so that they do not print. Evan has finished updating his list and is ready to print it. He begins by previewing the list.

QuickTip

You can print multiple ranges in your worksheets at the same time by clicking the Print area box in the Sheet tab of the Page Setup dialog box. Then simply drag to select areas in the worksheet you wish to print.

1. Click the **Print Preview button** [icon] on the Standard toolbar
   Notice that the status bar reads Page 1 of 2. You want all the fields in the list to fit on a single page, but you'll need two pages to fit all the data. So you set the page orientation to landscape and adjust the Fit to options.

2. From the Print Preview window, click **Setup**, click the **Page tab**, under Orientation click the **Landscape option button**, under Scaling click the **Fit to option button**, double-click the **tall box** and type **2**, then click **OK**
   The list still does not fit on a single page. Check to see what is on page 2.

3. Click **Next**
   Because the records on page 2 appear without column headings, you can set up the first row of the list, containing the field names, as a repeating print title.

4. Click **Close** to exit the Print Preview window, click **File** on the menu bar, click **Page Setup**, click the **Sheet tab**, under Print titles click the **Rows to repeat at top box**, then click any cell in row 1
   When you select row 1 as a print title, Excel automatically inserts an absolute reference to a beginning and ending row to repeat at the top of each page—in this case, the print title to repeat beginning and ending with row 1. See Figure H-16.

5. Click **Print Preview**, click **Next** to view the second page, then click **Zoom** to get a closer look
   Setting up a print title to repeat row 1 causes the field names to appear at the top of each printed page. Next, change the header to reflect the contents of the list.

6. Click **Setup**, click the **Header/Footer tab**, click **Custom Header**, click the **Center section box**, type **Nomad Ltd—New Customer List**

7. Select the header text in the Center section box, click the **Font button** [A], change the font size to **14** and the style to **Bold**, click **OK**, click **OK** again to return to the Header/Footer tab, then click **OK** to preview the list
   Page 2 of the report appears as shown in Figure H-17.

8. Save, print, then close the workbook

FIGURE H-16: Sheet tab of the Page Setup dialog box

Indicates row 1 will appear at top of each printed page

Indicates which columns will appear at left of each printed page

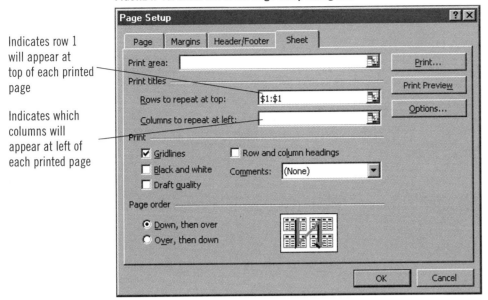

FIGURE H-17: Print Preview window showing page 2 of completed report

List header ———

Row 1 of list repeated as a print title

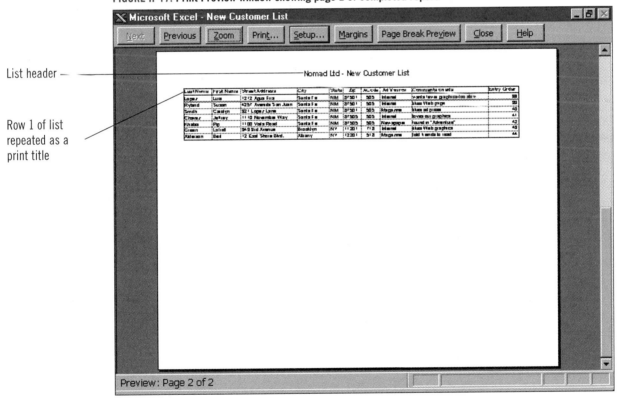

<img name="CLUES TO USE" />

Setting page printing order

You can control the order Excel creates pages from your worksheet in the Sheet tab of the Page Setup dialog box. See the Page order option in Figure H-16. Normally, Excel prints pages by selecting a pageful of data going down the rows first, then across columns. You also can print by first filling pages going across the columns and then down the rows.

Practice

► Concepts Review

Label each of the elements of the Excel screen shown in Figure H-18.

FIGURE H-18

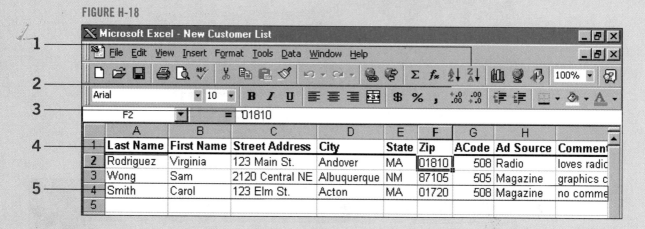

Match each statement with the term it describes.

6. Arrange records in a particular sequence
7. Organized collection of related information in Excel
8. Row in an Excel list
9. Type of software used for lists containing more than 65,536 records
10. Label positioned at the top of the column identifying data for that field

a. List
b. Record
c. Database
d. Sort
e. Field name

Select the best answer from the list of choices.

11. Which of the following Excel sorting options do you use to sort a list of employee names in A-to-Z order?
    a. Ascending
    b. Absolute
    c. Alphabetic
    d. Descending

12. Which of the following series is in descending order?
    a. 4, 5, 6, A, B, C
    b. C, B, A, 6, 5, 4
    c. 8, 7, 6, 5, 6, 7
    d. 8, 6, 4, C, B, A

13. Once the _____ is defined, any new records added to the list using the data form are included in the _____.
    a. Database, database
    b. Data form, data form
    c. Worksheet, worksheet
    d. List range, list range

14. When printing a list on multiple pages, you can define a print title containing repeating row(s) to
    a. Include appropriate fields in the printout.
    b. Include field names at the top of each printed page.
    c. Include the header in list reports.
    d. Exclude from the printout all rows under the first row.

▶ Skills Review

1. Create a list.
    a. Create a new workbook, then save it as "M.K. Electric Employee List".
    b. In cell A1, type the title "M.K. Electric Employees".
    c. Enter the field names and records using the information in Table H-4.
    d. Apply bold formatting to the field names.

Excel 97

TABLE H-4

Last name	First name	Years	Position	Pension	Union
Smith-Hill	Janice	8	Office Manager	Y	N
Doolan	Mark	3	Customer Service	N	N
Coleman	Steve	4	Senior Installer	N	Y
Quinn	Jamie	7	Junior Installer	N	Y
Rabinowicz	Sarah	11	Field Manager	Y	Y

    e. Center the entries in the Years, Pension, and Union fields.
    f. Adjust the column widths to make the data readable.
    g. Save, then print the list.

2. Add records with the data form.

   a. Select all the records in the list, including the field names, then define the range as "Database".

   b. Open the data form and add a new record for David Gitano, a newly hired junior installer at M.K. Electric. David is not eligible for the employee pension, but he is a member of the union.

   c. Add a new record for George Worley, the company's new office assistant. George is not eligible for the employee pension, and he is not a union member.

   d. Save the list.

3. Find and delete records.

   a. Find the record for Jamie Quinn.

   b. Delete the record.

   c. Save the list.

4. Sort a list by one field.

   a. Select the Database list range.

   b. Sort the list alphabetically in ascending order by last name.

   c. Save the list.

5. Sort a list by multiple fields.

   a. Select the Database list range.

   b. Sort the list alphabetically in ascending order first by union membership and then by last name.

   c. Save the list.

6. Print a list.

   a. Add a header that reads, "Employee Information".

   b. Print the list, then save and close the workbook.

   c. Exit Excel.

1. Your advertising firm, Personalize IT, specializes in selling specialty items imprinted with the customer's name and/or logo such as hats, pens, and T-shirts. Plan and build a list of information with a minimum of 10 records using the three items sold. Your list should contain at least five different customers. (Some customers will place more than one order.) Each record should contain the customer's name, item sold, and its individual and extended cost. Enter your own data and make sure you include at least the following list fields:

- Item—Describe the item.
- Cost-Ea.—What is the item's individual cost?
- Quantity—How many items did the customer purchase?
- Ext. Cost—What is the total purchase price?
- Customer—Who purchased the item?

To complete this independent challenge:

1. Prepare a list plan that states your goal, outlines the data you'll need, and identifies the list elements.
2. Sketch a sample list on a piece of paper, indicating how the list should be built. What information should go in the columns? In the rows? Which of the data fields will be formatted as labels? As values?
3. Build the list first by entering the field names, then by entering the records. Remember you will invent your own data. Save the workbook as "Personalize IT".
4. Reformat the list, as needed. For example, you might need to adjust the column widths to make the data more readable. Also, remember to check your spelling.
5. Sort the list in ascending order by Item, then by Customer, then by Quantity
6. Preview the worksheet; adjust any items as needed; then print a copy.
7. Save your work before closing.
8. Submit your list plan, preliminary sketches, and final printouts.

2. You are taking a class titled "Television Shows: Past and Present" at a local community college. The instructor has provided you with an Excel list of television programs from the '60s and '70s. She has included fields tracking the following information: the number of years the show was a favorite, favorite character, least favorite character, the show's length in minutes, the show's biggest star, and comments about the show. The instructor has included data for each show in the list. She has asked you to add a field (column label) and two records (shows of your choosing) to the list. Because the list should cover only 30-minute shows, you need to delete any records for shows longer than 30 minutes. Also, your instructor wants you to sort the list by show name and format the list as needed prior to printing. Feel free to change any of the list data to suit your tastes and opinions.

To complete this independent challenge:

1. Open the workbook titled XL H-2, then save it as "Television Shows of the Past".
2. Using your own data, add a field, then use the data form to add two records to the list. Make sure to enter information in every field.
3. Delete any records having show lengths other than 30. (*Hint*: Use the Criteria data form to set the criteria, then find and delete any matching records.)

Excel 97

4. Make any formatting changes to the list as needed.

5. Save the list prior to sorting.

6. Sort the list in ascending order by show name.

7. Preview, then print the list. Adjust any items as needed so that the list can be printed on a single page.

8. Sort the list again, this time in descending order by number of years the show was a favorite.

9. Change the header to read "Television Shows of the Past: '60s and '70s".

10. Preview, then print the list.

11. Save the workbook.

3. You work as a sales clerk at Nite Owl Video. Your roommate and co-worker, Albert Lee, has put together a list of his favorite movie actors and actresses. He has asked you to add several names to the list so he can determine which artists and what kinds of films you enjoy most. He has recorded information in the following fields: artist's first and last names, life span, birthplace, the genre or type of roles the artist plays most (for example, dramatic or comedic), the name of a film for which the artist has received or been nominated for an Academy Award, and finally, two additional films featuring the artist. Using your own data, add at least two artists known for dramatic roles and two artists known for comedic roles.

To complete this independent challenge:

1. Open the workbook titled XL H-3, then add at least four records using the criteria mentioned above. Remember, you are creating and entering your own movie data for all relevant fields.

2. Save the workbook as "Film Star Favorites". Make formatting changes to the list as needed. Remember to check your spelling.

3. Sort the list alphabetically by Genre. Perform a second sort by Last Name.

4. Preview the list, adjust any items as needed, then print a copy of the list sorted by Genre and Last Name.

5. Sort the list again, this time in descending order by the Life Span field, then by Last Name.

6. Print a copy of the list sorted by Life Span and Last Name.

7. Save your work, then submit your printouts.

4. Because Web users are located all over the world, you can use the World Wide Web (WWW) to locate almost any type of information, in just about any country around the globe. Travel information is especially helpful when you are planning vacations. You have decided to travel to Hawaii for one month over the summer. Your choice of accommodations includes a condominium close to the beach with full kitchen facilities. Use your choice of search engines on the WWW to locate information on condo rentals in Hawaii, and then build an Excel list with the information you gather.

To complete this independent challenge:

1. Open a new workbook, then save it as "Hawaiian Vacation".
2. Create a list with the following field names: Complex Name, Island, Ocean View?, Peak Season Rate, Off-Season Rate (rates per night), Max # of Bedrooms, On-Site Pool?, On-Site Golf?, Air Conditioning?, and Web Site Address.
3. Log on to the Internet and use your Web browser to go to http://www.course.com. From there, click the link Student Online Companions, then click the Excel link for Unit H.
4. Use any combination of the following sites to search for and compile your data: Yahoo!, WebCrawler, or Alta Vista. (*Hint:* When using Web search engines, the + (plus sign) before a word means that the word must appear in the Web document. Therefore, a suggested search string would be +Hawaii +Condo +Rentals.) Be sure to gather information on 10 different possible vacation sites (minimum 10 records). While on the Web, print at least two graphics of sites chosen to accompany your worksheet data.
5. Add the Web data as records in your list.
6. Format the worksheet as desired to increase readability.
7. Save and print the workbook, then submit your printouts.

► Visual Workshop

Create the worksheet shown in Figure H-19. Save the workbook as "Famous Jazz Performers". Once you've entered the field names and records, sort the list by Contribution to Jazz and then by Last Name. Change the page setup so that the list is centered on the page horizontally and the header reads "Famous Jazz Performers". Preview and print the list, then save the workbook. Submit your printouts.

FIGURE H-19

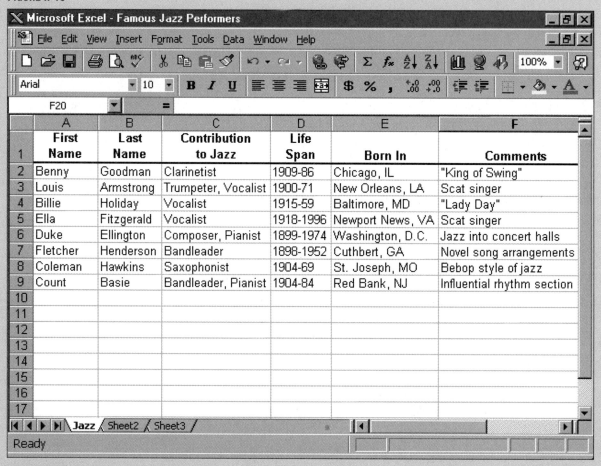

Analyzing
List Data

Objectives

- ► Retrieve records with AutoFilter
- ► Create a custom filter
- ► Filter a list with Advanced Filter
- ► Extract list data
- ► Create automatic subtotals
- ► Look up values in a list
- ► Summarize list data
- ► Use data validation for list entries

There are many ways to **analyze**, or manipulate, list data with Excel. One way is to filter a list so that only the rows that meet certain criteria are retrieved. In this unit you will retrieve records using AutoFilter, create a custom filter, and filter a list using Excel's Advanced Filter feature. In addition, you will learn to insert automatic subtotals, use lookup functions to locate list entries, and apply database functions to summarize list data that meets specific criteria. You'll also learn how to restrict entries in a column using data validation.

Nomad Ltd has recently acquired a new division to sell health-related products and services and to manage a chain of health clubs. Evan Brillstein has taken a job as the assistant to the director, Megan Grahs. One of Evan's first tasks was to create a list of all the new members for his manager. Megan suggested that Evan add two other fields: one for membership identification numbers and another for additional membership information. She also asked him to manipulate the list to produce specific reports.

Retrieving Records with AutoFilter

Excel's AutoFilter feature searches for records that meet criteria specified by the user and then lists those matching records. One way is to **filter** out, or hide, data that fails to meet certain criteria. You can filter specific values in a column, use the predefined Top 10 option to filter records based on upper or lower values in a column, or create a custom filter. For example, you can filter a customer list to retrieve only those names of customers residing in Hawaii. You also can filter records based on a specific field and request that Excel retrieve only those records having an entry (or no entry) in that field. Once you create a filtered list, you can print it or copy it to another part of the worksheet to manipulate it further. ◢━━━ Evan has added the appropriate fields Megan requested to the new member list and now is ready to work on his reports. He begins by retrieving data on only those new members who live in Albuquerque, New Mexico.

Steps 1 2 3 4

1. Open the workbook titled **XL I-1**, then save it as Health Club, New Member List

You will use the AutoFilter feature to retrieve the records for the report.

2. Click **Data** on the menu bar, point to **Filter**, then click **AutoFilter**

List arrows appear to the right of each field name. Clicking the City list arrow initiates the first filter.

3. Click the **City list arrow**

An AutoFilter list containing the different city options appears below the field name, as shown in Figure I-1. Because you want to retrieve membership data for only those members who live in Albuquerque, you'll specify "Albuquerque" as your **search criteria.**

4. In the filter list, click **Albuquerque**

Only those records containing Albuquerque in the City field are retrieved, as shown in Figure I-2. The status bar indicates the number of matching records (in this case, 2 of 35), the color of the row numbers changes for the matching records, and the color of the list arrow for the filtered field changes. Next, you want to retrieve information about those members who were charged the highest two membership rates. To do so, you must clear the previous filter.

5. Click **Data** on the menu bar, point to **Filter**, then click **Show All**

All the records reappear.

6. Scroll right until columns G through N are visible, click the **Initial Fee list arrow**, then click **(Top 10...)**

The Top 10 AutoFilter dialog box opens. To select only those records that have the two highest fees, you need to change the current default value from 10 to 2.

7. With 10 selected in the middle box, type **2**, then click **OK**

The records are retrieved for the new members who paid the two highest fees ($325 and $350). See Figure I-3. Now you can print the report, clear the filter, and then move the pointer back to the beginning of the worksheet.

8. Click the **Initial Fee list arrow**, click **(All)**, press **[Ctrl][Home]**, then print the list

Because you didn't make any changes, there is no need to save the file.

Trouble?

If the column label in cell A1 covers the column headers, making it difficult to find the appropriate columns, select A2 before scrolling.

FIGURE I-1: Worksheet showing AutoFilter options

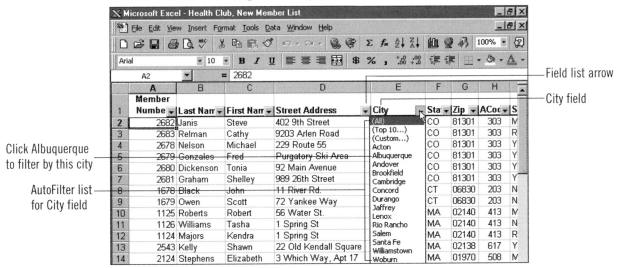

Field list arrow

City field

Click Albuquerque to filter by this city

AutoFilter list for City field

FIGURE I-2: List filtered with AutoFilter

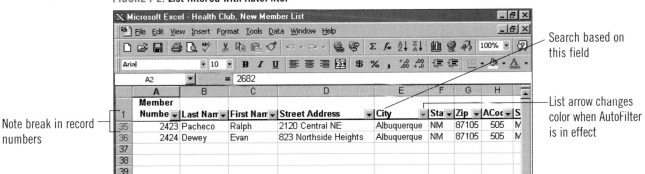

Search based on this field

List arrow changes color when AutoFilter is in effect

Note break in record numbers

FIGURE I-3: List filtered with Top 10 AutoFilter criteria

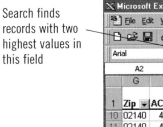

Search finds records with two highest values in this field

Creating a Custom Filter

So far, you have used the AutoFilter command to filter rows based on an entry in a single column. You can perform more complicated filters using options in the Custom AutoFilter dialog box. For example, you could filter rows based on two entries in a single column or use comparison operators such as "greater than" or "less than" to display only those records with amounts greater than $50,000 in a particular column. Evan's next filtering task is to locate those new members who live west of the Rocky Mountains, who bought a Single type membership, and who heard about Nomad Limited's health clubs through a magazine advertisement.

Steps

QuickTip
When specifying criteria in the Custom AutoFilter dialog box, use the ? wildcard to specify any single character and the * wildcard to specify any series of characters.

Trouble?
If no records are displayed in the worksheet, you may have forgotten to type the apostrophe before the number 81000. Repeat Steps 2 and 3, making sure you include the leading apostrophe.

1. **Click the Zip list arrow, then click (Custom...)**
   The Custom AutoFilter dialog box opens. Because you know that all residents west of the Rockies have a Zip code greater than 81000, you specify this criteria here. Because all the Zip codes in the list were entered originally as labels with leading apostrophes, you need to include this apostrophe when entering the Zip code value.

2. **Click the Zip list arrow, click is greater than, press [Tab], then type '81000**
   Your completed Custom AutoFilter dialog box should match Figure I-4.

3. **Click OK**
   The dialog box closes, and only those records having a Zip code greater than 81000 appear in the worksheet. Now, you'll narrow the list even further by displaying only those members with a Single type of membership.

4. **Scroll right until columns G through N are visible, click the Member Type list arrow, then click Single**
   The list of records retrieved has narrowed. Finally, you need to filter out all the members except those who heard about the health clubs through a magazine advertisement.

5. **Click the Source list arrow, then click Magazine**
   Your final filtered list should match Figure I-5. Now, you're ready to print this list for Evan's manager. You'll use the existing print settings—landscape orientation, scaled to fit on a single page.

6. **Preview, then print the worksheet**
   The one-page report looks good. Now you can clear the filter and re-list all the records.

7. **Click Data on the menu bar, point to Filter, click AutoFilter to deselect it, then press [Ctrl][Home]**
   AutoFilter is turned off, and all records are listed.

FIGURE I-4: Custom AutoFilter dialog box

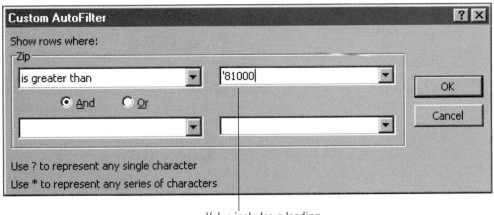

Value includes a leading
apostrophe

FIGURE I-5: Results of custom filter

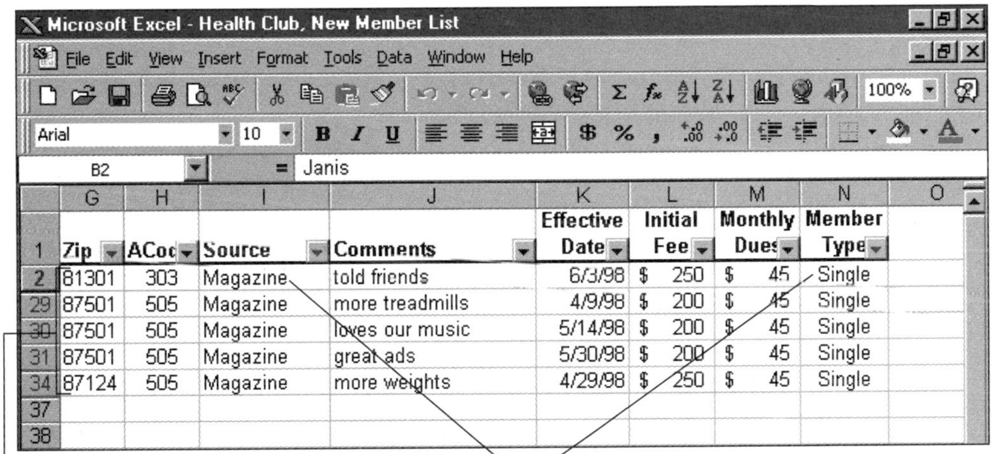

Zip codes greater
than 81000

Fields used in custom filter

And and Or Logical Conditions

You can narrow a search even further by using the And or Or buttons in the Custom AutoFilter dialog box. For example, you can select records for those customers living in Colorado *and* New Mexico as well as select records for customers living in Colorado *or* New Mexico. See Figure I-6. When used in this way, "And" and "Or" are often referred to as logical conditions. When you search for customers living in Colorado *and* New Mexico, you are specifying an And condition. When you search for customers living either in Colorado *or* New Mexico, you are specifying an Or condition.

FIGURE I-6: Using "Or" in the Custom AutoFilter dialog box

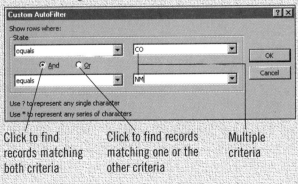

Click to find
records matching
both criteria

Click to find records
matching one or the
other criteria

Multiple
criteria

Filtering a List with Advanced Filter

The Advanced Filter command allows you to search for data that matches complicated criteria in more than one column, using And and Or conditions. To use advanced filtering, you must define a criteria range. A **criteria range** is a cell range containing one row of labels (usually a copy of the column labels) and at least one additional row underneath the row of labels that contains the criteria you want to match. ◀▬▬ Evan's next task is to identify those new members whose memberships were effective in April and who paid an initial fee less than or equal to $300. He will use the Advanced Filter command to retrieve this data. Evan begins by defining the criteria range.

Steps

Trouble?

If the column labels make it difficult for you to drag the pointer to cell; N7, try clicking N7 first; then drag the pointer all the way left to cell A7.

1. Select rows 1 through 6, click Insert on the menu bar, then click Rows; click cell A1, type Criteria Range, click cell A6, type List Range, then click the Enter button ☑ on the formula bar

   See Figure I-7. Six blank rows are added above the list. The labels "Criteria Range" and "List Range" are not required by Excel, but they are useful because they help organize the worksheet. Next, you copy the column labels to row 2.

2. Select range A7:N7, click the Copy button 🖹 on the Standard toolbar, click cell A2, then press [Enter]

   Next, you need to specify that you want records for only those new members whose memberships were effective prior to May 1 and who paid an initial fee of no more than $300. In other words, you need records with a date before (less than) May 1, 1998 (<5/1/98) and an initial fee that is less than or equal to $300 (≤300).

3. Scroll right until columns H through N are visible, click cell K3, type < 5/1/98, click cell L3, type <=300, then click ☑

   This enters the criteria in the cells directly beneath the criteria range labels. See Figure I-8. Placing the criteria in the same row indicates that the records you are searching for must match both criteria; that is, it specifies an And condition.

4. Press [Ctrl][Home], click Data on the menu bar, point to Filter, then click Advanced Filter

   The Advanced Filter dialog box opens, with the list range already entered. Notice that the default setting under Action is to filter the list in its current location rather than copy it to another location. Now, you need to enter the criteria range you just created.

5. Click the Criteria range box, if necessary move the dialog box to select range A2:N3 in the worksheet, then click OK

   The filtered list contains the records that match both the criteria. You'll filter this list even further in the next lesson.

CLUES TO USE

Understanding the criteria range

When you define the criteria range in the Advanced Filter dialog box, Excel automatically creates a name for this range in the worksheet (Criteria). The criteria range includes the field names and any criteria rows underneath.

FIGURE I-7: Using the Advanced Filter command

New rows —
New labels

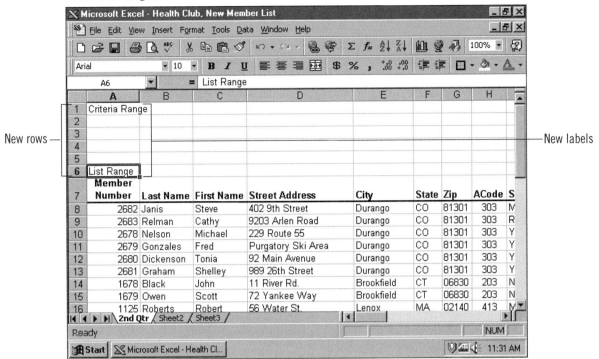

FIGURE I-8: Criteria in the same row

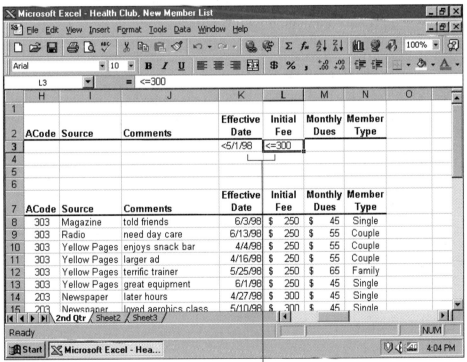

Subsequent filtered
records will match
these criteria

Extracting List Data

Whenever you take the time to specify a complicated set of search criteria, it's a good idea to extract the matching records. That way, you won't accidentally clear the filter or lose track of the records you spent time compiling. When you **extract** data, you place a copy of a filtered list in a range you specify in the Advanced Filter dialog box. ✐━━ Evan needs to filter the previous list one step further to reflect only those members who heard of Nomad Ltd's clubs through the Internet or a magazine ad. To complete this filter, he will specify an Or condition by entering two sets of criteria in two separate rows. He decides to save the matching records by extracting them to a different location in the worksheet.

Steps 1 2 3 4

1. **Click cell I3, type Internet, then press [Enter]; in cell I4, type Magazine, click the Enter button ☑ on the formula bar, then copy the criteria in K3:L3 to K4:L4**
   See Figure I-9. Next, in the Advanced Filter dialog box, you'll indicate that you want to copy the filtered list to a range beginning in cell A50.

2. **Click Data on the menu bar, point to Filter, then click Advanced Filter; under Action, click the Copy to another location option button, click the Copy to box, then type A50**
   The last time you filtered the list, the criteria range only included rows 2 and 3. Now you need to change the criteria range to include row 4.

Trouble?

Make sure the criteria range in the Advanced Filter dialog box includes the field names and the number of rows underneath that contain criteria. If you leave a blank row in the criteria range, Excel filters nothing and shows all records.

3. **Click the Criteria Range box, edit the current formula to read $A$2:$N$4, click OK; then scroll down until row 50 is visible**
   The matching records are copied to the range beginning in cell A50. The original list (starting in cell A7) contains the records filtered in the previous lesson. Now you are ready to select and then print the filtered list.

4. **Select range A50:N55, click File on the menu bar, click Print, under Print what, click the Selection option button, click Preview, then click Print**
   Next, you will re-list the records in the range, save your changes, and then close the file.

5. **Press [Ctrl][Home], click Data on the menu bar, point to Filter, then click Show All**
   You return to the original list.

6. **Save, then close the workbook**

FIGURE I-9: Criteria in separate rows

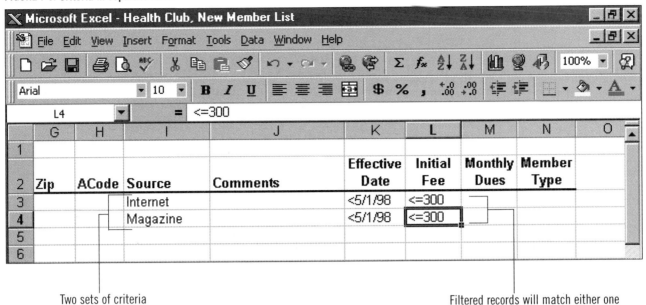

Two sets of criteria

Filtered records will match either one
set of criteria or the other

Understanding the criteria range and the copy-to location

When you define the criteria range and/or copy-to location in the Advanced Filter dialog box, Excel automatically creates names for these ranges in the worksheet (Criteria and Extract). The criteria range includes the field names and any criteria rows underneath. The extract range includes just the field names above the extracted list. To extract a different list, simply select Extract as the copy-to location. Excel will automatically delete the old list in the extract area and generate a new list under the field names. Make sure the worksheet has enough blank rows underneath the field names for your data.

Creating Automatic Subtotals

Excel's subtotals feature provides a quick, easy way to group and summarize data in a list. Usually, you create subtotals with the SUM function. You also can subtotal groups with functions such as COUNT, AVERAGE, MAX, and MIN. Your list must have field names and be sorted before you can issue the Subtotal command. ◤ Evan wants to create a list grouped by advertising source, with subtotals for initial fee and monthly dues. He starts by sorting the list in ascending order—first by advertising source, then by state, and, finally, by city.

Steps

1. **Open the workbook titled XL I-1, then save it as Health Club, New Members List 2**
   You sort the list by selecting the appropriate options in the Sort Dialog box.

2. **Click the Name Box list arrow, click Database, click Data on the menu bar, then click Sort; click the Sort by list arrow, click Source, click the first Then By list arrow, click State, click the Ascending option button to set the Then by sort order; click the second Then By list arrow, click City, then click OK**
   The list is sorted in ascending order, first by advertising source, then by state, and, finally, by city. Before you use the Subtotals command, you must position the cell pointer within the list range (in this case, range A1:N36).

Trouble?

If you receive the following message: "No list found. Select a single cell within your list and Microsoft Excel will select the list for you.", you did not select the list before issuing the Subtotals command. Click OK, then repeat Step 3.

3. **Press [Ctrl][Home], click Data on the menu bar, then click Subtotals**
   The Subtotal dialog box opens. In the At each change in list box, you specify the items you want to be subtotaled while the Use function list box options designate a specific function to apply to the values. Finally, the values to be summarized are indicated in the Add subtotal to list box.

4. **Click the At each change in list arrow, click Source, click the Use function list arrow, click Sum, in the Add subtotal to list, click the Initial Fee and Monthly Dues check boxes to select them; if necessary, click the Member Type check box to deselect it; then, if necessary, click the Replace current subtotals and Summary below data check boxes to select them**
   Your completed Subtotal dialog box should match Figure I-10.

5. **Click OK**
   The subtotaled list appears, showing the calculated subtotals and grand total in columns L and M. See Figure I-11. Notice that Excel displays an outline to the left of the worksheet showing the structure of the subtotaled lists.

6. **Preview and print the worksheet using the current settings**
   Now that you have the subtotals you need, you can turn off the subtotaling feature.

7. **Press [Ctrl][Home], click Data on the menu bar, click Subtotals, then click Remove All**
   The subtotals are removed, and the Outline feature is turned off automatically. Because you did not alter the worksheet data in any way, there's no need to save the file.

Show or hide details in an Excel outline

Once subtotals have been generated, all detail records are displayed in an outline. See Figure I-12. You can then click the Hide Details button ▬ of your choice to hide that group of records. You also can click the Show Details button ➕ for the group of data you want to display. To show a specific level of detail, click the row or column level button for the lowest level you want to display. For example, to display levels 1 through 3, click 3.

FIGURE I-10: Completed Subtotal dialog box

Field to group with

Function to be applied

Subtotal these fields

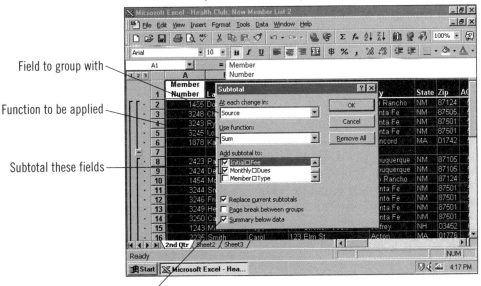

Check to generate grand totals

FIGURE I-11: Portion of subtotaled list

Number 9 indicates
the SUM function

Range to be subtotaled

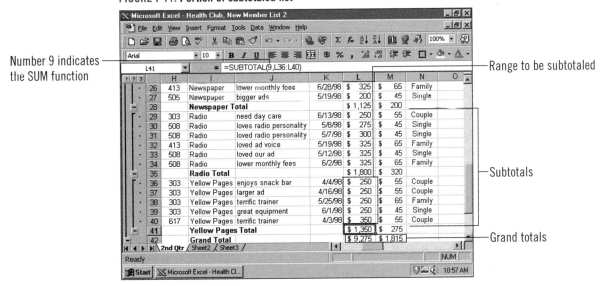

Subtotals

Grand totals

FIGURE I-12: Subtotaled list with level 2 details hidden

Row level symbols

Show details buttons

Hide details button

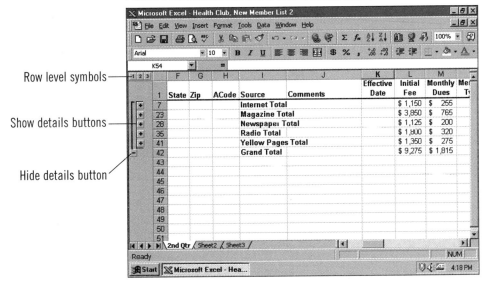

Looking Up Values in a List

Excel's VLOOKUP function helps you locate specific values in a list. The VLOOKUP searches vertically (V) down the leftmost column of a list and then reads across the row to find the value in the column you specify. The process of looking up a number in a phonebook uses the same logic as Excel's VLOOKUP function: you locate a person's name and then read across the row to find the phone number you are looking for. ✐ At times, Evan wants to find out what type of membership a person bought simply by entering his or her specific membership number. To do this, he uses the VLOOKUP function. He begins by creating a special list, or table, containing the membership numbers he wants to look up. Then he copies the related field names to a separate location.

Steps 1 2 3 4

1. Click cell **C2**, click **Window** on the menu bar, then click **Freeze Panes**; scroll right until columns N through T and rows 1 through 15 are visible

2. Click cell **P1**, type **VLOOKUP Function**, click the **Enter button** ☑ on the formula bar; copy the contents of cell A1 to cell R1, then copy the contents of cell N1 to cell S1
   See Figure I-13. Next, you'll enter the first member number.

3. Click cell **R2**, type **3247**, then press [→]
   Next, you will open the Paste Function dialog box and enter a VLOOKUP function that will find the record for member number 3247. This record will then indicate the customer's associated member type.

Trouble?

If the Office Assistant activates for this task, select the "No" option to indicate you don't want to learn more about this function at the present time. Continue with Step 5.

4. Make sure cell S2 is still selected, click the **Paste Function button** ƒₓ on the Standard toolbar, under Function Category click **Lookup & Reference**, under Function name click **VLOOKUP**, then click **OK**
   The VLOOKUP dialog box opens. Since the value you want to find is in cell R2, you'll enter "R2" in the Lookup_value box. The list you want to search is the membership list, so you'll enter its name ("Database") in the Table_array box.

5. Drag the VLOOKUP dialog box down so that at least rows 1 and 2 of the worksheet are visible; with the insertion point in the Lookup_value box, click cell **R2**, click the **Table_array box**, then type **DATABASE**
   The column you want to search (Member Type) is the 14th column from the left, so you'll enter "14" in the Col_index_num box. You want to find an exact match for the value in cell R2, so you'll set the Range_lookup argument to FALSE.

6. Click the **Col_index_num box**, type **14**, click the **Range_lookup box**, then type **FALSE**
   Your completed VLOOKUP dialog box should match Figure I-14.

Trouble?

If an exact match is not returned, make sure the Range_lookup is set to FALSE.

7. Click **OK**
   Excel searches down the leftmost column of the membership list until it finds a value matching the one in cell R2. Then it finds the member type for that record ("Single") and displays it in cell S2. Now, you'll use this function to determine the membership type for one other member.

Time To

↳ Return to the top of the worksheet
↳ Save the workbook

8. Click cell **R2**, type **2125**, then click ☑
   The VLOOKUP function returns the value Family in cell S2.

FIGURE I-13: Worksheet with headings for VLOOKUP

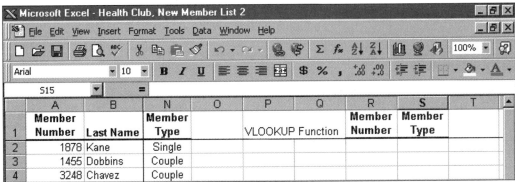

FIGURE I-14: Completed VLOOKUP dialog box

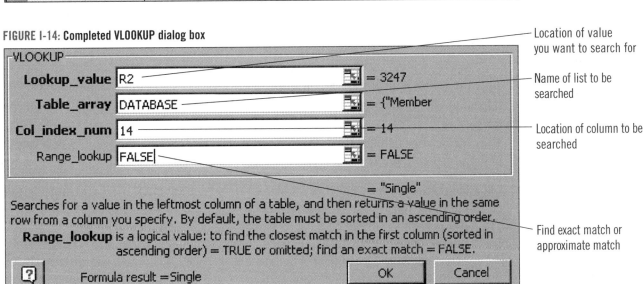

Location of value
you want to search for

Name of list to be
searched

Location of column to be
searched

Find exact match or
approximate match

Using the HLOOKUP Function

The VLOOKUP (Vertical Lookup) function is useful when your data is arranged vertically in columns. The HLOOKUP (Horizontal Lookup) function is useful when your data is arranged horizontally in rows. HLOOKUP searches horizontally across the topmost row of a list until the matching value is found, then looks down the number of rows you specify. The arguments for this function are identical to those for the VLOOKUP function, with one exception. Instead of a Col_index_number, HLOOKUP uses a Row_index_number, which indicates the location of the row you want to search. For example, if you want to search the fourth row from the top, then the Row_index_number would be 4.

ANALYZING LIST DATA   EX I-13

Summarizing List Data

Database functions allow you to summarize list data in a variety of ways. For example, you can use them to count, average, or total values in a field for only those records that meet specified criteria. When working with a sales activity list, for instance, you can use Excel to count the number of client contacts by sales representative or total the amount sold to specific accounts by month. The format for database functions is explained in Figure I-15. ▰▰▰▰ Evan wants to summarize the information in his list in two ways. First, he wants to find the total initial fees for each advertising source. Also, he wants to count the number of records for each advertising source. He begins by creating a criteria range that includes a copy of the column label for the column he wants to summarize, as well as the criteria itself.

Steps 1 2 3 4

1. **With the panes still frozen, scroll down until row 31 is the top row underneath the frozen headings, then enter and format the five labels, shown in Figure I-16, in the range: I39:K41**

   The criteria range in I40:I41 tells Excel to summarize records with the entry "Yellow Pages" in the Source column. You will enter the functions in cells L39 and L41.

QuickTip

You can use a column label, such as "City," in place of a column number. Type the text exactly as it is entered in the list and enclose it in double quotation marks.

2. **Click cell L39, type =DSUM(DATABASE,12,I40:I41), then click the Enter button ☑ on the formula bar**

   The result in cell L39 is 1350.

   For the range named Database, Excel totaled the information in column 12 (Initial Fee) for those records that meet the criteria of Source=Yellow Pages. Next, you'll use the DCOUNTA function to determine the number of nonblank records meeting the criteria Source = Yellow Pages.

Trouble?

If the result you receive is incorrect, make sure you entered the formula correctly, using the letter "I" in the criteria range address, and the number one (1) for the column number.

3. **Click cell L41, type =DCOUNTA(DATABASE,1,I40:I41), then click ☑**

   The result in cell L41 is 5.

   This function uses the first field in the list, Member Number, to check for nonblank cells within the criteria range Source = Yellow Pages. Evan also wants to see total fees and a count for the magazine ads. To do this, he enters "Magazine" in cell I41.

4. **Click cell I41, type Magazine, then click ☑**

   The high value revealed when the criteria was changed to Magazine indicates that magazine advertising does not seem to be the most effective way of generating new memberships for Nomad Ltd's health clubs. Compare your results with Figure I-17.

5. **Press [Ctrl][Home], then save and close the workbook**

FIGURE I-15: Format of a database function

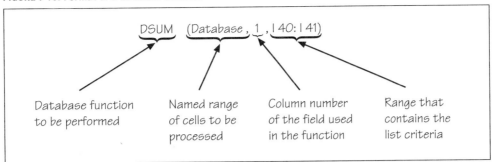

DSUM (Database, 1, I 40: I 41)

Database function   Named range   Column number   Range that
to be performed   of cells to be   of the field used   contains the
                           processed   in the function   list criteria

FIGURE I-16: Portion of worksheet showing summary area

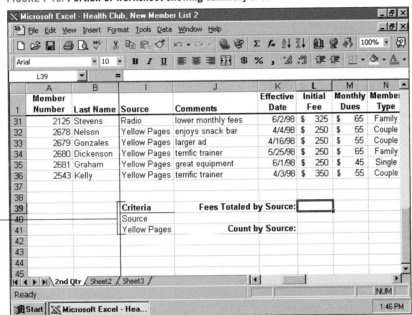

Summary area

FIGURE I-17: Result generated by database function

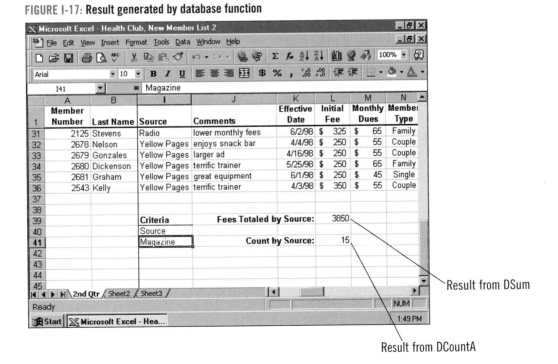

Result from DSum

Result from DCountA

Using Data Validation for List Entries

Excel's Data Validation feature allows you to specify what data is valid for a range of cells. You can restrict data to whole numbers, decimal numbers, or text, or set limits on entries. Also, you can specify a list of acceptable entries. Once you've specified what data is considered valid, Excel prevents users from entering any other data (considered invalid) except your specified choices. ◀━━ Evan wants to make sure that information in the Member Type column is entered consistently in the future. He decides to restrict the entries in that column to three options: Couple, Single, and Family. First, he selects the column he wants to restrict.

Steps 1 2 3 4

1. Open the workbook titled **XL I-1**, then save it as Health Club, New Members List 3

2. Scroll right until column N is displayed, then click the **Column N column header**
   Next, you'll use the Validation command to restrict entries to a brief list of options.

QuickTip

To restrict entries to decimal or whole numbers, dates, or times, select the appropriate option in the Allow list.

3. Click **Data** on the menu bar, click **Validation**, if necessary, click the **Settings tab**, click the **Allow list arrow**, then click **List**
   Selecting "List" enables you to type a list of specific options. Next, you need to enter the list of acceptable entries.

QuickTip

To specify a long list of valid entries, type the list in a column elsewhere in the worksheet, then type the address of the list in the Source box.

4. Click the **Source box**, then type **Couple, Single, Family**
   See Figure I-18. To display a list of valid entries whenever you click a cell in the Member Type column, you need to make sure the In-cell Dropdown check box is selected.

5. If necessary, click the **In-cell Dropdown check box**, then click **OK**
   The dialog box closes, and you return to the worksheet. The new data restrictions will only apply to new entries in the Member Type column. You'll try adding an entry now.

6. Click cell **N37**, then click the **dropdown list arrow** to display the list of valid entries
   See Figure I-19. You could click an item in the list to have it entered in the cell. But first, you'll see what happens if you enter an invalid entry.

7. Click the **dropdown list arrow** to close the list, type **Individual**, then press [Enter]
   A warning dialog box appears to prevent you from entering the invalid data. You'll enter valid data now.

Time To

✔ Save the workbook
✔ Close the workbook
✔ Exit Excel

8. Click **Cancel**, click the **dropdown list arrow**, then click **Family**
   The cell accepts the valid entry. The data restriction ensures that new records will contain the correct entries for the Member Type column. Also, the membership list is finished and ready for future data entry.

FIGURE I-18: Creating data restrictions

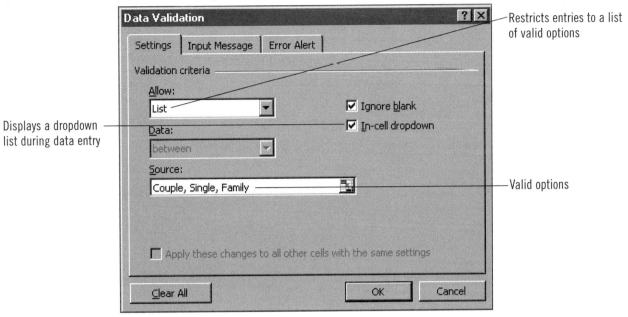

Restricts entries to a list of valid options

Displays a dropdown list during data entry

Valid options

FIGURE I-19: Entering data in restricted cells

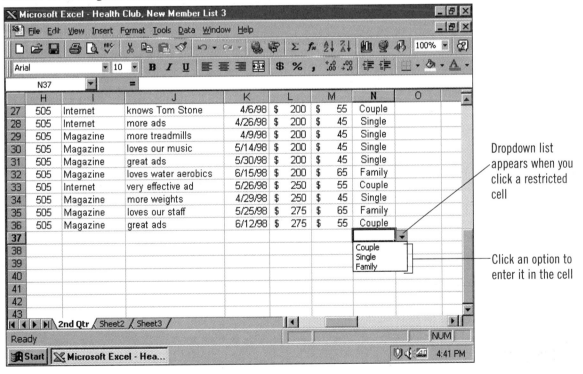

Dropdown list appears when you click a restricted cell

Click an option to enter it in the cell

Practice

► Concepts Review

Label each element of the Excel screen shown in Figure I-20.

FIGURE I-20

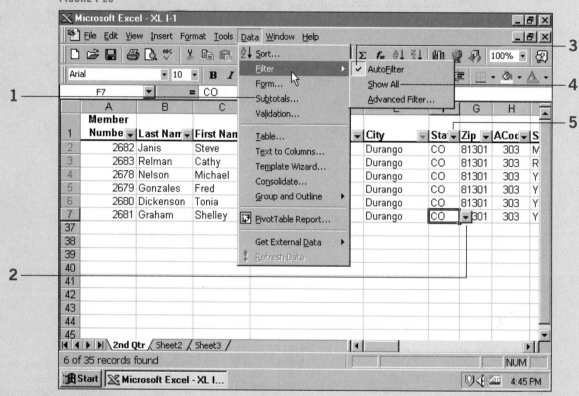

Match each statement with the term it describes.

6. Cell range when advanced filter results are copied to another location
7. Range in which search conditions are set
8. Restricts list entries to specified options
9. Range used to specify a database in database functions
10. Function used to total list values that meet specified criteria

a. DSUM
b. Extracted list
c. Data validation
d. Criteria range
e. List range

Select the best answer from the list of choices.

11. You might perform an AutoFilter and search for nonblank entries in order to
   a. Identify missing data
   b. Find records with data in a particular field
   c. Sum records with data in a particular field
   d. b and c

12. **What does it mean when you select the Or option when creating a custom filter?**
    a. Neither criteria has to be 100% true.
    b. Either criterion can be true to find a match.
    c. Both criteria must be true to find a match.
    d. Custom filter requires a criteria range.

13. **What must a list have before automatic subtotals can be inserted?**
    a. Enough records to show multiple subtotals
    b. Grand totals
    c. Column or field headings
    d. Formatted cells

 ## Skills Review

1. **Retrieve records with AutoFilter.**
    a. Open the workbook titled XL I-2, then save it as "Compensation Summary".
    b. You will use AutoFilter to retrieve records for employees in the Accounting department; then locate the employee in that department with the highest annual salary. Click Data on the menu bar, point to Filter, then click AutoFilter.
    c. Click the Dept. list arrow, then click Accounting.
    d. Click the Annual Salary list arrow, click Top 10, type 1 in the selected box, then click OK.

2. **Create a custom filter.**
    a. You will create a custom filter showing employees hired prior to 1/1/90 or after 1/1/94. Click Data on the menu bar, point to Filter, then click Show All.
    b. Click the Hire Date list arrow, then click Custom.
    c. Click the list arrow under Hire Date, click "is less than," then type 1/1/90 in the box.
    d. Click the Or button.
    e. Click the second list arrow under Hire Date, click "is greater than," type 1/1/94 in the box, then click OK.
    f. Preview, then print the list.
    g. Click the Hire Date list arrow, then click All to redisplay all records.
    h. Click Data on the menu bar, point to Filter, then click AutoFilter to deselect it.

3. **Filter a list with Advanced Filter.**
    a. You will retrieve a list of employees who were hired prior to 1/1/90 and earn over $60,000 a year. Define a criteria range by copying the field names in range A1:J1 to cell A14.
    b. In cell D15, type < 1/1/90, then in cell G15 type >60000.
    c. Press [Ctrl][Home].
    d. Click Data on the menu bar, point to Filter, then click Advanced Filter.
    e. Click the Copy to Another Location button, click the Criteria Range box and select range A14:J15, click the Copy to box, type A18, then click OK.
    f. Scroll so that rows 18 through 20 are visible to confirm that the retrieved list meets the criteria.
    g. Change the page setup to landscape orientation, then select and print the extracted list in range A18:J20.
    h. Select range A14:J20. Click Edit on the menu bar, point to Clear, then click All.

4. Create automatic subtotals.

a. Move to cell A1. Sort the list in ascending order by department, then in descending order by monthly salary.

b. Click Data on the menu bar, then click Subtotals.

c. Click the At each change in list arrow, then select Dept.

d. Click the Use function list arrow, then click Sum if necessary.

e. Click Monthly Salary in the Add Subtotal to list box to select it, click Annual Comp to deselect it, then click OK.

f. AutoFit the width of column E.

g. Preview, then print just the subtotaled list using landscape orientation.

h. Click Data on the menu bar, click Subtotals, then click Remove All.

5. Look up values in a list.

a. Locate annual compensation information by entering a social security number. Scroll so that columns I through Q are visible.

b. In cell N2, type 556-53-7589.

c. In cell O2, type the following function: =VLOOKUP(N2,A2:J11,10,FALSE), then click the Enter button on the formula bar.

d. Enter another social security number, 356-93-2123, in cell N2.

e. Save your worksheet.

6. Summarize list data.

a. Enter a database function to average the annual salaries by department. Use the Marketing department as the initial criteria.

b. Define the criteria area. In cell C14, type "Criteria"; in cell C15, type "Dept." (make sure you type the period); then in cell C16, type "Marketing".

c. In cell E14, type "Average Annual Salary by Department:".

d. In cell H14, type the following database function: =DAVERAGE(Database,7,C15:C16). Click the Enter button on the formula bar.

e. Test the function further by entering the text "Finance" in cell C16. When the criteria is entered, cell H14 should display 53,475 as the result.

f. Save the workbook, then close it.

7. Use data validation for list entries.

a. Open the workbook titled XL I-2 again, then save it as "Compensation Summary 2".

b. Click the Column E column header.

c. Click Data, click Validation, click the Settings tab, click the Allow list arrow, then click List.

d. Type a list in the Source box that restricts the entries to "Accounting", "Finance", and "Marketing". Remember to use a comma between each item in the list.

e. Make sure the In-cell Dropdown box is checked, then close the dialog box.

f. Click cell E12, then select "Finance" in the dropdown list.

g. Click the Column E column header.

h. Click Data, click Validation, click the Settings tab, click the Allow list arrow, then click Whole Number.

i. In the minimum box, type 1000. In the Maximum box type 20000. Close the dialog box.

j. Click cell F12, type 25000, then press [Enter].

k. Click Cancel, then type 19000.

l. Save, then close the workbook. Exit Excel.

▶ Independent Challenges

1. Your neighbor, Phillipe, brought over his wine cellar inventory workbook file on disk and asked you to help him manipulate the data in Excel. Phillipe would like to filter the list to show two subsets: all wines with a 1985 vintage, and Chardonnay wines with a vintage, prior to 1985. Also, he would like to subtotal the list and show the total dollar value by type of wine as well as restrict entries in the Type of Wine column to eight possibilities.

To complete this independent challenge:

1. Open the workbook titled XL I-3, then save it as "Wine Cellar Inventory".
2. Use AutoFilter to generate a list of wines with a 1985 vintage. Preview, then print the list.
3. Use Advanced Filter to extract a list of Chardonnay wines with a vintage prior to 1985. Preview, then print the list.
4. Clear the filter, and insert subtotals for Total $ according to type of wine. (*Hint:* Make sure to sort the list by type of wine prior to creating the subtotals.) Print the subtotaled list. Turn off subtotaling.
5. Beginning in cell H1, type the list of eight wine types in column H. The list should include: Cabernet, Champagne, Chardonnay, Muscat, Pinot Noir, Riesling, Sauvignon Blanc, and Zinfandel.
6. Open the Data Validation dialog box, then click List in the Allow box. Enter the range address for the list of wine types in the source box. Make sure the In-cell Dropdown check box is selected. Close the dialog box.
7. Use your Web browser to go to the Vintage Village Web page. If you have trouble finding the page, go to http://www.course.com. From there, click Student Online Companions, click the link for this textbook, then click the Excel link for Unit I. Search the Wine List for three new wines (of the accepted types) to add to the database. Use the dropdown list arrow to enter data in the Wine Type column.
8. Save, then close the workbook.

2. Your neighbor, Phillipe, was thrilled when you delivered his filtered and subtotaled wine inventory list. After viewing your printouts, he asks you to help him with a few more tasks. He wants the list to be sorted by wine label. In addition, he wants to be able to type in the vintage year (starting with 1985) and get a total bottle count and average cost per bottle for that vintage. (*Hint:* You need to define a criteria area outside the list to contain the two database functions.) Finally, Phillipe wants you to provide him some form of documentation on how to accomplish the summaries.

To complete this independent challenge:

1. Open the workbook titled XL I-3, then save it as "Wine Cellar Inventory 2".
2. Sort the list alphabetically by wine label.
3. Define an area either above or below the list with the label "Criteria". Add appropriate column labels and criteria. Use 1985 as the vintage year for the criteria.
4. Near the criteria area, type labels for the two database functions.
5. Enter the database functions to find total bottle count and average price per bottle for a particular vintage.
6. Save your work. Preview and then print the list. Display the worksheet formulas, then preview and print the criteria area. Hide the formulas again.
7. Create a separate worksheet that documents the functions you used. Format the two cells containing the database functions as text by adding leading apostrophes. Widen any columns as necessary. Print a second copy of the list with the two database functions. Change the page setup so that the gridlines and row and column headings are printed.
8. Save, then close the workbook.

3. A few months ago, you started your own business, called Books 4 You. You create and sell personalized books for special occasions. You bought a distributorship from an already-established book company and the rights to use several of the company's titles. Using your personal computer, specialized software, and preprinted book pages, you create personalized books on your laser printer. All you need from a customer is the name of the book's "star," his or her special date, if appropriate (i.e., birth or anniversary date), and the desired book title. Using the software, you enter the data and generate book pages, which you later bind together. After several months of struggling, you are starting to make a profit. You decided to put together an invoice list to track sales, starting in October. Now that you have this list, you would like to manipulate it in several ways. First, you want to filter the list to retrieve only children's books ordered in the first half of the month (prior to 10/16). Next, you want to subtotal the unit price, sales tax, and total cost columns by book title. Finally, you want to restrict entries in the Order Date column.

To complete this independent challenge:

1. Open the workbook titled XL I-4, then save it as "Books 4 You, Invoice Database".
2. Filter the list to show children's books ordered prior to 10/16/98. Print the filtered list on a single page with gridlines and row and column headings. Clear the filter, then save your work.
3. Create subtotals in the unit price, sales tax, and total cost columns by book title. Print the subtotaled list on a single page without gridlines, row, or column headings. Clear the subtotals.
4. Use the Data Validation dialog box to restrict entries to those with order dates between 12/31/97 and 1/1/99. Select "Date" in the Allow list, then enter the appropriate dates in the Start Date and End Date boxes. Test the data restrictions by attempting to enter an invalid date.
5. Save, then close the workbook.

4. You are pleased with the ease with which you are able to manipulate the invoice list data for your new company, Books 4 You. You decide to attempt further list manipulation. As your list grows, it will be more difficult to find specific records. Therefore, you want to be able to retrieve a book title and order date by entering only a customer's invoice number. Also, you would like to access the list to determine how many of the different birthday books are selling, during any given month, starting with October. You decide to place these functions to the right of the list because you will be adding more records below the existing ones.

To complete this independent challenge:

1. Open the workbook titled XL1-4, then save it as "Books 4 You, Lookup".
2. Enter a VLOOKUP function to retrieve a customer's book title, based on that invoice number. Enter a second VLOOKUP function to look up the order date. Format the cell displaying the date in a date format, then save your work.
3. Below the VLOOKUP area, and to the right of the invoice list, define an area in which to count the number of birthday books ordered in any given month, starting with October. (*Hint:* You can use wildcards in your criteria; for example, you can use Birthday* to find the birthday books.) Save your work.
4. Print the list on a single page, if possible.
5. Provide documentation for any functions used. Then print the worksheet functions with gridlines and row and column headings on a single page, if possible.
6. Save, then close the workbook.

Visual Workshop

Create the worksheet shown in Figure I-21. Save the workbook as "Commission Lookup" to your Student Disk. (*Hints:* The formula in cell D5 accesses the commission from the table. Calculate the commission by multiplying the amount of sale by the commission value. If an exact amount for the amount of sale does not exist, the next highest or lowest dollar value is used.) Preview, then print the worksheet.

FIGURE I-21

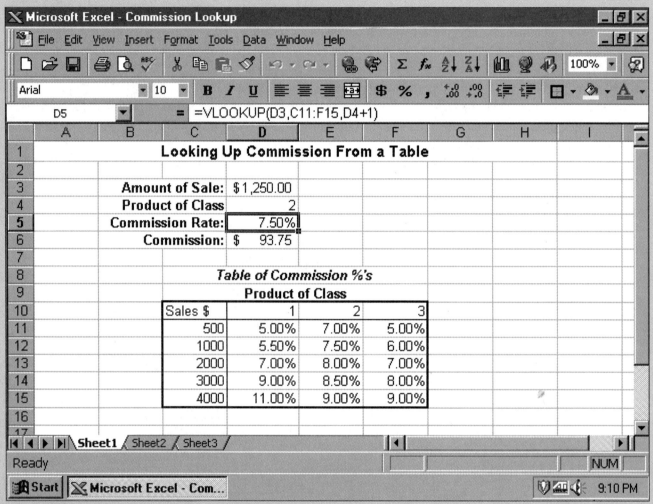

Enhancing
Charts and Worksheets

Objectives

► **Select a custom chart type**
► **Customize a data series**
► **Format a chart axis**
► **Add a data table to a chart**
► **Rotate a chart**
► **Enhance a chart with WordArt**
► **Rotate text**
► **Map data**

There are many ways to revise a chart or a worksheet to present its data with greater impact. In this unit, you enhance both charts and worksheets by selecting a custom chart type, customizing a data series, formatting axes, adding a data table, and rotating a chart. You also add special text effects and rotate text. Finally, you increase the impact of geographical data by plotting it on a map. Keep in mind that your goal in enhancing charts or worksheets is to increase the effectiveness of the data. Avoid excessive customization, which can be visually distracting.

Nomad Ltd's health division markets a line of health food products. Evan's manager, Megan Grahs, asks him to produce two charts showing the sales of these products in the first two quarters. She encourages Evan to enhance the charts and the worksheet data to improve their appearance and make the data more accessible. Finally, she asks Evan to create a map illustrating the sales by state of one product.

Selecting a Custom Chart Type

Excel's Chart Wizard offers a choice between standard and custom chart types. With a **standard chart type**, you need to add the formatting and any options you want to appear in your chart. A **custom chart type**, in contrast, is already formatted and contains numerous options, such as a legend, gridlines, data labels, colors, and patterns. When you need to control exactly which elements to include in your chart, start with a standard chart type. Custom chart types, however, save you time and produce better-looking charts. ◢━━━ Evan's first task is to create a chart showing the number of cases sold for each health food product for the first quarter. To save time, he decides to use a custom type for this chart.

Steps 1 2 3 4

1. **Open the workbook titled XL J-1, then save it as Health Food Products**
   The first step is to select the data you want to appear in the chart. In this case, you want the row labels in cells A6:A10, and the data for January and February in cells B5:C10.

2. **Select the range A5:C10**
   Next, open the Chart Wizard, where you'll specify a Custom chart type.

3. **Click the Chart Wizard button 📖 on the Standard toolbar, click the Custom Types tab in the First Chart Wizard dialog box, then under Select from, click the Built-in option button to select it if necessary**
   See Figure J-1. When the built-in option button in the Custom Types tab is selected, all of Excel's custom chart types are displayed in the Chart type box, and a sample of the default chart appears in the Sample box. Once you make a selection in the Chart type box, the default chart disappears and a preview of the selected chart type appears in the Sample box. Select a chart type now.

4. **Click Columns with Depth in the Chart type box**
   A preview of the chart appears in the Sample box. Notice that this custom chart type, with its 3-D bars and white background, has a more elegant appearance than the default column chart shown in Figure J-1. Unlike the previous default chart, this chart doesn't have gridlines, and the column labels are formatted for readability. Now, you'll finish creating the chart, inserting it below the worksheet data.

5. **Click Next**

6. **Make sure ='TotalSales'!A$5:$C$10 appears as the data range in the Data range box in the second Chart Wizard dialog box, then click Next**

7. **In the third Chart Wizard dialog box, click Next; if necessary, click the As object option in option button in the fourth Chart Wizard dialog box to select it; then click Finish**
   The completed chart appears, covering part of the worksheet data, along with the Chart toolbar. The Chart toolbar can appear anywhere within the worksheet window. As you complete the following steps, you may need to drag the toolbar to a new location. Finally, you move the chart and enlarge it to make it easier to read.

Trouble?

Remember to drag the Chart toolbar out of the way if it blocks your view of the chart.

8. **Scroll down the worksheet until rows 13 through 28 are visible, click the chart border and drag the chart left and down until its upper-left corner is in cell A13, drag the middle right sizing handle right to the border between Column H and Column I, then drag the bottom middle sizing handle down to the border between rows 25 and 26**
   The new chart fills the range A13:H25, as shown in Figure J-2.

9. **Save the workbook**

FIGURE J-1: **Custom Types tab settings**

Displays Excel's chart types

Custom Types tab

Custom chart types

Default chart

Default chart has only basic formatting

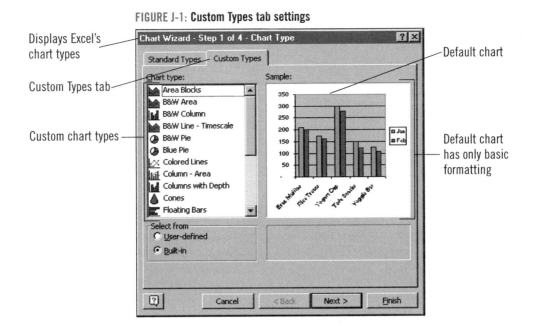

FIGURE J-2: **New chart**

Chart fills range A13:H25

Chart toolbar

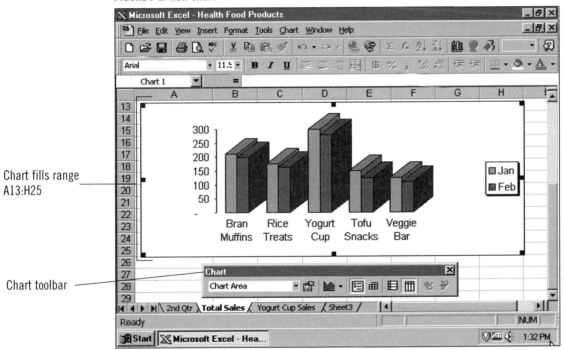

CLUES TO USE

Creating a Custom Chart type

You can create your own custom chart type by starting with a standard chart and then adding elements (such as a legend, color or gridlines) that suit your needs. After you've finished creating the chart, click it to activate the Chart menu, click Chart Type, click the Custom Types tab, then click User-defined. Click Add, then type a name for your chart type in the Name box. To use your custom type when creating additional charts, open the Chart Wizard dialog box, then click the User-defined button in the Custom Types tab.

Customizing a Data Series

A **data series** is the information, usually numbers or values, that Excel plots on a chart. You can customize the data series in a chart easily by altering the spreadsheet range that contains the chart data *or* by entering descriptive text, called a **data label**, that appears above a data marker in a chart. As with other Excel elements, you can change the borders, patterns, or colors of a data series. Evan notices that he omitted the data for March when he created his first-quarter sales chart. He needs to add this information to make the chart accurately reflect the entire first-quarter sales. Also, he wants to customize the updated chart by adding data labels to one of the data series to make it more detailed. Then he'll change the color of another data series so its respective column figures will stand out more. He starts by adding the March data.

1. **Click the chart to select it, scroll up until row 5 is the top row in the worksheet area, select the range D5:D10, position the pointer over the lower border of cell D10 until it changes to ⬚, drag the selected range anywhere within the chart area, then scroll down the worksheet until the entire chart is in view**
   The chart now includes data for the entire first quarter: January, February, and March. Next, you will add data labels to the March data series. The first step is to use the Chart toolbar to select the item you want to format.

2. **Click the Chart Objects list arrow in the Chart toolbar, then click Series "Mar"**
   See Figure J-3. Selection handles appear on each of the columns representing the data for March. Now that the data series is selected, you can format it by adding labels.

QuickTip

If you have difficulty identifying the Chart Objects list arrow, rest your pointer on the first list arrow to the left on the Chart toolbar until the name "Chart Objects" appears.

3. **Click the Format Object button 🖼 on the Chart toolbar, then click the Data Labels tab in the Format Data Series dialog box**
   The Data Labels tab opens. You want the value to appear on top of each selected data marker.

4. **Under Data labels, click the Show value option button, then click OK**
   The data labels appear on the data markers, as shown in Figure J-4. Although these data labels appear distorted on the screen, they will be more distinct when they are printed. Next, you change the color of the February data series so that it will stand out more.

5. **Click the Chart Object list arrow on the Chart toolbar, click Series "Feb", click 🖼, then click the Patterns tab in the Format Data Series dialog box**
   The Patterns tab opens. See Figure J-5. The maroon color in the Sample box matches the current color displayed in the chart for the February data series. You decide that the series would show up better in a brighter shade of red.

QuickTip

You also can click outside the chart to deselect it.

6. **Under Area, click the red box (third row, first color from the left), click OK, press [Esc] to deselect the data series, press [Esc] again to deselect the entire chart, then save the workbook**
   The February data series now appears in a more noticeable shade of red.

FIGURE J-3: Selected data series

Columns represent data for March

Selection handles

Format Object button

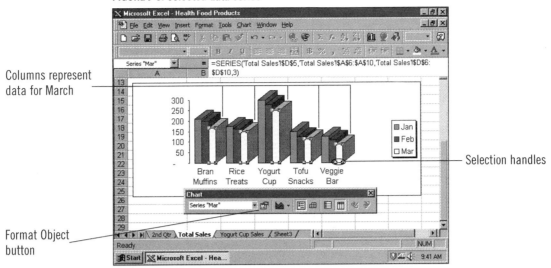

FIGURE J-4: Chart with data labels

Data labels

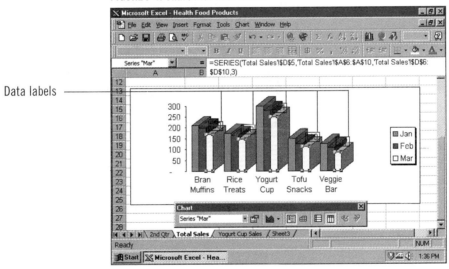

FIGURE J-5: Patterns tab settings

Bright red color choice

Current color of February data series

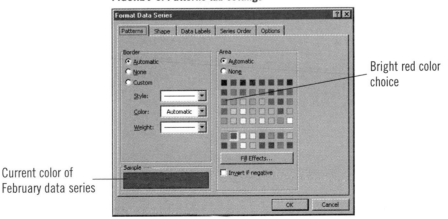

CLUES TO USE

Removing, inserting, and formatting legends

To insert or remove a legend, click the Legend button ▣ on the Chart toolbar to toggle the legend on or off. To format legend text, click Legend in the Chart Objects list box of the Chart Toolbar. Then click the Format Object button on the Chart toolbar, and choose the options you want in the Font tab.

Formatting a Chart Axis

Excel automatically plots and formats all chart data and places chart axes within the chart's **plot area.** As Figure J-6 shows, data values in two-dimensional charts are plotted on the value (*y*) axis and categories are plotted on the category (*x*) axis. Excel creates a scale for the value (*y*) axis that is based on the highest and lowest values in the data series. Then Excel determines the intervals in which the values occur along the scale. In three-dimensional charts, Excel generates three axes, with the third axis—the value (*z*) axis—usually containing the scale. For a list of the axes Excel uses to plot data, see Table J-1. You can override Excel's default formats for chart axes at any time by using the Format Axis dialog box. Because the highest column is so close to the top of the chart, Evan wants to increase the maximum number on the value axis, which in this case, is the *y*-axis, and change its number format. To begin, he selects the object he wants to format.

Steps

1. **Click the chart, click the Chart Objects list arrow on the Chart toolbar, then click Value Axis**
   Now that the *y*-axis is selected, you can format it.

2. **Click the Format Object button on the Chart toolbar, then click the Scale tab**
   The Scale tab of the Format Axis dialog box opens. The check marks under Auto indicate the default scale settings. You can override any of these settings by entering a new value.

3. **In the Maximum box select 300, type 400, then click OK**
   The chart adjusts so that 400 appears as the maximum value on the value axis. Additionally, Excel automatically revises the scale so that tick marks appear at 100-point intervals. Next, you want the minimum value to appear as a zero (0) and not as a hyphen (-).

4. **With the Value Axis still selected in the Format Object box, click on the Chart toolbar, then click the Number tab**
   The Number tab of the Format Axis dialog box opens. Currently, a custom format is selected under Category, which instructs Excel to use a hyphen instead of 0 as the lowest value.

5. **Under Category click General, click OK, press [Esc] twice, then save the workbook**
   The chart now shows 0 as the minimum value, as shown in Figure J-7.

TABLE J-1: Axes used by Excel for chart formatting

axes in a two-dimensional chart	axes in a three-dimensional chart
Category (*x*) axis (horizontal)	Category (*x*) axis (horizontal)
Value (*y*) axis (vertical)	Series (*y*) axis (depth)
	Value (*z*) axis (vertical)

FIGURE J-6: Chart elements

Tick marks

Maximum value

Value (y) axis with scale

Minimum value

Plot area

Category (x) axis

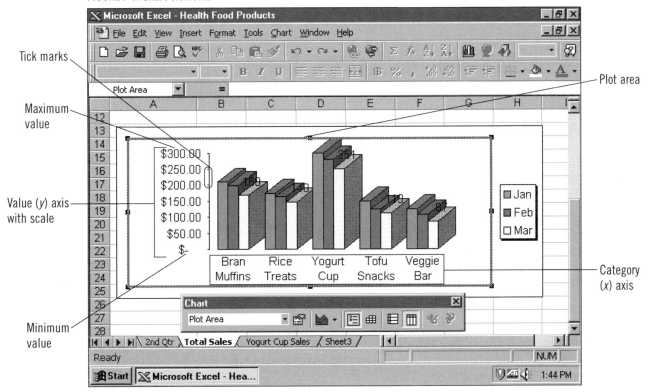

FIGURE J-7: Chart with formatted axis

New maximum value

New interval between points

New minimum value

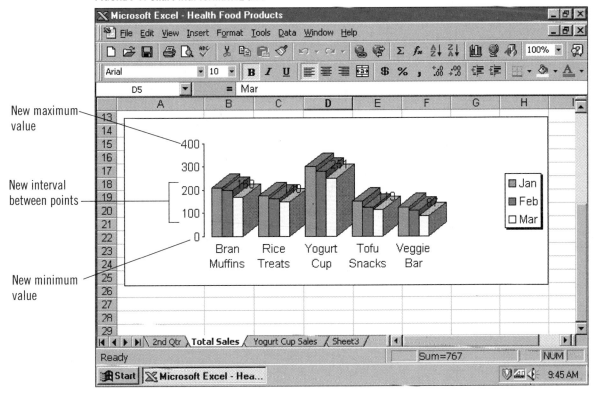

Excel 97

Adding a Data Table to a Chart

A **data table**, attached to the bottom of a chart, is a grid containing the chart data. Data tables are useful because they highlight the data used to generate a chart, which might otherwise be difficult to find. Data tables can be displayed in line, area, column, and bar charts, and print automatically along with a chart. It's good practice to add data tables on chart sheets to charts stored separately from worksheet data. ➤ Evan wants to emphasize the first-quarter data used to generate his chart. He decides to add a data table.

1. Click the **chart** to select it, click **Chart** on the menu bar, click **Chart Options**, then click the **Data Table tab**
The Data Table tab of the Chart Options dialog box opens, as shown in Figure J-8. The preview window displays the selected chart.

> **QuickTip**
> You also do this when creating a chart in the third Chart Wizard dialog box.

2. Click the **Show data table check box** to select it
The chart in the preview window changes to show what the chart will look like with a data table added to the bottom. See Figure J-9. The data table crowds the chart labels, making them hard to read. You'll fix this problem after you close the Chart Options dialog box.

> **QuickTip**
> To hide a data table, open the Data Table tab in the Chart Options dialog box, then clear the Show data table check box.

3. Click **OK**, then, if necessary, scroll down to display the chart
The chart and the newly added data table look too crowded inside the current chart area. If you were to drag the chart borders to enlarge the chart, you wouldn't be able to see the entire chart displayed on the screen. It's more convenient to move the chart to its own sheet.

4. If necessary, click the **chart** to select it, click **Chart** on the menu bar, click **Location**, click the **As new sheet option button** under Place chart, then click **OK**
The chart is now located on a new sheet, where it is fully displayed in the worksheet window. See Figure J-10.

5. Print the chart sheet, then save the workbook

FIGURE J-8: Data Table tab settings

Click to add a
data table

Click the Data Table tab

Preview window

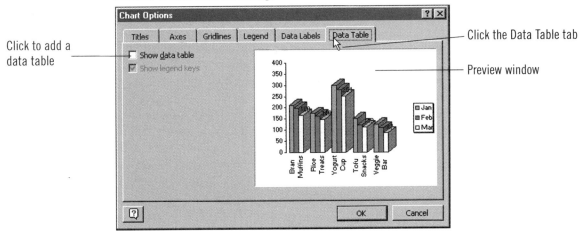

FIGURE J-9: Show Data Table box selected

Chart labels are
hard to read

Data table

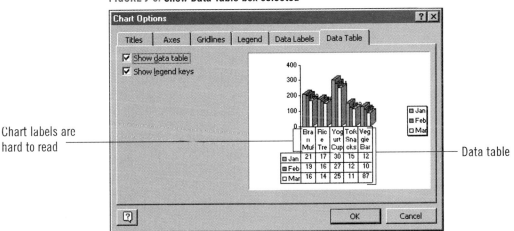

FIGURE J-10: Chart moved to chart sheet

Entire chart visible
in window

Data table

New sheet tab

Labels fully
displayed

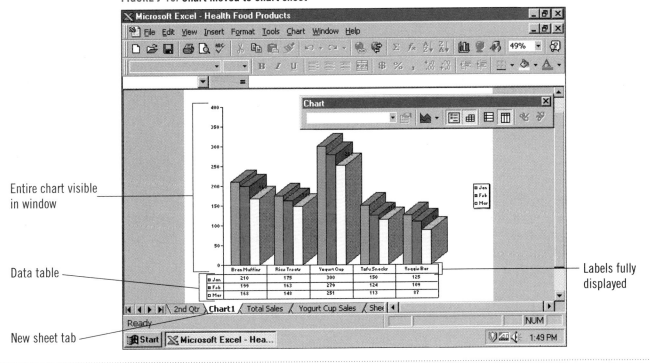

Excel 97

Rotating a Chart

Three-dimensional (3-D) charts do not always display data in the most effective way. In many cases, data in these charts can be obscured by one or more of the chart's data markers. By rotating and/or elevating the axes, you can improve the visibility of the chart's data. With Excel, you can adjust the rotation and elevation of a 3-D chart by dragging it with the mouse or using the 3-D View command on the Chart menu. For a detailed explanation of the options in the Format 3-D View dialog box, look up "Rotating 3-D charts" in Excel's Help index. Evan's workbook already contains a 3-D chart illustrating the sales data for the second quarter. He will activate that chart, then rotate it so that the June columns are easier to see.

1. **Click the 2nd Qtr sheet tab, click the Chart Object list arrow on the Chart toolbar, then click Corners**
   Selection handles appear on the corners of the chart, as shown in Figure J-11. Now, you'll rotate the chart by dragging the lower-right corner handle.

2. **Click the lower-right corner handle of the chart, press and hold the left mouse button, then drag the chart left approximately 2" until it looks like the object shown in Figure J-12, then release the mouse button**
   The June columns are still not clearly visible. When using the dragging method to rotate a three-dimensional chart, you might need to make several attempts before you're satisfied with the view. It's usually more efficient to use the 3-D View option on the Chart menu.

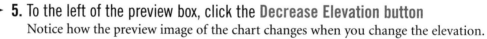

Trouble?

Don't worry if your 3-D View dialog box settings are different from the ones shown in Figure J-13.

3. **Click Chart on the menu bar, click 3-D View, then drag the 3-D View dialog box to the upper-right corner of the screen**
   See Figure J-13. The preview box in the 3-D View dialog box allows you to preview changes to the chart's orientation in the worksheet. To begin adjusting the chart's position, you first reset the chart defaults.

4. **Click Default**
   The chart returns to its original position. Next, Evan decreases the chart's elevation, the height from which the chart is viewed.

Trouble?

If you have difficulty locating the Decrease elevation button, refer to Figure J-13.

5. **To the left of the preview box, click the Decrease Elevation button**
   Notice how the preview image of the chart changes when you change the elevation.

6. **Click Apply**
   With an elevation of 10, the viewpoint shifts downward, and the chart gains some vertical tick marks. Next, you'll change the rotation and **perspective**, or depth, of the chart.

7. **In the Rotation box, select the current value, then type 55; in the Perspective box, select the current value, type 0, then click Apply**
   The chart is reformatted, and all of the columns are visible. You notice, however, that the columns appear crowded. To correct this problem, you change the height as a percent of the chart base.

Time To

✔ Save the workbook

8. **In the Height box, select the current value, type 70, click Apply, then click OK**
   The 3-D dialog box closes. The chart columns now appear less crowded, making the chart easier to read.

FIGURE J-11: **Chart corners selected**

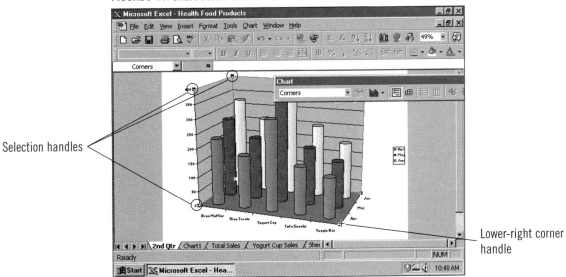

Selection handles

Lower-right corner handle

FIGURE J-12: **Chart rotation in progress**

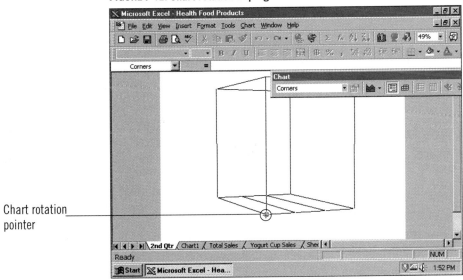

Chart rotation pointer

FIGURE J-13: **Screen with chart and 3-D View dialog box**

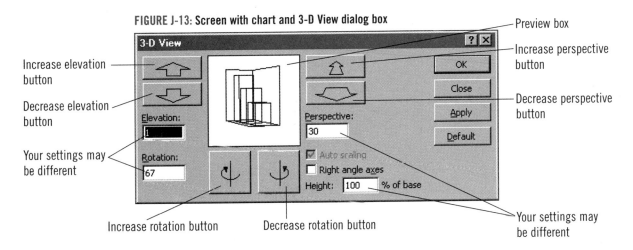

Increase elevation button

Decrease elevation button

Your settings may be different

Increase rotation button

Decrease rotation button

Preview box

Increase perspective button

Decrease perspective button

Your settings may be different

Enhancing a Chart with WordArt

You can enhance your chart or worksheet by adding specially formatted text using the WordArt tool on the Drawing toolbar. Once you've added a piece of WordArt to your workbook, you can edit or format it using the tools on the WordArt toolbar. Text formatted as WordArt is considered a drawing object, rather than text. This means that WordArt objects cannot be treated as if they were labels entered in a cell; that is, you cannot sort, spell-check, or use their cell references in formulas. Evan decides to add a WordArt title to the second-quarter chart. He begins by displaying the Drawing toolbar.

1. **Click the Drawing button** 🔏 **on the Standard toolbar**
   The Drawing toolbar appears at the bottom of the Excel window. Now, you can create the WordArt text, which will be your chart title.

2. **Click the Insert WordArt button** 🔏 **on the Drawing toolbar**
   The WordArt Gallery dialog box opens. This is where you select the style for your text.

3. **In the second row, click the second style from the left**, as shown Figure J-14; then **click OK**
   The Edit WordArt Text dialog box opens, as shown in Figure J-15. This is where you enter the text you want to format as WordArt. You also can adjust the point size or font of the text or select bold or italic styles.

4. **Type 2nd Quarter Sales, click the Bold button** **B** , **if necessary, select Times New Roman in the Font list box and 36 in the Size list box, then click OK**
   The Edit Word Art Text dialog box closes, and the chart reappears with the new title in the middle of the chart. You'll drag this title to a better location.

5. **Place the pointer over 2nd Quarter Sales (the WordArt title) until the pointer changes to** ⤬ **, then drag 2nd Quarter Sales up until it appears centered over the top of the chart**
   The title is repositioned as shown in Figure J-16. Next, you decide to edit the WordArt to change "2nd" to the word "Second." To do this, you'll use the Edit Text button on the WordArt toolbar.

6. **Click the Edit Text button on the WordArt toolbar, in the Edit WordArt Text box double-click 2nd, type Second, then click OK**
   The Edit WordArt Text dialog box closes, and the edited title appears over the chart. The chart is finished, so you can close the Drawing toolbar, save your work, and print it.

7. **Press [Esc] to deselect the WordArt, click** 🔏 **, print the chart sheet, then save the workbook**

QuickTip

To delete a piece of WordArt, click it to make sure it is selected, then press [Delete].

QuickTip

To change the style of a piece of WordArt, click the WordArt Gallery button on the WordArt toolbar and select a new style in the WordArt Gallery.

FIGURE J-14: Selecting a WordArt style

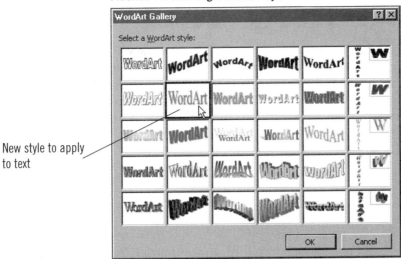

New style to apply
to text

FIGURE J-15: Entering the WordArt text

Default font for this
style

Replace with your
text

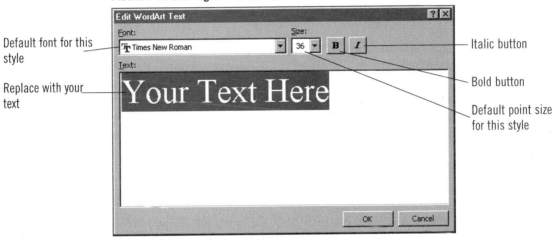

Italic button

Bold button

Default point size
for this style

FIGURE J-16: Positioning the WordArt

New location
for title

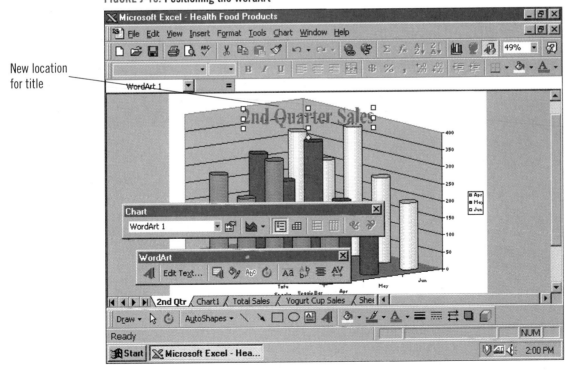

Rotating Text

By rotating text within a worksheet cell, you can draw attention to column labels or titles, without turning the text into a drawing object (as in WordArt). Unlike WordArt, rotated text retains its usefulness as a worksheet entry, which means you can still sort it, spell-check it, and use its cell reference in formulas. ◀━━ Now that he's finished enhancing the two charts in his workbook, Evan wants to improve the worksheet's appearance. He decides to rotate the column labels in cells B5 through G5.

Steps

1. **Click the Total Sales sheet tab, then scroll down until row 5 is the top row in the worksheet area, then select cells B5:G5**
   Now that you've selected the cells you want to format, open the Format Cells dialog box, where you'll rotate the text entries.

2. **Click Format on the menu bar, click Cells, then click the Alignment tab**
   The Alignment tab of the Format Cells dialog box opens. See Figure J-17. The settings under Orientation enable you to change the rotation of cell entries. Clicking the Vertical Text box on the left (the narrow one) allows you to display text vertically in the cell. To rotate the text to another angle, drag the rotation indicator in the Right Text box to the angle you want, or type the degree of angle you want in the Degrees box. You'll use the Degrees box to rotate the text entries.

3. **Double-click the Degrees box, type 45, then click OK**
   The Format Cells dialog box closes. Next, you deselect the column labels.

4. **If necessary, scroll up until row 1 is the top row in the worksheet area, then click cell A1**
   The column labels for January through June now appear at a 45-degree angle in their cells, as shown in Figure J-18. The worksheet is now finished, so you save and print it.

5. **Save, then print the worksheet**

FIGURE J-17: Alignment tab settings

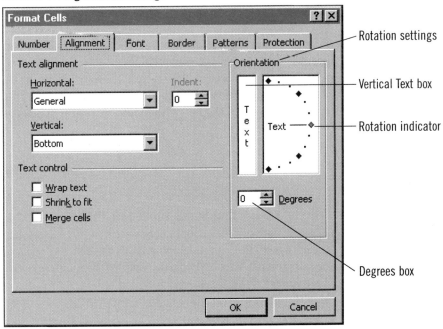

FIGURE J-18: Rotated column labels

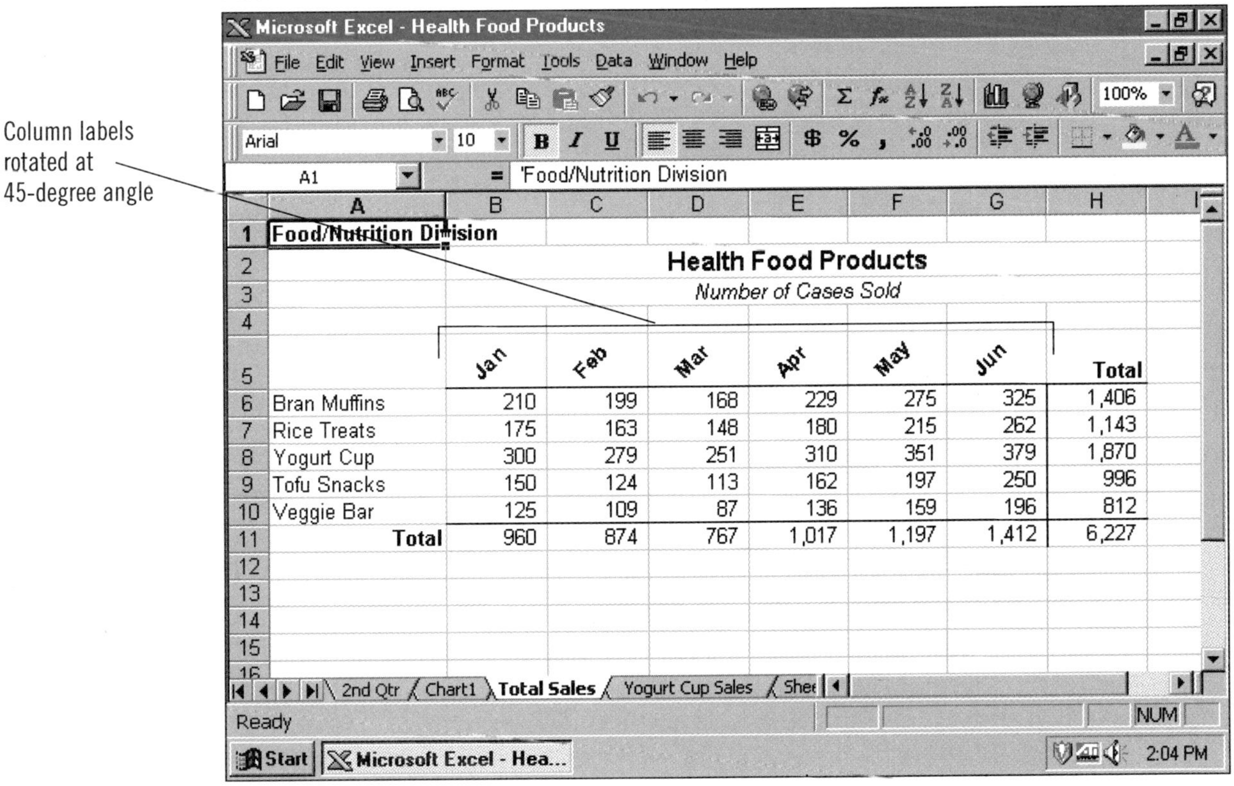

Column labels rotated at 45-degree angle

Rotating Chart Labels

You can easily rotate the category labels on a chart by using the buttons on the Chart toolbar. First, you select the Category Axis in the Chart Objects list box.

Then you click either the Angle Text Downward button or the Angle Text Upward button on the Chart toolbar.

ENHANCING CHARTS AND WORKSHEETS EX J-15 ◄

Excel 97

Mapping Data

A **data map** shows geographic features and their associated data. To create a simple data map, arrange your worksheet data in two columns—the first containing geographic data, such as the names of countries or states, and the second column containing the related data. 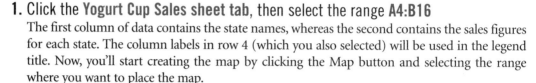 Evan has compiled detailed sales figures for Yogurt Cups by state. Now, he wants to create a map that clearly illustrates which states have the highest sales. He begins by selecting the data he wants to map.

Steps

1. **Click the Yogurt Cup Sales sheet tab, then select the range A4:B16**
   The first column of data contains the state names, whereas the second contains the sales figures for each state. The column labels in row 4 (which you also selected) will be used in the legend title. Now, you'll start creating the map by clicking the Map button and selecting the range where you want to place the map.

2. **Click the Map button 🌐 on the Standard toolbar, drag the pointer from the middle of cell C4 to the lower-right corner of cell H23, then release the mouse button**
   The map range is outlined on the worksheet, and the Multiple Maps Available dialog box opens on top. Now, you'll choose the most appropriate map.

3. **Click United States (AK & HI Inset), then click OK**
   The map and the Microsoft Map Control dialog boxes appear.

4. **Drag the Microsoft Map Control dialog box to the lower-left corner of the screen, then scroll up until the entire map is visible in your screen**
   See Figure J-19. Excel automatically divides the sales data into intervals and assigns a different shade of gray to each interval, as the map legend indicates. The rectangular border indicates that the map is in Edit mode. Next, you need to add a more appropriate title.

5. **Double-click the United States (AK & HI Inset) map title, drag the pointer to select the default text, type Yogurt Cup Sales, then press [Enter]**
   The new title replaces the default map title. Next, to highlight the sales data more dramatically, you'll change the way values are represented using the Microsoft Map Control dialog box, shown in Figure J-20. You adjust the way data is represented on the map by dragging format buttons into the Format box. You want to change the format from shading to dots of varying density.

6. **Click the Dot Density button ▨, then drag it over the top of the Value Shading button in the Format box**
   When you release the mouse button, the map display changes from shading to dots, with one dot equal to seven cases of yogurt cups.

7. **Click Map on the Menu bar, click Features, under Fill Color click the Custom option button, click the Custom list arrow, click the turquoise square, then click OK**
   The map's background color changes to turquoise, as shown in Figure J-21. Finally, you'll change the legend title to something more descriptive.

8. **Double-click the map legend; if necessary, in the Format Properties dialog box click the Legend Options tab; select the default text in the Title box, type 1st and 2nd Quarter, then click OK**
   The map is finished, so you can save the workbook and print the Yogurt Cup Sales sheet.

9. **Press [ESC] three times to deselect the map, print the worksheet, save the workbook, and exit Excel**

Trouble?

If you don't see the Map button on the Standard toolbar, then the Map feature for Excel is not installed on your computer. See your instructor or technical support person for assistance.

QuickTip

Click the Map Refresh button 🗺 to incorporate any changes to the data range into an existing map.

Trouble?

If your map doesn't print, your printer may not have enough memory. Try using another printer.

FIGURE J-19: Newly created map

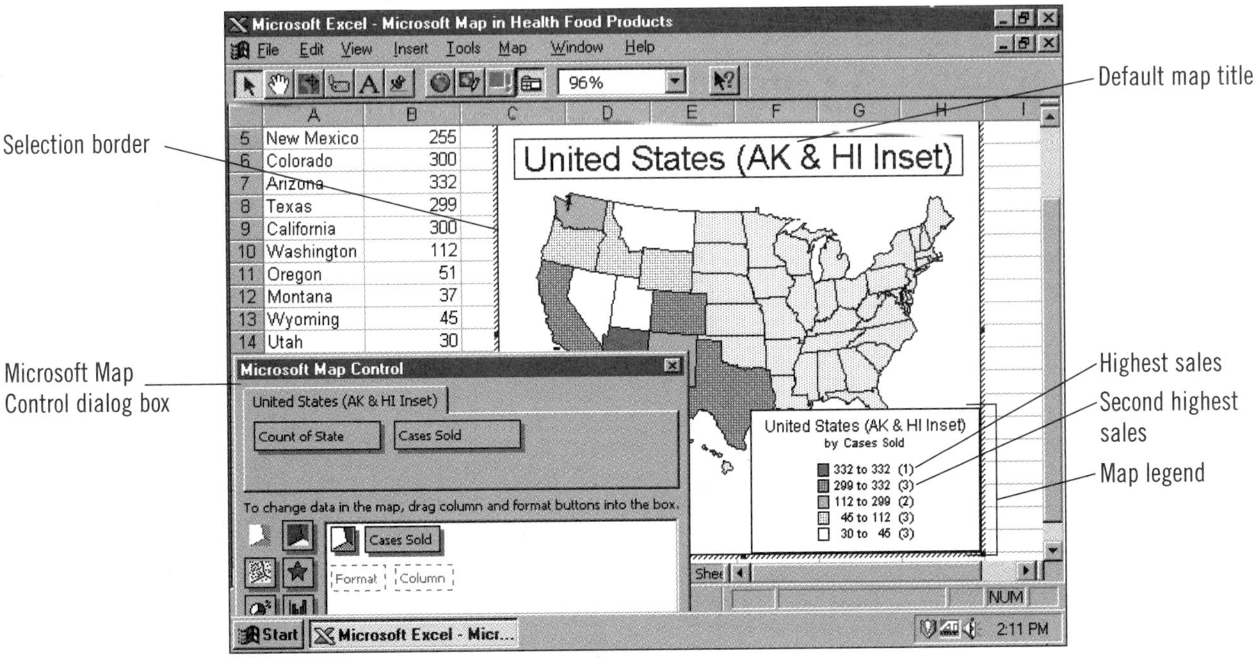

Selection border

Microsoft Map Control dialog box

Default map title

Highest sales

Second highest sales

Map legend

FIGURE J-20: Microsoft Map Control dialog box

Value Shading button

Dot Density button

Format buttons

Columns in data range

Format box

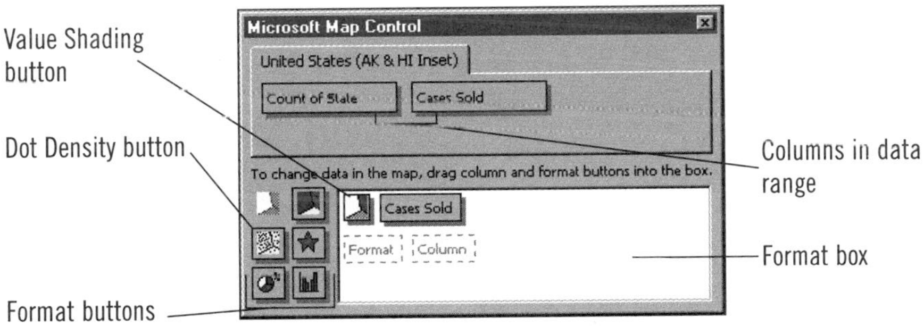

FIGURE J-21: Values formatted as dots

Dot Density button replaces Value Shading button

Dots

Turquoise background

Updated legend

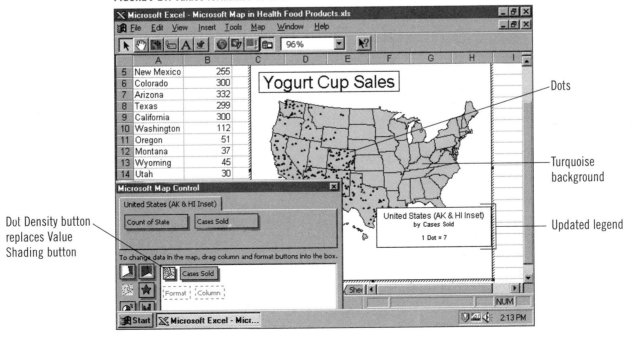

Practice

► Concepts Review

Label each element of the Excel screen shown in Figure J-22.

FIGURE J-22

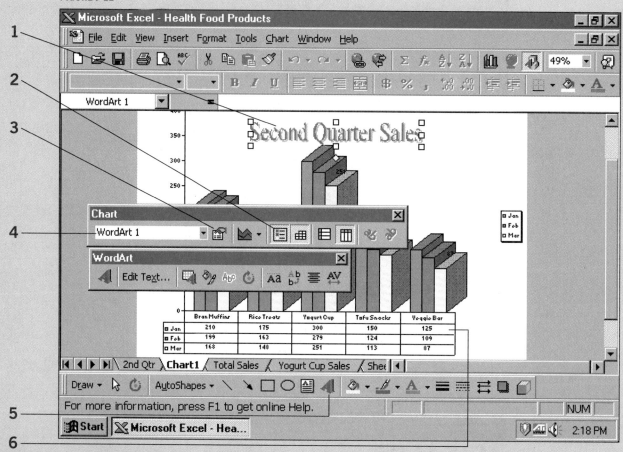

Match each statement with the button it describes.

7. **Opens the WordArt dialog boxes.**
8. **Use to format the selected chart object.**
9. **Use to create a data map.**
10. **Use to change the style of a piece of WordArt.**
11. **Use to display the Drawing toolbar.**

a.
b.
c.
d.
e.

Select the best answer from the list of choices.

12. **A chart's scale**
    a. Appears on the category (*x*) axis.
    b. Displays values on the value (*y*) axis or the value (*z*) axis.
    c. Always appears on the value (*y.*) axis.
    d. Cannot be modified.

13. **What is the most efficient method of rotating a 3-D chart?**
    a. Click Edit on the menu bar, then click Default.
    b. Adjust settings in the 3-D View dialog box.
    c. Select the chart corners, then drag a corner.
    d. Delete the chart, and start over with a new one.

14. **How can you change the way data is represented on a map?**
    a. Drag format buttons in the Microsoft Data Control dialog box.
    b. Click Map, then click Data Representation.
    c. Click the Map Refresh button.
    d. None of the above.

15. **Which statement best describes the difference between two- and three-dimensional column charts?**
    a. Two-dimensional charts have category (x) and value (y) axes; three-dimensional charts have category (x), series (y), and value (z) axes.
    b. Two-dimensional charts show the data in three dimensions.
    c. Three-dimensional charts show the data in four dimensions.
    d. Two-dimensional charts have a value scale on the x-axis, and three-dimensional charts have a value scale on the z-axis.

16. **What is a data table?**
    a. A three-dimensional arrangement of data on the y-axis.
    b. Worksheet data arranged geographically.
    c. A customized data series.
    d. The data used to create a chart displayed in a grid.

17. **A custom chart type**
    a. Contains no formatting.
    b. Looks less polished than a standard chart type.
    c. Contains numerous options such as colors, patterns, and gridlines.
    d. All of the above.

18. **To rotate text in a worksheet cell**
    a. Adjust settings on the Alignment tab of the Format cells dialog box.
    b. Click the Rotate button on the Standard toolbar.
    c. Select the text, and drag to rotate it the desired number of degrees.
    d. Format the text as WordArt, then drag the WordArt.

▶ Skills Review

1. Select a custom chart type.
   a. Open the workbook titled XL J-2, then save it as "Number of PCs Sold".
   b. If necessary, click the 1st Quarter sheet, then select the range A4:B7.
   c. Click the Chart Wizard button, click the Custom Types tab in the Chart Wizard dialog box, then make sure the Built-in option button is selected.
   d. Click Blue Pie in the Chart type box.
   e. Click Next in the first Chart Wizard dialog box.
   f. Make sure the data range in the second Chart Wizard dialog box is correct, then click Next.
   g. In the third Chart Wizard dialog box, click Next.
   h. In the fourth Chart Wizard dialog box, make sure the As Object In button is selected, then click Finish.
   i. Drag the chart to a better location in the worksheet.
   j. Save, preview, then print the worksheet data and chart.

2. Customize a data series.
   a. Click the 2nd Quarter sheet tab.
   b. Select range D4:D7.
   c. Drag the selection into the chart's plot area.
   d. Scroll the chart into view to ensure the data for June is added.
   e. Use the Chart Object list arrow to select the data series for June.
   f. Click the Format Object button on the Chart toolbar, then click the Data Labels tab in the Format Data Series dialog box.
   g. Display data labels for the June data, then close the dialog box.
   h. Use the Format Data Series dialog box to change the color of the May data series to bright red.
   i. Save the workbook.

3. Format a chart axis.
   a. Make sure the chart is in Edit mode. Note that the value (z) axis scale ranges from 0 to 30.
   b. Use the Chart Object list arrow to select the Value axis.
   c. Click the Format Object button on the Chart toolbar, then click the Scale tab.
   d. Change the value in the Maximum box to 40.
   e. Click the Number tab.
   f. Under Category, click Accounting to add a dollar sign and two decimal places to the values, then close the dialog box.
   g. Save the workbook.

4. Add a data table to a chart.
   a. Make sure the chart is in Edit mode.
   b. Click Chart, click Chart Options, then click the Data Table tab.
   c. Click the Show data table check box to select it.
   d. Close the dialog box, then scroll down to display the chart.
   e. Use the Location command on the Chart menu to move the chart to its own sheet.
   f. Click the Third Quarter sheet tab.
   g. Use the Data Table tab in the Chart Options dialog box to hide the data table.
   h. Remove the chart legend.
   i. Save the workbook.

5. Rotate a chart.
- **a.** Click the Chart1 tab.
- **b.** Use the Chart Object list arrow to select the chart corners.
- **c.** Drag a chart corner to rotate the chart.
- **d.** Click Chart on the menu bar, then click 3-D View.
- **e.** Return the chart to its default rotation.
- **f.** Change the rotation to 315.
- **g.** Change the elevation to 13.
- **h.** Press [Esc] to deselect the chart corners.
- **i.** Save the workbook.

6. Enhance a chart with WordArt.
- **a.** Display the drawing toolbar.
- **b.** Click the Insert WordArt button on the Drawing toolbar.
- **c.** Select the second style from the right in the second row, then click OK.
- **d.** In the Edit WordArt dialog box, type "Second Quarter Sales".
- **e.** Click the Italic button, then close the dialog box.
- **f.** Position the new title over the top of the chart.
- **g.** Make sure the WordArt is still selected, then use the WordArt Gallery button on the WordArt toolbar to select a new style for the title.
- **h.** Save the workbook.
- **i.** Close the Drawing toolbar.

7. Rotate text.
- **a.** Click the 1st Quarter sheet tab.
- **b.** Select cells B4:D4.
- **c.** Click Format on the menu bar, click Cells, then click the Alignment tab.
- **d.** Double-click the Degrees box, type 45, then close the dialog box.
- **e.** Click the 2nd Quarter sheet tab.
- **f.** Select the range B4:D4.
- **g.** Open the Alignment tab in the Format Cells dialog box, then drag the rotation indicator to 45 degrees.
- **h.** Click the 3rd Quarter sheet tab, then rotate the Category Axis labels downward.
- **i.** Save the workbook.

8. Map worksheet data.
- **a.** Click the Mail Order Contacts sheet tab.
- **b.** Select the range A4:B16.
- **c.** Click the Map button on the Standard toolbar.
- **d.** Position the map in the range C4:H23, and use the United States (AK & HI Inset) map.
- **e.** Change the map title to "Western Region Contacts".
- **f.** Change the map's background color to bright pink.
- **g.** Change the data formatting to dot density.
- **h.** Change the legend title to Mail Order.
- **i.** Click cell B9, then change the data for California to 25.
- **j.** Double-click the map to put it in Edit mode, then click the Map Refresh button to update the map.
- **k.** Save the workbook, then select, preview, and print each sheet in the workbook.

▶ Independent Challenges

1. You are the owner of Sandwich Express, a metropolitan delicatessen. Each week, you order several pounds of cheese: Cheddar, Monterey Jack, Swiss, Provolone, and American. Last month was especially busy, and you ordered an increasing amount of cheese each week in every category except American, which is declining in popularity. Recently, your spouse has joined you in the business and wants to develop a more efficient forecast of the amount of cheese to order each week. To help your spouse analyze last month's cheese orders, you developed a worksheet with a three-dimensional stacked bar chart. Now, you want to enhance the chart by adding data labels, reformatting the value (z) axis, increasing the elevation, and adding several titles.

To complete this independent challenge:

1. Open the workbook titled XL J-3, then save it as "Cheese Order Tracking".
2. Customize the data series. Add the data for 8/22 and 8/29 to the chart. Then add data labels to all data markers.
3. Reformat the value (z) axis to show values every 40 pounds instead of every 50 pounds.
4. Increase the chart's elevation.
5. Add a WordArt title that reads "Cheese Ordered in August".
6. Move the chart to a chart sheet, and add a data table.
7. Preview and print the worksheet and chart together, then save the workbook.

2. As the owner of Sandwich Express, you meet quarterly with your dairy product salesman, James Snyder, to discuss trends in dairy product usage at your delicatessen. These quarterly meetings seem to take longer than necessary, and you are not always sure he has retained all the information discussed. You decide to use charts to communicate during these meetings. As part of your presentation at the end of the third quarter, you decide to generate an additional chart showing what percentage of the total cheese orders for each month each cheese type represents, starting with August. Because this chart will compare parts of a whole, you create a three-dimensional pie chart. Also, to ensure the intended messages are communicated effectively, you add a few enhancements to the chart and worksheet. First, you need to add totals to the worksheet.

To complete this independent challenge:

1. Open the workbook titled XL J-3, then save it as "Cheese Order Pie".
2. Select and delete the current 3-D bar chart from the worksheet.
3. Add monthly totals in column G that total each cheese type across all five weeks. Then calculate a grand total for the month. (*Hint:* To double-check your monthly total, add totals for each week in row 10. Then select the totals in B10:F10 and note the sum in the AutoCalculate box in the Status bar.)
4. Use the Chart Wizard to create a custom type chart showing what percentage of the total cheese ordered in August (1,745 pounds) each type of cheese represents. (*Hint:* Use the Control key to select nonadjacent ranges of cheese types and totals to be charted before you open the Chart Wizard.) Place the chart on its own sheet.
5. Add the WordArt title "Sandwich Express—August Cheese Orders".
6. Add an italicized WordArt subtitle that reads "(% of total pounds ordered)".
7. In the August worksheet, rotate the dates in Row 4 to a 45-degree angle.
8. Preview and print the worksheet, then the chart. Then save the workbook.

3. You are a real estate agent for Galaxy Properties, which specializes in residential real estate. In September, you were voted salesperson of the month. Your sales manager has asked you to assemble a brief presentation on your sales activity during September for the new agents in the office. You decide to include a chart showing how many properties you closed and their respective dollar amounts in each of three areas: single-family homes, condominiums, and townhouses. Using your own data, create a worksheet and accompanying chart to present the data. Enhance the chart as outlined below.

To complete this independent challenge:

1. Create a new workbook, then save it as "September Sales, Galaxy Properties".
2. Enter your own worksheet labels, data, and formulas.
3. Create a custom bar chart showing your September sales activity.
4. Include data labels on the condominium data series.
5. Add a WordArt title.
6. Add new data to the worksheet for rental properties, then add the data series to the chart.
7. Move the chart to a chart sheet, and add a data table.
8. Rotate the column labels in the worksheet.
9. Preview and print the worksheet and chart, then save the workbook.

4. As a trade consultant for numerous multinational corporations, you regularly check the U.S. Census Bureau's home page on the World Wide Web (WWW) for information on international trade. For an upcoming presentation, you want to create a map illustrating data on international trade in goods and services for January 1996. After you create the map, you will enhance it as outlined below.

To complete this independent challenge:

1. Create a new workbook, then save it as "International Trade".
2. Use your Web browser to go to the U.S. Census Bureau home page. If you have trouble finding this page, go to http://www.course.com. From there, click Student Online Companions, click the link for this textbook, then click the Excel link for Unit J. On the U.S. Census Bureau home page, click Subjects A–Z; in the alphabetical list of topics in the next page, click Foreign Trade; under Spotlight in the next page, click Historical Trade Data; under Years Available in the next page, click 1996; then in the next page, click January.
3. Click Exhibit 14: Exports, Imports and Balance of Goods by Selected Countries and Geographic Areas, then print that page.
4. Enter the January data for the European Union (EU) into your worksheet. (Do not include the data for "other EU.") Add a column label for the numerical column explaining the units used for the data. (*Hint:* The units are explained in the paragraph above the data in the Web page.) Be sure to format your data in columns.
5. Create a map of Europe based on the information you have entered in the worksheet.
6. Enhance the map's appearance by changing the background color, adding a better title, and adding a better legend title.
7. Drag a sizing handle to adjust the map's size to make it easy to read.
8. Preview and print the worksheet and map, then save the workbook.

▶ Visual Workshop

Create the worksheet and accompanying custom chart shown in Figure J-23. Save the workbook as "The Blossom House". Study the chart and worksheet carefully to make sure you start with the most appropriate custom chart type, and then make all the modifications shown. Preview, then print the worksheet and chart together in landscape orientation. (*Hint:* You might need to adjust the plot area so that the chart objects are less crowded.)

FIGURE J-23

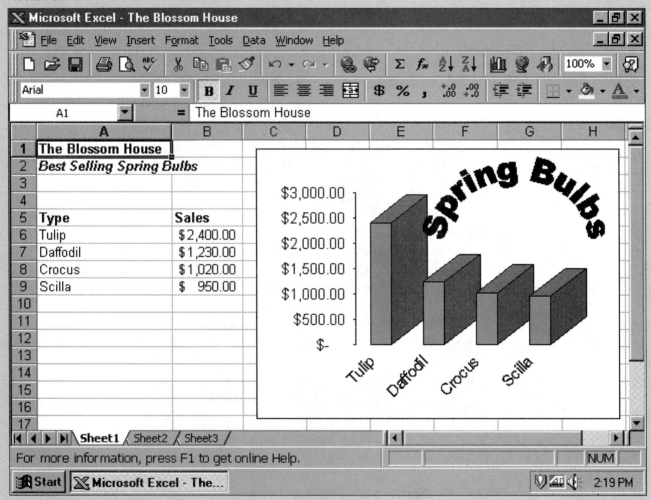

Using
What-If Analysis

Objectives

- ► Define a what-if analysis
- ► Track a what-if analysis with Scenario Manager
- ► Generate a scenario summary
- ► Project figures using a data table
- ► Create a two-input data table
- ► Use Goal Seek
- ► Set up a complex what-if analysis with Solver
- ► Run Solver and generate an Answer Report

Each time you use a worksheet to answer the question "what if?," you are performing a **what-if analysis**. For example, what would happen to a firm's overall expense budget if company travel expenses decreased by 30%? Using Excel, you can perform a what-if analysis in many ways. In this unit, you will learn to track what-if scenarios and generate summary reports using Excel's Scenario Manager. You will design and manipulate one-input and two-input data tables to project multiple outcomes. Also, you will use Excel's Goal Seek feature to solve a what-if analysis. Finally, you will use Solver to perform a complex what-if analysis involving multiple variables. ✎—— Nomad Ltd's Health Division is considering the purchase of several company cars for transporting personnel to off-site events. Evan Brillstein's manager, Megan Grahs, has asked him to research various payment options and to help select the best mix of vehicles. Evan will use Excel to perform a what-if analysis to provide the necessary information.

Defining a What-If Analysis

A what-if analysis in a worksheet can provide immediate answers to questions such as "What if we sell 30% more of a certain product?" or "What happens if interest rates rise 2 points?" A worksheet used to produce a what-if analysis is often referred to as a **model** because it acts as the basis for multiple outcomes. A what-if analysis in a worksheet is generated by changing the value in one or more **input cells** (cells in which data, rather than formulas, are entered) and observing the effects in dependent cells. A **dependent cell** is a cell—usually containing a formula—that can be located either in the same worksheet as the changing value or in another worksheet. ▄▄▄ Evan has created a worksheet model to perform an initial what-if analysis of car-loan payments. See Figure K-1. Evan follows the guidelines below to perform a what-if analysis.

Details

 Understand and state the purpose of the worksheet model.
The worksheet model is designed to calculate a fixed rate, monthly car-loan payment.

 Determine the data input value(s) that, if changed, affect the dependent cell results.
The model contains three data input values (labeled Loan Amount, Annual Interest Rate, and Term in months), in cells B4, B5, and B6, respectively.

 Identify the dependent cell(s), usually containing formulas, that will contain adjusted results once different data values are entered.
There are three dependent cell formulas (labeled Monthly Payment, Total Payments, and Total Interest). The results appear in cells B9, B10, and B11, respectively.

 Formulate questions you want the what-if analysis to answer.
Evan wants to answer the following questions with his model: (1) What happens to the monthly payments if the interest rate is 10%? (2) What happens to the monthly payments if the loan term is 60 months (5 years) instead of 48 months (4 years)? (3) What happens to the monthly payments if a less-expensive car with a lower loan amount is purchased?

 Perform the what-if analysis and explore the exact relationships between the input values and the dependent cell formulas, which depend on the input values.
Evan wants to see what effect a 10% interest rate has on the dependent cell formulas. Because the interest rate is located in cell B5, any formula that references cell B5 will be directly affected by a change in interest rate—in this case, the Monthly Payment formula in cell B9. Because the formula in cell B10 references cell B9 and the formula in cell B11 references cell B10, however, a change in the interest rate in cell B5 affects these other two formulas as well. Figure K-2 shows the result of the what-if analysis described in this example.

FIGURE K-1: Worksheet model for a what-if analysis

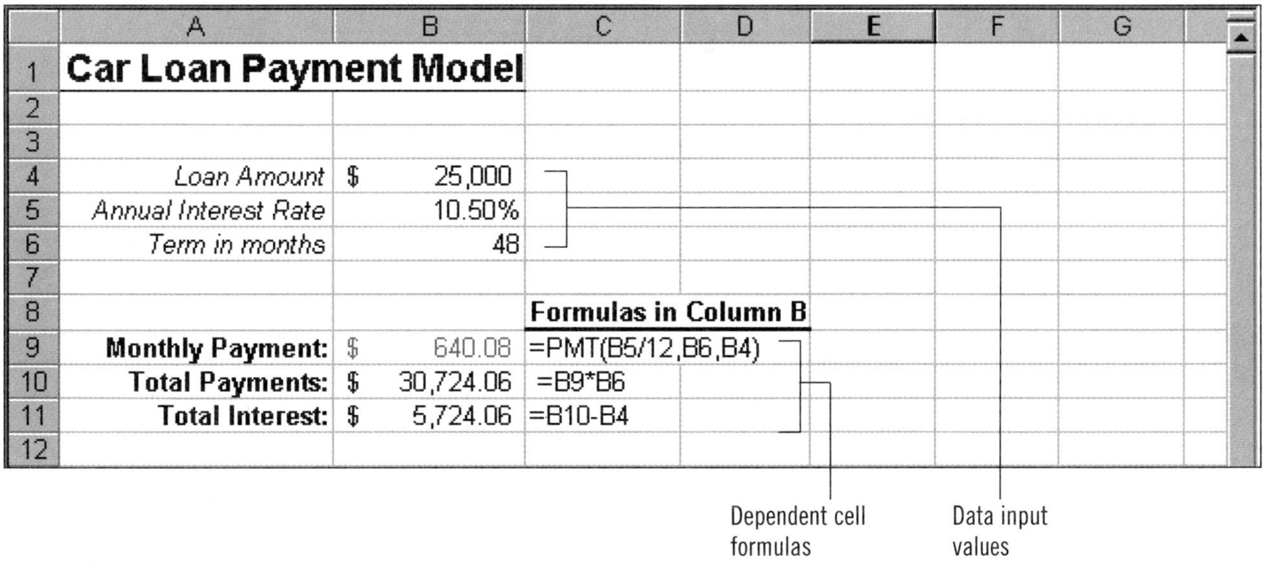

	A	B	C	D	E	F	G	
1	**Car Loan Payment Model**							
2								
3								
4	*Loan Amount*	$ 25,000						
5	*Annual Interest Rate*	10.50%						
6	*Term in months*	48						
7								
8			**Formulas in Column B**					
9	**Monthly Payment:**	$ 640.08	=PMT(B5/12,B6,B4)					
10	**Total Payments:**	$ 30,724.06	=B9*B6					
11	**Total Interest:**	$ 5,724.06	=B10-B4					
12								

Dependent cell formulas

Data input values

FIGURE K-2: What-if analysis with changed input value and dependent formula results

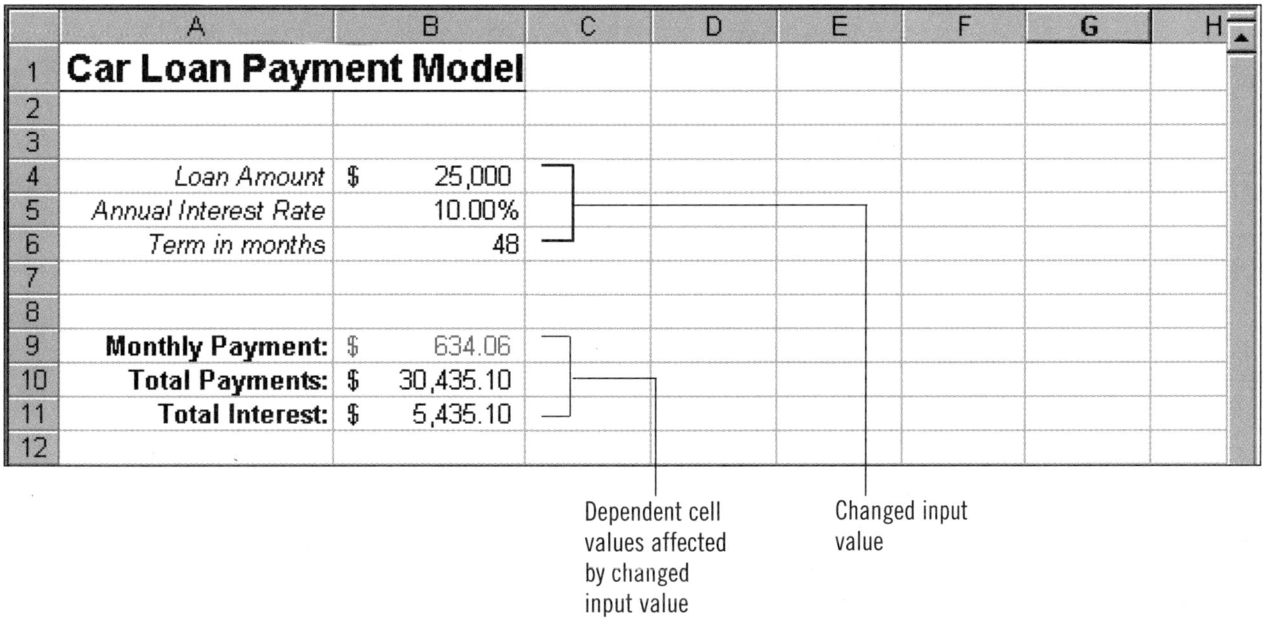

	A	B	C	D	E	F	G	H
1	**Car Loan Payment Model**							
2								
3								
4	*Loan Amount*	$ 25,000						
5	*Annual Interest Rate*	10.00%						
6	*Term in months*	48						
7								
8								
9	**Monthly Payment:**	$ 634.06						
10	**Total Payments:**	$ 30,435.10						
11	**Total Interest:**	$ 5,435.10						
12								

Dependent cell values affected by changed input value

Changed input value

Tracking a What-If Analysis with Scenario Manager

A **scenario** is a set of values you use to forecast worksheet results. Excel's Scenario Manager simplifies the process of what-if analysis by allowing you to name and save different scenarios with the worksheet. Scenarios are particularly useful when you work with uncertain or changing variables. If you plan to create a budget, for example, but are uncertain of your revenue, you can assign several different values to the revenue and then switch between the scenarios to perform a what-if analysis. ▶ Evan uses Scenario Manager to consider three car-loan scenarios: (1) the original loan quote, (2) a longer-term loan, and (3) a reduced loan amount.

1. Open the workbook titled **XL K-1**, then save it as **Evan's Car Payment Model**
   First, you select the cells that will change in the different scenarios; these are known as **changing cells**.

2. Select range **B4:B6**, click **Tools** on the menu bar, then click **Scenarios**
   The Scenario Manager dialog box opens with the following message: "No Scenarios defined. Choose Add to add scenarios." Now you add the scenario name.

3. Click **Add**, drag the Add Scenario dialog box to the right until columns **A** and **B** are visible, then in the Scenario name box, type **Original loan quote**
   The range in the Changing Cells box reflects your initial selection, as shown in Figure K-3.

4. Click **OK** to confirm the Add Scenario settings
   The Scenario Values dialog box opens, as shown in Figure K-4. Notice that the existing values appear in the changing cell boxes. Because this first scenario reflects the original loan quote input values, you confirm, rather than change, the current values listed.

5. Click **OK**
   The Scenario Manager dialog box reappears with the new scenario listed in the Changing cells box. You define the second scenario by changing the loan term from 48 to 60 months.

6. Click **Add**; in the Scenario name box type **Longer term loan**, click **OK**; in the Scenario Values dialog box, select **48** in the third changing cell box, type **60**, then click **Add**
   The Add Scenario dialog box reappears with the second scenario listed in the Changing cells box. Finally, you define the third scenario.

7. In the Scenario name box, type **Reduced loan amount**, click **OK**; in the Scenario Values dialog box, select **25000** in the first changing cell box, type **21000**, then click **OK**
   The Scenario Manager dialog box reappears. See Figure K-5. All three scenarios are listed, with the most recent—Reduced loan amount—selected. Now you can apply the different scenarios to your worksheet.

8. Make sure Reduced loan amount is still selected, click **Show**, notice that the monthly payment in the worksheet changes from $640.08 to $537.67; click **Longer term loan**, click **Show**, notice that the monthly payment is now $537.35; click **Original loan quote**, click **Show** to return to the original values, then click **Close**

Time To
✔ Save the workbook

Merging scenarios

If you must bring scenarios from another workbook into the current workbook, click the Merge button in the Scenario Manager dialog box. The Merge Scenarios dialog box opens, which you can use to select scenarios from other workbooks.

FIGURE K-3: Add Scenario dialog box

Scenario name

Cell range to be changed

Your user name and date will be different

Click to confirm scenario settings

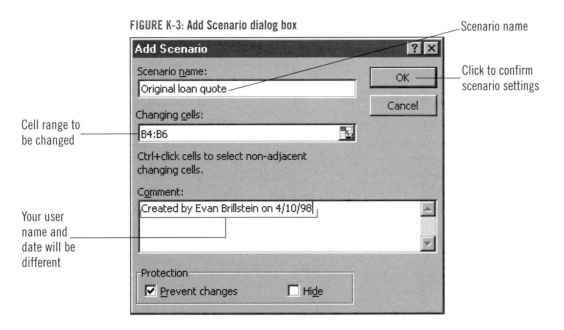

FIGURE K-4: Scenario Values dialog box

Changing cell boxes

Click to return to Scenario Manager dialog box

Click to add current scenario and to return to Add Scenario dialog box

Current cell values in B4, B5, B6

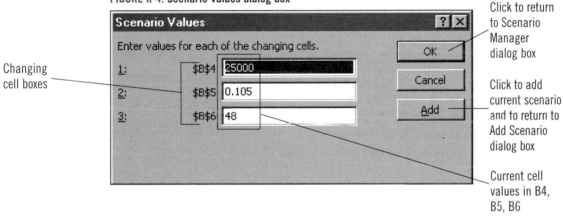

FIGURE K-5: Scenario Manager dialog box with three scenarios listed

Three scenarios

Click to show selected scenario

Click to delete selected scenario

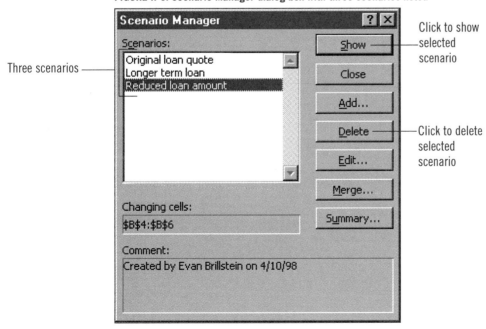

Generating a Scenario Summary

Although switching between different scenarios when analyzing data may be useful, in most cases, you will want to refer to a single report summarizing the results of the scenarios in a worksheet. A **scenario summary** is an Excel table that compiles data from the changing cells and corresponding result cells for each scenario. You can use a scenario summary to illustrate the best, worst, and most-likely case scenarios for a particular set of circumstances. Now that he's defined his scenarios, Evan needs to generate and print a scenario summary report. Naming the cells makes the summary easier to read because the names, not the cell references, are listed in the report. Evan begins by creating cell names in column B based on the labels in column A (the left column).

1. Select range **A4:B11**, click **Insert** on the menu bar, point to **Name**, click **Create**, if necessary click the **Left column check box** to select it, then click **OK**
You now confirm that the cell names were created.

2. Click cell **B4**, make sure Loan_Amount appears in the name box, then click the **name box list arrow**
All six names appear in the name box list, confirming that they were created. See Figure K-6. Now you are ready to generate the scenario summary report.

3. Press **[Esc]**, click **Tools** on the menu bar, click **Scenarios**, then in the Scenario Manager dialog box, click **Summary**
The Scenario Summary dialog box opens. Notice that Scenario summary is selected, indicating that it is the default report type.

4. If necessary, double-click the **Result cells box**, then select range **B9:B11** in the worksheet
The references in the Result cells box adjust to reflect those cells affected by the changing cells. See Figure K-7. With the report type and result cells specified, you are now ready to generate the report.

QuickTip

Scroll right to see all three scenarios included in the report. The scenario summary is not linked to the worksheet. If you change cells in the worksheet, you must generate a new scenario summary.

5. Click **OK**
The summary of the worksheet's scenarios appears on a new sheet. The report appears in outline format so that you can hide or show report details. Because the Current Values column shows the same values as the Original loan quote column, you delete column D.

6. Press **[Ctrl][Home]**, click the **Current Values column header** for column D, click the **right mouse button**, then in the pop-up menu, click **Delete**
The column containing the current values is deleted and the Original loan quote column data shifts right to fill column D. Next, you will delete the notes at the bottom of the report because they refer to the column that no longer exists. You also want to make the report title more descriptive.

Time To

✔ Save the worksheet
✔ Print the report

7. Select range **B13:B15**, press **[Delete]**, select cell **B2**, edit its contents to read **Scenario Summary for Car Loan**, then click cell **A1**
The completed Scenario summary is shown in Figure K-8. Now you can save your work and print the report using landscape orientation.

FIGURE K-6: List box containing newly created names

Name box list arrow

Names match labels in column A

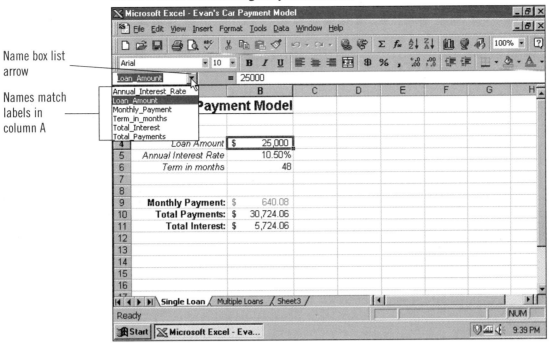

FIGURE K-7: Scenario Summary dialog box

Default report type

Cells to be recalculated when a new scenario is applied

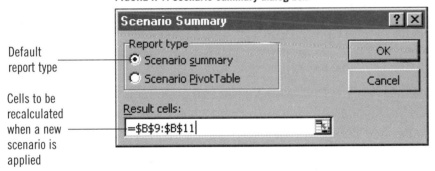

FIGURE K-8: Completed Scenario summary report

Column D now contains original loan quote

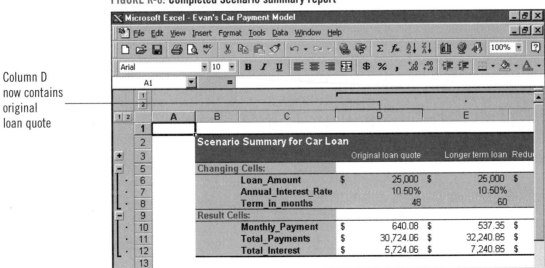

Projecting Figures Using a Data Table

Another way to answer what-if questions in a worksheet is by using a data table. A **data table**, sometimes referred to as a **one-input data table**, is a range of cells that shows the resulting values when one input value is varied in a formula. For example, you could use a data table to calculate your monthly mortgage payment based on several different interest rates. Now that he's completed his analysis, Evan wants to find out how the monthly car payments would change as interest rates increase by increments of 0.25%. He estimates that the lowest interest rate would be about 9.75% and the highest 11.25%. To project these figures, Evan will generate a one-input data table. First, he creates a table structure, with the varying interest rates listed in the left column.

1. Click the **Single Loan sheet tab**, select cell **D4**, type **Interest**, select cell **D5**, type **9.75%**, select cell **D6**, type **10.00%**; select range **D5:D6**, drag the fill handle to select range **D7:D11**, then release the mouse button
   With the varying interest rates (that is, the input values) listed in column D, you now enter a formula reference to cell B9. This tells Excel to use the formula in cell B9 to calculate multiple results in column E, based on the changing interest rates in column D.

2. Click cell **E4**, type **=B9**, then click the **Enter button** ✓ on the formula bar
   Notice that the value in cell B9, $640.08, now appears in cell E4, and the formula reference (=B9) appears in the formula bar. See Figure K-9. Because the value in cell E4 isn't a part of the data table (Excel only uses it to calculate the values in the table), you will hide the contents of cell E4 from view using a custom number format.

3. With cell E4 selected, click **Format** on the menu bar, click **Cells**, in the Format Cells dialog box click the **Number tab**; under Category click **Custom** if necessary, select the contents of the Type box, type **;;**, then click **OK**
   With the table structure in place, you can now generate monthly payment values for the varying interest rates. To do this, you must highlight the range that makes up the table structure.

Trouble?

If you receive the message "Selection not valid," repeat Step 4, taking care to select the entire range D4:E11.

4. Select range **D4:E11**, click **Data** on the menu bar, then click **Table**
   The Table dialog box opens, as shown in Figure K-10. This is where you indicate in which worksheet cell you want the varying input values (the interest rates in column D) to be substituted. Because the monthly payments formula in cell B9 (which you just referenced in cell E4) uses the total interest value in cell B5, you'll enter a reference to cell B5. You'll place this reference in the Column input cell box, rather than the Row input cell box, because the varying input values are arranged in a column.

QuickTip

You cannot delete individual values in a data table; instead, you must clear all resulting values at once.

5. Click the **Column input cell box**, click cell **B5**, then click **OK**
   Excel generates monthly payments for each interest rate. The monthly payment values are displayed next to the interest rates in column E. Next, you add formatting to the new data and the heading in cell D4.

6. Click cell **D4**, click the **Bold button** **B**, then click the **Align Right button** ≣ (both on the Formatting toolbar)

7. Select range **E5:E11**, click the **Currency Style button** $ on the Formatting toolbar, deselect the range, then save and print the worksheet
   The completed data table appears as shown in Figure K-11. Notice that the monthly payment amount for a 10.50% interest rate is the same as the original loan quote in cell B9 and the reference to it in cell E4. You can use this information to cross-check the values Excel generates in data tables.

FIGURE K-9: One-input data table structure

Reference to formula in cell B9

Value displayed in cell B9

Varying interest rates

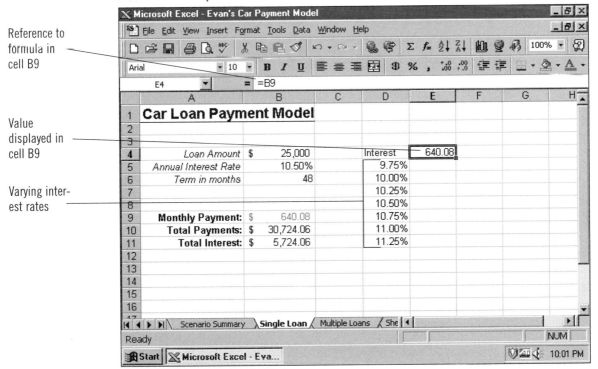

FIGURE K-10: Table dialog box

Enter reference to interest-rate input cell here

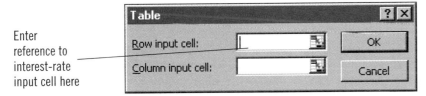

FIGURE K-11: Completed data table with resulting values

Monthly payments

Formatted heading

Completed data table

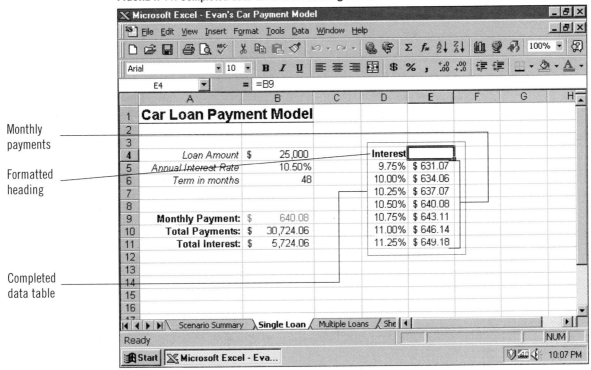

Creating a Two-Input Data Table

A **two-input data table** shows the resulting values when two different input values are varied in a formula. You could, for example, use a two-input data table to calculate your monthly mortgage payment based on varying interest rates and varying loan terms. In a two-input data table, different values of one input cell appear across the top row of the table, while different values of a second input cell are listed down the left column of the table. ➤ Evan wants to use a two-input data table to see what happens if the various interest rates are applied across several different loan terms, such as 3, 4, and 5 years. He begins by changing the structure of the one-input data table to accommodate a two-input data table.

Steps 1 2 3 4

1. Move the contents of cell **D4** to cell **C7**; click cell **C8**, type **Rates**, click the **Enter button** ☑ on the formula bar, then click the **Align Right button** ▤ and the **Bold button** **B** (both on the Formatting toolbar)

   The left table heading is in place. Now, you delete the old data table values and enter a heading for the values along the top row of the table.

2. Select range **E4:E11**, press **[Delete]**, click cell **F3**, type **Months**, click ☑, then click **B**

3. Click cell **E4**, type **36**, click ☑, click the **Comma Style button** ▸ on the Formatting toolbar, click the **Decrease decimal button** ▦ twice on the Formatting toolbar, press **[→]**, in cell F4 type **48**, press **[→]**, in cell G4 type **60**, then click ☑

   With both top row and left column values and headings in place, you are ready to reference the monthly payment formula in the upper-left cell of the table. Again, this is the formula Excel will use to calculate the values in the table. Because it is not part of the table (Excel only uses it to calculate the values in the table), you will hide the cell contents from view.

4. Click cell **D4**, type **=B9**, click ☑, click **Format** on the menu bar, click **Cells**, in the Format Cells dialog box click the **Number tab** if necessary, click **Custom**, select the contents of the Type box, type **;;** then click **OK**

   The two-input data table structure is complete, as shown in Figure K-12. Next, you select the table structure and then open the Table dialog box.

5. Select range **D4:G11**, click **Data** on the menu bar, then click **Table**

   The Table dialog box opens. The loan terms are arranged in a row, so you'll enter a reference to the loan term input cell (B6) in the Row input cell box. The interest rates are arranged in a column; you'll enter a reference to the interest rate input cell (B5) in the Column input cell box.

6. With the insertion point positioned in the Row input cell box, click cell **B6** in the worksheet, click the **Column input cell box**, then click cell **B5**

   See Figure K-13. The row input cell (B6) references the loan term, and the column input cell (B5) references the interest rate. Now, you can generate the data table.

7. Click **OK**, select range **F5:G11**, click the **Currency Style button** ⑤ on the Formatting toolbar, then click cell **F8**

   The resulting values appear, as shown in Figure K-14. The value in cell F8 matches the original quote: a monthly payment of $640.08 for a 48-month loan term at a 10.50% interest rate. Now you can preview, print, and save your work.

8. Preview and print the worksheet, then save the workbook

FIGURE K-12: Two-input data table structure

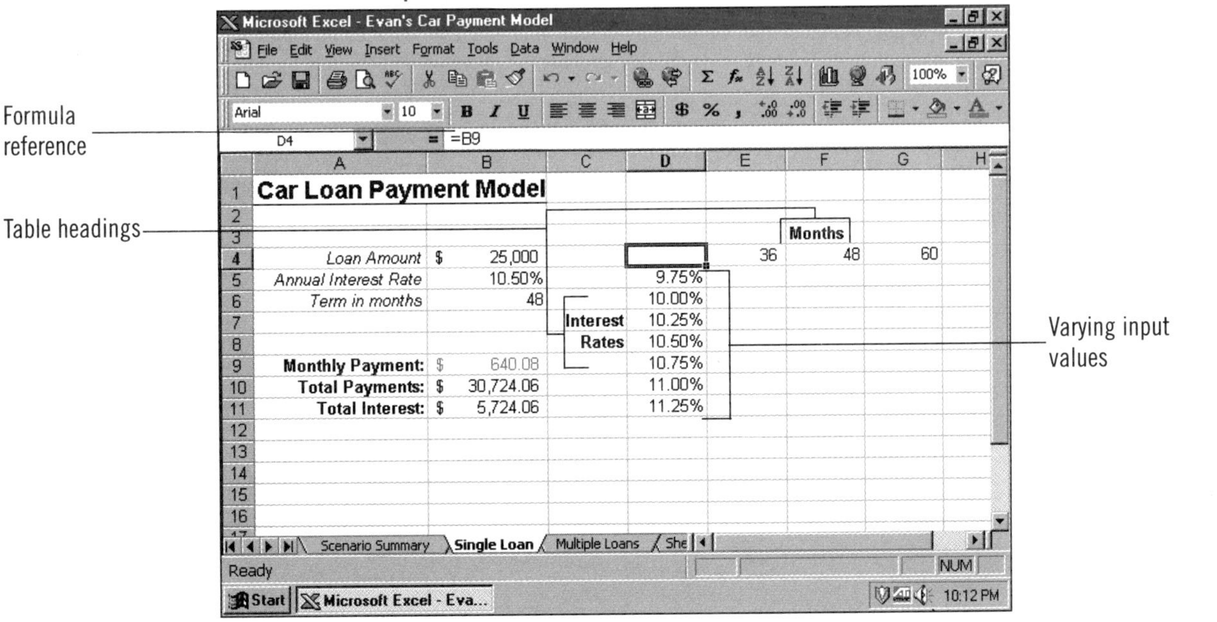

Microsoft Excel - Evan's Car Payment Model
D4 = =B9
Car Loan Payment Model
Months
36 48 60
Loan Amount $ 25,000
Annual Interest Rate 10.50%
Term in months 48
Interest Rates
9.75% 10.00% 10.25% 10.50% 10.75% 11.00% 11.25%
Monthly Payment: $ 640.08
Total Payments: $ 30,724.06
Total Interest: $ 5,724.06
Scenario Summary
Single Loan
Multiple Loans
Formula reference
Table headings
Varying input values

FIGURE K-13: Table dialog box

Table
Row input cell: $B$6
Column input cell: $B$5
OK
Cancel
Loan term input cell
Interest-rate input cell

FIGURE K-14: Completed two-input data table

Microsoft Excel - Evan's Car Payment Model
F8 = {=TABLE(B6,B5)}
Car Loan Payment Model
Months
36 48 60
9.75% $ 803.75 $ 631.07 $ 528.11
10.00% $ 806.68 $ 634.06 $ 531.18
10.25% $ 809.62 $ 637.07 $ 534.26
10.50% $ 812.56 $ 640.08 $ 537.35
10.75% $ 815.51 $ 643.11 $ 540.45
11.00% $ 818.47 $ 646.14 $ 543.56
11.25% $ 821.43 $ 649.18 $ 546.68
Loan Amount $ 25,000
Annual Interest Rate 10.50%
Term in months 48
Interest Rates
Monthly Payment: $ 640.08
Total Payments: $ 30,724.06
Total Interest: $ 5,724.06
Hidden reference to cell B9
Monthly payments for varying rates and terms
Original loan quote information

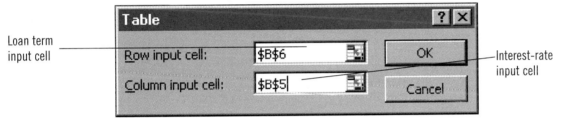

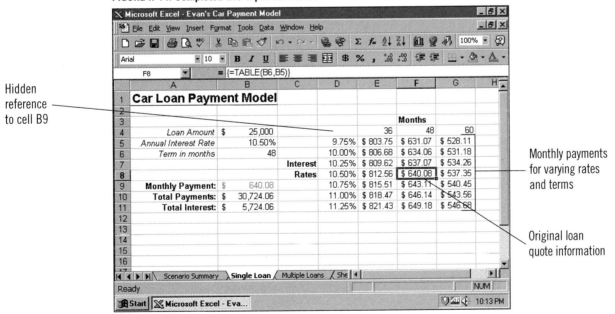

Using Goal Seek

You can think of goal seeking as a what-if analysis in reverse. In goal seeking, you specify a solution and then find the input value that produces the answer you want. Backing into a solution in this way, sometimes referred to as **backsolving**, can save a significant amount of time. For example, you can use Goal Seek to determine how many units must be sold to reach a particular sales goal or to determine the expenses that must be cut to meet a budget.　After reviewing his data table, Evan has a follow-up question: How much money could Nomad Ltd borrow if the company wanted to keep the total payment amount of all the cars to $28,000? Evan uses Goal Seek to answer this question.

Steps

1. Click cell B10

The first step in using Goal Seek is to select a goal cell. A **goal cell** contains a formula in which you can substitute values to find a specific value, or goal. You use cell B10 as the goal cell because it contains the formula for total payments.

2. Click Tools on the menu bar, then click Goal Seek

The Goal Seek dialog box opens. Notice that the Set cell box contains a reference to the Total Payments cell you selected in Step 1. Next, you specify the goal for total payments, 28000.

3. Click the To value box, then type 28000

The 28000 figure represents the desired solution that will be reached by substituting different values in the goal cell. Last, you specify which cell will be changed to reach the 28000 solution.

4. Click the By changing cell box, then click cell B4

See Figure K-15. With the target value in the target cell specified, you can begin the Goal Seek.

5. Click OK

The Goal Seek Status dialog box opens with the following message: "Goal Seeking with Cell B10 found a solution." Notice that by changing the loan amount figure in cell B4 from $25,000 to $22,783, Goal Seek achieves a total payments result of $28,000.

6. Click OK

Changing the loan amount value in cell B4 affects the entire worksheet. See Figure K-16.

7. Print, then save the workbook

QuickTip

Before you select another command, you can return the worksheet to its status prior to the Goal Seek by pressing [Ctrl][Z].

FIGURE K-15: Completed Goal Seek dialog box

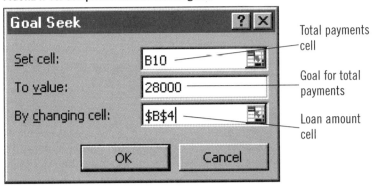

Total payments
cell

Goal for total
payments

Loan amount
cell

FIGURE K-16: Worksheet with new values

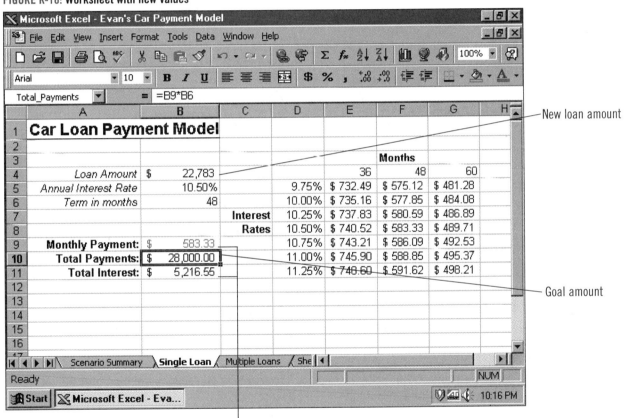

New loan amount

Goal amount

Monthly payment
and total interest
also changed
along with loan
amount

Excel 97

Setting Up a Complex What-If Analysis with Solver

Excel's Solver finds the most appropriate value for a formula by changing the input values in the worksheet. The cell containing the formula is called the **target cell**. Cells containing the values that change are called **changing cells**. Solver is helpful when you need to perform complex what-if analysis involving multiple input values or when the input values must conform to specific constraints. After seeing Evan's analysis of interest rates and payments, Megan decides that the best plan is to purchase a combination of vans, sedans, and compact cars that will accommodate a total of 44 passengers, the number of people the company routinely needs to transport to off-site conferences and conventions. In addition, the total monthly payments for the vehicles should not exceed $3700. Megan asks Evan to use Solver to find the best possible combination of vehicles.

Steps

Trouble?

If Solver is not an option on your Tools menu, you need to install the Solver add-in. See your instructor or technical support person for assistance.

Trouble?

If your Solver Parameters dialog box has entries in the By Changing Cells box or in the Subject to the Constraints box, click Reset All, then click OK, and continue with Step 3.

1. **Click the Multiple Loans sheet tab**
   See Figure K-17. This worksheet is designed to calculate total loans, payments, and passengers for a combination of vans, sedans, and compact cars. It assumes an annual interest rate of 10% and a loan term of 48 months. You will use Solver to change the purchase quantities in cells B7:D7 (the changing cells) in order to achieve your target of 44 passengers in cell B15 (the target cell). Your solution will include a constraint on cell C14, specifying that the total monthly payments must be less than or equal to $3700. The first step is to open the Solver dialog box.

2. **Click Tools, then click Solver**
   The Solver Parameters dialog box opens. This is where you indicate the target cell, the changing cells, and the constraints under which you want Solver to work. You begin by changing the value in the target cell to 44.

3. **With the insertion point in the Set Target Cell box, click cell B15 in the worksheet, in the Solver Parameters dialog box click Value of, then type 44**
   $B$15 appears in the Set Target Cell box, and 44 appears in the Value of box. Next, you specify the changing cells.

4. **Click the By Changing Cells box, then select cells B7:D7 in the worksheet**
   $B$7:$D$7 appears in the By Changing Cells box. Now, you need to specify the constraints on the worksheet values.

5. **Click Add**
   The Add Constraint dialog box opens. This is where you specify the total monthly payment amount—in this case, no higher than $3700.

6. **Click the Cell Reference box, click cell B14 in the worksheet, in the Add constraint dialog box click the list arrow, if necessary, select <=, click the Constraint check box to select it, then type 3700**
   See Figure K-18. The Change Constraint dialog box specifies that cell B14 should contain a value that is less than or equal to 3700. Next, you need to specify that the purchase quantities should be as close as possible to integers. They should also be greater than or equal to zero.

7. **Click Add, click the Cell Reference box, select range B7:D7, in the Add constraint dialog box click the list arrow, then select int**

8. **Make sure "integer" appears in the Constraint box, click Add, click the Cell Reference box, select cells B7:D7 in the worksheet, in the Add Constraint dialog box, click the list arrow, select >=, click the Constraint box, type 0, then click OK**
   The Solver Parameters dialog box reappears, with the constraints listed as shown in Figure K-19. In the next lesson, you will run Solver and generate an answer report.

FIGURE K-17: Worksheet setup for complex what-if analysis

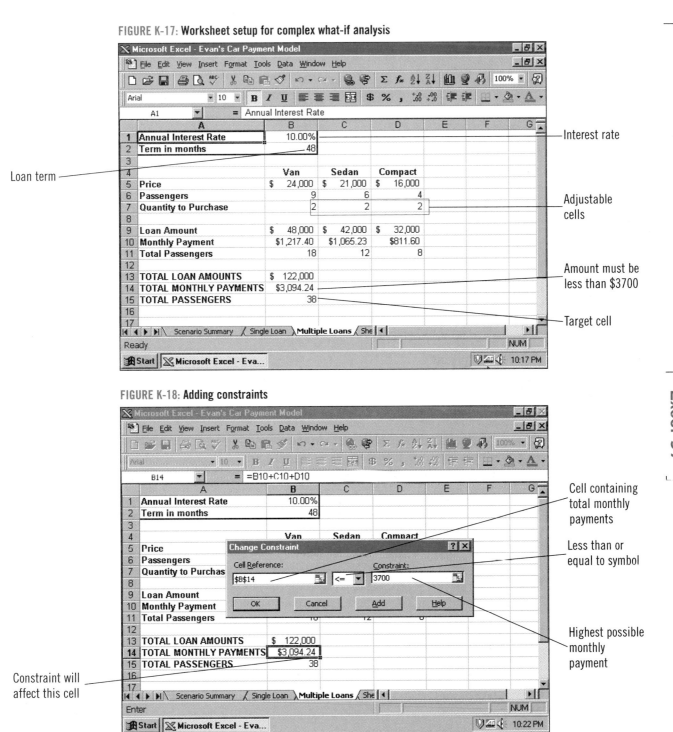

Loan term

Interest rate

Adjustable cells

Amount must be less than $3700

Target cell

FIGURE K-18: Adding constraints

Constraint will affect this cell

Cell containing total monthly payments

Less than or equal to symbol

Highest possible monthly payment

FIGURE K-19: Completed Solver Parameters dialog box

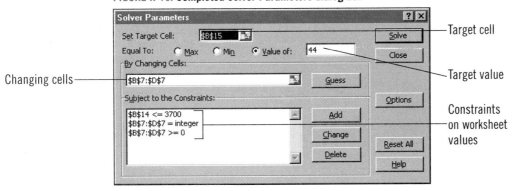

Changing cells

Target cell

Target value

Constraints on worksheet values

Running Solver and Generating an Answer Report

After entering all the parameters into the Solver Parameters dialog box, you can run Solver to find an answer. In some cases, Solver may not be able to find a solution that meets all of your constraints; in which case, you would need to enter new constraints and try again. Once Solver finds a solution, you can choose to create a special report explaining the solution. ◄───── Evan has finished entering his parameters in the Solver Parameter dialog box. Now he's ready to run Solver and create an answer report.

1. Make sure your Solver Parameter dialog box matches Figure K-19 in the previous lesson

2. Click **Solve**
   After a moment, the Solver Results dialog box opens, indicating that Solver has found a solution. See Figure K-20. The solution values appear in the worksheet, but you decide to move them to a special Answer Report and display the original values in the worksheet.

3. Click **Restore Original Values**, in the Reports list box click **Answer**, then click **OK**
   The Solver Results dialog box closes, and the original values are displayed in the worksheet. The Answer Report appears on a separate sheet.

4. Click the **Answer Report 1 sheet tab**
   The Answer Report displays the solution to the vehicle-purchase problem, as shown in Figure K-21. In order to accommodate 44 passengers and keep the monthly payments to less than $3700, you need to purchase two vans, three sedans, and two compact cars. Notice that Solver's solution includes two long decimals that are so small as to be insignificant. You'll now format the worksheet cells to display only integers. Also, because the Original Value column doesn't contain any useful information, you'll delete it.

5. Press [Ctrl], click cell **E8** and cell **E14**, click the **Decrease Decimal button** .00 on the Standard toolbar until the cells display no decimal places

6. Right-click the **column D column header**, in the pop-up menu click **Delete**, press **[Ctrl][Home]**, then save the workbook and print the worksheet
   You've successfully found the best combination of vehicles using Solver. The settings you specified in the Solver Parameters for the Multiple Loans worksheet are saved along with the workbook.

7. Close the workbook and exit Excel

FIGURE K-20: Solver Results dialog box

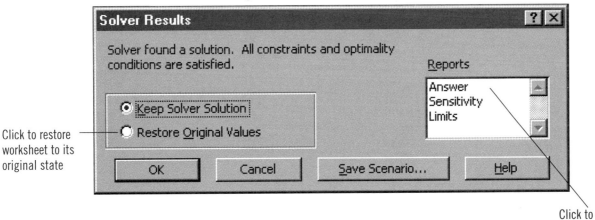

Click to restore worksheet to its original state

Click to create a report summarizing Solver's answer

FIGURE K-21: Answer report

Column to be deleted

Values in work-sheet before running Solver

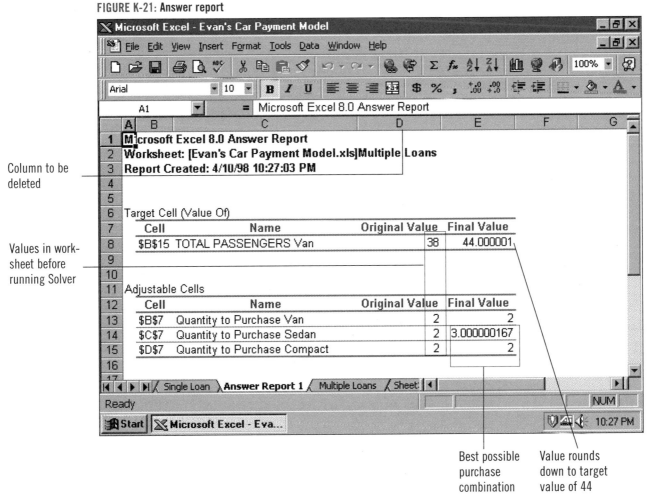

Best possible purchase combination

Value rounds down to target value of 44

Practice

▶ Concepts Review

Label each element of the Excel screen shown in Figure K-22.

FIGURE K-22

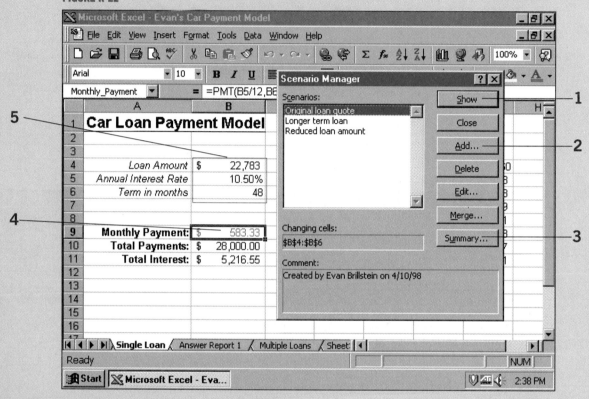

Match each statement with the term it describes.

6. Add-in that helps you solve complex what-if scenarios.
7. Separate sheet with results from the worksheet's scenarios.
8. Generates values resulting from a formula and input values variations across the top row and left column.
9. Helps you backsolve what-if scenarios.
10. Generates values resulting from a formula and input values variations across the top row or left column.

a. Two-input data table
b. Scenario summary
c. Goal Seek
d. One-input data table
e. Solver

Select the best answer from the list of choices.

11. A scenario is
a. A worksheet model.
b. A set of values used to forecast worksheet results.
c. The same as a changing cell.
d. The same as a dependent cell.

12. **What are changing cells?**
    a. Input cells that change, depending on their formulas.
    b. Formulas that change, depending on their input cells.
    c. Input cells whose values can be changed in a scenario.
    d. Cells that change positions during a what-if analysis.

13. **Dependent cells are usually**
    a. Formula cells that depend on input from other cells.
    b. Data cells that depend on their formulas.
    c. Input cells that depend on the results of a data table.
    d. Formula cells that depend on the results of a scenario.

14. **When using Solver, the cell containing the formula is called the**
    a. Changing cell.
    b. Input cell.
    c. Output cell.
    d. Target cell.

▶ Skills Review

1. **Define a what-if analysis.**
   a. Open the workbook titled XL K-2, then save it as "Car Brake Pad Replacement Model".
   b. State the purpose of the worksheet model.
   c. Locate the data input cells.
   d. Locate any dependent cells.
   e. Write three questions this what-if analysis model could answer.

2. **Track a what-if analysis with Scenario Manager.**
   a. Set up the most likely scenario with the current data input values. Select range B3:B5, click Tools on the menu bar, click Scenarios, then click Add. In the Scenario name box, type Most Likely, click OK, click OK to confirm the current values, then click Add.
   b. Add the best-case scenario using the same changing cells. In the Scenario name box, type Best Case, then click OK. In the Scenario Values dialog box, change the value in the box labeled $B$3 to 50, change the value in the box labeled $B$4 to 45, then change the value in the box labeled $B$5 to .75. Click Add.
   c. Add the worst-case scenario. In the Scenario name box, type Worst Case, then Click OK. In the Scenario Values dialog box, change the value in the box labeled $B$3 to 75, change the value in the box labeled $B$4 to 70, then change the value in the box labeled $B$5 to 2. Click OK.
   d. If necessary, drag the Scenario Manager dialog box to the right until columns A and B are visible.
   e. With the Worst Case scenario selected, click Show. Note the results.
   f. Select the Best Case scenario, then click Show. Note the results. Finally, click Most Likely, then click Show. Note the results.
   g. Close the Scenario Manager dialog box.
   h. Save your work.

3. **Generate a scenario summary.**
   a. Create names for the input value cells and the dependent cell. Select range A3:B7, click Insert on the menu bar, point to Name, click Create, make sure the Left Column check box is selected, then click OK.
   b. Deselect the range, then click the name box list arrow to verify that the names were created.
   c. Click Tools on the menu bar, click Scenarios, then click Summary.

d. In the Scenario Summary dialog box, make sure the report type selected is Scenario Summary and the result cell is B7, then click OK.

e. Edit cell B2 to read "Scenario Summary for Front Brake Pad Replacement".

f. Delete the Current Values column.

g. Delete the notes beginning in cell B11.

h. Press [Ctrl][Home].

i. Save your work.

j. Print the scenario summary report in landscape orientation.

4. Project figures using a data table.

a. Click the Single Job Sheet tab.

b. Enter the name label and varying input values. Click cell D3, type Labor $, then click the Enter button.

c. Adjust the formatting of the label so that it is boldfaced and right-aligned.

d. In cell D4, type 50; then in cell D5, type 55.

e. Select range D4:D5, then use the fill handle to extend the series to cell D9.

f. Reference the job cost formula in the upper-right corner of the table structure. In cell E3, enter =B7.

g. Format the contents of cell E3 as hidden, using the ;; Custom formatting type on the Number tab of the Format Cells dialog box.

h. Generate the new job costs based on the varying labor costs. Select range D3:E9, click Data on the menu bar, then click Table. In the Table dialog box, click the Column Input Cell box, click cell B3, then click OK.

i. Format range E3:E9 as currency.

j. Save the workbook, then preview and print the worksheet.

5. Create a two-input data table.

a. Move the contents of cell D3 to cell C6.

b. Delete the range E4:E9.

c. Format cell E3 using the Comma style button, then move the contents of cell E3 to cell D3.

d. Format the contents of cell D3 as hidden, using the ;; Custom formatting type on the Number tab of the Format Cells dialog box.

e. Click cell F2, type "Hrs per job", click the Enter button, then change the formatting of the label so it is boldfaced.

f. In cell E3 type 1, in cell F3 type 1.5, then in cell G3 type 2.

g. Select range D3:G9, click Data on the menu bar, then click Table.

h. In the Row input cell box, click cell B5, in the Column input cell box, click cell B3, then click OK.

i. Format range F4:G9 as currency.

j. Save the workbook, preview, then print the worksheet.

6. Use Goal Seek.

a. Determine what the parts would have to cost so that the cost to complete the job is $125. Click cell B7. Click Tools on the menu bar, then click Goal Seek.

b. In the To value box, type 125, click the By changing cell box, click cell B4, then click OK.

c. In the Goal Seek Status dialog box, click OK to return to the worksheet. Note the cost of the parts.

d. Save the workbook.

e. Determine what the labor would have to cost so that the cost to complete the job is $100. Note the result.

f. Save the workbook.

g. Determine what the number of hours would have to be for the cost to complete the job to equal $90. Note the result.

h. Save the workbook.

i. Preview, then print the worksheet.

j. On the printout, write the cost of the parts when the job cost equals $125, the labor costs when the job cost equals $100, and the hours when the job cost equals $90.

7. Perform a complex what-if analysis with Solver and generate an Answer Report.

a. Click the Multiple Jobs sheet tab to make it active, then open the Solver dialog box.

b. Make B16 the target cell, with a target value of 146.

c. Use cells B6:D6 as the changing cells.

d. Specify that cell B14 must be greater than or equal to 4000.

e. Specify that cell B15 must be greater than or equal to 6000.

f. Use Solver to find a solution.

g. Generate an Answer Report and restore the original values to the worksheet.

h. Edit the Answer Report to delete the original values column.

i. Save the workbook.

j. Preview and print the Answer Report, then close the workbook.

▶ Independent Challenges

1. You are an independent mortgage broker who has been working on your own for several years. One of your clients is a couple who wants to buy their first home and has qualified for a $150,000 loan. You have created a preliminary worksheet model to determine their monthly payment based on several different interest rates and loan terms. Although they are still saving for a down payment, the couple predicts they will be ready to buy in about six months. Interest rates are on the rise, and you want to show your clients a few different mortgage-payment scenarios. The couple wants to secure either a 15-year or a 30-year fixed loan. Using Scenario Manager, create the following three scenarios: the original quote, a 30-year loan at 8%; a 30-year loan at 10%; and a 15-year loan at 7.75%. Then create a scenario summary report showing the details.

To complete the independent challenge:

1. Open the workbook titled XL K-3, then save it as "Fixed-rate Mortgage Loan Payment Model".

2. Using Scenario Manager and assuming a constant loan amount of $150,000, create the following three scenarios: one with the current input values called 30-year loan at 8%; a 30-year loan at 10%; and a 15-year loan at 7.75%. Use cells B4:B6 as the changing cells for each scenario.

3. Show each scenario to make sure it performs as intended.

4. Generate a scenario summary titled "Scenario Summary for Fixed-rate Mortgage Loan Payment". Eliminate any references to current values in the report.

5. Preview, then print the scenario summary.

6. Save the worksheet, then close the workbook.

2. Your real-estate clients are grateful for the information you provided in the what-if scenarios. The couple asks if you can show them what the monthly payments would be for a $150,000 loan, over 15- and 30-year terms, with interest rates ranging in 0.5% increments. Using the workbook provided, create a two-input data table that shows the results of varying loan term and interest rates. Use the Web page address provided to find the current rate for a 30-year fixed loan.

To complete this independent challenge:

1. If you completed Independent Challenge 1, open and use the workbook titled "Fixed-Rate Mortgage Loan Payment Model". Otherwise, open the workbook titled XL K-3, then save it as "Fixed-rate Mortgage Loan Payment Model".
2. Go to the Microsurf Web page. If you have trouble finding the page, go to http://www.course.com. From there, click Student Online Companions, click the link for this textbook, then click the Excel link for Unit K. Find the lowest interest rate for your state for a 15-year fixed loan for a principal less than $214,600, with 0 points.
3. Create a data table structure with varying interest rates for 15- and 30-year terms. Use the lowest 15-year interest rate from the Microsurf Web page as the lowest possible rate. Make the highest possible interest rate 3% greater than the lowest, and vary the rates in-between by 0.25%.
4. Reference the appropriate cell in the table.
5. Generate the two-input data table.
6. Preview, then print the scenario summary.
7. Save the worksheet, then close the workbook.

3. As the owner of Micros Unlimited, a small personal computer (PC) store, you assemble your own PCs to sell to the home and business markets. You have created a PC Production financial model to determine the costs and profits associated with your three models: PC-1, PC-2, and PC-3. You need to show the results of varying hourly costs from $15 to $45 in $5 increments. Also, you want to show how the hourly cost affects total profit for each PC model your company produces. To do this, you decide to use a one-input data table. Use the workbook provided to create a one-input data table.

To complete this independent challenge:

1. Open the workbook titled XL K-4, then save it as "PC Production Model".
2. Create a data table structure with varying hourly costs, in $5 increments, from $15 to $45. Reference multiple profit formulas across the top of the table.
3. Generate the one-input data table.
4. Preview, then print the worksheet.
5. Save the worksheet, then close the workbook.

4. In addition to the data table you already created for your company, Micros Unlimited, you need to do a what-if analysis regarding the effect of Hours per Unit on Total Profit. Specifically, you want to find out how much you have to reduce hours per unit by in order to increase total profits to a specific target value. You decide to solve the problem by changing the Hours only for PC-3, using Goal Seek. If that doesn't work, you'll specify more complicated parameters using Solver.

To complete this independent challenge:

1. If you completed Independent Challenge 3, open the workbook titled "PC Production Model". Otherwise, open the workbook titled XL K-4, then save it as "PC Production Model".
2. Open the Goal Seek dialog box and set cell H9 to 25000 by changing cell B8. Click OK to find a solution.
3. Save the workbook, then print the worksheet.
4. Open the Solver dialog box. Set cell H9 as the target cell, with a value of 24500. Use cells B6:B8 as the changing cells. Specify that cells B6:B8 must be greater than or equal to 0 (zero) and less than or equal to 2.
5. Generate an Answer Report and restore the original values to the worksheet.
6. Save the workbook, preview and print the Answer Report, then close the workbook.

▶ Visual Workshop

Create the worksheet shown in Figure K-23. Make sure to generate the table on the right as a data table. Save the workbook as "Color Laptop Loan Payment Model". Preview, then print the worksheet. Print the worksheet again with the formulas displayed.

FIGURE K-23

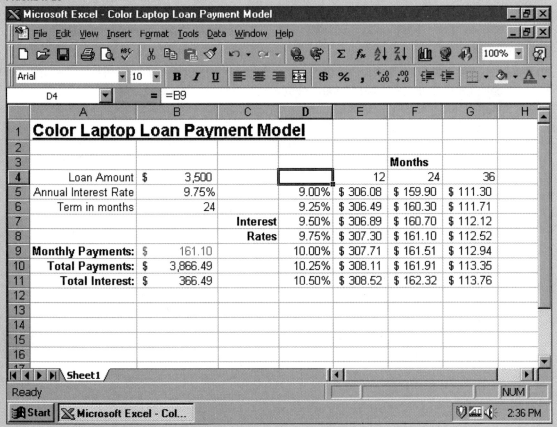

Summarizing
Data with PivotTables

Objectives

- ▶ **Plan and design a PivotTable**
- ▶ **Create a PivotTable**
- ▶ **Change the summary function of a Pivot Table**
- ▶ **Analyze three-dimensional data**
- ▶ **Update a PivotTable**
- ▶ **Change the structure and format of a PivotTable**
- ▶ **Create a chart from a PivotTable**
- ▶ **Use the GETPIVOTDATA function**

With Excel's PivotTable feature, you can summarize selected data in a
worksheet, then list and display that data in a table format. The interactive
quality of a PivotTable allows you to freely rearrange, or "pivot," parts of the
table structure around the data and summarize any data values within the
table. You also can designate a PivotTable page field that lets you view list
items three-dimensionally, as if they were arranged in a stack of pages. In
this unit, you will plan and design, create, update, and change the layout
and format of a PivotTable. Also, you will add a page field to a PivotTable,
then create a chart from the table. ◀━━━ It's nearing the end of the fiscal
year and Nomad Ltd's health division director, Megan Grahs, has asked
Evan Brillstein to develop a departmental salary analysis for each of the
new division's management positions. Evan uses a PivotTable to do this.

Planning and Designing a PivotTable

Creating a PivotTable involves only a few steps. Before you begin, however, you need to review the data and consider how a PivotTable can best summarize it. ◆——— Evan plans and designs his PivotTable using the following guidelines:

 Review the list information.

Before you can effectively summarize list data in a PivotTable, you need to know what information each field contains and understand the list's scope. Evan is working with a list of managers that he received from Miguel Garcia, the division's human resource manager. This list is shown in Figure L-1.

 Determine the purpose of the PivotTable, and write down the names of the fields you want to include.

The purpose of Evan's PivotTable is to summarize management salary information by position across various departments. Evan will include the following fields in the PivotTable: department, position, and annual salary.

 Determine which field contains the data you want summarized and which summary function will be used.

Evan intends to summarize salary information by averaging the salary field for each department and position. He'll do this by using Excel's Average function.

 Decide how you want the data arranged.

The layout of a PivotTable is crucial in delivering its intended message. Evan will define department as a column field, position as a row field, and annual salary as a data summary field. See Figure L-2.

 Determine the location of the PivotTable.

You can place a PivotTable in any worksheet of any workbook. Placing a PivotTable on a separate worksheet makes it easier to locate, however, and prevents you from accidentally overwriting parts of an existing sheet. Evan decides to create the PivotTable as a new worksheet in the current workbook.

FIGURE L-1: Management salary worksheet

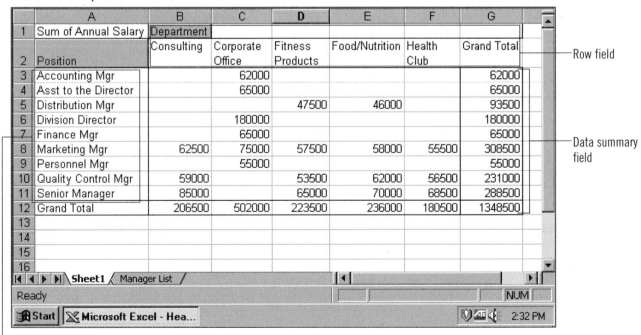

	First Name	Last Name	Hire Date	Department	Position	Mgmt Level	Annual Salary	Perf Rating
1								
2	Evan	Brillstein	2/1/98	Corporate Office	Asst to the Director	2	65,000	5
3	Helen	Brown	1/5/98	Consulting	Senior Manager	3	85,000	4
4	Kelly	Chow	2/10/98	Health Club	Quality Control Mgr	2	56,500	2
5	Arron	Darling	3/3/98	Fitness Products	Marketing Mgr	2	57,500	3
6	George	Erlinger	4/7/98	Fitness Products	Quality Control Mgr	2	53,500	4
7	Miguel	Garcia	3/12/98	Corporate Office	Personnel Mgr	2	55,000	4
8	Larry	Harlow	3/19/98	Health Club	Marketing Mgr	2	55,500	3
9	Louis	Lopez	8/1/98	Food/Nutrition	Marketing Mgr	2	58,000	3
10	Jake	Low	5/2/98	Food/Nutrition	Quality Control Mgr	2	62,000	4
11	Grahs	Megan	1/2/98	Corporate Office	Division Director	4	180,000	5
12	Fred	Neely	9/5/98	Corporate Office	Finance Mgr	2	65,000	3
13	Richard	Olson	2/8/98	Consulting	Quality Control Mgr	2	59,000	2
14	Lisa	Robinson	5/24/98	Food/Nutrition	Distribution Mgr	1	46,000	3
15	Sandra	Ruiz	10/18/98	Consulting	Marketing Mgr	2	62,500	3
16	Maria	Santos	1/10/98	Food/Nutrition	Senior Manager	3	70,000	4

Manager List

Ready   NUM

Start   Microsoft Excel - Hea...   2:26 PM

FIGURE L-2: Example of a PivotTable

	A	B	C	D	E	F	G
1	Sum of Annual Salary	Department					
2	Position	Consulting	Corporate Office	Fitness Products	Food/Nutrition	Health Club	Grand Total
3	Accounting Mgr		62000				62000
4	Asst to the Director		65000				65000
5	Distribution Mgr			47500	46000		93500
6	Division Director		180000				180000
7	Finance Mgr		65000				65000
8	Marketing Mgr	62500	75000	57500	58000	55500	308500
9	Personnel Mgr		55000				55000
10	Quality Control Mgr	59000		53500	62000	56500	231000
11	Senior Manager	85000		65000	70000	68500	288500
12	Grand Total	206500	502000	223500	236000	180500	1348500
13							
14							
15							
16							

Row field

Data summary field

Column field

Sheet1 / Manager List

Ready   NUM

Start   Microsoft Excel - Hea...   2:32 PM

Creating a PivotTable

Once you've planned and designed your PivotTable, you can create it. The PivotTable Wizard takes you through the process step-by-step. 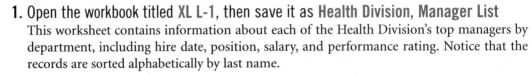 With the planning and design stage complete, Evan is ready to create a PivotTable that summarizes management salary information. Megan will use this information to budget salaries for the coming year.

1. Open the workbook titled **XL L-1**, then save it as **Health Division, Manager List**
This worksheet contains information about each of the Health Division's top managers by department, including hire date, position, salary, and performance rating. Notice that the records are sorted alphabetically by last name.

2. Click cell **A1** if necessary, click **Data** on the menu bar, then click **PivotTable Report**
The first PivotTable Wizard dialog box opens. This is where you specify the type of data source you want to use for your PivotTable: an Excel list or database, an external data source (for example, a Microsoft Access file), or multiple consolidation ranges (another term for worksheet ranges).

3. Make sure the **Microsoft Excel list or database option button** is selected, then click **Next**
The second PivotTable Wizard dialog box opens. Because the cell pointer was located within the list before you opened the PivotTable Wizard, Excel automatically completes the Range box with the table range that includes the selected cell—in this case, $A$1:$H$21. You can either type a new range in the Range box or confirm that the PivotTable will be created from the existing range.

4. Click **Next**
The third PivotTable Wizard dialog box opens, as shown in Figure L-3. You use this dialog box to specify the data arrangement you want. In this case, you want the information for each department arranged in columns and the information for each position arranged in rows.

5. Drag the **Department field button** from the right side of the dialog box to the **COLUMN** area, then drag the **Position field button** to the **ROW** area
See Figure L-4. This format will create a PivotTable with the departments as column headers and the management positions as row labels. In the next lesson, you indicate how you want the salary data to be summarized.

Trouble?

If the Office Assistant opens along with the PivotTable Wizard dialog box, click the No, don't provide help now option button, then continue with Step 3.

QuickTip

Long field names often are only partially displayed on field buttons. To display the entire field name in the PivotTable Wizard dialog box, place the pointer over the field button.

FIGURE L-3: Third PivotTable Wizard dialog box

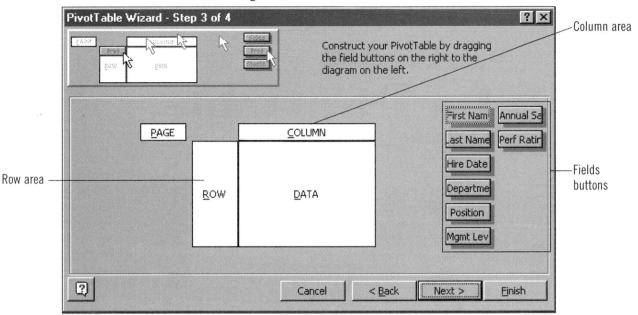

Row area ——

Column area

Fields buttons

FIGURE L-4: Revised positions of Field buttons

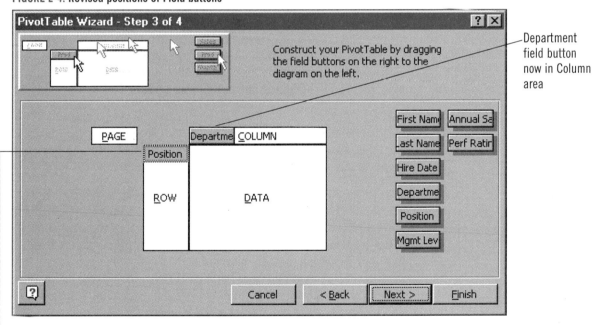

Department field button now in Column area

Position field button now in Row area

Excel 97

Changing the Summary Function of a PivotTable

A PivotTable's **summary function** controls what type of calculation is applied to the table data. Unless you specify otherwise, Excel applies the SUM function to numeric data and the COUNT function to data fields containing text. However, you can easily change the summary function in the PivotTable Wizard dialog box to a different function, such as AVERAGE (which calculates the average of all values in the field), PRODUCT (which multiplies all the values in a field), or MAX (which finds the highest value in a field).   Evan wants to average each of the manager's salaries using the AVERAGE function. He begins by specifying the field he wants to summarize in the third PivotTable Wizard dialog box.

Steps

QuickTip

You can use more than one summary function in a PivotTable by simply dragging multiple field buttons to the DATA area.

1. **With the third PivotTable Wizard dialog box still open, drag the Annual Salary field button to the DATA area**
   See Figure L-5. Because SUM is Excel's default function for data fields containing numbers, this button is renamed Sum of Annual Salary. Next, you'll open the PivotTable Field dialog box to change the summary function from SUM to AVERAGE.

2. **Double-click the Sum of Annual Salary field button**
   The PivotTable Field dialog box opens. The functions listed in the Summarize by list box designate how the data will be calculated. In this case, you'll select the AVERAGE function.

3. **In the Summarize by list box, click Average, then click OK**
   The PivotTable Field dialog box closes, and you return to the third PivotTable Wizard dialog box. The name of the field button in the Data area has changed from Sum of Annual Salary to Average of Annual Salary. Now that you've specified how the data will be arranged and summarized, you confirm the current settings and finish creating the PivotTable.

4. **Click Next**
   The fourth PivotTable Wizard dialog box opens. This is where you indicate the desired location for the new PivotTable. Evan decided during the planning and design stage that he wanted the PivotTable to appear on a new worksheet.

Trouble?

If your PivotTable toolbar does not appear, click View on the menu bar, click Toolbars, then click PivotTable to select it. If the PivotTable toolbar blocks your view of the worksheet, drag it to the lower-left corner of the worksheet window.

5. **Make sure the New worksheet option button is selected, then click Finish**
   The PivotTable reappears in a new worksheet (Sheet1), and the PivotTable toolbar appears as well. See Figure L-6. Notice that the position titles now appear as row labels in the left column, and the department names are listed across the columns as field names. The data area of the PivotTable shows the average salary for each position by department. After reviewing the data, you decide that it would be more useful to sum the salary information, rather than average it. You can quickly change the summary field again using the PivotTable Field button on the PivotTable toolbar to access the PivotTable Field dialog box.

6. **Click the PivotTable Field button** 🔳 **on the PivotTable toolbar; in the Summarize by list box, click Sum; then click OK**
   The PivotTable Field dialog box closes and Excel recalculates the PivotTable—this time, summing the salary data instead of averaging it. See Figure L-7. Finally, you'll rename the new sheet, then save and print the PivotTable.

7. **Rename Sheet1 PivotTable, save the workbook, then print the worksheet**

FIGURE L-5: Specifying the field to summarize

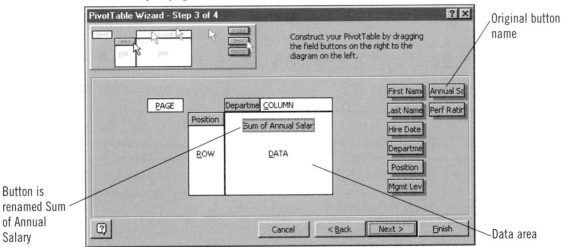

Original button name

Button is renamed Sum of Annual Salary

Data area

FIGURE L-6: Completed PivotTable

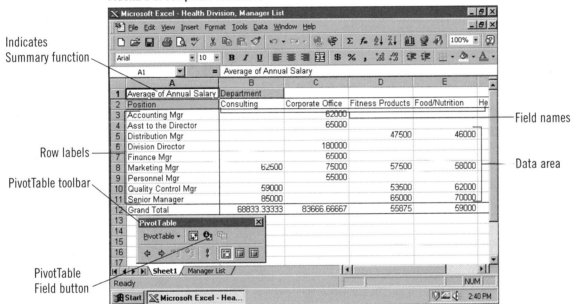

Indicates Summary function

Field names

Row labels

Data area

PivotTable toolbar

PivotTable Field button

FIGURE L-7: PivotTable with new summary function

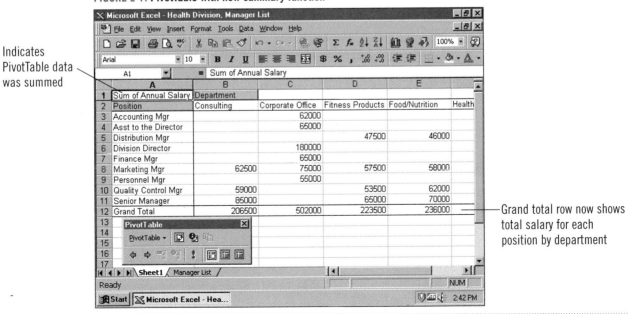

Indicates PivotTable data was summed

Grand total row now shows total salary for each position by department

Analyzing Three-Dimensional Data

When row and column field positions are established in a PivotTable, you are working with two-dimensional data. You can convert a PivotTable to a three-dimensional data analysis tool by adding a **page field**. Page fields make the data appear as if it is stacked in pages, thus adding a third dimension to the analysis. When using a page field, in effect, you are filtering data through that field. To add the page field, open the PivotTable Wizard using the PivotTable Wizard button on the PivotTable toolbar. Other buttons on the PivotTable toolbar are explained in Table L-1. Evan wants to filter the PivotTable so that only one department's data is visible at one time. He uses the PivotTable Wizard to add the Department page field.

Steps 1 2 3 4

1. **Click anywhere within the data area of the PivotTable, then click the PivotTable Wizard button 🔳 on the PivotTable toolbar**
   Because the cell pointer was positioned inside the PivotTable when the button was selected, Excel assumes you want to edit the table and automatically opens the third PivotTable Wizard dialog box. Now, you'll add a page field to the PivotTable so that data for only one department will appear.

2. **Drag the Department field button from the COLUMN area to the PAGE area**

3. **Click Finish**
   The PivotTable is re-created with a page field showing data for each department. See Figure L-8. You can select and view the data for each department, page by page, by clicking the Department list arrow and selecting the page you want to view.

4. **Click the Department list arrow**
   Because column B is narrow, the names of the available page options aren't fully displayed in the Department list box. For example, the Corporate Office option appears simply as Corporate. You'll select that option now to display the salary data for that department.

5. **Click Corporate**
   The PivotTable displays the salary data for the Corporate Office only, as shown in Figure L-9.

6. **Save the workbook, then print the worksheet**

QuickTip

You can use the Show Pages button 🔳 on the PivotTable toolbar to display each page of the page field on a separate worksheet.

TABLE L-1: PivotTable toolbar buttons

button	description	button	description
PivotTable ▾	Displays menu of PivotTable commands	🔳	Starts PivotTable Wizard
🔳	Modifies PivotTable field	🔳	Shows multiple PivotTable pages on separate worksheets
⇦	Ungroups selected rows or columns	⇨	Groups selected rows or columns
🔳	Hides detail in table groupings	🔳	Shows detail in table groupings
🔳	Updates list changes within the table	🔳	Selects the summary function label
🔳	Selects the PivotTable data	🔳	Selects both the summary function and the PivotTable data

FIGURE L-8: PivotTable with page field

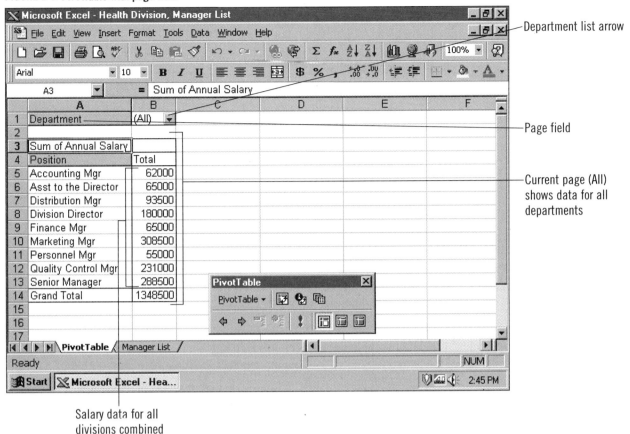

Department list arrow

Page field

Current page (All) shows data for all departments

Salary data for all divisions combined

FIGURE L-9: Corporate Office PivotTable page

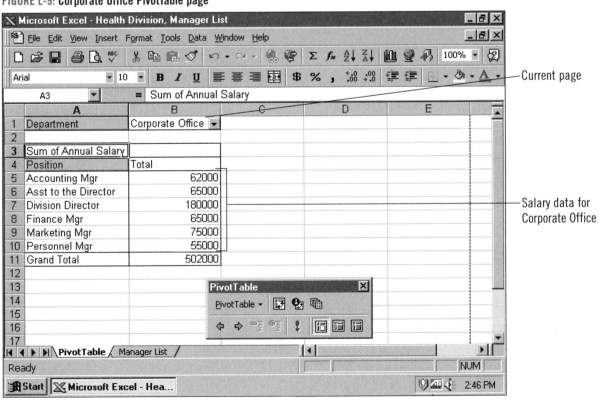

Current page

Salary data for Corporate Office

Updating a PivotTable

The data displayed in a PivotTable looks like typical worksheet data. Because the PivotTable data is linked to a source list, however, the values and results in the PivotTable are read-only values. That means you cannot move or modify part of a PivotTable by inserting or deleting rows, editing results, or moving cells. To change PivotTable data, you must edit the items directly in the list you used to create the table, called the **source list**, and then update, or **refresh**, the PivotTable to reflect the changes. Evan just learned from Miguel Garcia that a new training manager, Howard Freeberg, has been hired. Evan needs to add information about this new manager to the current list. He starts by inserting a row for Freeberg's information.

Steps

1. **Click the Manager List sheet tab**
   By inserting the new row in the correct position alphabetically, you will not need to sort the list again. Also, by adding the new manager within the named range, Database, the new row data will be included automatically in the named range.

2. **Right-click the Row 7 row header; then on the pop-up menu, click Insert**
   A blank row appears as the new row 7, and the data in the old row 7 moves down to row 8. You'll enter the data on Freeberg in the new row 7.

3. **Enter the data for the new manager based on the following information**

field name	new data item
First Name	Howard
Last Name	Freeberg
Hire Date	10/29/98
Department	Corporate Office
Position	Training Mgr
Mgmt Level	2
Annual Salary	59,000
Perf Rating	2

   The next step is to refresh the PivotTable so that it reflects the additional amount incurred by Freeberg's salary.

4. **Click the PivotTable sheet tab, then make sure the Corporate Office page is in view**
   Notice that the Corporate Office list does not currently include a training manager, and the grand total is 502,000. Before you select the Refresh Data command to refresh the PivotTable, you need to make sure the cell pointer is situated within the current table range.

5. **Click anywhere within the table range (A3:B11), then click the Refresh Data button on the PivotTable toolbar**
   A message dialog box opens with the message "PivotTable was changed during Refresh Data operation" to confirm that the update was successful.

6. **Click OK**
   The PivotTable now includes the training manager data in row 11, and the grand total has increased by the amount of his salary (59,000) to 561,000. See Figure L-10.

7. **Save the workbook, then print the worksheet**

QuickTip
Clicking a row label in a PivotTable selects the entire row. Clicking a data cell selects only that cell.

FIGURE L-10: Refreshed PivotTable

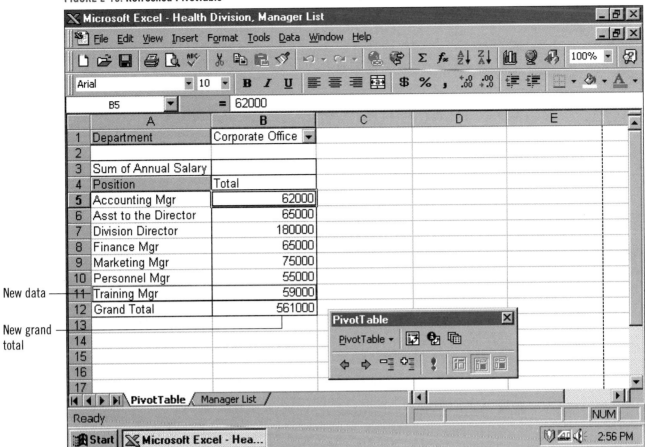

New data

New grand total

Maintaining original table data

Once you select the Refresh Data command, you cannot undo the operation. If you want the PivotTable to display the original source data, you must change the source data list, then re-select the Refresh Data com-

mand. If you're concerned about the effect refreshing the PivotTable might have on your work, save a second (working) copy of the workbook so that your original data remains intact.

Excel 97

Changing the Structure and Format of a PivotTable

Although you cannot change the actual data in a PivotTable, you can alter the structure and format of a PivotTable at any time. You might, for example, want to rename a PivotTable field button, add another column field, or switch the positions of existing fields. Alternatively, you may want to enhance the appearance of a PivotTable by changing the way the text or values are formatted. It's a good idea to format a PivotTable using AutoFormat, because once you refresh a PivotTable, any formatting applied to the cells other than an AutoFormat is removed. ✐ Evan wants to add the performance ratings to the PivotTable in order to supply Megan with additional data needed for salary budgeting. Once the new field is added, Evan will format the PivotTable.

Steps

1. Make sure that the **PivotTable sheet** is active, that the Corporate Office page is in view, and that the cell pointer is located anywhere inside the PivotTable (range A3:B12)
   You'll use the PivotTable Wizard to add the new column field.

2. Click the **PivotTable Wizard button** 🖅 on the PivotTable toolbar

3. In the third PivotTable Wizard dialog box, drag the **Perf Rating button** to the **COLUMN** area, then click **Finish**
   The PivotTable is re-created, and the new field is added. See Figure L-11. In addition to displaying the manager's position and annual salary on each department page, each manager's last performance rating on a scale from 1 to 5 appears as column labels. Now you are ready to format the PivotTable. First, you'll format the annual salary field. Start by selecting a cell within the salary field area.

4. Click cell **B5**, click the **PivotTable Field button** 🖭 on the PivotTable toolbar, then in the PivotTable Field dialog box, click **Number**

5. Under Category in the Format Cells dialog box, click **Accounting**, edit the Decimal Places box to read **0**, click **OK**, then click **OK** again
   The PivotTable Field dialog box closes, and the annual salaries are formatted with commas and dollar signs. Next, you'll select the PivotTable in order to apply a predefined AutoFormat to the entire table.

6. Click cell **A3**; click **Format** on the menu bar; click **AutoFormat**; under Table Format in the AutoFormat dialog box, click **Classic 2**; click **OK**; then deselect the range
   The PivotTable appears as shown in Figure L-12. The AutoFormat is applied to all pages of the PivotTable, as the next step shows.

7. Click the **Department list arrow**, then click **Health Club**

8. Save the workbook, then preview and print the active sheet

FIGURE L-11: Revised PivotTable

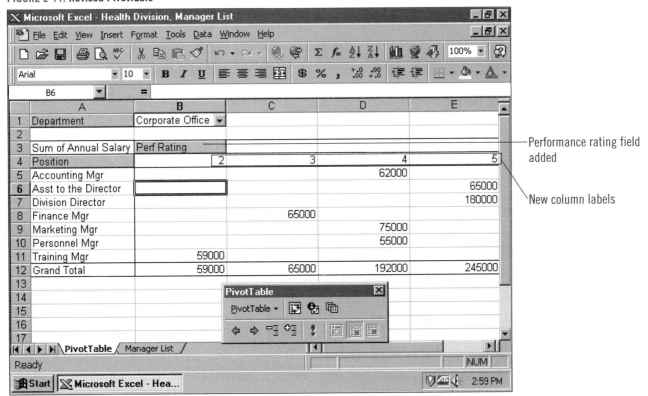

Performance rating field added

New column labels

FIGURE L-12: Corporate Office page with AutoFormat applied

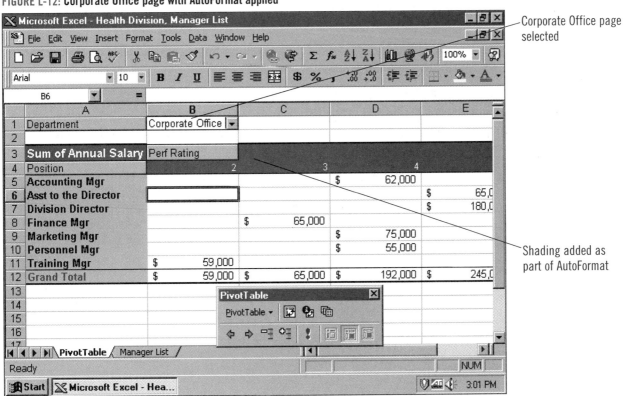

Corporate Office page selected

Shading added as part of AutoFormat

Creating a Chart from a PivotTable

You can further illustrate worksheet data by creating a chart from a PivotTable. Excel's Chart Wizard treats the information in a PivotTable like ordinary worksheet data, offering the usual selection of chart options. ✍ Evan wants to chart the annual salary and performance rating information for the Food/Nutrition Department. He uses Excel's Chart Wizard to create a column chart from the PivotTable data.

Steps

1. **Click the Department list arrow, then click Food/Nutrition**
   As with any chart, you begin by selecting the range you want to chart. Because selecting only part of a PivotTable can be tricky, you'll select the entire PivotTable, then edit the data range in the Chart Wizard dialog box.

2. **Double-click cell A3, then click the Chart Wizard button 📊 on the Standard toolbar**
   The first Chart Wizard dialog box opens.

3. **Make sure that under Chart type, Column is selected and that in the Chart subtype box, the upper-left corner chart is selected, then click Next**
   The second Chart Wizard dialog box opens, which is where you edit the data range to indicate the cells you want to include in the chart.

4. **Edit the information in the Data range box to read = PivotTable$A$5:$C$8, then click Next**
   The third Chart Wizard dialog box opens showing a sample of the charted data. See Figure L-13. Now you'll add a chart title.

5. **Click the Chart title box, type Food/Nutrition Department; click Next; in the fourth Chart Wizard dialog box, click the As new sheet option button; then click Finish**
   The finished chart appears in a new sheet. Next, you'll edit the current legend text, which only displays "Series1" and "Series2", to make it more descriptive.

6. **Click Chart on the menu bar, click Source Data, then click the Series tab**
   The Series tab of the Source Data dialog box opens, as shown in Figure L-14. This is where you type replacement text for the existing legend.

7. **In the Series list box, make sure Series1 is selected, click the Name text box and type Perf Rating 3; in the Series list box, click Series2, click the Name text box and type Perf Rating 4; then click OK**
   The Source Data dialog box closes, and your finished chart reappears. Notice the revised text in the chart legend box. See Figure L-15. Now you can save the workbook and print the chart.

8. **Save the workbook, then preview and print the chart**

FIGURE L-13: Third Chart Wizard dialog box

Sample of charted data —

Legend text

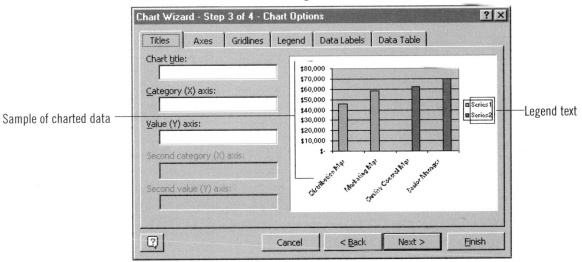

FIGURE L-14: Series tab settings

Existing legend text —

Type new legend text here

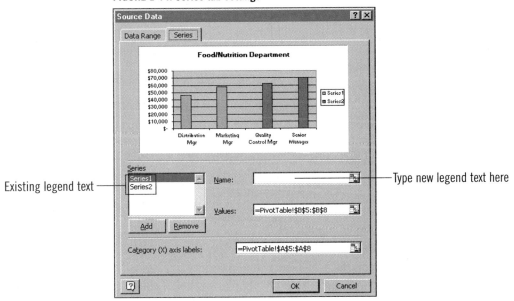

FIGURE L-15: Completed chart

Chart toolbar may not appear on your screen

Revised chart legend information

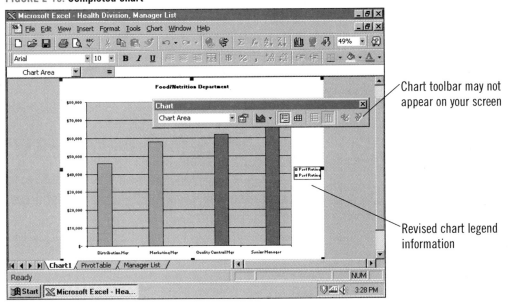

Excel 97

Using the GETPIVOTDATA Function

Because a PivotTable is rearranged so easily, you can't use an ordinary cell reference when you want to reference a PivotTable cell in another worksheet. If you change the way data is displayed in a PivotTable (for example, by displaying a different page) the data moves, rendering an ordinary cell reference incorrect. Instead, to retrieve summary data from a PivotTable, you need to use Excel's GETPIVOTDATA function. Its syntax is explained in Figure L-16. ➤ In creating next year's budget, Megan is considering allocating money toward a new marketing manager position. She asks Evan to include the current total salary for marketing managers on the Manager List sheet. Evan uses the GETPIVOTDATA function to retrieve this information from the PivotTable.

Steps 1234

QuickTip

When you switch to a new page, the chart you created from the Food/Nutrition page no longer shows the correct data. To redisplay the Food/Nutrition chart with the correct information, you need to redisplay the Food/Nutrition page in the PivotTable.

1. **Click the PivotTable sheet tab**

   The Food/Nutrition page is currently visible. Because you need the salary information for marketing managers in all departments, you switch to the (All) page.

2. **Click the Department list arrow, then click (All)**

   The PivotTable displays the salary data for all positions. Next, you will reference the total for marketing managers in the Manager List sheet. Start by entering a label explaining the data.

3. **Click the Manager List sheet tab, click cell D26, type Total Salary for Marketing Managers:, click the Enter button ✓ on the Formula bar, click the Align Right button ▤ on the Formatting toolbar, then click the Bold button B on the Formatting toolbar**

   The new label appears formatted in cell D26. Now, you'll enter a GETPIVOTDATA function in cell E26 that will retrieve the total salary for marketing managers from the PivotTable.

4. **Click cell E26, click the Paste Function button _f_ₓ on the Standard toolbar; under Function category in the Paste Function dialog box, click Database; under Function name, scroll down and click GETPIVOTDATA; then click OK**

   The GETPIVOTDATA dialog box opens. The function's first argument, Pivot_table, includes a reference to any cell within the PivotTable range. The second argument, Name, includes the row or column label for the summary information you want (in this case, Marketing Mgr) enclosed in quotation marks. You'll enter these arguments now.

5. **With the pointer in the Pivot_table box, click the PivotTable sheet tab; click cell F15 (or any other cell in the PivotTable range); in the GETPIVOTDATA dialog box, click the Name box; then type "Marketing Mgr"**

   See Figure L-17. Next format the result of the GETPIVOTDATA function.

6. **Click OK, then click the Currency Style button 🏦 on the Standard toolbar**

   The current total salary for marketing managers is $308,500.00, as shown in Figure L-18. This is the same value displayed in cell F10 of the PivotTable. The GETPIVOTDATA function will only work correctly when the total salary for all Marketing Managers is displayed in the PivotTable. You'll verify this by displaying a different page in the PivotTable and viewing the effect on the Manager List worksheet.

7. **Click the PivotTable sheet tab, click the Department list arrow, click Health Club, then click the Manager List sheet tab**

   The error message in cell E26 will disappear when you redisplay the (All) page.

8. **Click the PivotTable sheet tab, click the Department list arrow, click (All), then click the Manager List sheet tab**

   Note that the correct value—$308,500.00—is once again displayed in cell E26.

Time To

✔ Preview and print the Manager List worksheet

✔ Save and close the workbook

FIGURE L-16: GETPIVOTDATA function

GETPIVOTDATA(pivot_table,name)

Reference to any page in the PivotTable that shows the data you want to retrieve

The row or column label (enclosed in quotation marks) describing the summary value you want to retrieve. For example, "January 1998" for the grand total for January 1998

FIGURE L-17: Completed GETPIVOTDATA dialog box

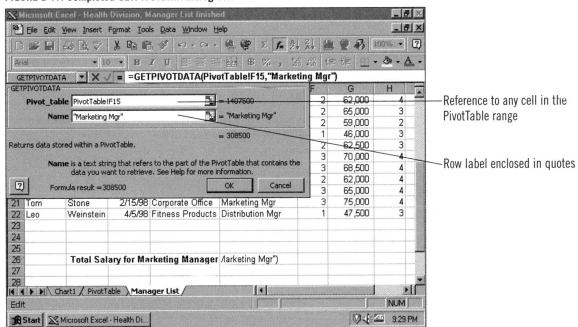

Reference to any cell in the PivotTable range

Row label enclosed in quotes

FIGURE L-18: GETPIVOTDATA function entered into the worksheet

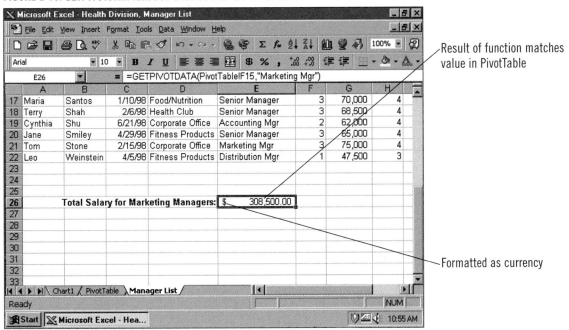

Result of function matches value in PivotTable

Formatted as currency

Excel 97

Practice

► Concepts Review

Label each element of the Excel screen shown in Figure L-19.

FIGURE L-19

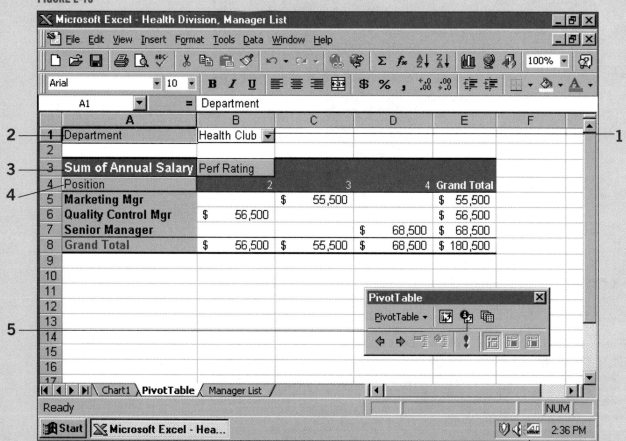

Match each statement with the term it describes.

6. Determines how data will be calculated.
7. Displays fields as column labels.
8. Shows data for one item at a time in a table.
9. Displays summarized values.
10. Retrieves information from a PivotTable.

a. COLUMN area
b. GETPIVOTDATA function
c. DATA area
d. PivotTable page
e. Summary function

Select the best answer from the list of choices.

11. A PivotTable is best described as an Excel feature that
   a. Displays columns and rows of data.
   b. "Stacks" pages of data.
   c. Allows you to display, summarize, and analyze list data.
   d. Requires a source list.

12. **Which PivotTable field allows you to average values?**
    a. Row field
    b. Data field
    c. Page field
    d. Column field

13. **To make changes to PivotTable data, you must**
    a. Create a page field.
    b. Edit cells in the source list and then refresh the PivotTable.
    c. Edit cells in the PivotTable and then refresh the source list.
    d. Drag a column header to the column area.

► Skills Review

1. **Plan and design a PivotTable.**
   a. Open the workbook titled XL L-2, then save it as "Creative Juices".
   b. You'll create a PivotTable to show the sum of sales across products and regions. Study the list, then write down the field names you think should be included in the PivotTable. Determine which fields you think should be column fields, row fields, and data fields, then sketch a draft PivotTable.
   c. Generate a PivotTable, then change the summary function.
   d. Make sure the cell pointer is in the table, click Data on the menu bar, then click PivotTable Report.
   e. Make sure Microsoft Excel list or database is selected, click Next, then click Next to confirm $A$1:$E$16 as the source list range.
   f. Drag the Product field button to the ROW area, then drag the Region field button to the COLUMN area.
   g. Drag the Sales $ field button to the DATA area.
   h. Double-click the Sum of Sales button, select Average as the summary function in the PivotTable Field dialog box, then click OK to close the PivotTable Field dialog box.
   i. Click Next, then click Finish in the fourth PivotTable dialog box.
   j. Click the PivotTable Field button on the PivotTable toolbar, then change the summary function to Sum.
   k. Rename the new sheet "Oct-98 PivotTable".
   l. Save your work.

2. **Analyze three-dimensional data.**
   a. Make sure the cell pointer is inside the PivotTable.
   b. Click the PivotTable Wizard button on the PivotTable toolbar.
   c. Drag the Sales Rep field button to the PAGE area.
   d. Click Finish.
   e. Click the Sales Rep list arrow, then click L. James.
   f. Click the Sales Rep list arrow, then click (All).
   g. Click the Sales Rep list arrow, then click M. Chang.
   h. Save your work.

3. Update a PivotTable.

a. Click the Sales List sheet tab.

b. Right-click the row header for row 8, then click Insert on the menu bar.

c. Using the data in Table L-2, add the new data items in the new blank row 8 of the table.

d. Click the Oct-98 PivotTable sheet tab.

e. Click the Refresh Data button on the PivotTable toolbar.

f. Save your work.

TABLE L-2: New data for sales list

field name	new data item
Period	Oct-98
Product	Lemon-Lime delight
Region	Northeast
Sales $	13,112
Sales Rep	M. Chang

4. Change the structure and format of a PivotTable.

a. In the PivotTable, drag cell B3 (Region) to cell A5. The orientation of the PivotTable changes.

b. Click Undo.

c. Select the range A3:D9.

d. Click Format on the menu bar; click AutoFormat; under Table Format, click Accounting 1; then click OK.

e. Press [Ctrl][Home] to deselect the range and return to cell A1.

f. Use the Sales Rep list arrow to verify that the AutoFormat was applied to all pages of the PivotTable. When you're finished, display the (All) page.

g. Save your work.

5. Create a chart from a PivotTable.

a. Double-click cell A3 to select the PivotTable.

b. Click the Chart Wizard button on the Standard toolbar.

c. In the first Chart Wizard dialog box, click Next to confirm the Column chart type.

d. In the second Chart Wizard dialog box, edit the data range to read ='Oct-98PivotTable'!$A$4:$E$9, then click Next.

e. In the third Chart Wizard dialog box, enter "Total Sales" as the chart title, then click Next.

f. In the fourth Chart Wizard dialog box, make sure the As new sheet option button is selected, then click Finish.

g. Preview, then print the chart.

h. Save the workbook.

6. Retrieve data with the GETPIVOTDATA FUNCTION.

a. Create a function to retrieve the total sales for Tangerine Tickler. Click the Sales List sheet tab.

b. Scroll down the worksheet, then click cell D20.

c. Click the Paste Function button on the Standard toolbar.

d. Select the GETPIVOTDATA function in the Paste Function dialog box, then click OK.

e. With the pointer in the Pivot_table text box, select any cell in the PivotTable.

f. Click the Name text box and type "Tangerine Tickler", then click OK.

g. Format cell D20 as currency.

h. Save the workbook, then preview and print the worksheet.

i. Close the workbook and exit Excel.

► Independent Challenges

1. You are the bookkeeper for the small accounting firm called Chavez, Long, and Doyle. Until recently, the partners had been tracking their hours manually in a log. Recently, you created an Excel list to track basic information: billing date, partner name, client name, nature of work, and hours spent. You used abbreviated field names to simplify the reports. It is your responsibility to generate a table summarizing this billing information by client. You will create a PivotTable that sums the hours by accountant and date for each project. Once the table is completed, you will print the PivotTable for the partners and the summary page for the managing partner, Maria Chavez, for approval.

To complete this independent challenge:

1. Open the workbook titled XL L-3, then save it as "Partner Billing Report".
2. Create a PivotTable that sums hours by partner and dates according to client. Use Figure L-20 as a guide.
3. Format the PivotTable using the AutoFormat of your choice.
4. Preview and print two copies of the PivotTable, one for each of the three partners. Then preview and print only the (All) page for Maria Chavez.
5. Save the worksheet, then close the workbook.

FIGURE L-20

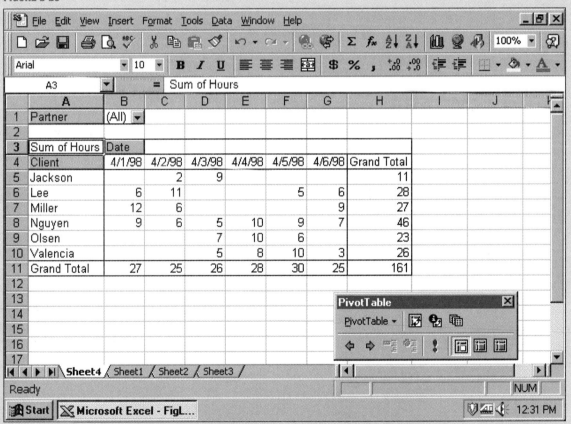

2. You are the owner of three mid-sized computer stores called PC Assist. One is located downtown, one is in the Plaza Mall, and one is in the Sun Center shopping center. You have been using Excel to maintain a sales summary list for the first-quarter sales in the following three areas: hardware, software, and miscellaneous items. You want to create a PivotTable to analyze and graph the sales in each category by month and store.

To complete this independent challenge:

1. Open the workbook titled XL L-4, then save it as "PC Assist—First Qtr Sales".
2. Create a PivotTable that sums the sales amount for each store across the rows and each category of sales down the columns. Add a page field for month.
3. Change the summary function to Average to show the average sales amount in each category.
4. Format the PivotTable using the Accounting 2 AutoFormat.
5. On a separate sheet, create a column chart for the January sales data in all three stores. (*Hint*: In the second Chart Wizard dialog box, change the data range to =Sheet4!$A$4:$D$8.) Remember to add a descriptive title to your chart.
6. Print the PivotTable and the chart.
7. Save, then close the workbook.

3. You manage a group of sales offices in the Western region for a cellular phone company called Digital Ear. Management has asked you to provide a summary table showing information on your sales staff, their locations, and their titles. You will create a PivotTable summarizing this information.

To complete this independent challenge:

1. Open the workbook titled XL L-5, then save it as "Western Sales Employees".
2. Create a PivotTable that lists the number of employees in each city, with the names of the cities listed across the columns and the titles listed down the rows. (*Hint*: Remember that the default summary function for cells containing text is Count.)
3. Add and format the label "Total Seattle Staff:" in cell C19 of Sheet1.
4. Create a formula in cell D19 that retrieves the total number of employees located in Seattle.
5. Preview, then print the PivotTable and the Staff List.
6. Save the worksheet, then close the workbook.

4. You are the managing director of WeCare, a nonprofit agency devoted to advocating better, more affordable daycare options nationwide. Next week, you will be giving a presentation to the top management of several corporations as part of an ongoing campaign to increase the availability of on-site daycare centers. As part of your presentation, you need to provide some summary information about conventional dayc are centers. You will retrieve the information you need from the US Census Department Web page and then create a PivotTable summarizing the data.

To complete this independent challenge:

1. Use your Web browser to go to the US Census Department home page at http://www.census.gov. (If you have trouble finding the page, go to http://www.course.com. From there, click Student Online Companions, click the link for this textbook, then click the Excel link for Unit L.) Click Subjects A–Z, in the alphabetical list click Child Care, then click Percent of Children Under 5 in Selected Child Care Arrangements: 1977–1993.
2. Print Table C1.
3. Open a new workbook and create a data list using the information from the Web page. Use the following field names: Date, Family Status, % of Kids in Day Care Cntrs or Nursery School. Enter the relevant data for all dates listed in the census table and for all three family statuses.
4. Create a PivotTable that shows the highest value in each category, using MAX as the summary function. List the dates down the rows and family status across the columns.
5. Format the PivotTable using the AutoFormat of your choice. Be sure to format the data as percentages.
6. Save the workbook as "Childcare Arrangements".
7. Preview, then print the data list and the PivotTable.
8. Close the workbook.

▶ Visual Workshop

Open the workbook titled XL L-6, then save it as "Corner Fruit Stand". Using the data in the workbook provided, create the PivotTable shown in Figure L-21. (*Hint:* There are two data summary fields.) Preview, then print the PivotTable. Save the worksheet, then close the workbook.

FIGURE L-21

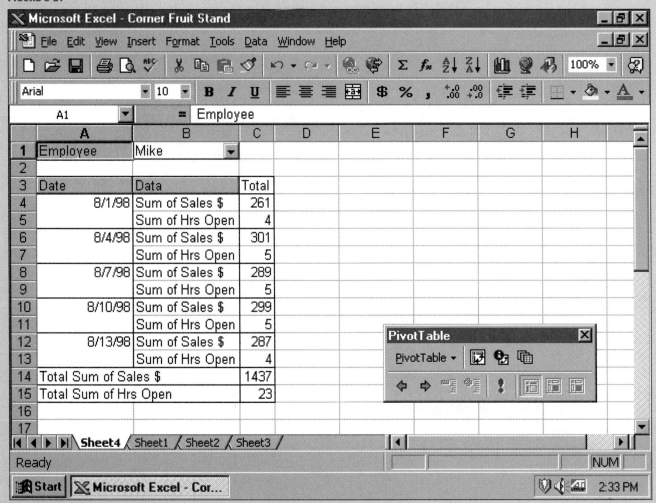

Exchanging
Data with Other Programs

Objectives

► **Plan a data exchange**
► **Import a text file**
► **Import a database table**
► **Insert a graphic file in a worksheet**
► **Embed a worksheet**
► **Link a worksheet**
► **Paste an Excel chart into a PowerPoint slide**
► **Convert a list to an Access table**

In a Windows environment, you can freely exchange data between Excel and most other Windows programs. In this unit, you will plan a data exchange with Excel. ➤ Megan Grahs, director of Nomad Ltd's health division, recently was approached by a business broker regarding the purchase of Ergonomic Enhancers, a mail-order catalog firm specializing in products that promote good health for office workers. Megan has asked Evan Brillstein, her assistant, to review the broker's paper documents and electronic files and develop a presentation on the feasibility of acquiring this company. To complete this project, Evan will exchange data between Excel and other programs.

Planning a Data Exchange

Because the tools available in Windows and Windows-supported programs are so flexible, exchanging data between Excel and other programs is easy. The first step involves planning what you want to accomplish with each data exchange. ◆ Evan uses the following guidelines to plan data exchanges between Excel and other programs in order to complete the business analysis project for Megan.

Steps

1. **Identify the data you want to exchange, its file type, and, if possible, the program used to create it**
   Whether the data you want to exchange is contained in a graphic file or a worksheet or consists only of text, it is important to identify the data's **source program**, the file type and the program used to create it. Once the source program has been identified, you can determine options for exchanging that data with Excel. Evan has been asked to analyze a text file containing the Ergonomic Enhancers product data. Although he does not know the source program, Evan knows that the file contains unformatted text. A file that consists of text but no formatting is sometimes referred to as an **ASCII file**. Because an ASCII file is a universally accepted text file format, Evan can easily import it into Excel.

2. **Determine the program with which you want to exchange the specified data**
   You might want to insert a graphic object into an Excel worksheet or add a spreadsheet to a WordPad document. Data exchange rules vary from program to program. Besides knowing which program created the data to be exchanged, you must also identify which program will receive the data (that is, the **destination program**). Evan received a database table of Ergonomic Enhancers' corporate customers created with the dBASE IV program. After determining that Excel can import dBASE IV tables, he plans to import that database file into Excel to perform his analysis.

3. **Determine the goal of your data exchange**
   Although it is convenient to use the Clipboard to cut, copy, and paste data within and among programs, you cannot retain a connection with the source program or document using this method. However, there are two ways to transfer data within and among programs that allow you to retain some connection with the source document and/or the source program. These data-transfer options involve using a Windows technology known as object linking and embedding, or **OLE**. The data to be exchanged, referred to as an **object**, may consist of text, a worksheet, or any other type of data. You use **embedding** to insert a copy of the original object in the destination document and, if necessary, to subsequently edit this data separately from the source document. This process is illustrated in Figure M-1. You use **linking** when you want the information you inserted to be updated automatically when the data in the source document changes. This process is illustrated in Figure M-2. Embedding and linking are discussed in more detail later on in this unit. Evan has determined that he needs to use both object embedding and object linking for his analysis and presentation project.

4. **Set up the data exchange**
   When you exchange data between two programs, it is best to start both programs prior to initiating the exchange. You also might want to tile the programs on the screen either horizontally or vertically so that you can see them both while the data is exchanged. Evan will work with Excel and WordPad when exchanging data for this project.

5. **Execute the data exchange**
   The steps you use will vary, depending on the type of data exchanged. Evan is eager to attempt the data exchanges to complete his business analysis of Ergonomic Enhancers.

FIGURE M-1: Embedded object

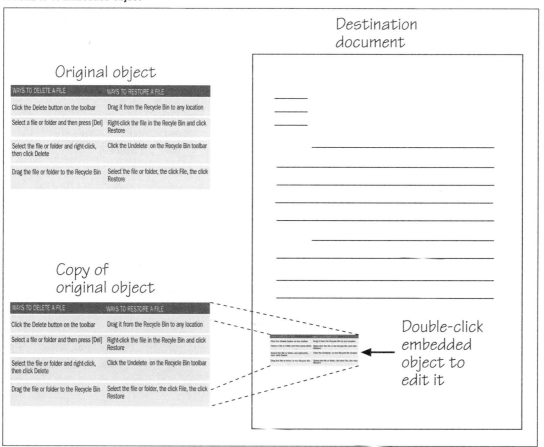

FIGURE M-2: Linked object

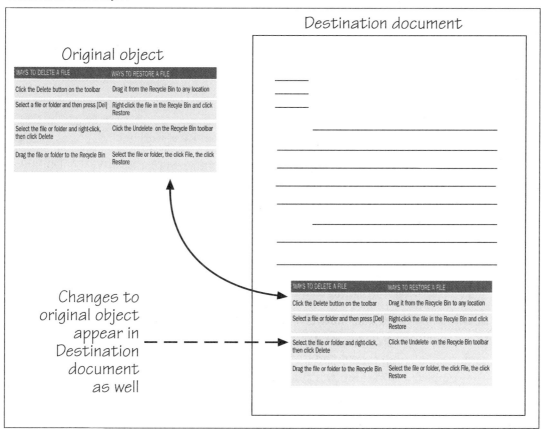

Excel 97

Importing a Text File

You can import data stored in other programs into Excel by simply opening the file, as long as Excel can read its file type. See Table M-1 for a list of file formats that Excel can import. After importing the file, you then use the Save As command on the File menu to save the data in Excel's own format. Text files utilize a tab or space as the **delimiter**, or column separator, in order to separate columns of data. When you import a text file into Excel, the Text Import Wizard automatically opens and describes how text is separated in the imported file. Now that he's planned his data exchange, Evan wants to import a delimited text file containing product cost and pricing data from Ergonomic Enhancers.

Trouble?

If the Preview window in the Text Import Wizard dialog box contains odd-looking characters, make sure you selected the correct Original Data Type.

1. In a blank workbook, click the **Open button** 📂 on the Standard toolbar, click the **Look in list arrow**, then click the drive containing your Student Disk
   The Open dialog box shows only those files that match the file types listed in the Files of type box—usually Microsoft Excel Files. To import the delimited text file, you need to select Text Files from the list of available file types.

2. Click the **Files of type list arrow**, click **Text Files**; if necessary, click **XL M-1**, then click **Open**
   The first Text Import Wizard dialog box opens. See Figure M-3. Notice that under Original data type, the Delimited option button is selected. In the Preview of file box, line 1 indicates that the file contains three columns of data: Item, Cost, and Price. Because no changes are necessary in this dialog box, you can continue.

3. Click **Next**
   The second Text Import Wizard dialog box opens. Under Delimiters, the tab character is selected as the delimiter, and the Data preview box contains an image of the text formatted in columns.

4. Click **Next**
   The third Text Import Wizard dialog box opens with options for formatting the three columns of data. Notice that under Column data format, the General option button is selected currently. This is the best formatting option for text mixed with numbers.

5. Click **Finish**
   Excel imports the text file into the blank worksheet as three columns of data: Item, Cost, and Price. Now, you can save the converted text file as an Excel workbook.

6. Click **File** on the menu bar, click **Save As**, make sure the drive containing your Student Disk appears in the Save in box, click the **Save as type list arrow**, click **Microsoft Excel Workbook**, edit the File name box to read **Ergonomic Enhancers - Product Info**, then click **Save**
   The file is saved as a workbook, and the new name appears in the title bar. To improve the appearance of the new worksheet, you widen column A. Then you'll add a column to show the difference between the cost of each item and its price (the profit). You finish by adding bold and centered formatting to the column labels.

7. Double-click the border between the **Columns A and B headers**, click cell **D1**, type **Profit**, click cell **D2**, type **=C2-B2**, copy the contents of cell D2 to range **D3:D23**, then center the column labels and apply bold formatting
   The completed worksheet, which analyzes the text file imported into Excel, is shown in Figure M-4. Now, you'll print and save your work.

8. Preview and print the list in portrait orientation, then save and close the workbook

FIGURE M-3: First Text Import Wizard dialog box

Original data type is delimited

Three-column headings

Preview of file box

Text appears in three columns

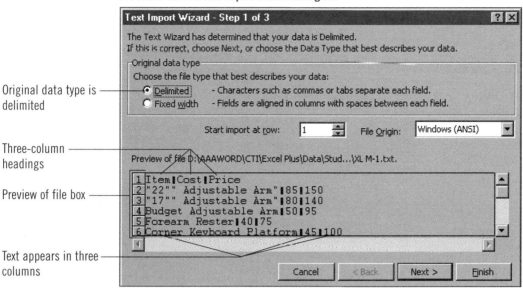

FIGURE M-4: Completed worksheet with imported text file

Columns from text file

Column A widened to fit longest entry

Added column with new profit data

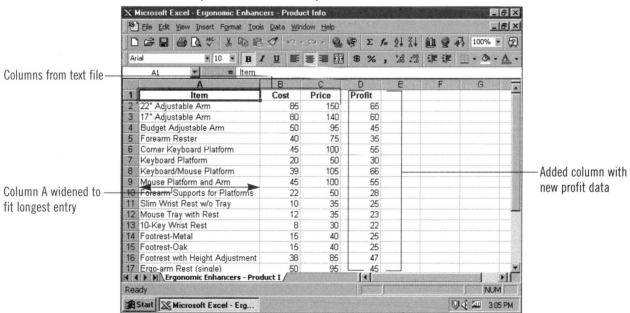

TABLE M-1: Importable file formats and extensions

file format	file extension(s)	file format	file extensions
dBASE II, III, IV	DBF	CSV (Comma Separated Values)	CSV
Excel 4.0	XLS, XLW, XLC, XLM	DIF (Data Interchange Format, i.e., VisiCalc)	DIF
Excel 5.0/7.0	XLS, XLT	Formatted Text (Space or column delimited)	TXT, PRN
Lotus 1-2-3	WKS, WK1, WK3, ALL, FMT, WK3, FM3, WK4	Text (Tab delimited)	TXT
Quattro/Quattro Pro	WQ1, WBI	SYLK (Symbolic Link: Multiplan, Microsoft Works)	SLK

Importing a Database Table

In addition to text files, you also can use Excel to import files from other Microsoft Office programs or database tables. To import files that contain supported file formats, simply open the file. Then you are ready to work with the data in Excel. ✏️ Evan received a database table of Ergonomics Enhancers corporate customers, which was created with dBASE IV. He will import this table into Excel, then format, sort, and total the data.

Steps

1. **Click the Open button 🖿 on the Standard toolbar, make sure the drive containing your Student Disk appears in the Look in box, click the Files of type list arrow, scroll down and click dBase Files, click XL M-2, if necessary, then click Open**
   Excel opens the database table and names the sheet tab XL M-2. See Figure M-5. Before manipulating the data, you'll save the table as an Excel workbook.

2. **Click File on the menu bar; click Save As; make sure the drive containing your Student Disk appears in the Save in box; click the Save as type list arrow; scroll up, if necessary, and click Microsoft Excel Workbook; edit the File name box to read Ergonomic Enhancers - Corporate Customer Info; click Save; then rename the sheet tab Corporate Customer Info**
   Next, you will edit the truncated column labels in row 1 so that the text wraps to two lines.

3. **Edit cell A1 to read COMPANY NAME (no underscore), click cell F1, type 1994, press [Alt][Enter] to force a new line, type ORDER, press Tab, type 1995, press [Alt][Enter], type ORDER, then press [Enter]**
   Pressing [Alt][Enter] as you create cell entries forces the text to wrap to the next line. Next, you will widen columns F and G, then format all the column labels.

4. **Format columns F and G using the Comma Style with no decimal places, center and apply bold formatting to all the column labels, then widen the columns as necessary**
   Now you will save, then sort the list in descending order by the 1995 orders.

5. **Save the workbook, click cell G2, then click the Sort Descending button 🔽 on the Standard toolbar**
   With the list formatted and sorted, you are ready to add totals to columns F and G.

6. **Select range F19:G19, click the AutoSum button Σ on the Standard toolbar, then format the range F19:G19 with borders**
   To view your completed changes, you'll display the entire sheet on a single screen.

7. **Press [Ctrl][Home], click the Zoom Control box on the Standard toolbar, type 75, then press [Enter]**
   Your completed worksheet should match Figure M-6. Now, you'll print and save your work.

8. **Preview and print the list in landscape orientation, then save the workbook.**

FIGURE M-5: Imported dBASE table

Excel substitutes underscores in place of spaces

Truncated column labels

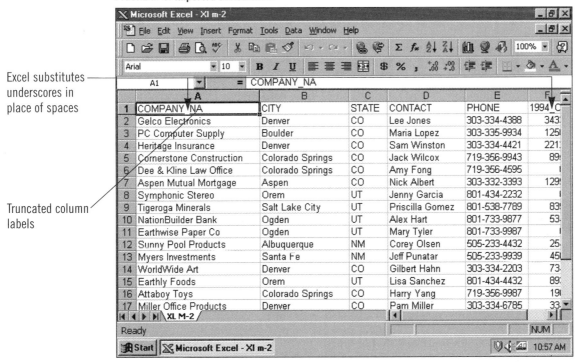

FIGURE M-6: Completed worksheet containing imported data

Adjusted and formatted column labels

New totals

Renamed sheet tab

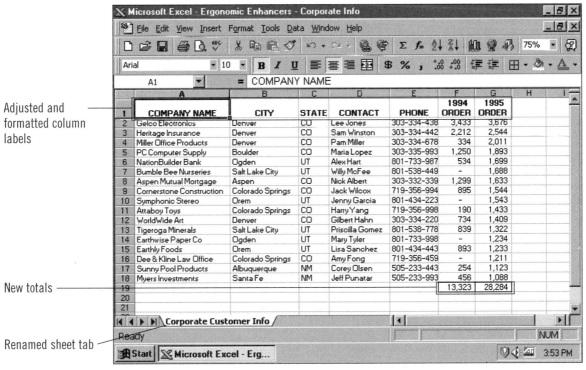

CLUES TO USE

Exporting Excel data

Most of the file types that Excel can import (listed in Table M-1) are also the file types to which Excel can export, or pass data to. Excel also can export Text and CSV formats for Macintosh and OS/2. Saving to a non-Excel format might result in the loss of formatting that is unique to Excel. To export an Excel worksheet, use the Save As command on the File menu, click the Save as type list arrow, then select the desired format.

Inserting a Graphic File in a Worksheet

A graphic object (such as a drawing, logo, or photograph) can greatly enhance a worksheet's visual impact. The Picture options on the Format menu make it easy to insert graphics into an Excel worksheet. Once you've inserted a picture, you can edit it using the tools available on Excel's Drawing and Picture toolbars. ◄▬▬ Evan wants to insert a copy of the Nomad Ltd Health Division logo at the top of his corporate customer database table. He has a copy of the logo, previously created by the company's marketing department, saved as a graphics file on a disk. He starts by returning the Zoom Control to 100%.

Steps

1. Click the **Zoom Control list arrow** on the Standard toolbar, then click **100%**
Before inserting the logo at the top of the worksheet, you must create space for it.

2. Select **rows 1** through **5**, click **Insert** on the menu bar, then click **Rows**
Next, you'll display the various Picture commands on the Insert menu.

3. Click cell **A1**, click **Insert** on the menu bar, then point to **Picture**
The Picture menu is displayed. See Figure M-7. This menu offers several options for inserting graphics. Because you already have a file that contains the company logo, you'll select From File.

4. Click **From File**; in the Insert Picture dialog box, make sure the drive containing your Student Disk appears in the Look in box; then click **XL M-3**
A preview of the selected graphic displays on the right side of the Insert Picture dialog box. See Figure M-8. Now, you are ready to insert a copy of the graphic on the worksheet.

Trouble?

If you don't see the Drawing toolbar displayed in your window, click the Drawing button 🔲 on the Standard toolbar, then continue with Step 6.

5. Click **Insert**
Excel inserts the graphic and opens both the Drawing and the Picture toolbars. See Figure M-9. To improve the look of the graphic, you'll use the Line Style button on the Drawing toolbar to add a border.

6. With the graphic still selected, click the **Line Style button** ▤ on the Drawing toolbar, click the **¼ pt** line style, press **[Esc]**, then click the **Drawing button** 🔲 on the Standard toolbar
The Drawing toolbar closes and the graphic is displayed in the worksheet with a border. Now, you are ready to preview and print the worksheet, save and close the workbook, and exit Excel.

7. Preview and print the worksheet in landscape orientation, then save and close the workbook and exit Excel

FIGURE M-7: **Picture menu**

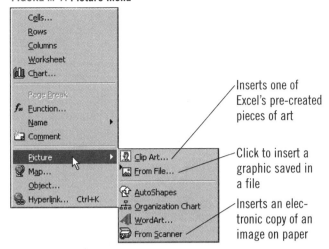

Inserts one of Excel's pre-created pieces of art

Click to insert a graphic saved in a file

Inserts an electronic copy of an image on paper

FIGURE M-8: **Insert Picture dialog box**

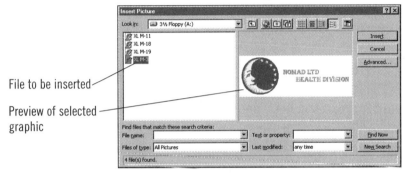

File to be inserted

Preview of selected graphic

FIGURE M-9: **Worksheet with embedded picture**

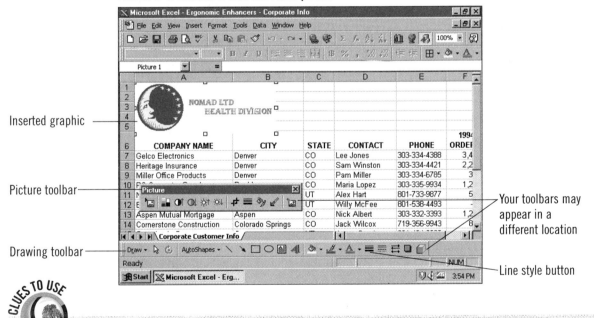

Inserted graphic

Picture toolbar

Drawing toolbar

Your toolbars may appear in a different location

Line style button

Creating and Modifying 3-D Shapes

Excel's Drawing toolbar makes it easy to create your own three-dimensional (3-D) graphics right in the worksheet, rather than importing them from another program. To create a 3-D graphic, first use the AutoShapes button on the Drawing toolbar to create a two-dimensional shape. Then select the shape, click the 3-D button on the Drawing toolbar, and click the 3-D effect you want. To modify a 3-D object—for example, its color or surface texture—click again, click 3-D Settings, then make the selections you want on the 3-D Settings toolbar.

Excel 97

Embedding a Worksheet

Microsoft Office programs work together to make it easy to copy an object (such as text, data, or a graphic) in a source program and then insert it into a document in a different program (the destination program). If you insert the object using a simple Paste command, however, you retain no connection to the source program. That's why it is often more useful to embed objects rather than simply paste them. **Embedding** allows you to edit an Excel workbook from within a different program using Excel's commands and tools. You can embed a worksheet so the data is visible in the destination program or so it appears as an icon in the destination document. To access data embedded as an icon, you simply double-click the icon. ◢ Evan decides to send an e-mail message to Megan updating her on the project status. He attaches a WordPad memo to this message, which includes the projected sales revenue worksheet embedded as an icon. First, he starts the WordPad program.

Steps

1. Press [Ctrl][Esc] to open the Windows Start menu; point to **Programs**; point to **Accessories**; click **WordPad**; then, if necessary, maximize the WordPad window
   The WordPad program opens, with a blank document displayed in the WordPad window. Now, you can open the previously created memo.

2. Click **File** on the WordPad menu bar, click **Open**, make sure the drive containing your Student Disk appears in the Look in box, click **XL M-4**, then click **Open**
   The memo opens. Before making any changes, you'll save the document with a new name.

3. Click **File** on the menu bar, click **Save As**, make sure the Save in box contains the drive containing your Student Disk, edit the File name box to read **Ergonomic Enhancers—Sales Projection Memo**, then click **Save**
   Because you want to embed the worksheet below the last line of the document, you'll move to the end of the memo and position the insertion point there.

4. Press [Ctrl][End], click **Insert** on the menu bar, then click **Object**
   The Insert Object dialog box opens. Because you are embedding an existing file, you choose the option that creates an embedded object from a file.

5. Click the **Create from File option button**
   Next, you select the name of the file you want to embed and indicate that the file should be embedded as an icon.

6. Click **Browse**, make sure the drive containing your Student Disk appears in the Look in box, click **XL M-5**, click **Insert**; then in the Insert Object dialog box, select the **Display As Icon check box**
   The Insert Object dialog box now shows the file to be embedded. See Figure M-10. You are now ready to embed the object.

7. Click **OK**, then click outside the object to deselect it
   The memo now contains an embedded copy of the sales projection worksheet, displayed as an icon. See Figure M-11. You double-click the icon to ensure it was embedded properly.

8. Double-click the **Microsoft Excel Worksheet icon** 📊
   The worksheet appears within the Excel program. See Figure M-12. Now, you can close it and return to the WordPad document.

9. Click **File** on the menu bar, click **Close & Return to Ergonomic Enhancers—Sales Projection Memo**, then save the memo

QuickTip

To edit an embedded object, double-click the object to open the source program, then make the desired changes. When you save and exit the source program, the embedded object reflects the changes.

Trouble?

If the entire worksheet appears, rather than just the icon, you might not have checked the Display As Icon box. Choose Object on the Insert menu, select the Display As Icon box, then continue with Step 8.

FIGURE M-10: Insert Object dialog box

Your drive may differ

Click to embed an existing worksheet

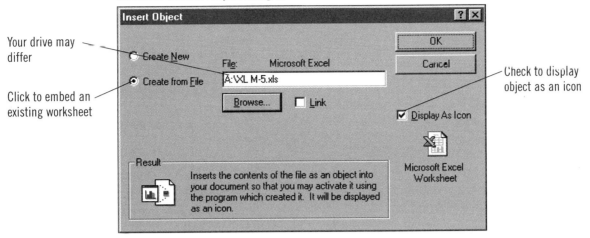

Check to display object as an icon

FIGURE M-11: Memo with embedded worksheet

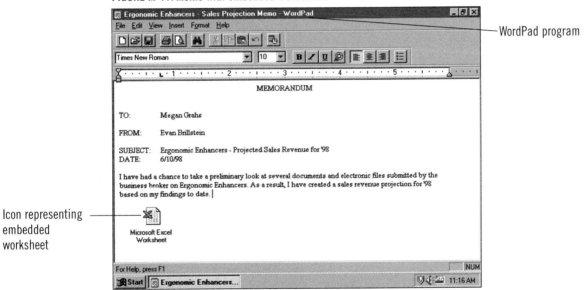

WordPad program

Icon representing embedded worksheet

FIGURE M-12: Embedded worksheet opened in Excel

Excel program

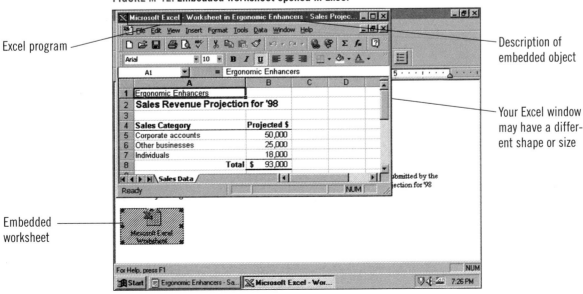

Description of embedded object

Your Excel window may have a differ-ent shape or size

Embedded worksheet

Linking a Worksheet to Another Program

You use **linking** when you want to insert a worksheet into another program and retain a connection with the original document as well as the original program. When you link a worksheet to another program, the link contains a pointer to the source document so that, when you double-click it, the source document opens for editing. Once you link a worksheet to another program, any changes you make to the original worksheet document are reflected in the linked object. Evan realizes he may be making some changes to the workbook he embedded in the memo to Megan. To ensure that these changes are reflected in this memo, he decides to link a copy of the worksheet to the source document, rather than simply embed it. First, he deletes the embedded worksheet icon, then replaces it with a linked version of the same worksheet.

Steps

1. With the WordPad memo still displayed in your window, if necessary, click the Microsoft Excel Worksheet icon 📄 to select it, then press **[Delete]**
   The embedded worksheet is removed. Now, you will link the same worksheet to the memo.

2. Make sure the insertion point is below the last line of the memo, click **Insert** on the WordPad menu bar, click **Object**, then in the Insert Object dialog box click the **Create from File option button**
   In the next step you select the file, then link the object.

3. Click **Browse**, make sure the drive containing your Student Disk appears in the Look in box, click **XL M-5**, click **Insert**, then select the **Link check box**
   With the file containing the worksheet object selected, you are ready to link the worksheet object to the memo.

4. Click **OK**; drag the worksheet's **lower right selection handle** to the right margin to enlarge the window, then click outside the worksheet to deselect it
   The memo now displays a linked copy of the sales projection worksheet. See Figure M-13. In the future, any changes made to the source file (XL M-5) will also be made to the linked copy in the WordPad memo. In the next step, you'll verify this by making a change to the source file and viewing its effect on the WordPad memo. First you save your changes, then exit WordPad.

QuickTip

When you open an Excel workbook containing a linked object, a dialog box will appear asking if you want to update the links.

5. Click the **Save button** 🖫 on the WordPad Standard toolbar, click **File** on the WordPad menu bar, then click **Exit**; start Excel, then open the file **XL M-5**
   The worksheet appears in the Excel window. You will test the link by changing the sales projection for individuals to 15,000.

6. Click cell **B6**, type **15,000**, then press **[Enter]**
   Now, you will open the WordPad memo to verify that the same change was made automatically to the linked copy of the worksheet.

Trouble?

If you can't read the worksheet clearly, select it, then drag the lower-right selection handle to enlarge it. Continue with Step 8.

7. Press **[Ctrl][Esc]** to open the Windows Start menu, point to **Programs**, point to **Accessories**, click **WordPad**; click **File** on the WordPad menu bar, then click **1 Ergonomic Enhancers - Sales Projection Memo**
   The memo re-displays on your screen with the new amount automatically inserted. See Figure M-14. Now that you know the link works correctly, you close the memo. Then you will close the worksheet without saving the change you made to cell B6.

8. Click **File** on the WordPad menu bar, click **Exit**, click **No** if you are asked if you want to save changes; click **File** on the Excel menu bar, click **Exit**, then click **No** to close the workbook without saving changes

FIGURE M-13: Memo with linked worksheet

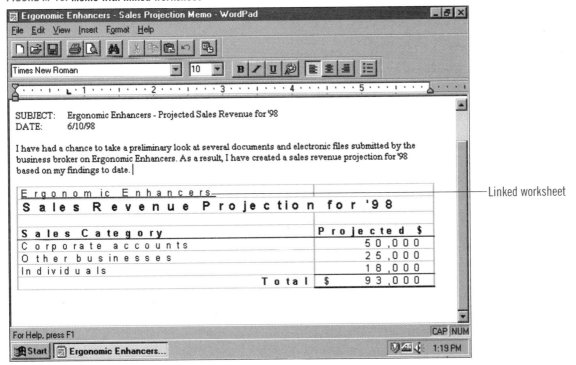

Linked worksheet

FIGURE M-14: Viewing updated WordPad memo

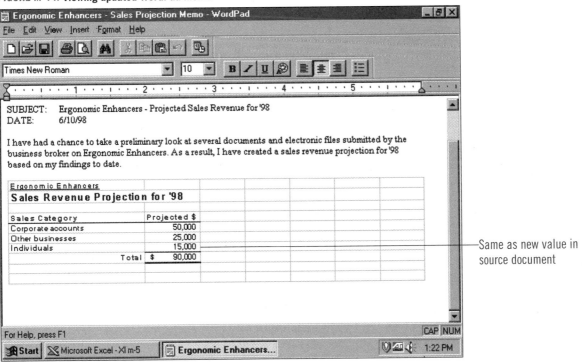

Same as new value in source document

Managing links

If changes have been made to the source file, the link is updated automatically each time you open the destination document. You can manage linked objects further by choosing Links on the Edit menu. This opens the Links dialog box, which allows you to update a link, or change the source file of a link. You also can **break**, or delete, a link by selecting the linked object, then pressing [Delete].

Pasting an Excel Chart into a PowerPoint Slide

Microsoft PowerPoint is a presentation graphics program, which means that you can use it to create slide show presentations. For example, you can create a slide show to present a sales plan to management or to inform potential clients about a new service. PowerPoint slides can include a mix of text, data, and graphics. Adding an Excel chart to a slide helps to illustrate complicated data, which gives your presentation added visual appeal. ◥━━━ Based on his analysis thus far, Megan asks Evan to brief the Marketing Department on the possible acquisition of Ergonomic Enhancers. Evan will make his presentation using PowerPoint slides. He decides to add an Excel chart to one of the presentation slides illustrating the 1998 Sales Projection data. He begins by starting PowerPoint.

Steps 1 2 3 4

Trouble?

If you don't see Microsoft PowerPoint on your Programs menu, look for something with a similar name somewhere on the Programs menu or the Start menu. If you still can't find it, Microsoft PowerPoint may not be installed on your computer. See your instructor or technical support person for assistance. If the Office Assistant opens when you start PowerPoint, click close and continue with Step 2.

1. Press **[Ctrl][Esc]** to open the Windows Start menu, point to **Programs**, then click **Microsoft PowerPoint**

   The PowerPoint dialog box opens within the Microsoft PowerPoint window. This is where you indicate whether you want to create a new presentation or open a previously created one. You want to open a previously created presentation.

2. Click the **Open an existing presentation option button**; click **OK**; make sure the drive containing your Student Disk appears in the Look in box; if necessary, click **XL M-6**; then click **Open**

   The presentation appears in Outline view, as shown in Figure M-15. Before you make any changes, you'll save the presentation with a new name.

3. Save the presentation as **Marketing Department Presentation**

   Notice that the outline of the presentation shows the title and text included on each slide. You will add an Excel chart to slide 2, "1998 Sales Projections". To add the chart, you first need to select the slide, then display it in Slide view.

4. Click the **slide 2 icon** ☐, click **View** on the PowerPoint menu bar, then click **Slide**

   The slide appears enlarged in its own window, as shown in Figure M-16. Although you could add new text to the slide at this point, you decide not to in order to keep the focus on the Excel chart. You'll begin adding the chart to slide 2 in the next step.

5. Click **Insert** on the PowerPoint menu bar, then click **Object**

   The Insert Object dialog box opens. You want to insert an object (the Excel chart) that has already been saved in a file.

QuickTip

The Insert Chart button allows you to create a new chart using a limited spreadsheet program called Microsoft Graph. Experienced Excel users will find it easier to create a chart in Excel.

6. Click the **Create from file option button**, click **Browse**, make sure the drive containing your Student Disk appears in the Look in box, click **XL M-7**, click **OK**; in the Insert Object dialog box click **OK** again, then press **[Esc]**

   A pie chart illustrating the 1998 sales projections appears in the slide with the words "Click to add text". The chart is difficult to read in Slide view, so you'll switch to Slide Show view to display the slide on the full screen. The words "Click to add text" will then disappear.

7. Click **View** on the PowerPoint menu bar, then click **Slide Show**

   After a pause, the first slide appears on the screen. You press [Enter] to move to the next slide.

8. Press **[Enter]**

   The finished sales projection slide appears, as shown in Figure M-17. The presentation for the Marketing Department is complete. Now you can return to Slide View, save the presentation, and exit Power Point.

QuickTip

The Excel worksheet you see in the PowerPoint slide is the one that was active when the workbook was last saved.

9. Press **[Esc]**, click the **Save button** 🖫 on the PowerPoint Standard toolbar, click **File** on the menu bar, then click **Exit**

FIGURE M-15: Presentation in Outline view

Slide 2 title

Slide 2 icon

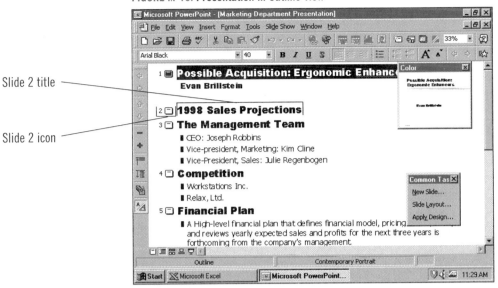

FIGURE M-16: Slide 2 in Slide view

No text added to this slide

Location to paste Excel chart

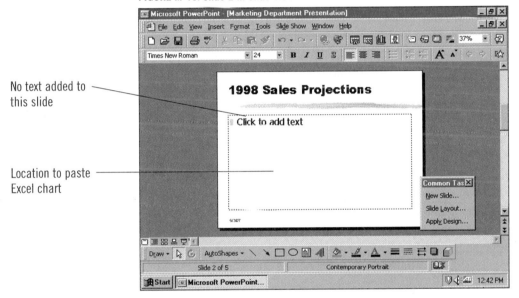

FIGURE M-17: Completed Sales Projections slide in Slide Show view

Excel chart inserted into slide

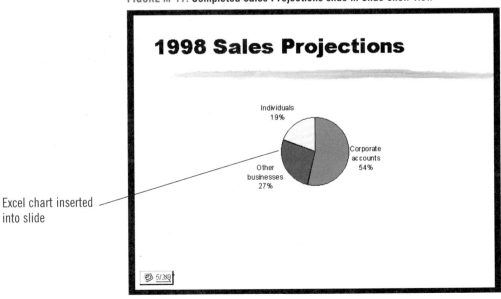

Converting a List to an Access Table

An Excel data list can be converted easily for use in Microsoft Access, a sophisticated database program. You need to make sure, however, that the list's column labels don't contain any leading spaces or any of the following special characters: a period (.), an exclamation point (!), an accent mark (`), or brackets ([]). Once converted to Access format, a data list is called a **table**. ⬛➤ Megan has just received a workbook containing salary information for the managers at Ergonomic Enhancers. She asks Evan to convert the list to a Microsoft Access table so that it can be added to Nomad Ltd's database of compensation information for all employees. Evan begins by opening the list in Excel.

Steps 1 2 3 4

1. Start Excel, open the workbook XL M-8, then save it as **Ergonomic Enhancers Management**

2. With cell A1 selected, click **Data** on the menu bar, then click **Convert to MS Access**; in the Convert to Microsoft Access dialog box make sure the **New database option button** is selected, then click **OK**

   The Microsoft Access window opens, followed by the First Import Spreadsheet Wizard dialog box. See Figure M-18. In the next step, you'll indicate that you want to use the column headings in the Excel list as the field names in the Access database.

3. Select the **First Row Contains Column Headings check box**, then click **Next**

   In the next Import Spreadsheet Wizard dialog box, you specify whether you want to store the Excel data in a new or an existing table. In this case, you want to store it as a new table.

4. Make sure the **In a New Table option button** is selected, then click **Next**

   The next Import Spreadsheet Wizard dialog box opens. This is where you specify information about the fields (the Excel columns) you are importing. Notice that the column headings from the Excel list are used as the field names. You also can indicate which columns from the Excel list you do not want to import. In this case, you do not want to import the Annual Salary column.

5. Scroll right until the **Annual Salary column** is in view; click anywhere in the column to select it, then, under Field Options, select the **Do not import field (Skip) check box**

   Your completed Import Spreadsheet Wizard dialog box should match Figure M-19. Now, you can continue importing the Excel data list.

6. Click **Next**

   The final Import Spreadsheet Wizard dialog box opens. This is where you specify the table's primary key. A **primary key** is the field that contains unique information for each record (or row) of information. Specifying a primary key allows you to retrieve data more quickly in the future. In this case, you use the Social Security field as the primary key because the social security number for each person in the list is unique.

7. Click the **Choose my own Primary Key option button**; make sure Social Security appears in the list box next to the selected option button; click **Next**; in the next Import Spreadsheet Wizard dialog box, click **Finish**; click **OK**; then click the **Maximize button 🔲** on the Microsoft Access window

   The new Access table is shown as an icon in the Tables tab of the new database. See Figure M-20. Next, you'll open the table to make sure it was imported correctly.

8. In the Tables tab, make sure **Compensation** is selected, then click **Open**

   The data from the Excel workbook is displayed in the new Excel table. Finally, you save the new database, then exit Access and Excel. When you click the Save button on the Access toolbar, Access automatically saves the database to the same location as the original Excel workbook.

9. Click the **Save button 🔲** on the Access toolbar, click **File** on the Access menu bar, then click **Exit**; in the Excel window save the workbook, then exit Excel

Trouble?

If you don't see the Convert to MS Access command on the Excel Data menu, you need to install the Microsoft AccessLinks Add-in program. See your instructor or technical support person for assistance.

QuickTip

If Access chooses your primary key, it will select a field with unique data or create a new field that assigns a unique number.

QuickTip

Because converting a list to Access format is permanent, it's a good idea to keep a copy of your Excel list.

FIGURE M-18: First Import Spreadsheet Wizard dialog box

Column labels will become field names

Preview of Access table

Unformatted dates will he formatted in final table

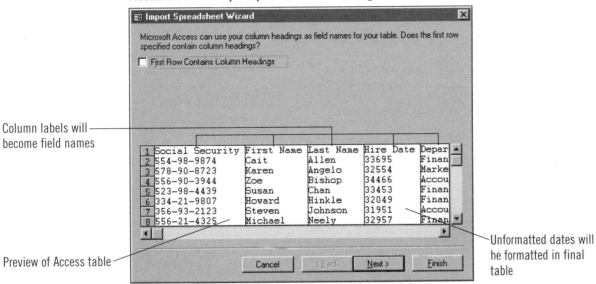

FIGURE M-19: Completed Input Spreadsheet Wizard dialog box

Click to select

Annual Salary column

Field names

Horizontal scroll bar

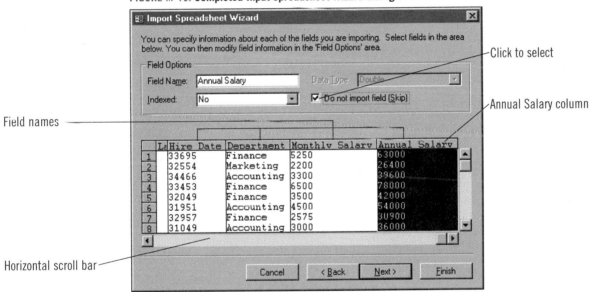

FIGURE M-20: Maximized Microsoft Access window

Database name taken from Excel workbook name

Icon indicates new table

New table name taken from sheet name in Excel workbook

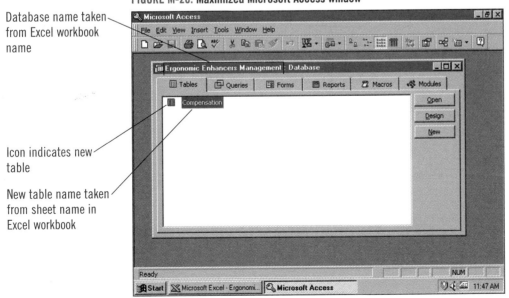

Practice

► Concepts Review

Label each element of the Excel screen shown in Figure M-21.

FIGURE M-21

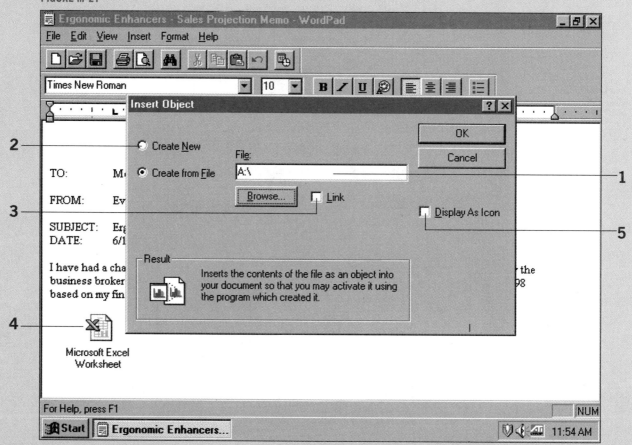

Match each statement with the term it describes.

6. Source document
7. Linking
8. Destination document
9. Embedding
10. Presentation program
11. Table

a. Used to create slide shows.
b. Copies and retains a connection with the source program and source document.
c. Document receiving the object to be embedded or linked.
d. An Excel list converted to Access format.
e. Copies and retains a connection with the source program.
f. File from which the object to be embedded or linked originates.

Select the best answer from the list of choices.

12. An ASCII file
    a. Contains formatting but no text.
    b. Contains an unformatted worksheet.
    c. Contains text but no formatting.
    d. Contains a PowerPoint presentation.

13. **An object consists of**
    a. Text only.
    b. Text, a worksheet, or any other type of data.
    c. A worksheet only.
    d. Database data only.

14. **Which of the following is true about converting an Excel list to an Access table?**
    a. The column labels cannot contain spaces.
    b. You must convert all the columns in the list to an Access table.
    c. The column labels can be used as the table's field names.
    d. All of the above.

15. **To view a worksheet that has been embedded as an icon in a WordPad document, you need to**
    a. Click View, then click Worksheet.
    b. Drag the icon.
    c. Click File, then click Open.
    d. Double-click the worksheet icon.

▶ Skills Review

1. **Import a text file.**
   a. Click File on the menu bar, click Open, make sure the drive containing your Student Disk appears in the Look in box, click the Files of type list arrow, click Text Files, click XL M-9, then click Open.
   b. Under Original data type in the first Text Import Wizard dialog box, make sure the Delimited option button is selected, then click Next.
   c. In the second Text Import Wizard dialog box, make sure the Tab box is selected, then click Next.
   d. In the third Text Import Wizard dialog box, click Finish.
   e. Save the file as an Excel workbook with the name "Sunshine Temporary—Income Summary".
   f. Widen the columns so that all the data is visible.
   g. Center the column labels and apply bold formatting.
   h. Save, preview, then print your work.
   i. Close the workbook.

2. **Import a database table.**
   a. Click File on the menu bar, click Open, make sure the drive containing your Student Disk appears in the Look in box, click the Files of type list arrow, click dBase Files, click XL M-10, then click Open.
   b. Save the file as an Excel workbook with the name "Sunshine Temporary—Company Budget".
   c. Rename the sheet tab "Company Budget".
   d. Change the column labels so they read as follows: BUDGET CATEGORY, BUDGET ITEM, MONTH, and AMOUNT BUDGETED.
   e. Use AutoSum to calculate a total in cell D26, then add a top and bottom border to the cell.
   f. Format range D2:D26 using the Comma Style with no decimal places.
   g. Add bold formatting to the column labels, then wrap the text on two lines.
   h. Manually adjust the columns as necessary.
   i. Save your work.

3. Embed a graphic file in a worksheet.

   a. Add four rows above row 1 to create space for the graphic file.

   b. Click cell A1, click Insert on the menu bar, point to Picture, then click From File.

   c. Make sure the drive containing your Student Disk appears in the Look in box.

   d. Click XL M-11, then click Insert.

   e. Drag the graphic's lower-right handle down to make the graphic easier to read.

   f. Open the Drawing toolbar, if necessary.

   g. Use the Line style button to add a border around the graphic.

   h. Press [Esc] to deselect the graphic, then close the Drawing toolbar.

   i. Preview, then print the worksheet.

   j. Save your work.

4. Embed a worksheet in another program.

   a. Type "For details on Green Hills salaries, then click icon:" in cell A33.

   b. Click cell D33, click Insert on the menu bar, then click Object.

   c. Click the Create from File tab, then click Browse.

   d. Make sure the drive containing your Student Disk appears in the Look in box.

   e. Click XL M-12, then click Insert.

   f. Select the Display as Icon check box, then click OK to embed the object.

   g. Double-click the icon to verify that the worksheet opens, then close it.

   h. Preview, then print the Sunshine Temporary—Company Budget worksheet.

   i. Save your work.

5. Link a worksheet.

   a. Click the embedded object icon to select it (if necessary), then press [Delete].

   b. Click cell A33, click Insert on the menu bar, then click Object.

   c. Click the Create from File tab, then click Browse.

   d. Make sure the drive containing your Student Disk appears in the Look in box.

   e. Click XL M-12, then click Insert.

   f. Make sure the Display as Icon check box is *not* selected, then select the Link to File check box.

   g. Click OK to link the object.

   h. Save, then close the Sunshine Temporary—Company Budget worksheet.

   i. Open the XL M-12 workbook, change the Manager salary to 5000, then open the Sunshine Temporary—Company Budget worksheet; click Yes when are asked if you want to update links, then verify that the manager salary has changed to 5000 in the linked workbook.

   j. Preview, then print the worksheet with the linked object on one page.

   k. Close both workbooks without saving changes, then exit Excel.

6. Paste an Excel chart into a PowerPoint slide.

   a. Press [Ctrl][Esc] to open the Windows Start menu, point to Programs, then click Microsoft PowerPoint.

   b. Click the Open an existing presentation option button, click OK, make sure the drive containing your Student Disk appears in the Look in box, click XL M-13, then click Open.

   c. Save the presentation as "Monthly Budget Meeting".

   d. Click the slide 2 icon to select the slide's title (January Expenditures), click View on the menu bar, then click Slide.

   e. Click Insert on the menu bar, then click Object.

f. Click the Create from file option button, click Browse, make sure the drive containing your Student Disk appears in the Look in box, click XL M-14, click OK, click OK again in the Insert Object dialog box, then press [Esc] to deselect the chart in the slide.

g. Click View on the menu bar, then click Slide Show.

h. Press [Enter] to display the slide with the chart.

i. Press [Esc] to return to Slide view, click the Save button on the PowerPoint Standard toolbar, click File on the menu bar, then click Exit to exit PowerPoint.

7. Converting an Excel list to an Access database.

a. Start Excel, open the workbook XL M-15, then save it as Budget List.

b. With cell A1 selected, click Data, then click Convert to MS Access; in the Convert to Microsoft Access dialog box make sure the New database option button is selected, then click OK.

c. Select the First Row Contains Column Headings check box, then click Next.

d. Make sure the In a New Table option button is selected, then click Next.

e. Click anywhere in the month column to select it, select the Do not import field (Skip) check box, then click Next.

f. Click the Let Access add Primary Key option button, then click Next.

g. Click Finish, click OK, then click the Maximize button on the Microsoft Access window.

h. Make sure January Budget is selected in the Tables tab, then click Open.

i. Drag the column borders as necessary to fully display the field names.

j. Click the Save button on the Access toolbar, click File on the menu bar, then click Exit to exit Access.

k. In the Excel window, save and print the worksheet (along with the conversion notice), then exit Excel.

▶ Independent Challenges

1. You are opening a new store, called Bridge Blades, that rents in-line skates. The store is located right outside Golden Gate Park in San Francisco, California. Recently, you heard that Tim Botano, the owner of Gateway In-line, a similar store, is planning to retire. You ask him for a list of his suppliers, and he agrees to sell it to you for a nominal fee. Because you have a personal computer (PC) running Excel, you ask him if he can put the list on a disk. The next day, you stop by his store and he sells you the text file containing the supplier information. You need to import this file and convert it to a workbook so that you can manipulate it in Excel. Then you will convert the file to an Access table, so that you can share it with your partner, who has Access, but not Excel, on her PC.

To complete this independent challenge:

1. Open the file titled XL M-16 (a text file). (*Hint*: The data type of the original file is delimited.)
2. Save the file as an Excel workbook titled "In-line Skate Supplier List".
3. Adjust the column labels and widths so that all the data is visible. Add or delete any formatting you feel is appropriate.
4. Sort the list in ascending order, first by item purchased, then by supplier.
5. Save your work, then preview and print your work on a single page.
6. Save the workbook with the new name "Supplier List Converted to Access," then convert the worksheet to an Access table. Use the column labels as the field names, store the data in a new table, import all columns in the list, and let Access add the primary key.
7. Open the Access table and adjust column widths to fully display the field names, then save the table and exit Access.
8. In the Excel window, save the open worksheet, print it (along with the conversion notice) on one page, then close the workbook.

2. You are the newly hired manager at Burger Pit, the local burger joint in your small town. A past employee, Roberta Carlson, has filed a grievance that she was underpaid in January 1996. The files containing the payroll information for early 1996 are in Lotus 1-2-3 (WK1) format. In June 1996, the owner switched the business records to Microsoft Excel. You have located the files containing the payroll information you need. You import the Lotus 1-2-3 file, convert it to an Excel workbook, and correct the formatting in order to verify the values and formulas, especially those for Roberta Carlson, to determine if she was indeed underpaid.

To complete this independent challenge:

1. Open the Lotus 1-2-3 file titled XL M-17.
2. Save the file as an Excel workbook titled "Burger Pit 1-1-96 Payroll Info".
3. Click Tools on the menu bar, click Options, click the View tab, then select the Gridlines check box to turn on the worksheet gridlines.
4. Check all values and formulas for discrepancies. If you find any, annotate them with a text box and an arrow. Do *not* change any spreadsheet formulas or values.
5. Correct the formatting. Delete any row(s) containing dashes or equal signs and add appropriate borders. Format all dollar values using the Comma Style with two decimal places. Add or delete any formatting you feel is appropriate.
6. Preview, then print your work on a single page.
7. Save the worksheet, then close the workbook.

3. You are a loan officer for a local bank. You have been asked to give a talk about the banking industry to a local high school economics class. As part of your talk, you decide to give a presentation explaining the most popular consumer loans. To illustrate your comments, you will add an Excel chart to one of your slides showing the most popular loan types and the number of applications received yearly for each.

To complete this independent challenge:

1. Create a worksheet containing popular loan types, then save it as "Most Popular Consumer Loans". Include the loans and the corresponding number of applications shown in Table M-2.
2. Create a pie chart from the loan data on a new sheet. Add an appropriate title to your chart.
3. Save the workbook, print the chart, then (with the chart sheet the active sheet) close the workbook.
4. Start PowerPoint, click the Blank presentation option button, then click OK.
5. In the New Slide dialog box, click the lay-out on the far-right in the bottom row (Blank), then click OK.
6. Make sure the slide is displayed in Slide View, then insert the Excel chart into the blank slide.
7. Click File on the PowerPoint menu bar, click Save As, then save the presentation as "Banking Industry Presentation".
8. Close the presentation, then exit PowerPoint and Excel.

TABLE M-2

loan type	number of applications
Fixed home loans	1456
New-car loans	5400
Used-car loans	3452
Adjustable home loans	760
Boat loans	250

4. Before becoming a lawyer, you worked your way through school as a wedding planner. Your best friend, who now works with you at a law firm, recently asked you to help with the budget for her wedding. Because you both have PCs, you can share files with each other. Your friend can afford to spend $6,000 on the wedding. Over lunch, you will create a preliminary budget for general categories and send it to her over the network. Then you will create a detailed food and drink worksheet. Finally, you will link the detailed food and drink worksheet at the bottom of the overall budget worksheet. To complete this independent challenge:

1. Go to the Way Cool Weddings home page, browse the various links, and make a list of common wedding expense categories. If you can't find the Way Cool Weddings home page, use your Web browser to go to http://www.course.com. From there, click Student Online Companions, click the link for this textbook, then click the Excel link for Unit M.
2. Create a worksheet, then save it as "Wedding Budget". Create a budget using the expense categories from the Way Cool Weddings home page. Enter estimated expenditures for each category. Add any formatting you feel is appropriate.
3. Create a new workbook and build a detailed food and drink budget. Save it as "Food and Drink Budget". Total the food and drink items and total the amount you budgeted in the Wedding Budget worksheet. Add any text formatting you feel is appropriate.
4. Just below the budget in the Wedding Budget worksheet, link the detailed food and drink budget. Do *not* display it as an icon. Add a note indicating that your friend can double-click the data to access the source file and make changes.
5. Preview, print, then save your work.
6. Close the workbook.

▶ Visual Workshop

Create the worksheet shown in Figure M-22. Insert the two graphic files XL M-18 (cup) and XL M-19 (pie) as shown. (*Hint*: Drag the selection handles as necessary to enlarge the art to the proper size.) Save the workbook as "Pie Menu". Preview, then print the worksheet.

FIGURE M-22

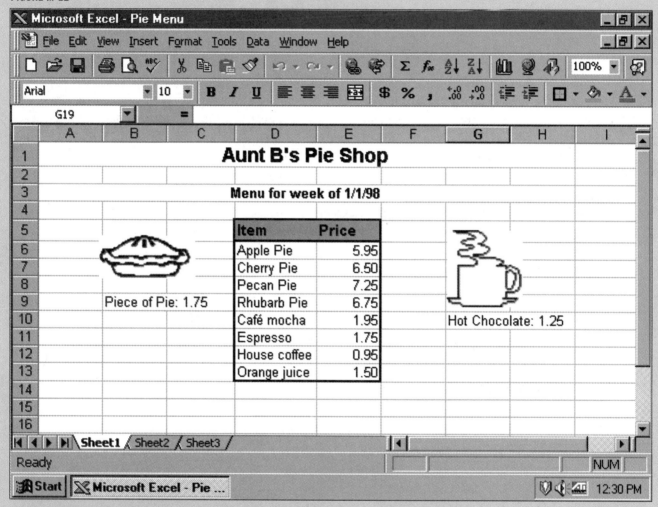

Working

with Excel and the Internet

Objectives

- ► **Define the Internet features of Excel**
- ► **Create hyperlinks between Excel files**
- ► **Browse Excel files using hyperlinks and the Web toolbar**
- ► **Create hyperlinks between Excel files and the Web**
- ► **Save an Excel file as an HTML document**
- ► **View Excel data in HTML format**
- ► **Create a Web form**
- ► **Run queries to retrieve data on the Web**

You can share Excel workbooks and reports by printing a hardcopy or by passing the electronic file to others to view and modify. Collaboration also is eased through the use of hyperlinks and other Excel features that allow you to place and retrieve data online over the Internet. In this unit, you will learn how to use Excel and the Internet to share data. ✍ Megan Grahs is preparing a presentation to the board of directors of Nomad Ltd on the health division's performance over the past quarter and their plans for future growth. She has asked her assistant, Evan Brillstein, to help her prepare for this presentation using Excel and the Internet.

Excel 97

Defining the Internet Features of Excel

Several Excel features rely on technology commonly associated with the Internet and the World Wide Web. The **World Wide Web** (commonly referred to as the **WWW** or the **Web**), is a structure of documents connected electronically over a large computer network made up of smaller networks and computers called the **Internet**. A **network** consists of two or more computers connected together for the purpose of sharing information and resources. The ability to share information **online**—over a network or the Internet—enables people to work together more efficiently. Evan Brillstein needs to collect the information Megan requested on Nomad's health division from a variety of sources. Using Excel, he can access and share information electronically in the following ways.

 Use hyperlinks to navigate between related files.

A **hyperlink** is an object (a filename, a word, a phrase, or a graphic) in a worksheet that you click to access another location in that worksheet, another worksheet, a document created in another program, or information on the Web. See Figure N-1. This system of linked information is called **hypertext**. Files containing hyperlinks are called **hyperlink documents**. You click a hyperlink to navigate, or **jump**, to a different document containing related information. The Excel online Help system is an example of a series of hyperlink documents. Evan can use hyperlinks to link workbooks containing data on the health division's products and services that Megan can use to prepare her presentation.

 Browse files on the Web.

The documents that make up the WWW also are connected by hyperlinks. Each of these documents is called a **Web document** or **Web page**. Web pages are stored on computers, called **Web servers** or **Web sites**, which are connected to the Internet. Web pages store different types of information including text, graphics, sound, animation, and video. A Web page often includes hyperlinks to other Web documents. You can use the Excel Web toolbar to navigate Web pages, or you can create hyperlinks in your worksheets that link you to relevant Web documents. For example, in the workbook containing information on Nomad's health clubs, Evan can create a hyperlink to the company's largest competitor. This will allow Megan to refer to the competitor's information as she prepares for her presentation.

 Publish workbook data on the Web.

Documents placed on the Web share a common file format called **HTML**, which stands for **HyperText Markup Language**. A software program, called a **Web browser**, enables users to access, view, and navigate all the documents on the Web. Web browsers only recognize files that are in HTML format. Excel workbook data can easily be converted to HTML format, which allows Evan to publish data on the health division's products and services on Nomad Ltd's Web site.

 Gather and retrieve data from the Web.

You can gather and retrieve information from the Web using Excel's Web Form Wizard, shown in Figure N-2. Using Excel, this data can then be organized and manipulated to generate useful worksheets, charts, pivot tables, and lists. Evan can use the Web Form Wizard to gather market research information from customers who visit Nomad Ltd's Web site.

FIGURE N-1: Excel worksheet with hyperlink

Blue color and underline indicates this is a hyperlink

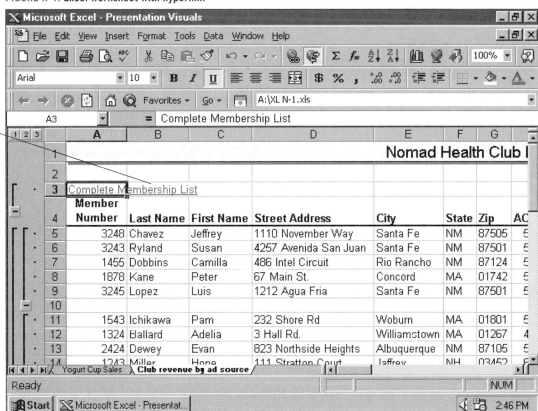

FIGURE N-2: Excel Web Form Wizard

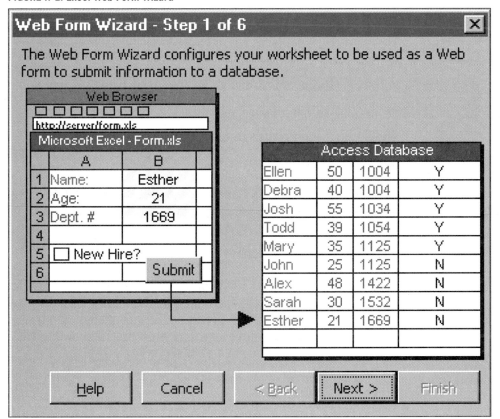

Creating Hyperlinks between Excel Files

Previously, when you navigated between two workbooks, you opened both workbooks, then used the Window menu to switch between the two. Hyperlinks offer another way of accessing related information that is in a different location. A hyperlink can be a filename, a word, a phrase, or a graphic that has been assigned an address to a different location in the worksheet or to a file located elsewhere. A hyperlink that consists of a filename or text will be displayed in color and as underlined text in the worksheet. If a hyperlink is a graphic, however, no visual cue displays until you position your mouse pointer over the graphic. Then, the mouse pointer changes to a pointing hand 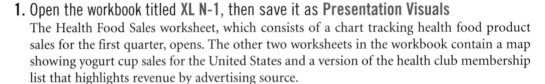 and displays the location of the link's destination file in a ScreenTip. When you click a hyperlink, the destination file, or **target**, is brought into memory and displayed on the screen. ◆▬▬▬ Evan has created a workbook containing charts on the division's health food sales as well as a table summarizing health club membership data. Before giving Megan the workbook, Evan wants to insert hyperlinks to the workbooks containing the data the charts and table summarize.

1. **Open the workbook titled XL N-1, then save it as Presentation Visuals**
   The Health Food Sales worksheet, which consists of a chart tracking health food product sales for the first quarter, opens. The other two worksheets in the workbook contain a map showing yogurt cup sales for the United States and a version of the health club membership list that highlights revenue by advertising source.

2. **If necessary, click cell A2, type Total Health Food Sales, then press [Enter]**
   This is the text you want to use as the hyperlink targeting the workbook containing the data on total health food sales. Now you specify the target for the hyperlink.

3. **Click cell A2, then click the Insert Hyperlink button**  **on the Standard toolbar**
   The Insert Hyperlink dialog box opens, as shown in Figure N-3. Here, you enter the address of the workbook containing the health food product total sales data, which would be its filename.

4. **In the Link to file or URL section of the Insert Hyperlink dialog box, click Browse**

5. **In the Link to File dialog box, click the filename Food Sales, click OK, then click OK again**
   The Insert Hyperlink dialog box closes, and you return to the worksheet. Notice the hyperlink text in cell A2 is colored and underlined, indicating that the text is a hyperlink.

6. **Click the Club revenue by ad source sheet tab, then, if necessary, click cell A3**
   In this worksheet, you want to insert a hyperlink to the workbook containing the full health club membership list.

7. **Type Complete Membership List, then press [Enter]**

8. **Click cell A3, click** **, in the Link to file or URL section of the Insert Hyperlink dialog box, click Browse, click the filename Club Members, click OK, then click OK again**
   The Insert Hyperlink dialog box closes, and the Complete Membership List hyperlink appears in the Club revenue by ad source worksheet, as shown in Figure N-4.

QuickTip

You also can have a graphical hyperlink. Simply select the graphic in the worksheet, then click the Insert Hyperlink button.

QuickTip

Make sure the "Use relative path for hyperlink" check box is selected so the path section of the dialog box will only show the name of the file and not the drive letters. Later, if you move the file to another folder, you will not have to insert a new address in the worksheet for the hyperlink to that file.

Time To

✔ Save

FIGURE N-3: Insert Hyperlink dialog box

Enter filename of hyperlink's target here

Click this button to locate file stored on hard drive or floppy disk

Make sure this check box is selected

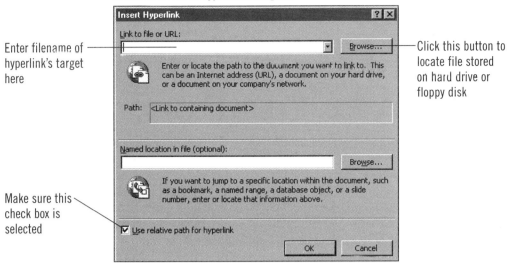

FIGURE N-4: Worksheet with hyperlinks

Hyperlink to Club Members workbook

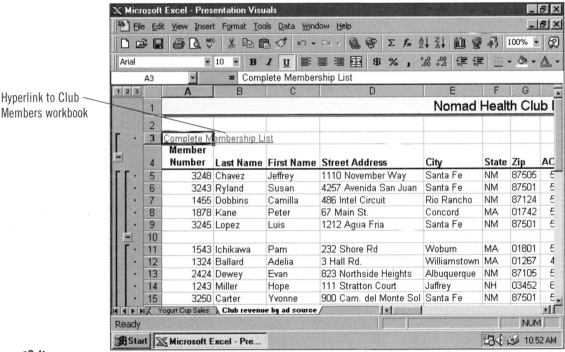

Editing a Hyperlink

After creating a hyperlink, you can easily edit its text or change its target. Simply right-click the hyperlink text, then click Hyperlink from the shortcut menu to display the submenu shown in Figure N-5. From this menu, you can click Hyperlink to select the hyperlink text for editing, or click Edit Hyperlink to change the target or remove the hyperlink from the worksheet entirely.

FIGURE N-5: Editing options on Hyperlink shortcut menu

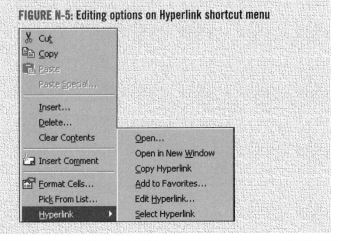

Browsing Excel Files Using Hyperlinks and the Web Toolbar

Once you have created hyperlinks between files, you need to test the links to make sure they are working properly. Then you can use these hyperlinks to quickly and easily navigate between, or **browse**, related files. You also can use the buttons on the Web toolbar to browse linked files. The hyperlinks Evan has created will allow Megan to browse between the Presentation Visuals workbook and the Food Sales and Club Members workbooks. However, before he gives the files to Megan, Evan wants to test the hyperlinks to make sure they work correctly. He starts by testing the Complete Membership List hyperlink.

Steps

1. **Position the mouse pointer over the text Complete Membership List, in cell A3**
   The pointer changes to a pointing hand ⍟, and a ScreenTip showing the address of the linked file appears, as shown in Figure N-6.

2. **Click the Complete Membership List hyperlink in cell A3**
   The Club Members workbook opens, as shown in Figure N-7. If the Web toolbar has not already displayed, it appears on your screen at this point. Table N-1 describes the function of each button on the Web toolbar.

3. **Click the Back button ⇐ on the Web toolbar**
   The Club revenue by ad worksheet re-displays. Notice that the hyperlink reference has changed color to indicate you have used the hyperlink at least once.

4. **Activate the Health Food Sales worksheet, then click the Total Health Food Sales hyperlink**
   The Food Sales workbook opens, and the Total Sales worksheet displays. Now return to the Health Food Sales worksheet in the Presentation Visuals workbook using the buttons on the Web toolbar.

5. **Click ⇐ on the Web toolbar**

6. **Click the Forward button ⇒ on the Web toolbar to jump to the Total Sales worksheet again, then click ⇐ on the Web toolbar**
   Once again, you return to the Presentation Visuals workbook. Now that you have browsed the links to make sure they are working correctly, you save your work.

7. **Save the workbook**

FIGURE N-6: Selecting a hyperlink

ScreenTip showing
hyperlink's target

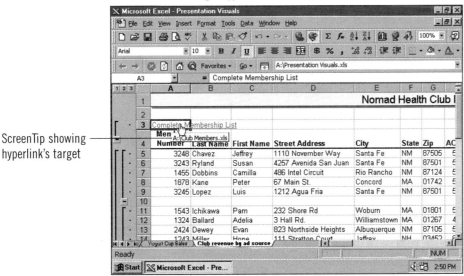

FIGURE N-7: Target document of hyperlink

Forward button

Web toolbar

Back button

Complete Members
workbook

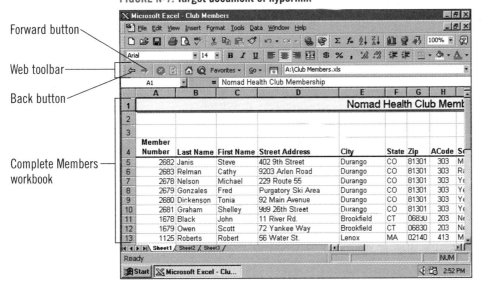

TABLE N-1: Web Toolbar Buttons

icon	button name	description
⇐	Back	Displays the previously visited hyperlink document.
⇒	Forward	Displays the hyperlink document visited after the current one displayed.
⊗	Stop Current Jump	Ends an initiated jump to a hyperlink document.
🗐	Refresh Current Page	Updates the information on a Web page or the current hyperlink document.
🏠	Start Page	Displays the home or start page of the current Web site.
🔍	Search the Web	Starts the installed Web browser to search the Web.
Favorites	Favorites	Adds address of files or Web sites to Favorites list for easy reference.
Go	Go	Displays a list of all Web commands on the toolbar.
⬜	Show Only Web toolbar	Hides all other toolbars so just the Web toolbar is displayed.
	Address	Shows a history of documents and sites visited.

Creating Hyperlinks between Excel Files and the Web

In addition to using hyperlinks to connect related Excel files, you also can create hyperlinks between files created in other Windows programs. You can even use hyperlinks to move between Excel files and information stored on the Web. Every Web page is identified by a unique address called a **Uniform Resource Locator (URL)**. You create a hyperlink to a Web page in the same way you create a hyperlink to another Excel file—by specifying the location of the Web page (its URL) in the Link to File or URL text box in the Insert Hyperlink dialog box. Evan decides to create a hyperlink to the Web page of Nomad's biggest competitor, FitnessCentral, in the Club Members worksheet. Megan can use this hyperlink to easily jump to this Web site to learn more about Nomad Ltd's competitor's offerings and membership guidelines and possibly use this information in her presentation.

Steps 1 2 3 4

1. Activate the **Club revenue by ad source worksheet**, click cell **D3**, type **FitnessCentral**, then press **[Enter]**

2. Click cell **D3**, then click the **Insert Hyperlink button** 🖫 on the Standard toolbar
   The Insert Hyperlink dialog box opens. This is where you specify the target for the hyperlink, the FitnessCentral Web page, by entering its URL in the Link to file or URL section of the Insert Hyperlink dialog box.

3. In the Link to File or URL text box, type **http://www.fitnesscentral.com/**
   Your completed Insert Hyperlink dialog box should match Figure N-8.

4. Click **OK**
   Now that you have created the hyperlink to FitnessCentral's Web page, test the hyperlink to make sure it links to the correct Web page. To test this hyperlink, you must have a modem, a Web browser installed on your computer, and access to an Internet Service Provider (ISP).

5. Click the **FitnessCentral** hyperlink in cell D3
   After a moment, the Web browser installed on your computer starts and displays the FitnessCentral Web page in your browser window.

6. If necessary, click the **Maximize button** 🔲 on the browser title bar to maximize the browser window.
   See Figure N-9. Now that you've confirmed the hyperlink works correctly, you return to the Club Members worksheet.

7. Click the **Back button** ⇦ on the Web toolbar

8. Save, then close the workbook

QuickTip

Make sure the URL address appears in the text box exactly as shown in Figure N-8. Every Web page URL begins with "http://". This acronym stands for HyperText Transfer Protocol, the method the Web page data uses to travel over the Internet to your computer.

FIGURE N-8: Completed Insert Hyperlink dialog box

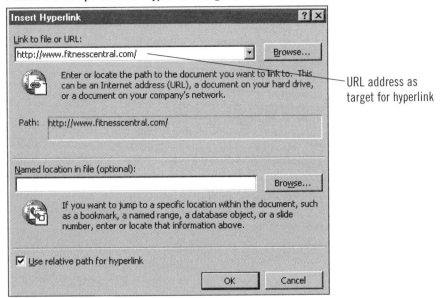

URL address as target for hyperlink

FIGURE N-9: Target document on the World Wide Web

Your Web browser may be different

Your screen may differ due to the dynamic nature of data on the Web

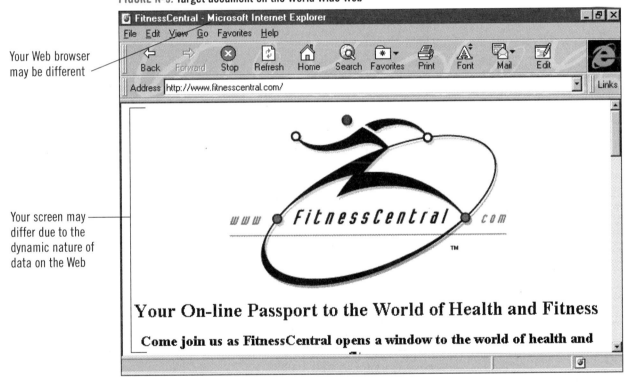

CLUES TO USE

Using Hyperlinks to navigate large worksheets

Previously, when you needed to locate and view different sections of a particularly large worksheet, you used the scroll bars, or, if there were range names associated with the different worksheet sections, the name box. You also can use hyperlinks to more easily navigate a large worksheet. To insert a hyperlink that targets a cell or a range of cells at another location in the worksheet or another sheet in the workbook, click the cell where you want the hyperlink to appear, then click the Insert Hyperlink button on the Standard toolbar. In the Insert Hyperlink dialog box, enter the cell address or range name of the hyperlink target in the Named location in file text box, then click OK.

Excel 97

Saving an Excel File as an HTML Document

Another way to share Excel data is to publish, or **post**, it online over a network. For example, you can post an Excel worksheet to a Web page so that anyone with access to a Web browser can view its contents. In order to post an Excel worksheet to the Web, you must make sure it is in HTML format. You use the Excel Internet Assistant Wizard to save a file in HTML format. 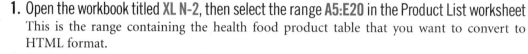 Megan anticipates that marketing Nomad's health food products on the Web will increase the division's sales. She asks Evan to create a Web page listing the health food products currently available, which she can show to the board of directors as a sample. Evan begins by opening the Excel file containing the product table, in order to select the data he wants to appear on the Web page.

1. **Open the workbook titled XL N-2, then select the range A5:E20 in the Product List worksheet**
   This is the range containing the health food product table that you want to convert to HTML format.

2. **Click File on the menu bar, then click Save as HTML**
   The first Internet Assistant Wizard dialog box opens, as shown in Figure N-10. This is where you specify the range(s) and charts you want to place on the Web page. The range you selected, $A$5:$E$20, is automatically inserted into the Ranges and charts to convert list box.

3. **Click Next**
   The second Internet Assistant Wizard dialog box opens. This is where you specify whether you want to create a completely new Web page or insert the range into an existing Web page. You want to create the Healthy Food Products table as a separate Web page, which is the default option.

4. **Make sure the Create an independent, ready-to-view HTML document option button is selected, then click Next**
   The third Internet Assistant Wizard dialog box opens. This is where you determine the layout of your Web page. Begin by editing the current default Web page title and inserting the text you want to appear in the title bar of the Web page.

5. **Triple-click the Title text box to select the default Web page title, then type Nomad Ltd Health Division**
   Now you will specify the text you want to appear above the health food products table on your Web page, then insert a horizontal line above the health food products table that will visually separate the table from the information that will appear above it on the Web page.

6. **Triple-click the Header text box, type Nomad Ltd Healthy Foods Product List, then if necessary, click the Insert a horizontal line before the converted data check box to select it**
   Now you'll enter the date the page was updated, the name of the person creating the Web page, and an e-mail address to contact for more information.

7. **Click the Last Update on text box, then edit it to read 10/1/99; in the By text box, type Evan Brillstein; then in the Email text box, type comments@nomad.com**
   Your completed third Internet Assistant Wizard dialog box should match Figure N-11. You are ready to complete the last dialog box of the Internet Assistant Wizard, in which you specify the location and name of the HTML file you are creating.

8. **Click Next; in the fourth Internet Assistant Wizard dialog box, make sure the Save the result as an HTML file option button is selected; triple-click the File path text box; if necessary, type a:\healthfood.htm, then click Finish**
   You are returned the product list worksheet. Excel has created the HTML formatted file and stored it on your Student Disk.

Trouble?

If the Save as HTML command does not appear on the File menu, you need to install the Internet Assistant. Click Tools on the menu bar, then click Add-Ins to display the Add-Ins dialog box. Click the Internet Assistant Wizard check box to select it, then click OK. If you don't see the Internet Assistant Wizard in the Add-Ins dialog box, check with your instructor or technical support person.

Trouble?

If you pressed [Enter] by mistake and advanced to the fourth Internet Assistant Wizard dialog box, click Back, then repeat Step 5.

QuickTip

All files that are in HTML format have the file extension .htm.

FIGURE N-10: First Internet Assistant Wizard dialog box

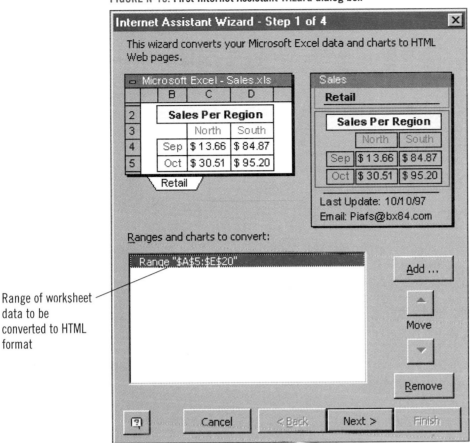

Range of worksheet
data to be
converted to HTML
format

FIGURE N-11: Completed third Internet Assistant Wizard dialog box

Title to appear in
Web browser title
bar when Web page
is displayed

Title to appear
above worksheet
data in Web page

Indicates a
horizontal line will
separate Excel data
from Web page title

Information to
appear at bottom
of Web page

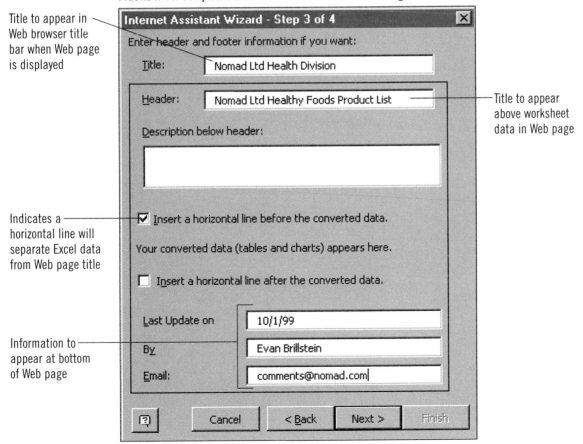

Viewing Excel Data in HTML Format

Once you have created your Web page, you should view it with a Web browser to ensure the layout appears as you want it to and that the Excel data retained the appropriate format during the conversion process. ◄━━━ Before Evan gives the newly created Web page to Megan, he views it with his Web browser.

1. **If the Web toolbar is not displayed, click View on the menu bar, point to Toolbars, then click Web**
   Excel displays the Web toolbar.

2. **Click the Go button** [Go] **on the Web toolbar, then click Open**
   The Open Internet Address dialog box opens, as shown in Figure N-12. This is where you specify the URL of the Internet site or the name of the HTML file you want to view. You can either type the information in the Address text box or use the Browse button to view the files stored on your computer or floppy disk.

3. **Click Browse**
   Excel displays the Browse dialog box.

4. **Click the Look In list arrow, click the drive that contains your Student Disk, in the File name list box, click healthfood, then click Open**
   You are returned to the Open Internet Address dialog box. Note that the address for the HTML file is now displayed in the Address textbox.

5. **Click OK**
   Excel starts Internet Explorer (or the Web browser installed on your computer) and displays the Nomad Ltd Healthy Foods Product List Web page. See Figure N-13.

6. **If necessary, maximize the browser window, scroll to view the full Web page, then click the Close button on the Web browser title bar**
   The Web page automatically closes when the Web browser closes.

7. **Click any cell in the Product List worksheet, then close the workbook without saving any changes**

Trouble?

If Excel opens a program other than a Web browser, such as Microsoft Word, a Web browser might not be installed on your computer. See your instructor or technical support person for assistance.

FIGURE N-12: Open Internet Address dialog box

Specify filename of Web page you want to view ⎯

Click here to view Web documents stored on your computer or floppy disk ⎯

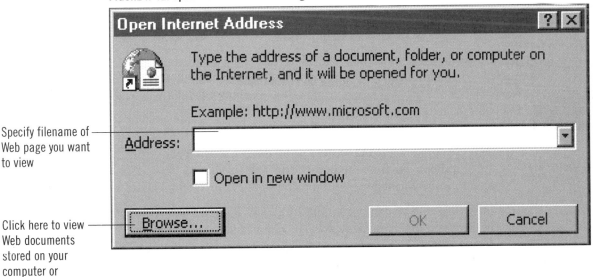

FIGURE N-13: Nomad Ltd Healthy Foods Product List Web page

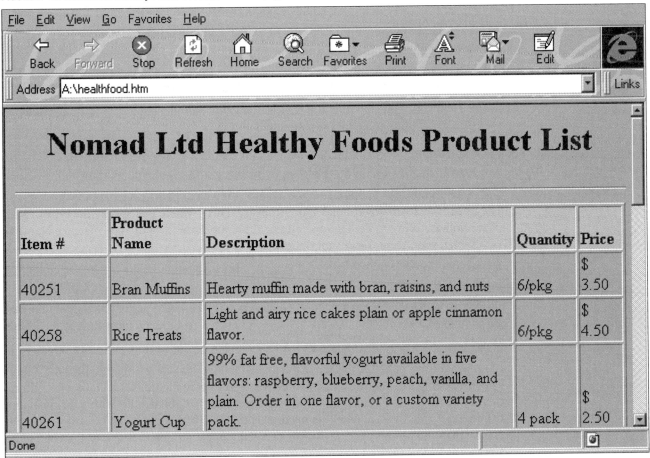

Excel 97

Steps 1 2 3 4

Creating a Web Form

You can use the Excel Web Form Wizard to create and display a form that visitors to your Web site can use to submit various types of information. Megan wants to include a Web form on Nomad's Web site that will enable customers to request more information about the new division. Evan uses the Excel Web Form Wizard to create this form.

1. Open the workbook titled **XL N-3**, then save it as **Request Info Form**
This workbook contains the order form that visitors to Nomad's Web pages can use to request more information about the division's products and services.

2. Click **Tools** on the menu bar, point to **Wizard**, then click **Web Form**
The first Web Form dialog box opens. This first dialog box introduces you to the Web Form Wizard.

3. Click **Next**
The second Web Form Wizard dialog box opens, as shown in Figure N-14. This is where you specify the location in the form (e.g., the range) where users will be entering their information. The Form Wizard automatically selects the cells for users to supply data based upon the location of these cells in the worksheet and the text labels in the adjacent cells. For example, the Form Wizard already displays the cells for users to enter their name, address, telephone, and e-mail in the Controls and cells list. However, the Form Wizard incorrectly selected cell A16 as a cell for users to enter data. You'll remove that entry, then add another cell that users can use to enter information on the form.

4. In the Controls and cells list, click **yespleasesendmeinformationonthefollow**, click **Remove**, click **Add a cell**; in the Type or select a cell text box in the Web Form Wizard dialog box, type **A17**, then click **OK**
The text "a17 $A$17" is added to the Controls and cells list box in the second Web Form Wizard dialog box. Now you change the field name of the cell to be more descriptive.

QuickTip

Field names must be entered in all lowercase and with no spaces.

5. In the Field name of the selected control text box, double-click **a17**, type the phrase **healthyfoods**, then click **Change Name**

6. Click **Add a cell**; in the Type or select a cell text box in the Web Form Wizard dialog box, type **A18**, click **OK**; in the Field name of the selected control text box, double-click **a18**; type **healthclubs**; click **Change Name**; then click **Next**
The third Web Form Wizard dialog box appears. This is where you specify the type of Web server you are using to gather your information. Since the default type matches Nomad's Web server, you accept the default option.

7. Make sure the **Microsoft Internet Information Server option button** is selected, then click **Next**
The fourth Web Form Wizard dialog box opens. This is where you specify how you want to save the completed form. In this case, you save the file as a Microsoft Excel file, which is the default.

8. Make sure the **Save the results as a Microsoft Excel file option button** is selected, in the File path text box triple-click **A:\MyForm.xls**, type **a:\requestinfo.xls**, then click **Next**
The fifth Web Form Wizard dialog box opens, as shown in Figure N-15. Once users submit their information using the Web form, another dialog box will display with a message confirming that their information has been received. The fifth Web Form Wizard dialog box enables you to specify the information that will appear in this message to the user. Now, specify the text of the first line of the message.

Time To

✔ Save
✔ Close

9. Triple-click the **Header text box**, type **Request for More Information**, click **Next**, then in the sixth Web Form Wizard dialog box, click **Finish**
Your Web form is completed.

FIGURE N-14: Second Web Form Wizard dialog box

Text from cell A16,
which is an
incorrect cell

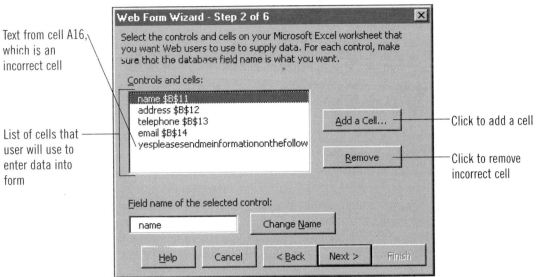

List of cells that
user will use to
enter data into
form

Click to add a cell

Click to remove
incorrect cell

FIGURE N-15: Fifth Web Form Wizard dialog box

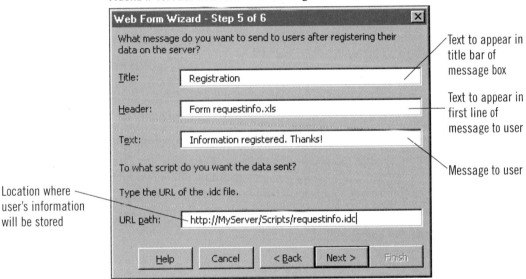

Text to appear in
title bar of
message box

Text to appear in
first line of
message to user

Message to user

Location where
user's information
will be stored

Viewing the Web Form

When you create a Web form from an Excel file, there are four files created that Excel and your Web server use to process information submitted by users. In the fourth Web Form Wizard dialog box, you specify one of those four files—the Excel file that contains the completed form. To view that form, you simply open the file in Excel. To view the Request for More Information form that you created for the Nomad Ltd Health Division, open the requestinfo.xls file, shown in Figure N-16. You will need to enable the macros associated with this file when you open it.

FIGURE N-16: Request for More Information form

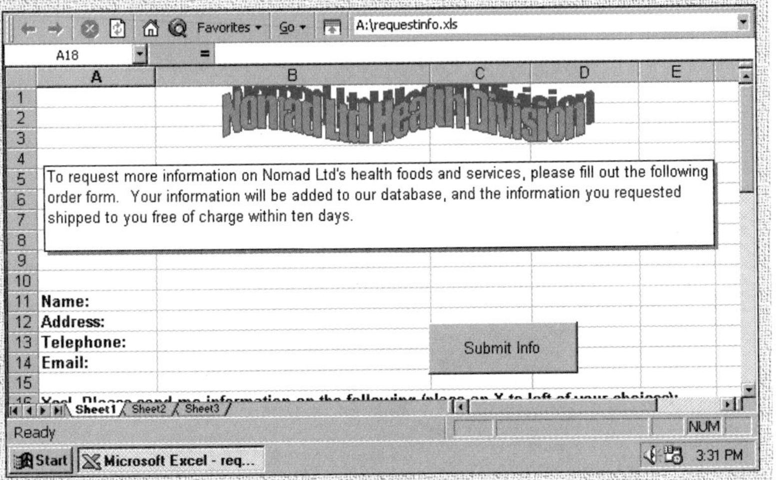

Run Queries to Retrieve Data on the Web

Excel 97

Often, you'll want to access information on the Web or the Internet to incorporate into an Excel worksheet. Using Excel, you can obtain data from a Web or an Internet site, or from an **intranet site**, an internet-like site that exists on a network within a company or organization, by running a **Web query**. You can then save the information as an Excel workbook and manipulate it in any way you choose. ◀━━ Evan is almost finished collecting the information Megan needs for her presentation to Nomad Ltd's board of directors. The last item she wants is stock information on Nomad's competitors in the health food products and services industry. Evan will run a Web query to obtain the most current stock information from the WWW.

1. Open a new workbook, then save it as **Stock Data**

2. Click **Data** on the menu bar, point to **Get External Data**, then click **Run Web Query**
   The Run Query dialog box opens, as shown in Figure N-17. This is where you select the Web query you want to run from a list of predefined queries.

QuickTip

Microsoft Excel includes sample Web queries, located in the Queries folder in the Microsoft Office directory.

3. Click the **Dow Jones Stocks by PC Quote, Inc**, then click **Get Data**
   The Returning External Data to Microsoft Excel dialog box opens, as shown in Figure N-18. This is where you specify the location to place the incoming data.

4. Make sure the **Existing worksheet option button** is selected, then click **OK**
   The External Data toolbar displays in the worksheet window, and the spinning world icon appears in the status bar, indicating that Excel is running the query. After a few moments, the Dow Jones Stocks information appears in the Excel window, as shown in Figure N-19. Now you have the stock information that Megan can use to research Nomad's competitors' stock values.

Trouble?

If you don't have a modem and access to the WWW through an ISP, check with your instructor or technical support person. If your ISP's connection dialog box opens, follow your standard procedure for getting online, then continue with Step 5.

5. Save and close the workbook, then exit Excel

Checking the Status of Your Query

You can check the status of a query that is taking a long time to return data. While the query is running, click the Refresh Status button 🛈 on the External Data toolbar. To cancel a query that is taking too long, click the Cancel Refresh button ✖ on the External Data toolbar.

FIGURE N-17: Run Query dialog box

List of predefined queries

Select this query

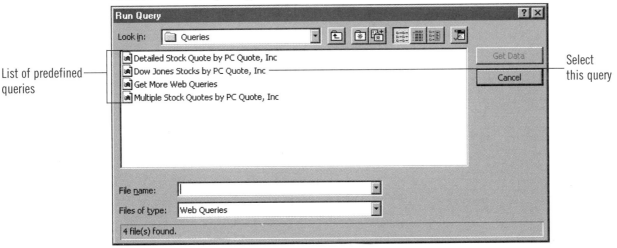

FIGURE N-18: Returning External Data to Microsoft Excel dialog box

Make sure this option is selected

Indicates location to place returned data

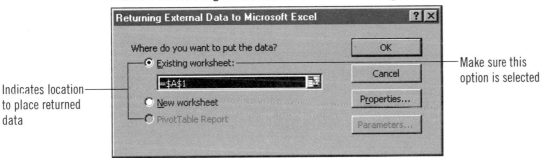

FIGURE N-19: Dow Jones Stocks data retrieved from Web query

The Web toolbar may or may not be displayed

External Data toolbar

Hyperlinks to Web pages of more stock data

Your screen may differ due to the dynamic nature of data on the Web

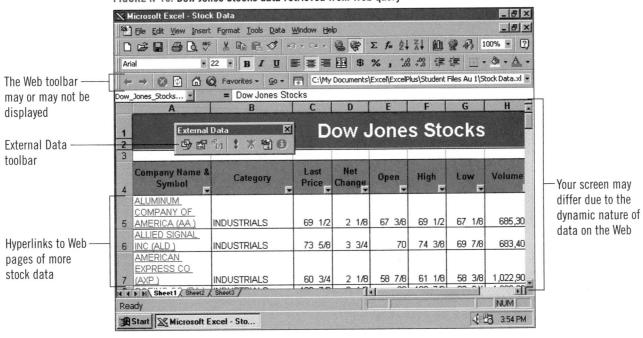

Practice

▶ Concepts Review

Label each of the elements shown in Figure N-20.

FIGURE N-20

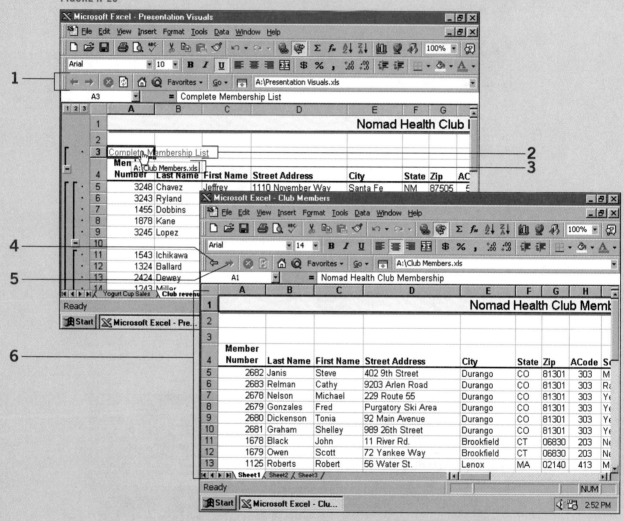

Match each statement with the item it describes.

7. Displays previously displayed hyperlink.
8. Displays hyperlink document visited after the currently displayed document.
9. Ends an initiated link.
10. Updates the currently displayed hyperlink document.
11. Starts the installed Web browser to search the WWW.

a. ⓠ
b. ⇦
c. ⊗
d. 🗗
e. ⇨

12. _____ is the format used to display documents on the Web.
   a. HTML
   b. Hypertext
   c. Visual Basic
   d. Web

13. Which of the following buttons can be used to stop an initiated jump to a hyperlink document?
   a. [Favorites]
   b. [icon]
   c. [icon]
   d. [icon]

14. Which Excel Wizard would you use if you wanted to convert an Excel file into HTML format?
   a. HTML Format Wizard
   b. Form Wizard
   c. Internet Assistant Wizard
   d. Convert Wizard

15. What file extension signifies a file is in HTML format?
   a. HTML
   b. XLS
   c. HTM
   d. GIF

16. What command from the Hyperlink shortcut menu would you use to change a hyperlink's target?
   a. New Target
   b. Select Hyperlink
   c. Edit
   d. Edit Hyperlink

▶ Skills Review

1. **Create hyperlinks between Excel files and browse using the Web toolbar.**
   a. Open the XL N-4 workbook, then save it as Sales Chart.
   b. Enter the text "Total Coffee Sales" in cell A1.
   c. Apply boldface formatting to cell A1.
   d. Click cell A1, then click the Insert Hyperlink button.
   e. Use the Browse button in the Link to file or URL section of the Insert Hyperlink dialog box to locate the file "Coffee Sales," and make this file the target of the Total Coffee Sales hyperlink.
   f. Click OK to close the Link to File dialog box, then click OK to close the Insert Hyperlink dialog box.
   g. Click the Total Coffee Sales hyperlink.
   h. Use the buttons on the Web toolbar to return to the Sales Chart workbook.
   i. Use the buttons on the Web toolbar to move to the worksheet containing the total coffee sales data.
   j. Use the buttons on the Web toolbar to return to the Sales Chart workbook, then save the workbook.

2. Create, test, and edit hyperlinks between Excel files and the Web.

a. Click cell B1, and enter the text "The Competition".

b. Apply boldface formatting to cell B1.

c. Click cell B1, then click the Insert Hyperlink button.

d. Type http://www.coffeeplantation.com/ in the Link to file or URL textbox of the Insert Hyperlink dialog box, then click OK.

e. Click the The Competition hyperlink to test the link. (*Note:* You must have a Web browser installed on your computer to test this hyperlink.)

f. Click the Back button to return to the Sales chart worksheet.

g. Right-click the hyperlink in cell B1, point to Hyperlink on the shortcut menu, then click Select Hyperlink. The hyperlink appears selected in the worksheet window.

h. Double-click the highlighted hyperlink, then type "The Competition's Web page".

i. Test the link again by selecting it.

j. Save, print, then close the workbook.

3. Save and view an Excel file as an HTML document.

a. Open the XL N-5 workbook.

b. Select the range A1:D7.

c. Click File on the menu bar, then click Save As HTML.

d. Confirm that the correct range appears in the first Internet Assistant Wizard dialog box, then click Next.

e. Specify you want to create an independent, ready-to-view HTML document in the second Internet Assistant Wizard dialog box, then click Next.

f. In the third Internet Assistant Wizard dialog box, specify "Coffeeberries Gourmet Coffee" as the title of the Web page, then delete the default title in the header box.

g. Enter today's date in the Last Update on text box, your name in the By text box, comments@coffeeberries.com in the Email text box, then click Next.

h. In the fourth Internet Assistant Wizard dialog box, specify the file should be saved as an HTML file, enter a:\coffeeproducts.htm in the File path text box, then click Finish.

i. Click the Go button on the Web toolbar, then click Open.

j. Type a:\coffeeproducts.htm in the Address text box of the Open Internet Address dialog box, then click Open.

k. View the Web page, then close the Web browser window.

l. Close the XL N-5 workbook without saving it.

4. Create a Web Form.

a. Open the XL N-6 workbook, then save it as Order Information.

b. Click Tools on the menu bar, point to Wizard, click Web Form to display the Web Form Wizard, then click Next.

c. In the second Web Form Wizard dialog box, confirm that the Controls and Cells list box contains references to cells B10, B11, B12, and B13, and that the default field names assigned to these cells are appropriate.

d. Click Next to open the third Web Form Wizard dialog box, confirm that the Microsoft Internet Information Server option button is selected, then click Next.

e. In the fourth Web Form Wizard dialog box, confirm the form you are creating will be saved as a Microsoft Excel file, then type a:\orderinfo.xls in the File path text box.

f. Click Next to open to the fifth Web Form Wizard dialog box, then enter "Request for More Information" in the Header text box.

g. Click next, then click Finish.

h. Save, then close the workbook.

i. Open the orderinfo.xls file to view and print the form you created. Select Enable Macros when prompted.

j. Close the workbook.

5. Run a query to retrieve data on the Web.

a. Open a new workbook and save it as "Stock Info".

b. Click Data on the menu bar, point to Get External Data, then click Run Web Query.

c. Click Dow Jones Stocks by PC Quote, Inc., then click the Get Data button.

d. In the Returning External Data to Microsoft Excel dialog box, specify that the data should be retrieved to the existing worksheet.

e. Once the Dow Jones Stock information appears in the worksheet window, scroll the workbook and view the data.

f. Print the first two pages of the workbook, then save and close it.

► Independent Challenges

1. To help you organize your homework from Unit N, you decide to link the various files you have created for Coffeeberries Gourmet Coffee in the Skills Review exercises in this unit using hyperlinks.

To complete this independent challenge:

1. Open the Sales Chart workbook, then save it as Sales Chart2.
2. Enter "Related Files" in cell D1, then format this text in boldface and italics.
3. Enter "Coffee Products Web page" in cell D2, then use the Insert Hyperlink button to create a link to the file "coffeeproducts.htm," which will be located on your Student Disk if you completed Skills Review 3.
4. Enter "Order Information Form" in cell D3, then use the Insert Hyperlink button to create a link to the file, "orderinfo.xls," which will be located on your Student Disk if you completed Skills Review 4.
5. Enter "Stock Information" in cell D4, then use the Insert Hyperlink button to create a link to the file, "Stock Info," which will be located on your Student Disk if you completed Skills Review 5.
6. Test the links you created in Steps 3, 4, and 5.
7. Save, then close the Sales Chart2 workbook.

2. Business Initiatives, Inc. develops and delivers training programs to corporations on a variety of topics, from customer satisfaction to staff recruitment. Many of the people facilitating Business Initiatives programs are freelance trainers, who are people who contract their services for a fee. Once a trainer has conducted a training program, he or she submits an invoice to Business Initiatives for payment. As an accounts payable clerk at Business Initiatives, you want to find a more efficient way to process the invoices you receive from the trainers. Since many of the freelance trainers have access to the Internet and the Web, you decide to create a Web form the trainers can use to submit their invoices to you electronically.

To complete this independent challenge:

1. Open the workbook titled XL N-7, then save it as Invoice Form.
2. Use the Web Form Wizard to create a Web form from this worksheet.
3. In the second Web Form Wizard dialog box, use the Add and Remove buttons to specify the cells where the user will enter his or her data. Make sure for those cells you add, you specify an appropriate Field Name. (*Hint:* The trainer submitting the invoice should specify the invoice number, the date, his or her name, address, phone number, social security number, and the number of days worked. Remove the totalinvoice and termsforpayment cells from the form.)
4. Save the results of the form as an Excel file named "invoice.xls".

5. In the fifth Web Form Wizard dialog box, specify the appropriate title, header, and message text for the message box that will appear when the trainer submits the form.
6. Save, then close the worksheet.
7. Open the invoice.xls file to view the Web form.
8. Double right-click the Submit button to select it, then move the mouse pointer over the button until it changes to ⛶. Drag the Submit button to cell A17.
9. Print the form, then close it.

3. You are the office manager for Glory Gardens, a large greenhouse and garden center. The company has four stores along the East Coast and also sells their products through a mail-order catalog. Recently, the company established a Web site as another means of reaching its customers. The owner of Glory Gardens has asked you to create a table in Excel listing the company's new products for the season and to save it in HTML format so that it can be published on the company's Web pages.

To complete this independent challenge:

1. Use the data in Table N-2 to create a worksheet itemizing Glory Garden's new products.

TABLE N-2

item #	variety	description	zone	quantity	price
40251	Crocus Gipsy Girl	Yellow with burgundy strips	5–8	15/pkg	$2.95
40258	Crocus Lady Killer	Deep purple, opening white	5–8	15/pkg	$4.50
40261	Crocus Zonatus	Fall-flowering, rose lilac with gold throatflowers	5–8	12/pkg	$2.95
10324	Golden Apeldoorn Tulips	Yellow	5–8	25/pkg	$8.50
72211	Astilbe Assort.	Fanal/Red, Bridal Veil/White, Chinese Pumila/Purple, Europa/Rose	3–8	1 ea	$16.50
72621	Hybrid Daylily Assort.	Horentia/Yellow, Anzac/Red, Catherine Woodbury/Pink w/ Yellow, Flames of Fantasy/Yellow, Summerwine/Claret	3–9	1 ea	$20.50
74311	Garden Phlox Assort.	Starfire/Red, Prime Minister/White w/ Red, Blue Boy/Lavender Blue, Powder Puff/Pink	3–9	1 ea	$19.50
82480	Exactum Persian Violet	Dark lavender, part shade	9–10	6/pkg	$12.50
87345	Purple Verbena	Dark lavender	9–10	6/pkg	$18.50
87730	Salvia Cherry Blossom	White/Pink	9–10	6/pkg	$12.95

2. Format the data appropriately, and experiment with various fonts to create a visually interesting title for the worksheet.
3. Save the worksheet as "Glory Gardens".
4. Convert the newly created Glory Gardens' product table to HTML format, then view the Web page in your Web browser.
5. Print the Web page from the Web browser.

4. You are a junior planner at Sensible Investors, a group of personal financial planners that plan, develop, and manage investment portfolios for individuals. Recently, you upgraded your spreadsheet software to Microsoft Excel 97. As you familiarize yourself with the new features of the software, you realize there is an option in the Run Query dialog box that allows you to access up-to-the minute stock data whenever you wish. The Get More Queries option provides a list of hyperlinks to various financial information resources. You no longer need to wait for the evening or morning newspaper to find out how a particular stock is performing. To obtain this list of available resources, you decide to run a query. Then you can pass this list onto your clients so they may select any or all of these they might want you to retrieve for them.

To complete this independent challenge:

1. Open a new workbook, then save it as "Computer Stock Info".
2. Run a Web query, then select Get More Queries in the Run Query dialog box.
3. Once the query results display in the worksheet window, scroll the document and locate the table listing hyperlinks to available Web queries.
4. Print just the table listing the hyperlinks for Web queries available for download.
5. Save the workbook.

▶ Visual Workshop

Create the Web page shown in Figure N-21. Start by creating the table of data, then create the pie chart. Place the pie chart in the same worksheet as the data. (*Hint:* The placement of the chart in the worksheet itself doesn't matter; you need only select the table of data. The Internet Assistant Wizard automatically selects the chart, along with the range containing the data, and converts it to HTML format for placement on your Web page.) Save the HTML file as Pastry.htm. Preview, then print the converted Excel data and chart from your Web browser.

FIGURE N-21

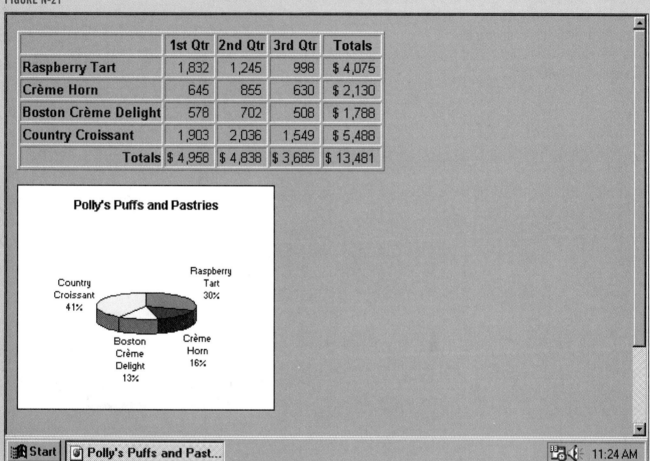

	1st Qtr	2nd Qtr	3rd Qtr	Totals
Raspberry Tart	1,832	1,245	998	$ 4,075
Crème Horn	645	855	630	$ 2,130
Boston Crème Delight	578	702	508	$ 1,788
Country Croissant	1,903	2,036	1,549	$ 5,488
Totals	$ 4,958	$ 4,838	$ 3,685	$ 13,481

Polly's Puffs and Pastries

Country Croissant 41%
Raspberry Tart 30%
Boston Crème Delight 13%
Crème Horn 16%

Start | Polly's Puffs and Past... | 11:24 AM

Gaining
Control over Your Work

Objectives

- ▶ **Find files**
- ▶ **Audit a worksheet**
- ▶ **Outline a worksheet**
- ▶ **Control worksheet calculations**
- ▶ **Create custom AutoFill lists**
- ▶ **Customize Excel**
- ▶ **Add a comment to a cell**
- ▶ **Save a workbook as a template**

Excel includes numerous tools and options designed to help you work as efficiently as possible. In this unit, you will learn how to use some of these elements to find errors and hide unnecessary detail. You'll also find out how to eliminate repetitive typing chores, save calculation time when using a large worksheet, as well as how to customize basic Excel features. Finally, you'll learn how to document your workbook and save it in a format that makes it easy to reuse and share with others. ◆───── Nomad Ltd's health division has recently acquired a health and wellness clinic to go along with its other newly acquired health-related services. Megan Grahs, Evan Brillstein's manager at Nomad Ltd, routinely asks him to perform a variety of spreadsheet-related tasks. The numerous options available in Excel help Evan perform his work quickly and efficiently.

Finding Files

The Open dialog box in Excel contains powerful searching tools, which make it easy for you to find files. You can search for a file in several ways, such as by name, or according to specific text located within a particular file. ▰▰▰ Recently, Evan's manager created a workbook that tracks the number of patient visits at the company health clinic. She can't remember the exact name of the file, so she asks Evan to search for it by the first few letters of the filename.

1. **Start Excel, then click the Open button ⬆ on the Standard toolbar**
   As referenced in Table O-1, the Open dialog box contains the Commands and Settings button, which you can use to open a menu of helpful options. This dialog box also contains four additional buttons that control the amount of information displayed about each file and folder. The amount of detail currently on your screen depends on the button that you clicked the last time this dialog box was opened. You'll choose the Details option in the next step, so that your screen will match the figure.

2. **Click the Details button ▦**
   The first step in searching for a file is to specify which drive and folder you want to look in.

3. **Click the Look in list arrow, then click the drive that contains your Student Disk**

4. **If the files for this unit are in a folder, click that folder in the Look box**
   Because you only know the first few letters of the filename, you'll use * (an asterisk) to substitute for the remaining unknown characters. In the next step, be sure to type the letter "O" and not a zero.

5. **Type XL O* in the File name box**
   Now you're ready to search your Student Disk for this file.

6. **Click Find Now**
   Excel displays five files that begin with "XL O," along with detailed information about the files. See Figure O-1. To narrow your search even further, you'll search for specific text contained within the workbook itself.

7. **Type Patient Visits in the Text or property box, then click Find Now**
   The file XL O-1 displays in the Look box. Because this is the file you are searching for, you'll open it now.

8. **Click Open, then save the workbook as Clinic Patient Visits**

> **Trouble?**
>
> If the message "0 file(s) found" appears in the lower left corner of the dialog box, you may have typed the letter "O" instead of a zero. Repeat Step 5, making sure to use a zero.

CLUES TO USE

File Properties

Excel automatically tracks specific file properties, such as author name, file size, and file type, and displays them when you click the Details button. You also can enter additional file properties, such as subject or a descriptive title. Simply right-click the file in the Open dialog box, click Properties to open the Properties dialog box, and then click the Summary tab. See Figure O-2. To search for a file by a specific property, enter the descriptive title, subject, or other relevant text in the Text or property box.

FIGURE O-1: Search results

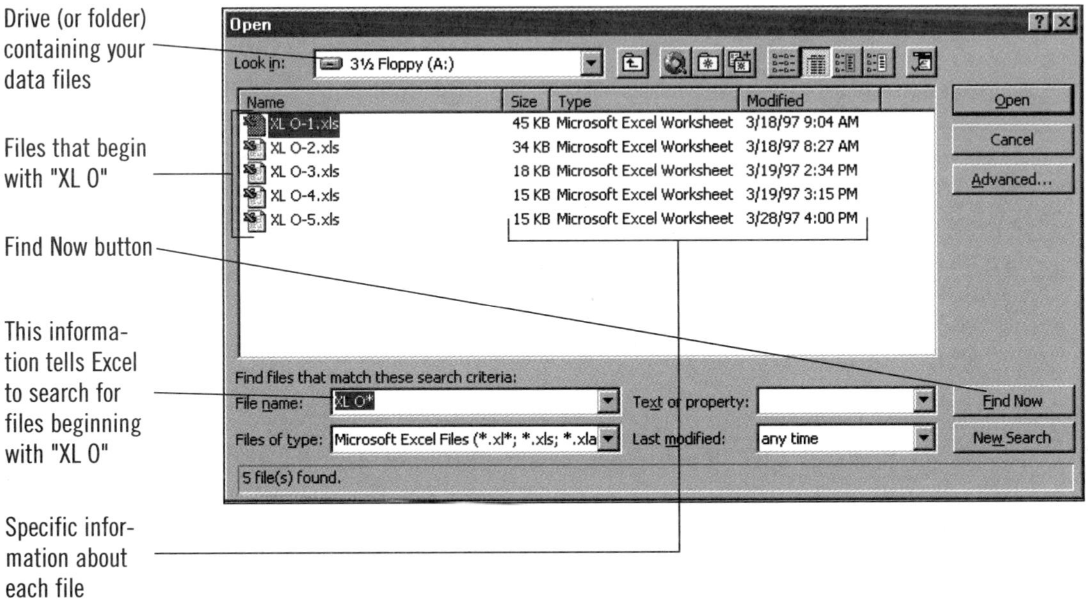

Drive (or folder) containing your data files

Files that begin with "XL O"

Find Now button

This information tells Excel to search for files beginning with "XL O"

Specific information about each file

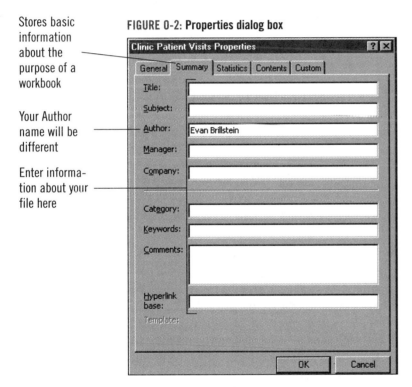

Stores basic information about the purpose of a workbook

Your Author name will be different

Enter information about your file here

FIGURE O-2: Properties dialog box

TABLE O-1: Open dialog box buttons

button	name	description
	List	Displays file and folder names
	Details	Displays file and folder names, along with the file type and the date last modified
	Properties	Displays information about the highlighted file, such as subject and keywords
	Preview	Displays the upper-left corner of the first sheet in a workbook
	Commands and Settings	Opens a menu with commands related to opening and searching for files

Auditing a Worksheet

Excel's auditing feature helps you track errors and determine worksheet logic—that is, how a worksheet is set up. Because worksheet errors and faulty logic can be introduced at any stage of development, it is important to include auditing as part of your workbook-building process. ➤ Megan asks Evan to audit the worksheet that tracks the number of patient visits to the company clinic and verify the accuracy of the year-end totals. Before beginning the auditing process, Evan adds a vertical pane to the window so he can view the first and last columns of the worksheet at the same time.

1. Drag the **vertical split box** (the small box to the right of the right horizontal scroll arrow) to the left until the vertical window pane divider is situated between columns A and B, then scroll the worksheet to the right until columns P through U are visible in the right pane

   See Figure O-3. Now you'll access the Auditing Toolbar.

2. Click **Tools** on the menu bar, point to **Auditing**, then click **Show Auditing Toolbar**

   See Figure O-4. The buttons on the Auditing toolbar identify any errors in your worksheet. Next, notice the #DIV/0! error in cell S6. These symbols indicate a **divide-by-zero error**, which occurs when you divide a value by zero. The Trace Error button on the auditing toolbar helps locate the source of this problem.

3. Click cell **S6**, then click the **Trace Error button** ◉ on the Auditing toolbar; if necessary, scroll down so row 16 is visible

   The formula bar reads =R6/$R$16, indicating that the value in cell R6 will be divided by the value in cell R16. Tracer arrows, or **tracers**, point from cells that might have caused the error to the active cell containing the error, as shown in Figure O-4. The tracers extend from cells R6 and R16 to cell S6. Note that cell R6 contains a value, whereas cell R16 is blank. In Excel formulas, blank cells have a value of zero. That means the value in cell R6 cannot be divided by the value in cell R16 (zero) because division by zero is impossible. To correct the error, you must edit the formula so that it references cell R15, the grand total of patient visits, not R16.

4. Press **[F2]** to switch to Edit mode, edit the formula to read **=R6/$R$15**, then click the **Enter button** ✓ on the formula bar

   The error message and trace arrows disappear, and the formula produces the correct result, 7%, in cell S6. Next, notice that the total for Dr. Ping in cell R5 is unusually high compared with the totals of the other physicians who practice holistic medicine. You can investigate this value by tracing the cell's precedents—the cells on which the active cell (R5) depends.

5. Click cell **R5**, click the **Trace Precedents button** ▤▸ on the Auditing toolbar, then scroll left until you identify the tracer's starting point

   The tracer arrow runs between cells B5 and R5, indicating that the formula in cell R5 reflects the quarterly *and* monthly totals of patient visits. Because both the quarterly totals and monthly totals are summed in this formula, the resulting figure is twice what it should be. You'll use AutoSum to correct this error so that only the quarterly totals are reflected in cell R5

6. If necessary, click cell **R5**, click the **AutoSum button** Σ on the Standard toolbar, then press **[Enter]**

   The tracer arrow disappears and the correct result, 276, appears in cell R5. Correcting the formula in cell R5 also adjusts the Grand Total percentage in cell S5 to 7%. Now that all the errors in the worksheet have been identified and corrected, you are finished auditing.

7. Save the workbook, click **Window** on the menu bar, click **Remove Split**, then close the Auditing toolbar

FIGURE O-3: Worksheet ready for auditing

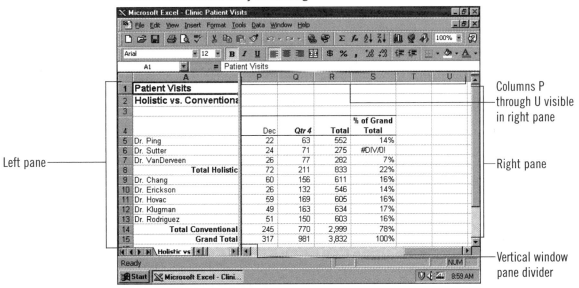

Left pane

Columns P
through U visible
in right pane

Right pane

Vertical window
pane divider

FIGURE O-4: Worksheet with traced error

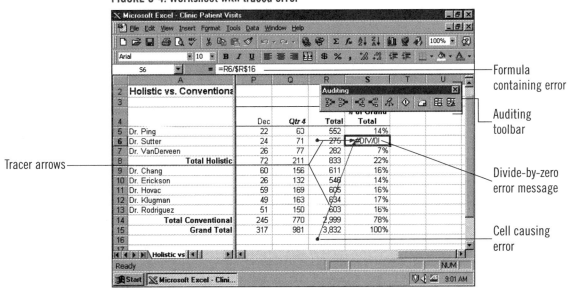

Tracer arrows

Formula
containing error

Auditing
toolbar

Divide-by-zero
error message

Cell causing
error

CLUES TO USE

Circular References

A cell with a **circular reference** contains a formula that refers to its own cell location. For example, if you entered the formula =B4+Q3 in cell B4, the result would be a circular reference, causing an error in the worksheet. If you accidentally enter a formula with a circular reference, a warning box will open alerting you to the problem. Click OK to open a Help window explaining how to find the circular reference using the Circular Reference toolbar. In simple formulas, a circular reference is easy to spot. To correct it, simply edit the formula to remove any reference to the cell where the formula is located.

Outlining a Worksheet

Excel's Outline command displays a worksheet with buttons that allow you to adjust the display of the worksheet to show only the critical rows and columns. For outlining to function properly, worksheet formulas must point consistently in the same direction. (If you're not sure which way your formulas point, click the Trace Precedents button on the Auditing toolbar.) Summary rows, such as subtotal rows, must be located below related data, whereas summary columns, such as grand total columns, must be located to the right of related data. ◄━━ Evan needs to give his manager the updated year-end totals. To emphasize the subtotals for both Holistic and Conventional physicians, as well as the grand total of patient visits, he decides to outline the worksheet first.

Steps 1 2 3 4

1. If necessary, press **[Ctrl][Home]** to display the upper-left corner of the worksheet

2. Click **Data** on the menu bar, point to **Group and Outline**, then click **Auto Outline**
   The worksheet is displayed in Outline view, as shown in Figure O-5. There are several ways to change the amount of detail in an outlined worksheet, but the easiest is by using the Column Level and Row Level buttons, which hide varying amount of detail. The Row Level 1 button hides everything in the worksheet except the most important row or rows—in this case, the Grand Total row.

3. Click the **Row Level 1 button** [1]
   This selection doesn't display enough information, so you'll try the Row Level 2 button, which hides everything except the second most important rows—in this case, the subtotal rows and the Grand Total row.

4. Click the **Row Level 2 button** [2]
   Now you can see the rows you want. Next, you'll display only the columns you choose—in this case, the Qtr 1-Qtr 4 columns, the Total column, and the % of Grand Total column. Like the Row Level 2 button, the Column Level 2 button displays the Grand Total column, along with its corresponding subtotals.

5. Click the **Column Level 2 button** [≡] then, if necessary, scroll right to bring columns E, I, M, Q, R, and S into view
   You're now ready to print the outlined worksheet so that Evan can give it to his manager.

6. Click the **Print button** [🖶] on the Standard toolbar
   Your printed worksheet should look like the one shown in Figure O-6. Next, you'll re-display all the rows and columns and turn off the Outline feature.

7. Click the **Row Level 3 button** [3], then click the **Column Level 3 button** [3]

8. Click **Data** on the menu bar, point to **Group and Outline**, then click **Clear Outline**

FIGURE O-5: Worksheet in Outline view

Column Level buttons

Row Level buttons

Row Level 1 button

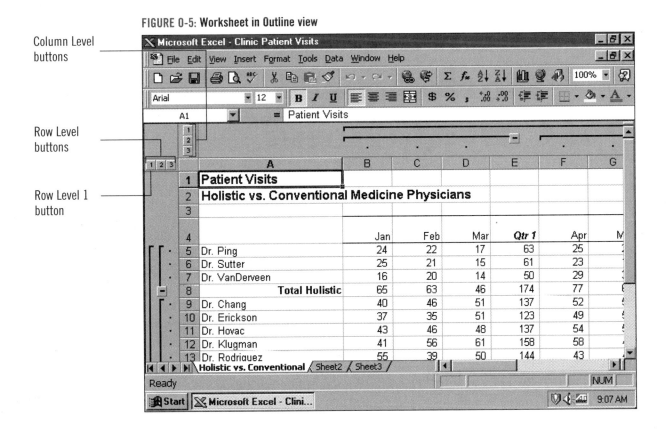

FIGURE O-6: Printed worksheet

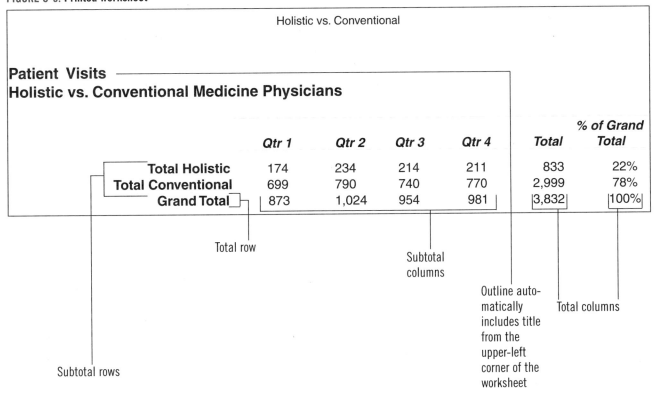

Holistic vs. Conventional

Patient Visits
Holistic vs. Conventional Medicine Physicians

	Qtr 1	Qtr 2	Qtr 3	Qtr 4	Total	% of Grand Total
Total Holistic	174	234	214	211	833	22%
Total Conventional	699	790	740	770	2,999	78%
Grand Total	873	1,024	954	981	3,832	100%

Total row

Subtotal columns

Outline automatically includes title from the upper-left corner of the worksheet

Total columns

Subtotal rows

Excel 97

Controlling Worksheet Calculations

Whenever you change a value in a cell, Excel automatically recalculates all the formulas in the worksheet based on that cell. This automatic calculation is efficient until you create a worksheet so large that the recalculation process slows down data entry and screen updating. At that point, you might want to selectively determine if and when you want Excel to perform calculations automatically. You do this by applying the manual calculation option. Once you change the calculation mode to manual, the manual mode is applied to all open worksheets. ◄◄◄ Because Evan knows that using specific Excel calculation options can help make worksheet building more efficient, he decides to change from automatic to manual calculation.

Steps 1234

1. **Click Tools on the menu bar, click Options, then click the Calculation tab**
   The Calculation tab of the Options dialog box opens, as shown in Figure O-7. This is the tab you use to specify the manual option.

2. **Under Calculation, click the Manual option button**
   Notice that the Recalculate before save box automatically contains a check mark when you select the Manual option. Now, anytime you reopen your workbook, you will be working with updated values.

3. **Click OK**
   Evan just received word that the December total for Dr. Chang is incorrect. You'll adjust the entry in P9 accordingly, but first you'll freeze the column and row headers to make the worksheet easier to read.

4. **Click cell B5, click Window on the menu bar, click Freeze Panes, then scroll right to bring columns P through S into view**

5. **Click cell P9, type 30, then click the Enter button ☑ on the formula bar**
   See Figure O-8. Notice that the formula results in the worksheet are *not* updated. (For example, the percentage in cell S9 is still 16%.) The word "Calculate" appears in the status bar to indicate that a specific value in the worksheet did indeed change and must be recalculated. You can press [F9] at any time to calculate all the open worksheets manually or [Shift][F9] to calculate just the active sheet.

QuickTip

When you are in manual calculation mode, make sure to recalculate your worksheet before you print and after you make changes.

6. **Press [Shift][F9], then save the workbook**
   See Figure O-9. The percentage in cell S9 is now 15% instead of 16%. The other formulas in the worksheet affected by the value in cell P9 changed as well. Because this is a relatively small worksheet that recalculates quickly, you will return to automatic calculation.

7. **Click Tools on the menu bar, click Options, if necessary, click the Calculation tab, under Calculation click the Automatic option button, then click OK**
   Now any additional changes you make to the worksheet will again be recalculated automatically.

FIGURE O-7: Calculation tab of the Options dialog box

Calculation tab

Manual option button

Some of your settings may differ

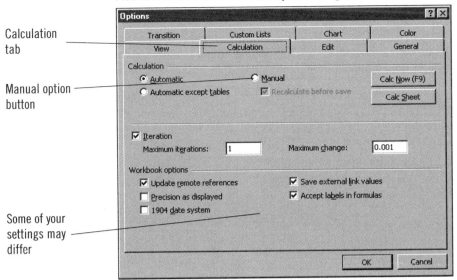

FIGURE O-8: Worksheet in manual calculation mode

Changed value

Value still needs to be updated

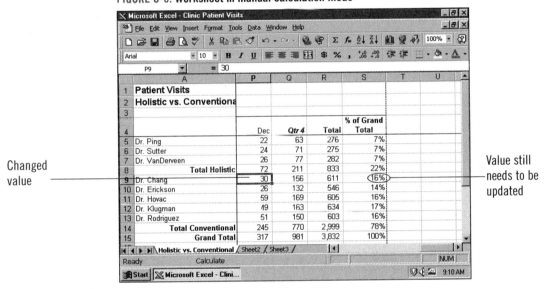

FIGURE O-9: Worksheet with updated values

Updated value

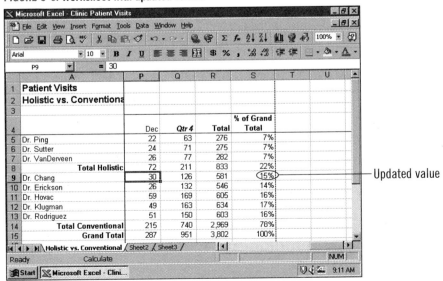

Creating Custom AutoFill Lists

Whenever you need to type a list of words regularly, you can save time by creating a custom AutoFill list. Then you only need to type the first entry in a blank cell. Excel will enter the rest of the information for you automatically when you drag the AutoFill handle, which is located in the lower-right corner of the cell. Figure O-10 shows some examples of AutoFill lists. Evan often has to repeatedly enter the names of the conventional-care physicians in the various worksheets. He decides to create an AutoFill list to save time in performing this task. He begins by selecting the names in the worksheet.

 Steps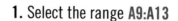

1. Select the range **A9:A13**

 Trouble?

If a list of doctors' names already appears in the Custom lists box, the person using the computer before you forgot to delete it. Click the list, click [Delete], and proceed with Step 3.

2. Click **Tools** on the menu bar, click **Options**, then click the **Custom Lists tab**
See Figure O-11. The Custom Lists tab shows the existing AutoFill lists. Notice that the Import list from cells box contains the range you selected in Step 1. Next, you'll add the text from that range to the Custom Lists box.

3. Click **Import**
The list of doctors' names is highlighted in the Custom lists box and displays in the List entries box. Now you can test your custom AutoFill list by placing it in a blank worksheet.

4. Click **OK**, click the **Sheet2 tab**, type **Dr. Chang** in cell A1, then click the **Enter button** on the formula bar

5. Position the pointer over the AutoFill handle in the lower right corner of cell A1
Notice that the pointer changes to $+$, as shown in Figure O-12.

 QuickTip

You also could drag the AutoFill handle to the right to fill the six cells in Row 1.

6. Click and drag the pointer down to cell **A5**, then release the mouse button
The highlighted range now contains the custom list of doctor names you created. Now that you've finished creating and applying your custom AutoFill list, you need to delete it from the Options dialog box if other students will be using your computer to complete the lesson. If no one else will be using the computer, skip Step 7 and proceed to the next lesson.

Time To

✔ Save the workbook

7. Click **Tools** on the menu bar, click **Options**, if necessary, click the **Custom Lists tab**, click the list of doctors' names in the Custom lists box, click **Delete**, click **OK** to confirm the delete, then click **OK** again

FIGURE O-10: Sample AutoFill lists

AutoFill handle —

Information entered automatically —

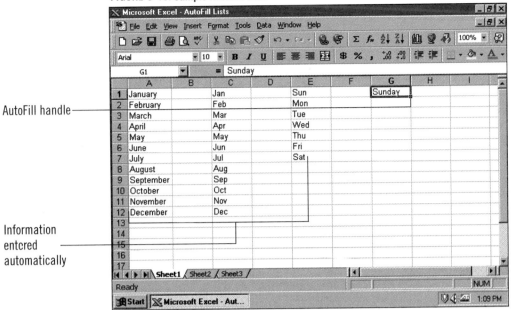

FIGURE O-11: Custom Lists tab

Existing AutoFill lists —

Range contains list of doctor's names —

Click to add doctors' names to dialog box —

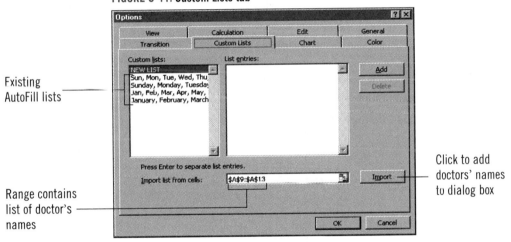

FIGURE O-12: Applying a custom AutoFill list

First name in the list —

AutoFill pointer —

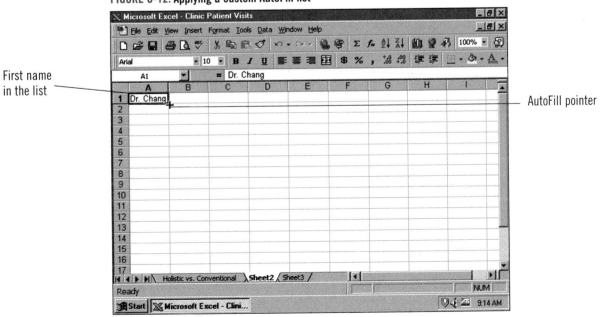

Excel 97

Customizing Excel

Excel's default settings for editing and viewing the worksheet are designed with the user's convenience in mind. However, you may find that a particular setting doesn't always fit your needs (for example, where the cell selector moves after you press [Enter]). The eight tabs of the Options dialog box allow you to customize Excel to suit your work habits and needs. You've already used the Calculation tab to switch to manual calculation and the Custom Lists tab to create your own AutoFill list. The most commonly used functions of the Options dialog box tabs are explained in more detail in Table O-4. ✐ Evan is curious about how he can customize Excel to allow him to work more efficiently. He decides to use a blank workbook to explore some of the features of Excel accessed through the Options dialog box.

 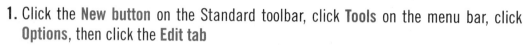

> **QuickTip**
>
> Do not change any settings in the Options dialog box other than those covered in this lesson.

1. Click the **New button** on the Standard toolbar, click **Tools** on the menu bar, click **Options**, then click the **Edit tab**

In some worksheets, it's more convenient to have the cell selector automatically move right one cell, rather than down one cell, after you press [Enter]. You'll change this setting now to see the effect on your worksheet.

2. Click the **Direction list arrow**, then click **Right**

See Figure O-13. Displaying the Properties dialog box when you save a file for the first time allows you to enter detailed information (or properties) about a workbook. This documentation may be useful to co-workers because it allows them to read a summary of your workbook without actually having to open it. You'll select this option now.

> **QuickTip**
>
> It's especially important not to adjust any other General tab settings if you're sharing a computer.

3. Click the **General tab**, then click the **Prompt for workbook properties check box**

Finally, you decide to turn off the worksheet gridlines to see how your worksheet will look.

4. Click the **View tab**, under Window options click the **Gridlines check box**

Keep in mind that this setting, as well as the others under "Window options," affects only the active worksheet. Now you'll close the Options dialog box to see the results of your new workbook settings.

5. Click **OK**, type **Accounts Receivable** in cell A1, then press **[Enter]**

The information in your new worksheet is displayed without any gridlines. In addition, the cell selector is now located to the right of cell A1. Next, as you save the workbook, you'll enter some information in the Properties dialog box. For more information about file properties, see the section on Finding files earlier in this unit.

6. Save the workbook as **Accounts** to your Student Disk, if necessary click the **Summary tab** in the Properties dialog box, then type **Sample workbook used to practice customizing Excel**

See Figure O-14.

> **QuickTip**
>
> In order to see a preview of a workbook in the Open dialog box, you need to click the Save Preview check box in the Properties dialog box.

7. Click **OK**

Now that you're finished exploring the Options dialog box, you need to reestablish the original Excel settings. Notice that you don't need to adjust the Gridlines settings because that change applied only to the active worksheet.

8. Click **Tools** on the menu bar, click **Options**, click the **Edit tab**, click the **Direction list arrow**, click **Down**, click the **General tab**, click the **Prompt for workbook properties check box** to uncheck it, click **OK**, then close the workbook

FIGURE O-13: Edit tab in the Options dialog box

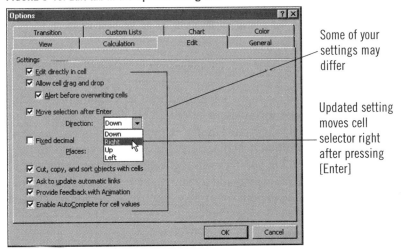

Some of your settings may differ

Updated setting moves cell selector right after pressing [Enter]

FIGURE O-14: Properties dialog box

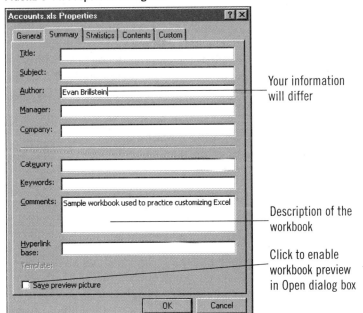

Your information will differ

Description of the workbook

Click to enable workbook preview in Open dialog box

TABLE O-4: Options dialog box tabs

tab	description
Calculation	Controls how the worksheet is calculated; choices include automatic versus manual
Chart	Controls how empty cells are treated in a chart and whether chart tips are displayed
Color	Allows you to copy a customized color palette from one workbook to another
Custom Lists	Allows you to add or delete custom AutoFill lists
Edit	Controls where the cell selector moves after you press [Enter], and whether you can edit directly in cells
General	Controls whether the Properties dialog box is displayed after saving a workbook, the number of sheets in a new workbook, and the drive and folder used in the Save dialog box by default; User name is also listed here
Transition	Provides options useful for users familiar with Lotus 1-2-3
View	Controls whether the Formula bar, Status bar, scroll bars, row and column headers, and gridlines are visible; also controls whether formulas are displayed in the worksheet

Excel 97

Adding a Comment to a Cell

Whenever you'll be sharing a workbook with others, it's a good idea to **document**, or make notes about, basic assumptions, complicated formulas, or questionable data. By reading your documentation, a co-worker then can quickly become familiar with your workbook. The easiest way to document a workbook is to use **cell comments**, which are notes you've written about your workbook that appear when you place the pointer over a cell.  Evan thinks one of the doctor's names may be misspelled. He decides to add a comment for Megan, pointing out the possible error. He begins by right-clicking the cell where he wants to add the comment, then proceeds to open the Comment box.

Steps

1. Click the **Holistic vs. Conventional sheet tab**, then right-click cell **A7**

QuickTip

You also can click the New Comment button on the Auditing toolbar to insert a comment.

2. Click **Insert Comment**
The comment box opens, as shown in Figure O-15. Notice that Excel automatically includes the user name at the beginning of the comment. The user name data was collected from information you previously entered in the General tab of the Options dialog box. Notice the white sizing handles on the border of the Comment box. You use these handles to change the size of the box by dragging as necessary. Next, make a note about the possible misspelling in the Comment box.

3. Type **Is this spelling correct? I think there might be a space after "Van."**
Notice how the text automatically wraps to the next line as necessary. Now, you close the Comment box.

4. Click outside the comment box
A red triangle appears in the upper-right corner of cell A7. The triangle indicates that a comment is attached to the cell. Next, you'll display the comment.

QuickTip

To edit an existing comment, select the cell where the comment is attached, click Insert, and then click Edit Comment.

5. Place the pointer over cell A7
The comment appears next to the cell. When you move the pointer outside of cell A7, the comment disappears. The worksheet is now finished and ready for printing. In order to fit the worksheet on a single page, you will use landscape orientation and scale it to fit. On a second printed page, you print only the cell comment along with its associated cell reference.

6. Click **File** on the menu bar, click **Page Setup**, if necessary click the **Page tab**, under Scaling, click the **Landscape option button**, click the **Fit to option button**, click the **Sheet tab**, under Print click the **Comments list arrow**, click **At end of sheet**, click the **Row and column headings check box**, click **Print**, then click **OK**
Excel prints two pages.

7. Save the workbook

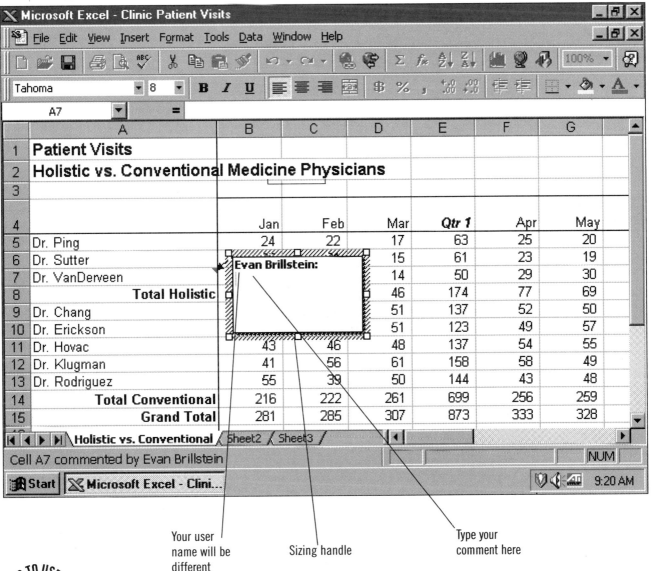

Your user
name will be
different

Sizing handle

Type your
comment here

Sharing Workbooks

Excel makes it easy for people to work on data collaboratively. The simplest way to share a workbook is to route it, via e-mail or on disk, to your co-workers. Propose that each person make suggestions using Cell Comments. When you receive the edited version, you can incorporate any valuable suggestions in your workbook.

If you prefer, you can send out multiple copies of the same workbook and then merge your co-workers' changes into one workbook. To find out exactly how to do this, search for "workbooks, merging" in the Help index.

In some cases, you may want your co-workers to be able to use the same workbook simultaneously. To do this, simply save the workbook as a shared workbook and then place it on a shared network directory or in a shared folder on your computer. Saving a workbook as a shared workbook activates the Change History feature, which shows information about changes to the shared workbook. To learn how to review and incorporate your co-workers' changes, search for "shared workbooks, incorporating changes" in Excel's Help Index.

To prepare a shared workbook, follow these steps:

1 Click **Tools**, click **Share Workbook**, then click the **Editing tab**

2 Click the **Allow Changes by More Than One User at the Same Time check box**, click **OK**, then click **OK** again

3 Click **File** on the menu bar, click **Save As**, then save the shared workbook to a network or shared folder

Saving a Workbook as a Template

A **template** is a workbook that contains text (such as column and row labels), formulas, macros, and formatting you use repeatedly. Once you save a workbook as a template, it provides a model for creating a new workbook without your having to reenter standard data. Excel provides several templates on the Spreadsheet Solutions tab of the New dialog box. In most cases, though, you'll probably want to create your own template from a worksheet you use regularly. ➤ Megan plans to use the same formulas, titles, frozen panes, and row and column labels that Evan used for the Clinic Patient Visits worksheet for subsequent yearly worksheets. She asks Evan to delete the extra sheets, comments, and data for each month, and then save the workbook as a template.

Steps 1 2 3 4

1. **Click the Sheet2 tab, press [Ctrl], click the Sheet3 tab, right-click the Sheet3 tab, click Delete, then click OK**

2. **Right-click cell A7, then click Delete Comment**
   Now that you've removed the extra sheets and the comment, you'll delete the data on patient visits. However, you'll leave the formulas in rows 8, 14, and 15, and in columns E, I, M, Q, R, and S so that another user can simply begin entering data without having to re-create the formulas.

3. **Press [Ctrl], select the ranges B5:D7, B9:D13, F5:H7, F9:H13, J5:L7, J9:L13, N5:P7, N9:P13, press [Delete], then click anywhere to deselect the ranges**
   See Figure O-16. The hyphens in the subtotal and total rows and columns indicate that the current value of these cells is zero. The divide by zero error messages in Column S are only temporary and will disappear as soon as you open the template, save it as a workbook, and begin to enter next year's data. To make subsequent template use easier, you scroll the right pane back to display the January column and select the first cell where data can be entered.

4. **Scroll left to bring columns B through G into view, then click cell B5**
   Notice that when you save the file as a template, the original workbook (which you saved in the previous lesson) remains intact on your Student Disk. Now you're ready to save the template.

5. **Click File, then click Save As**

6. **Click the Save As Type list arrow, then click Template (*.xlt)**
   Excel adds the .xlt extension to the filename and automatically switches to the Templates folder, as shown in Figure O-17. However, to keep your files organized, you save your template to your Student Disk instead.

7. **Click the Save in list arrow, click the drive and folder containing your Student Disk, click Save, close the workbook, then exit Excel**
   Next year, when Megan or Evan needs to compile the information for patient visits, they can simply open the Clinic Patient Visits template and begin entering data. When this new work is saved for the first time, Excel will automatically save the template as a regular workbook. The original template remains intact.

Trouble?

If you accidentally delete a formula, insert a copy from the appropriate adjoining cell; or click the Undo button and repeat Step 2.

FIGURE O-16: Preparing the template

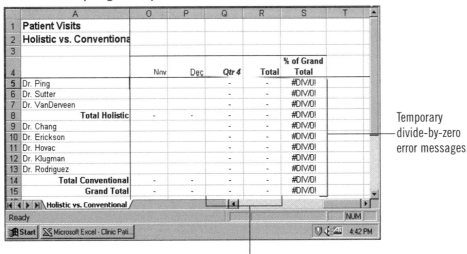

	A	O	P	Q	R	S	T
1	Patient Visits						
2	Holistic vs. Conventiona						
3							
4		Nov	Dec	Qtr 4	Total	% of Grand Total	
5	Dr. Ping			-	-	#DIV/0!	
6	Dr. Sutter			-	-	#DIV/0!	
7	Dr. VanDerveen			-	-	#DIV/0!	
8	Total Holistic	-	-	-	-	#DIV/0!	
9	Dr. Chang			-	-	#DIV/0!	
10	Dr. Erickson			-	-	#DIV/0!	
11	Dr. Hovac			-	-	#DIV/0!	
12	Dr. Klugman			-	-	#DIV/0!	
13	Dr. Rodriguez			-	-	#DIV/0!	
14	Total Conventional	-	-	-	-	#DIV/0!	
15	Grand Total	-	-	-	-	#DIV/0!	

Holistic vs. Conventional

Ready — NUM

Start — Microsoft Excel - Clinic Pati... — 4:42 PM

Temporary divide-by-zero error messages

Hyphens indicate value of zero

FIGURE O-17: Saving a template

Default folder containing templates

Your folders will be different

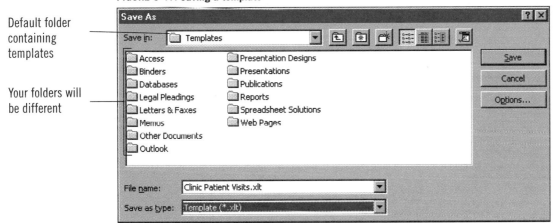

Save As

Save in: Templates

- Access
- Binders
- Databases
- Legal Pleadings
- Letters & Faxes
- Memos
- Other Documents
- Outlook
- Presentation Designs
- Presentations
- Publications
- Reports
- Spreadsheet Solutions
- Web Pages

Save
Cancel
Options...

File name: Clinic Patient Visits.xlt

Save as type: Template (*.xlt)

<p>Excel 97</p>

CLUES TO USE

Opening a Template

If you're using your own computer, you may want to save your templates in one of the Template subfolders, shown in Figure O-17. Then you can quickly open your template from the New dialog box by clicking File, then clicking New.

The New dialog box contains an assortment of tabs containing icons for workbook templates, as shown in Figure O-18. The Spreadsheet Solutions tab in the New dialog box contains several ready-made templates you can use for business-related tasks, such as creating invoices or purchase orders. The other tabs in the New dialog box depend on which subfolders you used to save your templates. For instance, if you saved a template named "Personnel" in the Other Documents subfolder, then you would see an Other Documents tab in the New dialog box, with the Personnel template as an option. To open the Personnel template, click it, then click OK.

FIGURE O-18: New dialog box

New

General | Spreadsheet Solutions | Other Documents

Personnel.xlt

Preview

OK   Cancel

Contains the basic Excel workbook template

This template was saved originally in the Other Documents subfolder

Tabs correspond to subfolders shown in Figure O-17

Contains ready-made templates

Practice

► Concepts Review

Label each element of the Excel screen shown in Figure O-19.

FIGURE O-19

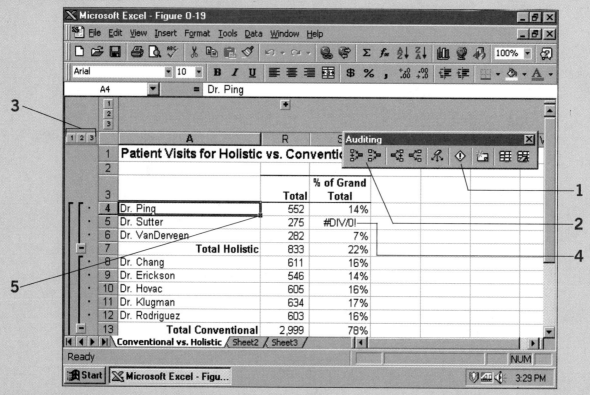

Match each statement with the term it describes.

6. Contains settings for customizing Excel
7. Note that appears when you place the pointer over a cell
8. Occurs in a formula that refers to its own cell location
9. Calculates the worksheet manually
10. Automatically enters a list in a worksheet
11. Used to track errors and determine worksheet logic
12. A powerful searching tool that makes it easy to find files
13. Allows you to display the most important columns and rows

a. Open dialog box
b. Options dialog box
c. Auditing toolbar
d. Outlining a worksheet
e. Circular reference
f. [Shift][F9]
g. AutoFill
h. Comment

Select the best answer from the list of choices.

14. When searching for a file, which of these characters can substitute for unknown characters in a filename?
  a. #   b. &   c. *   d. !

15. If you want several people to use a workbook simultaneously, you need to save it as a(n)
  a. Multiple Workbook.   b. Active Workbook.   c. Edited Workbook.   d. Shared Workbook.

16. You can search for a file by
  a. name.   b. text within the file.   c. property.   d. All of the above.

17. The _____ button locates the cells used in the active cell's formula.
   a. Trace Precedents   **b.** Trace Antecedents   **c.** Function   **d.** Validation Circle
18. The _____ automatically hides everything in the worksheet except the most important row or rows.
   a. Column Level 1 button
   b. Row Level 1 button
   c. Trace Precedents button
   d. Outline feature
19. To create a custom AutoFill list you should first
   a. Press [Shift][F9].
   b. Click the AutoFill tab in the Edit dialog box.
   c. Drag the AutoFill handle.
   d. Select the list in the worksheet.
20. The _____ tab in the Options dialog box controls whether the Properties dialog box is displayed when you save a workbook.
   a. General   **b.** Edit   **c.** Properties   **d.** View

▶ Skills Review

1. **Find files.**
   a. Display the Open dialog box.
   b. In the Look in box, click the drive that contains your Student Disk.
   c. If the files for this unit are in a folder, click that folder in the Look in box.
   d. If necessary, click the Details button to display information about each file.
   e. Click the Properties button to display file properties.
   f. Click the List button to display only filenames.
   g. Search for all files that begin with XL O.
   h. To narrow your search, search for the text "Household" contained within a workbook.
   i. Open the workbook XL O-2.
   j. Save the workbook as "Household Budget."

2. **Audit a worksheet.**
   a. Click Tools, point to Auditing, then click Show Auditing Toolbar.
   b. Drag the toolbar to the lower-right corner of the worksheet window.
   c. Click cell E4, click the New Comment button on the Auditing toolbar, type "Took quarter off to travel," then click outside the Comments box to close it.
   d. Click cell C17, click the Trace Precedents button on the Auditing toolbar, then scroll to see where the tracer ends.
   e. Edit the formula in cell C17 to read =SUM(C9:C16), then click the Enter button on the Formula bar.
   f. Click cell H10, then click the Trace Error button on the Auditing toolbar.
   g. Edit the formula in cell H10 to read =G10/$G$17.
   h. Click cell C19, then edit the formula to read =C6-C17.
   i. Remove the circular reference by editing the formula in cell C19 to read =C6-C17.
   j. Click the Close button on the Auditing toolbar, then save the workbook.

3. **Outline a Worksheet and Control Worksheet Calculation.**
   a. Move to the upper-left corner of the worksheet, then display the worksheet in outline view.
   b. Use the Row Level buttons to display only the most important rows in the budget.
   c. Use the Row Level buttons to display the second-most-important rows in the budget.
   d. Print the Outlined worksheet in Landscape orientation.
   e. Use the Row Level buttons to display all the rows in the budget.
   f. Clear the outline from the worksheet.
   g. Open the Options dialog box and switch to manual calculation.
   h. Click cell C5 and type 800.
   i. Calculate the worksheet manually using the appropriate key combination.
   j. Turn off manual calculation, and save the workbook.

4. **Create a custom AutoFill list.**
   a. Select the range B9:B16.
   b. Open the Custom Lists tab in the Options dialog box.
   c. Import the selected text into the dialog box.
   d. Close the dialog box.
   e. Click the Sheet2 tab.
   f. Enter "Mortgage" in cell A1.
   g. Drag A1's fill handle to cell A8.
   h. Select cell A1 again, and drag its fill handle to cell H1.
   i. Open the Options dialog box again, and delete the list you just created.
   j. Save the workbook.

5. **Customize Excel.**
   a. Open the Options dialog box.
   b. In the Edit tab, change the direction of the cell selector to "Up."
   c. In the General tab, indicate that you want the Properties dialog box to appear when you save a workbook for the first time.
   d. In the View tab, turn off the worksheet gridlines.
   e. Close the dialog box and return to Sheet2, which is now displayed without gridlines.
   f. Click the Budget tab, and notice that this worksheet is displayed with gridlines.
   g. Open a new workbook.
   h. Type your name in cell C5, then press Enter. Check to make sure the cell selector moves up.
   i. Save the workbook to your Student Disk as "Customizing Excel," adding your name if necessary, and the comment "Sample workbook" to the Properties dialog box, then close the workbook.
   j. Open the Options dialog box and change the cell selector direction back to "Down." Then turn off the Properties dialog box and close the Options dialog box.

6. **Add a comment to a cell.**
   a. In the Budget sheet, click cell A19.
   b. Open the comment box by using the Comment command on the Insert menu.
   c. Type "Cash Flow is calculated by subtracting total expenses from total income. Negative numbers appear in parentheses."
   d. Drag the white handles on the borders of the comment box until you can see the entire note.
   e. Click anywhere outside the comment box to close it.

   f. Display the comment, and check for errors.

   g. Right-click cell A19, then click Edit Comment.

   h. Click to the left of the "N" in "Negative," then drag to select the entire second sentence.

   i. Press the Delete button, then close the Comment box.

   j. Right-click cell E4 (where you added a comment earlier), then click Delete Comment.

   k. Print the worksheet and your comment in landscape orientation.

   l. Save the workbook.

7. Save a workbook as a template.

   a. Delete sheets 2 and 3.

   b. Delete the comment in cell A19.

   c. Delete the budget data for all four quarters. Leave the worksheet formulas intact.

   d. Save the workbook to your Student Disk as a template.

   e. Close the template.

   f. Open the template using the Open command on the File menu.

   g. Enter data for all four quarters and in every budget category.

   h. Save the workbook as Household Budget 2.

   i. Print and close the workbook, and exit Excel.

▶ Independent Challenges

1. You are manager at Life Skills, a nonprofit agency devoted to helping people with severe learning disabilities become proficient computer users. Your department specializes in hands-on instruction for popular personal computer (PC) programs. During the month of October, you created a check register in Excel for department expenses. Before you begin generating a November register, however, you want to check the October one for errors. In your worksheet audit, you will look for missing check numbers, miscalculated totals, and faulty formula logic. Also, you want to add comments to document the worksheet.

   To complete this independent challenge:

1. Open the workbook titled XL O-3, then save it as "1998 Monthly Check Register".
2. Open the Auditing toolbar.
3. The balance in cell F16 does not reflect the RAM upgrade on 10/15/98. Use the Trace Precedents button to show the logic of the formula in F16. Once you identify the error in cell F16, edit the formula in cell F16 to subtract the RAM expense from the previous balance.
4. Due to illness, your Excel instructor taught only three hours of a six-hour course. Create a comment indicating this in cell C19.
5. Use the Trace Error button to determine the source of the problem in cell E24. Edit the formula to solve the problem, and then format the cell to display a percentage with no decimal places.
6. Save the workbook. Preview, then print the worksheet on one page and the comment on another.
7. Close the workbook.

2. As a manager at Life Skills, a nonprofit agency that helps learning-disabled people become proficient computer users, you need to keep track of regular monthly expenses. Your assistant compiled a list of fixed expenses in an Excel workbook but forgot the filename. Once you find the file using the search tools in the Open dialog box, you want to create a custom AutoFill list containing each expense item, to save time in preparing similar worksheets in the future. Finally, you will practice using manual calculation and then turn off the worksheet gridlines to make the expense data easier to read.

To complete this independent challenge:

1. Search your Student Disk for a file with the text "Printer paper" in the workbook. Search again for a file with the text "Fixed Monthly Expenses" in the workbook. Open the workbook, and save it as "Monthly Budget."
2. Select the cells containing the list of expense items. Then open the Options dialog box and import the list into the Custom Lists tab.
3. Close the Options dialog box and practice using the AutoFill handle to insert your list in a column in Sheet2. Insert the list a second time in a row in Sheet2.
4. Save the workbook, then preview and print Sheet2 on a single page.
5. Return to the Fixed Expenses sheet, then delete your custom list from the Options dialog box.
6. Use the Options dialog box to switch to manual calculation and to turn off the gridlines in the Fixed Expenses sheet.
7. Change the expense for Printer paper to 25.00. Calculate the worksheet manually.
8. Turn on automatic calculation again, then print the Fixed Expenses worksheet.
9. Save and close the workbook.

3. Your business, Babies Inc., helps parents find high-quality in-home childcare. In exchange for a one-time fee, you recruit and interview potential nannies, confirm references, and conduct a thorough background check. In addition, once a nanny has been hired, you provide training in child development and infant CPR. Currently, you are preparing your budget for the next four quarters. After you enter the data for each expense and income category, you will create a condensed version of the worksheet using Excel's outlining tools.

To complete this independent challenge:

1. Open a new workbook, then save it as "Babies Budget."
2. Enter a title and then the following row labels: Description, 1st Qtr, 2nd Qtr, 3rd Qtr, 4th Qtr, and Total.
3. Enter the following income items: Nanny Fee, Child Development Course, CPR Course. Subtotal the income items, and then enter at least six office-expense items.
4. Subtotal the expenses. Enter expenses and income data for each quarter. Create formulas for the total column and a cash flow row.
5. Display the worksheet in Outline view.
6. Contract the outline to display only the subtotal and total rows, then print the outline.
7. Re-display all the rows, then contract the outline again to eliminate the data for each quarter. Print the outline.
8. Clear the outline, then print the entire worksheet.
9. Save the workbook, and close it.

4. Bat Conservation International (BCI) is a worldwide organization dedicated to protecting all kinds of bats. According to BCI's Web page, bats are some of the "most gentle, beneficial and necessary" animals on earth. Unfortunately, because of centuries of myth and superstition, they also are among the world's least appreciated and most endangered animals. In order to get this message out, BCI spends 44% of its budget on public education. You'll find more details on BCI's revenues and expenses in the Revenue and Expenses Pie Chart page of its Annual Report. Create an income and expense template using categories from the pie chart.

To complete the independent challenge:

1. Use your Web browser to go to the home page for Bat Conservation International. If you have trouble finding the page, go to http://www.course.com. From there, click Student Online Companions, click the link for this textbook, then click the Excel link for Unit O. Click the Annual Report link, and then open the Revenue and Expenses Pie Chart.
2. Create an Income and Expense worksheet for four quarters using the categories shown on the pie chart. Do not include any actual data.
3. Create a total column, then create subtotals rows for Expenses as well as for Support and Revenues.
4. Print the empty template.
5. Save the workbook to your Student Disk as BCI Budget, in template format.
6. Open the template, and enter your own data for all four quarters. Print the worksheet.
7. Save the workbook as BCI Budget in workbook format. Close the workbook.

► Visual Workshop

Open the workbook titled XL O-5, then click Cancel to close the dialog box warning you of a circular reference. Save the workbook as "City Zoo Animal Count" to your Student Disk. Use the auditing techniques you have learned so far to correct any errors so that the worksheet entries and formulas match Figure O-20. Make sure to include a cell comment in cell E13. Preview, then print the worksheet and comment in landscape orientation showing row and column headings. In addition to the worksheet printout, include a printout of worksheet formulas showing row and column headings also.

FIGURE O-20

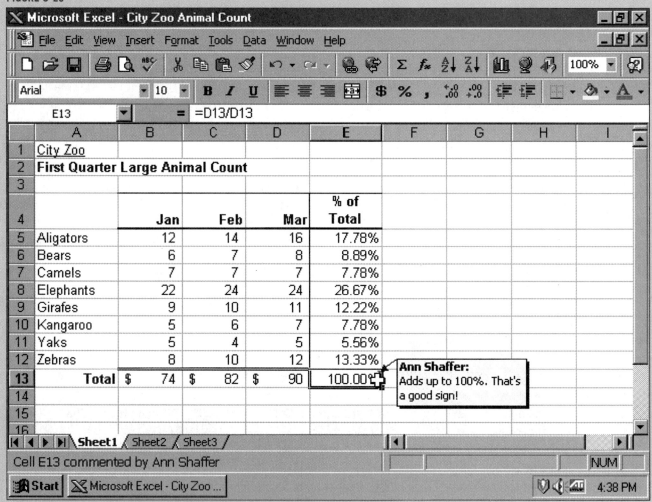

Programming
with Excel

▶ **View VBA code**
▶ **Analyze VBA code**
▶ **Write VBA code**
▶ **Add a conditional statement**
▶ **Prompt the user for data**
▶ **Debug a macro**
▶ **Create a main procedure**
▶ **Run a main procedure**

All Excel macros are written in a programming language called Visual Basic for Applications or, simply, **VBA.** When you create a macro with Excel's macro recorder, the recorder writes the required VBA instructions for you. You also can create an Excel macro by entering the appropriate VBA instructions manually. The sequence of VBA statements contained in a macro is called a **procedure.** In this unit, you view and analyze existing VBA code. Then you will write some VBA code on your own. You will learn how to add a conditional statement to a procedure, as well as how to prompt the user for information while the macro is running. You will also find out how to locate any errors, or bugs, in a macro. Lastly, you will combine several macros into one. ✐ Megan Grahs, Nomad's health division director, has asked her assistant, Evan Brillstein, to create five macros to automate some of the division's time-consuming tasks.

Viewing VBA Code

Before you can write Excel macro procedures, you must become familiar with the VBA (Visual Basic for Applications) programming language. A common method of learning any programming language is to view existing code. To do this, you start by opening the Visual Basic Editor, which contains a Project window, a Properties window, and a Code window. The VBA code for the macro procedure appears in the Code window. The first line of a procedure is called a **procedure header**. The procedure header defines the procedure's type, name, and arguments. Items listed in blue are **keywords**, which are words recognized to be part of the VBA programming language. **Comments**, which are notes explaining the code, are shown in green, and the remaining code is shown in black. You use the Editor to view or edit an existing macro procedure as well as to create a new macro procedure. ✐ Each month, Nomad Ltd's health division receives a text file from the KWIN radio station containing information about monthly radio ads. Megan already imported the text file into a worksheet but still needs to format it. Evan has begun work on a macro to automate the process of formatting this imported text file.

Trouble?

If the Virus warning dialog box shown in Figure P-1 appears, click Enable Macros. If a macro information dialog box opens informing you that Visual Basic macro modules are now edited in the Visual Basic Editor, click OK, then continue with Step 2.

1. **Open the workbook titled XL P-1, then save it as KWIN Procedures**
   The KWIN Procedures workbook opens with a blank worksheet. To view the FormatFile macro procedure, you need to open the Visual Basic Editor.

2. **Click Tools on the menu bar, point to Macro, then click Macros**
   The Macro dialog box appears with the FormatFile macro procedure selected in the list box. You now open this procedure in the Visual Basic Editor.

3. **Click Edit**
   The Visual Basic Editor opens and displays the FormatFile procedure in the Code window. See Figure P-2. If your Code window isn't maximized as in the figure, you can enlarge it in the next step. Also, if you don't see the Project window or the Properties window, you can display them.

4. **If necessary, click the Code window's Maximize button; if necessary, click the menu bar, click Properties, click View, then click Project Explorer**
   Now, you will familiarize yourself with the first few lines of the procedure code.

5. **Examine the top three lines of comments and the first line of code beginning with Sub FormatFile ( )**
   Notice that the different parts of the procedure appear in various colors. The third line of comments explains that the keyboard shortcut for this macro procedure is Ctrl+f. The keyword *Sub* in the procedure header indicates that this is a **Sub procedure**, or a series of Visual Basic statements that perform an action but do not return a value. In the next lesson, you will analyze the procedure code to see what each line does.

Understanding the Visual Basic Editor

A **module** is the Visual Basic equivalent of a worksheet. In it, you store macro procedures, just as you store data in worksheets. Modules, in turn, are stored in workbooks (or **projects**), along with worksheets. You view and edit modules in the Visual Basic Editor, which is made up of three windows, the Project Explorer (also called the Project window), the Code window, and the Properties window. The **Project Explorer** displays a list of all open projects (or workbooks) and the worksheets and modules they contain. To view the procedures stored in a module, you must first select the module in the Project Explorer (just as you would select a file in the Windows Explorer). The **Code window** then displays the selected module's procedures. The **Properties window** displays a list of characteristics (or **properties**) associated with the module. A newly inserted module has only one property, its name.

FIGURE P-1: Virus warning dialog box

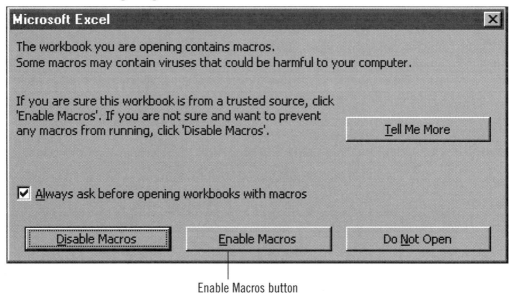

Enable Macros button

FIGURE P-2: Procedure displayed in the Visual Basic Editor

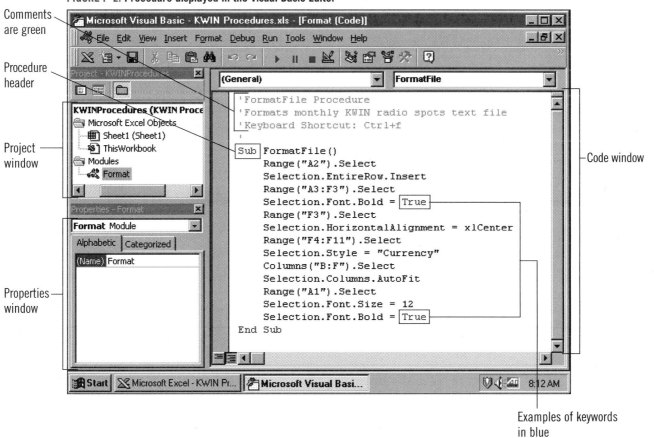

Comments are green

Procedure header

Project window

Properties window

Code window

Examples of keywords in blue

Excel 97

Analyzing VBA Code

You can learn a lot about the VBA language simply by analyzing the code generated by Excel's macro recorder. The more VBA code you analyze, the easier it will be for you to write your own programming code. ◀━━━ Before writing any new procedures, Evan analyzes the procedure he's already written.

Steps 1 2 3 4

1. **With the FormatFile procedure still displayed in the Code window, examine the next four lines of code beginning with Range("A2").Select**

   See Figure P-3. Every element of Excel, including a range, is considered an **object**. A **range object** represents a cell or a range of cells. The statement *Range("A2").Select* selects the range object cell A2. Notice that several times in the procedure a line of code (or **statement** selects a range, and then subsequent lines act on that selection. The next statement, *Selection.EntireRow.Insert*, inserts a row above the selection, which is currently cell A2. The next two lines of code select range A3:F3 and apply bold formatting to that selection. In VBA terminology, whether bold formatting is enabled is a value of an object's Bold property. A **property** is an attribute of an object that defines one of the object's characteristics (such as size) or an aspect of its behavior (such as whether it is enabled). To change the characteristics of an object, you simply change the values of its properties.

2. **Examine the remaining lines of code, beginning with Range ("F3").Select**

   The next two statements select the range object cell F3, then center its contents. Then the F4:F11 range object is formatted as currency. Column objects B through F are then selected and their widths set to AutoFit. Finally, the range object cell A1 is selected, its font size is changed to 12, and its Bold property is set to True. The last line, *End Sub*, indicates the end of the Sub procedure and is also referred to as a **procedure footer**. Next, you'll use the FormatFile procedure to format the text stored in a different workbook. First, though, you'll return to Excel to open and rename the workbook containing the unformatted text.

3. **Click the View Microsoft Excel button** ☒ **on the Visual Basic Editor Standard toolbar**

4. **Open the workbook titled XL P-2, then save it as KWIN Advertising 9-98**

   This workbook contains the text you want to format. Now, you'll use the keyboard shortcut, [Ctrl][F], to run the FormatFile procedure.

5. **Press [Ctrl][F]**

   The FormatFile procedure formats the text, as shown in Figure P-4. Now, you'll save and print the formatted worksheet.

6. **Save the workbook, then print the worksheet**

   Now that you've successfully viewed and analyzed code for a macro procedure, you will learn how to write your own code.

CLUES TO USE

Object Properties

The properties of an object are listed in the Properties window. To change the characteristics of an object, you simply change the values of its properties. For example, to apply bold formatting to a selected range, you assign the value True to the range's Bold property. To remove bold formatting, assign the value False.

FIGURE P-3: VBA code for the FormatFile procedure

Select range object cell A2

Inserts a row above cell A2

Applies bold formatting to range A3:F3

Centers contents of cell F3

Formats range F4:F11 as currency

Sets width of columns B–F to AutoFit

Adjusts font size and fomatting of cell A1

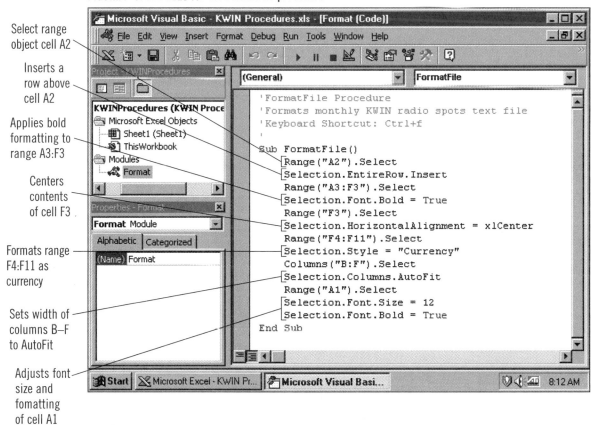

```
'FormatFile Procedure
'Formats monthly KWIN radio spots text file
'Keyboard Shortcut: Ctrl+f
'
Sub FormatFile()
    Range("A2").Select
    Selection.EntireRow.Insert
    Range("A3:F3").Select
    Selection.Font.Bold = True
    Range("F3").Select
    Selection.HorizontalAlignment = xlCenter
    Range("F4:F11").Select
    Selection.Style = "Currency"
    Columns("B:F").Select
    Selection.Columns.AutoFit
    Range("A1").Select
    Selection.Font.Size = 12
    Selection.Font.Bold = True
End Sub
```

FIGURE P-4: Worksheet formatted using FormatFile procedure

Formatted title

Row inserted

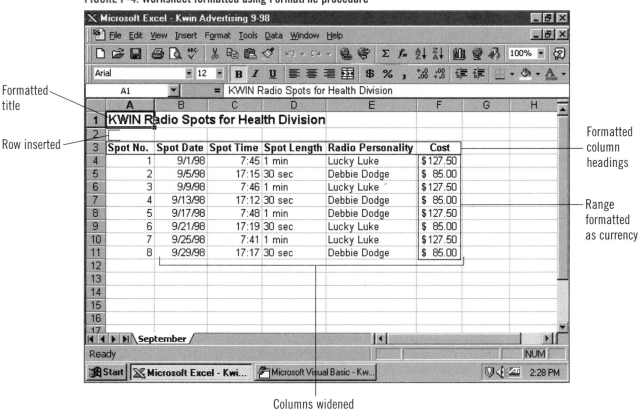

Formatted column headings

Range formatted as currency

Columns widened

Excel 97

Writing VBA Code

To write your own code, first you need to open the Visual Basic Editor, then add a module to the workbook. Then you can begin entering the procedure code. In the first few lines of a procedure, typically you include comments indicating the name and brief descriptions of the procedure and shortcut keys, if applicable. When writing Visual Basic code for Excel, you must follow the formatting rules, or **syntax**, of the VBA programming language exactly. Even an extra space or a period could cause a procedure to fail. It is important to review the procedure based on the code you've written before you actually run it. 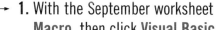 Each month, Megan asks Evan to total the cost of the radio ads. Evan decides to write a procedure that will automate this routine task. He starts by displaying the VBE.

QuickTip

You also can open the Visual Basic Editor by opening the Macro dialog box, selecting a macro, then clicking Edit.

1. **With the September worksheet still displayed, click** Tools **on the menu bar, point to** Macro, **then click** Visual Basic Editor
   The Format procedure is displayed again in the Visual Basic Editor. Now you can insert a new module into the active project, KWIN Procedures. You can tell that KWIN Procedures is the active project because one of its parts (the Format module in the Format folder) is selected in the Project Explorer window.

2. **Click** Insert **on the Visual Basic Editor menu bar, then click** Module
   A new, blank module, with the default name Module1, is inserted in the KWIN Procedures workbook. Before entering the code for the procedure, you'll change the default name to a more descriptive one.

3. **Click (Name) in the Properties window, type** Total, **then press [Enter]**
   Now you can type the new procedure as shown in Figure P-5. Notice that comments begin with an opening apostrophe and that pressing [Tab] indents the lines of code under "Sub AddTotal ( )". After you type *Sub AddTotal( )* (the procedure header) and press [Enter], the Visual Basic Editor will automatically enter *End Sub* (the procedure footer) in the Code window. As you type the code between the procedure header and footer, the Visual Basic Editor occasionally will display a list of words that can be used in the procedure statements. You could build your code by selecting words from the list, but until you become a more experienced programmer it's easier simply to type your code.

QuickTip

You edit text in the Code window by selecting and deleting characters or by clicking and typing new characters. To start a new line, press [Enter].

4. **Click in the Code window, then type the procedure code exactly as shown in Figure P-5**
   The lines that begin with *ActiveCell.Formula* insert the information that is enclosed in quotation marks into the active cell. For example, *ActiveCell.Formula = "Monthly Total:"* inserts the words "Monthly Total:" into cell E12, the active cell. The *With* clause near the bottom of the procedure is used to repeat several operations on the same object. Now that you've finished entering the code, review the procedure and save any changes before running it.

5. **Compare the procedure code you entered in the Code window with Figure P-5; if necessary, make any corrections; then click the** Save KWIN Procedures.xls button 🖫 **on the Visual Basic Editor Standard toolbar**
   With your work checked and saved, you switch to the KWIN Advertising 9-98 workbook and run the procedure.

Trouble?

If an error message appears, click Debug. Click the Reset button, correct the error by referring to Figure P-5, then repeat Steps 5 and 6.

6. **Click the** View Microsoft Excel button 🗷 **on the Visual Basic Editor Standard toolbar, verify that the KWIN Advertising 9-98 workbook appears on the screen, click** Tools **on the Excel menu bar, point to** Macro, **then click** Macros
   The Macro dialog box opens. This is where you select the macro procedure you want to run. Notice that the names of the macros have two parts. The first part ('KWIN Procedures.xls'!) indicates the workbook where the macro is stored. The second part (AddTotal or FormatFile) is the name of the procedure, taken from the procedure header.

Time To

✔ Save the workbook

7. **Click** 'KWIN Procedures.xls'!AddTotal, **then click** Run
   The AddTotal procedure inserts and formats the ad expenditure total in cell F12, as shown in Figure P-6.

FIGURE P-5: **VBA code for the AddTotal procedure**

Save KWIN
Advertising 9-98
button

Comments begin
with apostrophes

Press [Tab] to
indent lines

New module
name

With clause
repeats several
operations on
the same object

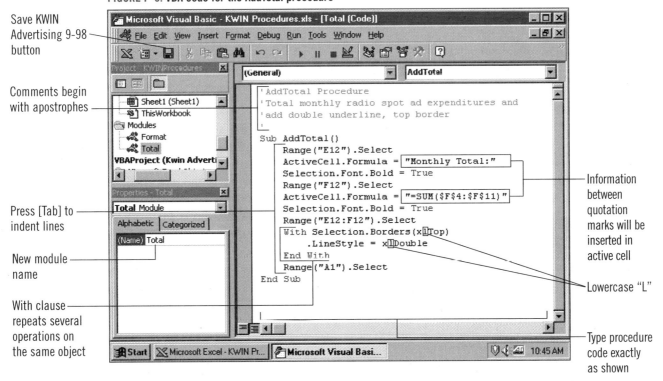

Information
between
quotation
marks will be
inserted in
active cell

Lowercase "L"

Type procedure
code exactly
as shown

FIGURE P-6: **Worksheet after running the AddTotal procedure**

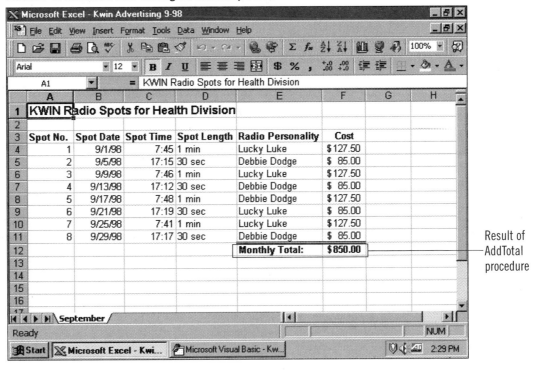

Result of
AddTotal
procedure

CLUES TO USE

Entering Code

To assist you in entering the macro code, Editor often displays a list of words that can be used in the macro statement. Typically, the list appears after you press the . (period). To include a word from the list in the macro statement, select the word in the list, then press [Tab].

For example, to enter the *Range("E12").Select* instruction, type *Range("E12")*, then press the . (period). Type *s* to select the Select command in the list, then press [Tab] to enter the word Select in the macro statement.

Adding a Conditional Statement

Sometimes, you may want a procedure to take an action based on a certain condition or set of conditions. For example, *if* a salesperson's performance rating is a 5 (top rating), *then* calculate a 10% bonus; otherwise (*else*), there is no bonus. One way of adding this type of conditional statement in Visual Basic is by using an **If...Then...Else statement**. The syntax for this statement is: If *condition* Then *statements* [Else *elsestatements*]. The brackets indicate that the Else part of the statement is optional. Megan wants to find out whether the amount spent on radio ads stays within or exceeds the $900 budgeted amount. Evan will use Excel to add a conditional statement that indicates this information. He starts by returning to the Visual Basic Editor and inserting a new module in the KWIN Procedures workbook.

1. With the September worksheet still displayed, click **Tools** on the menu bar, point to **Macro**, click **Visual Basic Editor**, verify that KWIN Procedures is the active project in the Project Explorer window, click **Insert** on the Visual Basic Editor menu bar, then click **Module**

   A new, blank module is inserted in the KWIN Procedures workbook. Before entering the code, you'll give the module a more descriptive name.

2. In the Properties window click **(Name)**, then type **Budget**

   Now you can create a procedure that uses an If...Then...Else statement to determine the monthly budget status.

3. Click in the Code window, then type the code exactly as shown in Figure P-7

   Notice the additional comment lines (in green) in the middle of the code. These extra lines help explain the procedure. Now that the BudgetStatus procedure is finished, you'll review it and save your work before running it.

4. Compare the procedure you entered with Figure P-7; if necessary, make any corrections; then click the **Save KWIN Procedures.xls button** 🖫 on the Visual Basic Editor Standard toolbar

   Next, you'll switch to the KWIN Advertising workbook and run the BudgetStatus procedure.

5. Click the **View Microsoft Excel button** 🖾 on the Visual Basic Editor toolbar; click **Tools** on the menu bar; point to **Macro**, click **Macros**; in the Macro dialog box, click **'KWIN Procedures.xls'!BudgetStatus**; then click **Run**

   The BudgetStatus procedure indicates the status—within budget—as shown in Figure P-8. Now you save your changes to the KWIN Advertising workbook.

6. Save your work

FIGURE P-7: VBA code for the BudgetStatus procedure

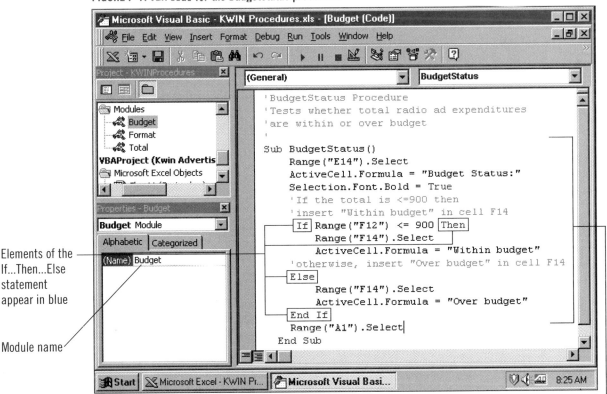

Elements of the If...Then...Else statement appear in blue

Module name

Type code exactly as shown

FIGURE P-8: Result of BudgetStatus procedure

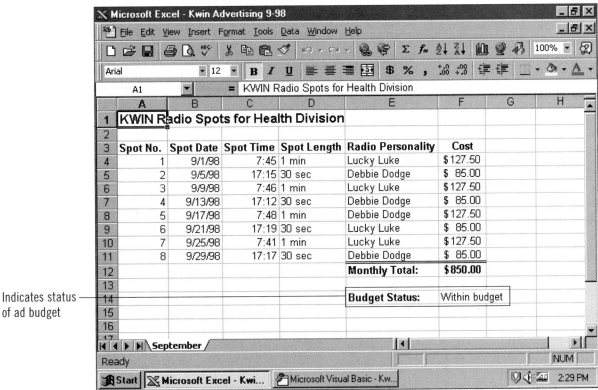

Indicates status of ad budget

Prompting the User for Data

Excel 97

When automating routine tasks, sometimes you need to pause a macro to allow user input. You use VBA's InputBox function to display a dialog box that prompts the user for information. A **function** is a predefined procedure that returns a value; in this case the value returned is the information the user enters The required elements of an InputBox function are: *object*.InputBox("*prompt*"), where "*prompt*" is the message that appears in the dialog box. For a detailed description of the InputBox function, use the Visual Basic Editor's Help menu. ⟵ Evan decides to create a procedure that will insert the user's name in the left-footer area of the workbook. He'll use the Input function to display a dialog box in which the user can enter his or her name. First, he returns to the Visual Basic Editor and inserts a new module.

QuickTip

To enlarge your Code window, place the mouse pointer on the left border of the Code window until it turns into ◂╫▸, then drag the border to the left until the Code window is the desired size.

1. With the September worksheet still displayed, click **Tools** on the menu bar, point to **Macro**, click **Visual Basic Editor**, click **Insert** on the Visual Basic Editor menu bar, then click **Module**

A new, blank module is inserted in the KWIN Procedures workbook. Before entering the code, you'll give the module a more descriptive name.

2. In the Properties window, click **(Name)**, then type **Footer**

Now you can create a procedure that inserts the user's name into the footer.

3. Click in the Code window, then type the procedure code exactly as shown in Figure P-9.

Notice that the Code window in Figure P-9 is enlarged so that you can read all of the code. Like the Budget procedure, this procedure also contains comments that explain the code. The first part of the code, *Dim LeftFooterText As String* **declares**, or defines, *LeftFooterText* as a text string variable. In Visual Basic, a **variable** is a slot in memory in which you can temporarily store one item of information. Dim statements are used to declare variables and must be entered in the following format: Dim *variablename* As *datatype*. In this case, you plan to store the information received from the input box in the temporary memory slot called LeftFooterText. Then you can place this text in the left-footer area. The remaining statements in the procedure are explained in the comment line directly above the statement. Now that the FooterInput procedure is finished, you review and then save your work.

4. Review your code for errors, make any changes if necessary, then click the **Save KWIN Procedures.xls** button 🖫 on the Visual Basic Editor Standard toolbar

Next, you will switch to the KWIN Advertising workbook and run the FooterInput procedure.

5. Click the **View Microsoft Excel** button ⊠ on the Visual Basic Editor toolbar, click **Tools** on the menu bar, point to **Macro**, click **Macros**, in the Macro dialog box click **'KWIN Procedures.xls'!FooterInput**, then click **Run**

The procedure begins, and a dialog box generated by the InputBox function appears, prompting you to enter the left-footer text. See Figure P-10. You want the user to enter his or her name in the left-footer area.

QuickTip

If your macro doesn't run correctly, it may contain a spelling or syntax error. You'll learn how to correct such macro errors in the next lesson.

6. With your pointer in the text box, type your name, then click **OK**

Next, you'll check the footer to make sure that a name appears on the left, the center section is blank, and the right section includes the date.

7. Click the Print Preview button 🔍 on the Standard toolbar

Although the customized footer is inserted on the sheet, notice that, due to an error, your name does *not* appear in the left section of the footer. In the next lesson, you will learn how to step through a procedure's code, line by line. This will help you locate the error in the Footer procedure. For now, you'll close the Preview window and return to the worksheet.

8. Click **Close**

FIGURE P-9: VBA code for the FooterInput Procedure

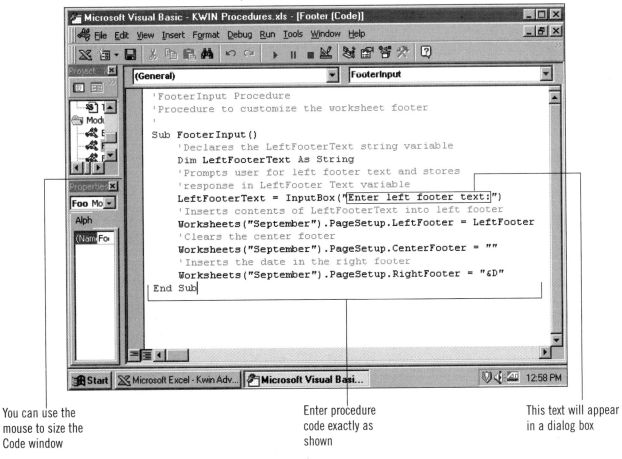

You can use the mouse to size the Code window

Enter procedure code exactly as shown

This text will appear in a dialog box

FIGURE P-10: InputBox function's dialog box

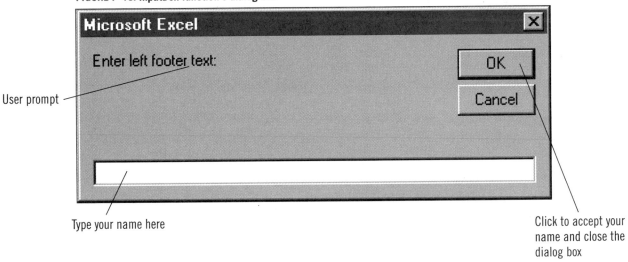

User prompt

Type your name here

Click to accept your name and close the dialog box

Debugging a Macro

When a macro procedure does not run properly, it can be due to an error, referred to as a **bug**, in the code. To assist you in finding the bug(s) in a procedure, you can use the Visual Basic Editor to step through the procedure's code, one line at a time. When you locate the error (bug), you can then correct, or **debug**, it. ⟶ Evan decides to debug the macro procedure to find out why it failed to insert his name in the worksheet's footer.

Steps

1. **With the KWIN Advertising 9-98 workbook still displayed, click Tools on the menu bar; point to Macro; click Macros; in the Macro dialog box, click 'KWIN Procedures.xls'! FooterInput; then click Step Into**
   The Visual Basic Editor appears with the statement selector positioned on the first statement of the procedure. See Figure P-11. You can continue stepping through the code by pressing [F8].

2. **Press [F8]**
   The statement selector skips over the comments and the line of code beginning with Dim. The Dim statement indicates that the procedure will store your name in a variable named LeftFooterText. Because Dim is a declaration of a variable and not a procedure statement, the statement selector skips it and moves to the line containing the InputBox function.

3. **Press [F8] again; with your pointer in the text box in the InputBox function dialog box, type your name, then click OK**
   The VBE reappears. The statement selector is now positioned on the *Worksheets ("September").PageSetup.LeftFooter = LeftFooter* instruction. This statement inserts your name (which you just typed in the Input Box) in the left section of the footer. This is the instruction that does not appear to be working correctly. In order to pinpoint the error, you'll examine the words at the end of the statement.

4. **If necessary, scroll right until the end of the LeftFooter instruction is visible, then place the mouse pointer ⌶ on LeftFooter, as shown in Figure P-12**
   The last part of the InputBox function should be the variable (LeftFooterText) where the procedure stored you name. Rather than containing your name, however, the variable at the end of the procedure is empty. That's because the InputBox function assigned your name to the LeftFooterText variable, not to the LeftFooter variable. Before you can correct this bug, you need to turn off the Step Into feature by clicking the Reset button.

5. **Click the Reset button ▪ on the Visual Basic Editor Standard toolbar, click at the end of the statement, then type Text**
   The revised statement now reads *Worksheets("September").PageSetup.LeftFooter = LeftFooterText*. With the bug corrected, you save your work and return to the KWIN Advertising 9-98 workbook.

6. **Click the Save KWIN Procedures.xls button 🖫 on the Visual Basic Editor Standard toolbar, then click the View Microsoft Excel button ⊠ on the Visual Basic Editor toolbar**
   You can now rerun the procedure.

7. **Click Tools on the menu bar, point to Macro, click Macros; in the Macro dialog box, click 'KWIN Procedures.xls'!FooterInput; click Run; when prompted, type your name; then click OK**
   Next, you'll open the Preview window to make sure the macro inserted your name in the worksheet footer.

8. **Click the Print Preview button 🔍 on the Standard toolbar**
   Your name now appears in the bottom-left section of the footer. You now close the Print Preview window, then save and print the KWIN Advertising worksheet.

9. **Click Close, save the workbook, then print your work**

FIGURE P-11: Statement selector positioned on first procedure statement

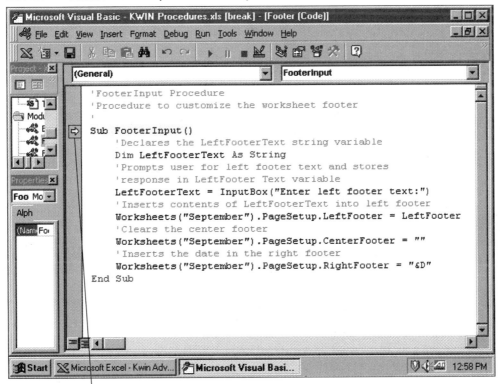

Statement selector

FIGURE P-12: Value contained in LeftFooter variable

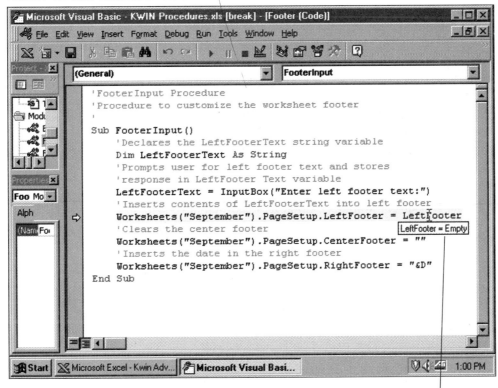

Indicates variable
at end of statement
is empty

Creating a Main Procedure

When you routinely need to run several macros one after another, you can save time by combining them into one procedure. The resulting procedure, which processes (or runs) multiple procedures in sequence, is referred to as the **main procedure**. To create a main procedure, you type a Call statement for each procedure you want to run. The syntax of the Call statement is Call *procedurename*, where *procedurename* is the name of the procedure you want to run. To avoid having to run his macros one after another every month, Evan decides to create a main procedure that will run (or call) each of the procedures in the KWIN Procedures workbook in sequence.

Steps

1. **With the September worksheet displayed, click Tools on the menu bar, point to Macro, then click Visual Basic Editor**
   Now, you'll insert a new module.

2. **Click Insert on the menu bar, then click Module**
   A new, blank module is inserted in the KWIN Procedures workbook. Next, you'll change the default module name to "MainProc," which is short for "Main Procedure."

3. **In the Properties window, click (Name), then type MainProc**
   Now you can enter the main procedure's code.

4. **Click the Code window, then enter the procedure code exactly as shown in Figure P-13**
   After entering the code, you need to review it and check for errors. Then you can save the main procedure.

5. **Compare the main procedure with Figure P-13, correct any errors if necessary, then click the Save KWIN Procedures.xls button 🔲 on the Visual Basic Editor Standard toolbar**
   Now that you're sure your code is correct, you can test the new main procedure. You'll do this on an unformatted version of the KWIN radio spot workbook. You need to return to the KWIN Advertising 9-98 workbook, close it, then open an unformatted version of the workbook.

6. **Click the View Microsoft Excel button 📉 on the Visual Basic Editor Standard toolbar, then close the KWIN Advertising 9-98 workbook**

7. **Open the workbook titled XL P-2, then save it as KWIN Advertising 9-98 Version 2**
   In the next lesson, you'll run the main procedure.

FIGURE P-13: **VBA code for MainProcedure procedure**

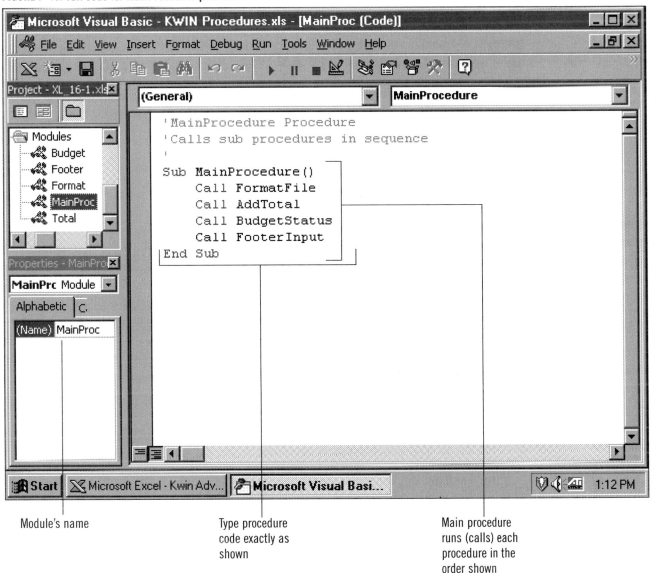

Module's name

Type procedure code exactly as shown

Main procedure runs (calls) each procedure in the order shown

Running a Main Procedure

Running a main procedure allows you to instantly run several macros in sequence. You can run a main procedure just as you would any other macro procedure—by selecting it in the Macro dialog box, then clicking Run. Evan has finished creating his main procedure and is now ready to run it. If the main procedure works correctly, it should format the worksheet, insert a budget status message, insert the ad expenditure total, and add Evan's name to the worksheet footer.

Steps

1. **With the September worksheet still displayed, click Tools on the menu bar, point to Macro, click Macros; in the Macro dialog box click 'KWIN Procedures.xls'! MainProcedure; click Run; when prompted type your name, then click OK**
   The MainProcedure runs the FormatFile, AddTotal, BudgetStatus, and FooterInput procedures in sequence. See Figure P-14. You can see the results of the FormatFile, AddTotal, and BudgetStatus procedures in the worksheet window. To view the results of the FooterInput procedure, you need to switch to the Preview window.

2. **Click the Print Preview button ⧉ on the Standard toolbar, verify that your name appears in the left footer area, then click Close**
   Next, in order to document your work, you'll print all the module sheets. First, you need to return to the Visual Basic Editor.

3. **Click Tools on the menu bar, point to Macro, then click Visual Basic Editor**
   You could print each procedure separately, but it's faster to print all the procedures in the workbook at one time.

4. **Click File on the Visual Basic Editor menu bar, then click Print**
   The Print KWINProcedures dialog box opens, as shown in Figure P-15. Collectively, all procedures in a workbook are known as a **project**. To print all the procedures at one time, you specify that you want to print the current project.

5. **Under Range in the Print - KWINProcedures dialog box, make sure the Current Project option button is selected, then click OK**
   Each procedure prints on a separate page. You are finished with the Visual Basic Editor, so you can return to Excel.

6. **Click the View Microsoft Excel button ⧉ on the Visual Basic Editor Standard toolbar**
   Now you can save the KWIN Advertising 9-98 Version 2 workbook, close all open workbooks, then exit Excel.

7. **Save the KWIN Advertising 9-98 Version 2 workbook and close it, close the KWIN Procedures workbook, then exit Excel**

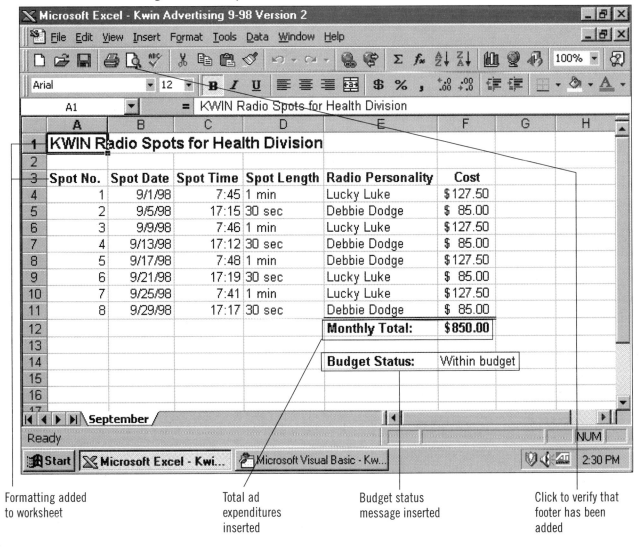

Formatting added
to worksheet

Total ad
expenditures
inserted

Budget status
message inserted

Click to verify that
footer has been
added

Excel 97

FIGURE P-15: Printing the macro procedures

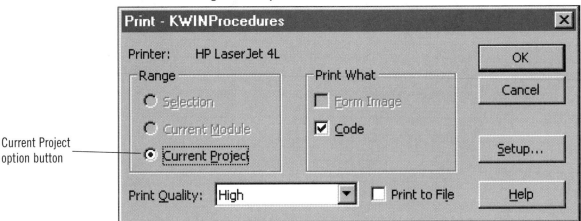

Current Project
option button

Practice

► Concepts Review

Label each element of the Visual Basic Editor screen shown in Figure P-16.

FIGURE P-16

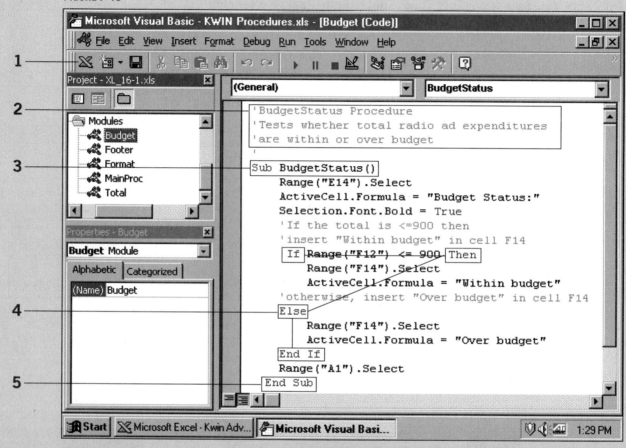

Match each statement with the term it describes.

6. Subprocedure
7. Procedure
8. Keywords
9. Function procedure
10. Comments

a. Another term for a macro in Visual Basic for Applications (VBA)
b. A procedure that returns a value
c. Words that are recognized as part of the programming language
d. A keyword
e. Descriptive text used to explain parts of a procedure

Select the best answer from the list of choices.

11. You enter the statements of a macro in
   a. The Macro dialog box
   b. Any blank worksheet
   c. The Properties window of the Visual Basic Editor
   d. The Code window of the Visual Basic Editor

12. What must you keep in mind when typing VBA code?
   a. Typographical errors can cause your procedures to fail.
   b. You can edit your code just as you would text in a word processor.
   c. The different parts of the code will appear in different colors.
   d. All of the above.

13. If your macro doesn't run correctly, you should
   a. Create an If, Then and Else statement.
   b. Select the macro in the Macro dialog box, click Step Into, and then debug the macro.
   c. Debug the macro in the worksheet window.
   d. Close the workbook and start over with a new macro.

▶ Skills Review

1. View and analyze VBA code.
   a. Open the workbook titled XL P-3, then save it as "Mission Medical Inc".
   b. Review the unformatted worksheet named Sheet1.
   c. Click Tools, point to Macro, then click Macros.
   d. Select the FormatList procedure, then click Edit.
   e. Write down what action you think each line of code will perform. (*Hint:* One of the statements will sort the list alphabetically by customer name.)
   f. Click the View Microsoft Excel button on the Visual Basic Editor Standard toolbar.
   g. Click Tools on the Excel menu bar, point to Macro, then click Macros.
   h. In the Macro dialog box, select the FormatList macro, then click Run.
   i. Save the workbook.

FIGURE P-17

2. Write VBA code.
   a. Click Tools, point to Macro, then click Visual Basic Editor.
   b. Click Insert, then click Module.
   c. In the Properties window, click (Name), then type Total.
   d. Click in the Code window.
   e. Type the procedure exactly as shown in Figure P-17.
   f. Compare your procedure to Figure P-17 and correct any errors.
   g. Click the View Microsoft Excel button on the Visual Basic Editor Standard toolbar.
   h. On the Excel menu bar, click Tools, point to Macro, then click Macros.
   i. In the Macro dialog box, select the SalesTotal macro, then click Run.
   j. Save the workbook.

```
'SalesTotal Procedure
'Totals monthly sales
Sub SalesTotal()
    Range("F17").Select
    ActiveCell.Formula="=SUM($F$2:$F$16)"
    Selection.Font.Bold=True
    With Selection.Borders(xlTop)
      .LineStyle=xlSingle
    End With
    Range("A1").Select
End Sub
```

3. Add a conditional statement.

a. Click Tools, point to Macro, then click Visual Basic Editor.

b. Click Insert, then click Module.

c. In the Properties window, click (Name) then type Goal.

d. Click in the Code window.

e. Type the procedure exactly as shown in Figure P-18.

f. Compare your procedure to Figure P-18 and correct any errors.

g. Click the View Microsoft Excel button on the Visual Basic Editor Standard toolbar.

h. On the Excel menu bar, click Tools, point to Macro, then click Macros.

i. In the Macro dialog box, select the SalesGoal macro, then click Run. If the procedure returns the message "Missed goal," the procedure worked as planned.

j. Save the workbook.

FIGURE P-18

```
'SalesGoal Procedure
'Tests whether sales goal was met
'
Sub SalesGoal()
    'If the total is >=225000, then insert "Met Goal"
    'in cell G17
    If Range("F17") >=225000 Then
        Range("G17").Select
        ActiveCell.Formula="Met goal"
    'otherwise, insert "Missed goal" in cell G17
    Else
        Range("G17").Select
        ActiveCell.Formula="Missed goal"
    End If
End Sub
```

4. Prompt the user for data

a. Click Tools, point to Macro, then click Visual Basic Editor.

b. Click Insert, then click Module.

c. In the Properties window, click (Name), then type Header.

d. Click in the Code window.

e. Type the procedure exactly as shown in Figure P-19.

f. Compare your procedure to Figure P-19 and correct any errors.

g. Click the View Microsoft Excel button on the Visual Basic Editor Standard toolbar.

h. Click Tools on the Excel menu bar, point to Macros, then click Macro.

i. In the Macro dialog box, select the HeaderFooter macro, then click Run. When you encounter a runtime error, click End.

j. Save the workbook

FIGURE P-19

```
'HeaderFooter Procedure
'Procedure to customize the header and footer
'
Sub HeaderFooter()
    'Inserts the filename in the header
    Worksheets("Sheet1").PageSetup.CenterHeader="&F"
    'Declares the variable LeftFooterText as a string
    Dim LeftFooterText As String
    'Prompts user for left footer text
    LeftFooter=InputBox("Enter your full name:")
    'Inserts response into left footer
    Workbooks("Sheet1").PageSetup.LeftFooter=LeftFooterText
    Workbooks("Sheet1").PageSetup.CenterFooter=""
    Workbooks("Sheet1").PageSetup.RightFooter="&D"
End Sub
```

5. Debug a macro.

a. Click Tools on the Excel menu bar, point to Macro, then click Macros.

b. In the Macro dialog box, select the HeaderFooter macro, then click Run. When you encounter a runtime error, click the Debug button.

c. The statement selector is positioned on the incorrect procedure statement: *Workbooks("Sheet1").PageSetup.LeftFooter = LeftFooterText.* (*Hint:* Note that Workbooks, instead of Worksheets, was entered in the statement.)

d. Click the Reset button on the Visual Basic Editor Standard toolbar.

e. Change *Workbooks* in the incorrect line of code to *Worksheets*. Do the same in the two following lines of code.

f. Return to Excel, then rerun the HeaderFooter procedure.

g. Preview the sheet to check the header and footer. Notice that the procedure does not display your name in the left section of the footer. Click Close.

h. Click Tools, point to Macro, then click Macros. Select the HeaderFooter procedure, then click Step Into to step through the procedure's code.

i. Use [F8] to step through the procedure's code. Find the error in the code, then click the Reset button and correct the code.

j. Return to Excel, then rerun the HeaderFooter procedure.

k. Preview the sheet to verify that your name now appears in the left section of the footer. Click Close.

l. Save the workbook.

6. Create and run a main procedure.

a. Return to the Visual Basic Editor and insert a new module.

b. In the Properties window, click (Name), then type MainProc.

c. Click in the Code window, then enter some comments that give the procedure's name (MainProcedure), and explain its purpose.

d. Enter the following procedure header: *Sub MainProcedure ().* (Be sure to type the empty parentheses at the end of the statement.)

e. Enter four Call statements that will run the FormatList, SalesTotal, SalesGoal, and HeaderFooter procedures in sequence.

f. Save the procedure and return to Excel.

g. Open the XL P-3 workbook, then save it as Medical Mission Inc Version 2.

h. Run the MainProcedure procedure. (*Hint:* In the Macro dialog box, the macro procedures you created will now have 'Medical Mission Inc.xls'! as part of their names. That's because the macros are stored in the Medical Mission Inc workbook, and not in the Medical Misson Inc Version 2 workbook.)

i. Save the Medical Mission Inc Version 2 workbook, print the worksheet, then close the Medical Mission Inc Version 2 workbook.

j. Return to the Visual Basic Editor to print the current project's code.

k. Return to Excel and close any open workbooks.

▶ Independent Challenges

1. Your officemate Smitty is on vacation for two weeks, and you have taken over his projects. The office manager, Su-ling, asks you to document the Excel procedure that Smitty wrote (called DoYourThing) for the company's auditors. You have located the workbook containing the procedure; now you will document it.

To complete this independent challenge:

1. Open the workbook titled XL P-4, then save it as "Mystery Procedure".
2. Run the DoYourThing procedure, noting anything you think should be mentioned in your documentation.
3. Select the DoYourThing procedure in the Macro dialog box, click Edit, then review the procedure in the Visual Basic Editor.
4. Print the procedures code.
5. Document the procedure by annotating the printed code, indicating the actions the procedure performs and the objects (ranges) that are affected.
6. Close the workbook.

2. You work in the sales office of a large automobile dealership called Auto Heaven. Each month you are required to produce a report stating whether sales quotas were met for the following five vehicle categories: compacts, sedans, sports/utility, vans, and trucks. This quarter the sales quotas for each month are as follows: compacts 50, sedans 35, sports/utility 20, vans 19, and trucks 40. The results this month (January) were 53, 32, 12, 25, and 35, respectively. You decide to create a procedure to automate your monthly task of determining the sales quota status for the vehicle categories. You would like the new clerk to take this task over when you go on vacation next month. Because the clerk has no previous experience with Excel, you decide to add input boxes that prompt the user to enter the actual sales results for the month.

To complete this independent challenge:

1. Create a workbook to be used as a monthly template, then save it as "Sales Quota Status".
2. Create a procedure using multiple If...Then...Else statements to determine automatically the sales quota status for each vehicle category.
3. Add input boxes to prompt the user for the actual sales data for each vehicle category. (*Hint:* You can use a combination of statements using InputBox and ActiveCell.)
4. Test the procedure. Correct any problems.
5. Save your work, then print the code.
6. Close the workbook.

3. You are an internal auditor for a large food manufacturer called Earthly Treats. You are responsible for ensuring that staff members document their Excel worksheets properly. To help the staff document their worksheets more efficiently, you decide to create two procedures. The first procedure will automate the process of displaying and printing worksheet formulas. The second will prompt the user for his or her department name and insert that information in the footer. The workbook name and date should appear in the footer as well. After you create the two procedures, you will create a main procedure to run them in sequence.

To complete this independent challenge:

1. Create a workbook, then save it as "Documentation Procedures".
2. Create a procedure that copies the active worksheet to a new worksheet, turns on formula display in the new sheet, and uses AutoFit to fit the new sheet's columns. The procedure should also print the new formula sheet, then delete the new sheet as the last step. (*Hint:* You can use the Macro Recorder to create the procedure.)
3. Save, test, then debug the procedure.
4. Create a procedure that creates the footer as described above.
5. Save, test, then debug the procedure.
6. Create a main procedure that calls the footer procedure and the print procedure in sequence.
7. Save, test, then debug the procedure.
8. Print the code for the current project.
9. Save your work, then close the workbook.

4. Many of the features that you may take for granted in Excel 97 were not included in earlier versions of the program. In fact, in the past, spreadsheet users and developers often had to write complex procedures to perform tasks that now require only a simple mouse click. (In some cases, these same tasks are now performed automatically by Excel.) You can find out more about the macro procedures built into Excel by searching for information on the Microsoft Corporation home page.

To complete this independent challenge:

1. Go to the Microsoft home page. If you can't find the Microsoft home page, use your Web browser to go to http://www.course.com. From there, click Student Online Companions, click the link for this textbook, then click the Excel link for Unit P.
2. Click the Search tab, and search for the topic "Programmability: Competitive Comparison." If you can't find that topic, search for information on the Visual Basic Editor.
3. List and explain four tasks that used to require complex procedures to accomplish, but which now require only a few mouse clicks.
4. List two spreadsheet-related tasks you envision performing regularly in the business world. Experiment with Excel to determine if features for performing the tasks are built into Excel, or if you would have to create a macro procedure to perform them.

Excel 97

Visual Workshop

Open the workbook titled XL P-5 and save it as "Big Time Audio". Create a macro procedure that will format the worksheet as shown in Figure P-20. (*Hint:* To write the first macro procedure in a workbook, click Tools, then click Visual Basic Editor. In the Visual Basic Editor, click Insert, click Module, rename the new module, and enter your code in the code window.)

FIGURE P-20

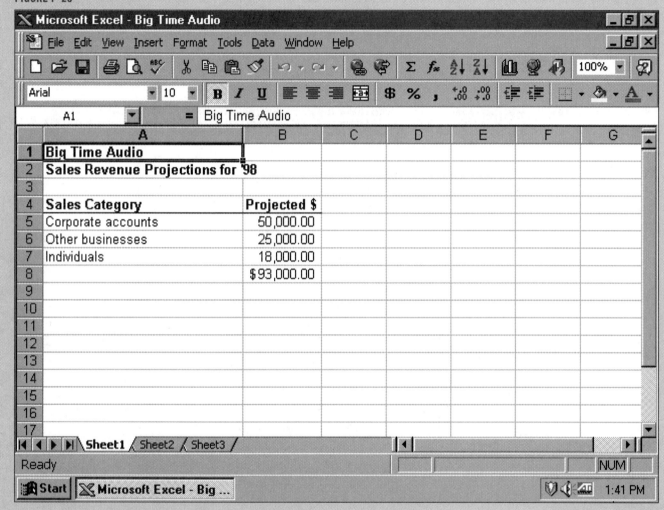

Glossary

Excel 97

Add-in An additional utility program that comes with Excel but is not automatically installed during a standard installation.

Alignment The horizontal placement of cell contents; for example, left, center, or right.

Analyze To manipulate list data.

Argument A value, range of cells, or text used in a macro or function. An argument is enclosed in parentheses; for example, =SUM(A1..B1).

Ascending order Data organized from A to Z or 0 to 9.

ASCII file A universally accepted text file format in which the file contains text but no formatting.

Attribute A styling feature such as bold, italics, and underlining that can be applied to cell contents.

Audit To examine a worksheet in order to track errors and determine the logic of worksheet formulas.

AutoCalculate area The area in the status bar that displays the sum (or function of your choice) of the values in the selected range.

AutoFill A feature that automatically enters a list into a range of cells.

Automatic Calculation The default option on the Calculation tab of the Options dialog box that tells Excel to recalculate the worksheet formulas automatically every time you change a value in a cell.

AutoSum A feature that automatically calculates worksheet totals accessed by a button on the Standard toolbar.

Backsolving In goal seeking, a process in which you specify a solution, and then find the input value that produces the answer you want.

Border Edges of a selected area of a worksheet. Lines and color can be applied to borders.

Break a link To delete the connection between linked objects.

Browse The act of moving between or navigating hyperlink documents.

Bug An error in a macro procedure's code.

Cell The intersection of a column and row.

Cell address Unique location identified by intersecting column and row coordinates.

Cell comments Notes attached to a cell that appear when you place the pointer over the cell.

Cell pointer A highlighted rectangle around a cell that indicates the active cell.

Cell reference The address or name of a specific cell; can be used in formulas and are relative or absolute.

Changing cells When using Solver, the cells that contain the values that change in order to produce the most appropriate value in the target cell.

Changing value In What-if Analysis, the value in an input cell that is adjusted to produce varying outcomes.

Check box A square box in a dialog box that can be clicked to turn an option on or off.

Clear A command on the Edit menu used to erase a cell's contents, formatting, or both.

Code window The part of the Visual Basic Editor that displays the selected module's procedures.

Comments Notes explaining the code in a Visual Basic for Applications procedure.

Criteria form A data entry window used to set search criteria in lists.

Criteria range A cell range containing one row of labels (usually a copy of the column labels) and at least one additional row underneath the row of labels that contains the criteria you want to match.

Custom chart type A kind of Excel chart (available on the Custom Types tab of the first Chart Wizard dialog box) that is already formatted and contains numerous options, such as a legend, gridlines, data labels, colors, and patterns.

Custom view A set of display and/or print settings that you can name and save, then access at a later time.

Data entry area The cells in a protected (locked) worksheet that must be unlocked because you need to change them.

Data exchange The process of importing data from other programs into Excel, and of exporting Excel data to other programs.

Data form A data entry window used to view or add records to a list.

Data label Descriptive text that appears above a data marker in a chart.

Data map A map that shows geographic features and the data associated with them.

Data series The information, usually numbers or values, that Excel plots on a chart.

Data table A grid attached to the bottom of a chart containing the chart data.

Database A collection of information organized by fields and records. A telephone book, a card catalog, and a list of company employees are all lists.

Database functions Excel functions that allow you to summarize list data in a variety of ways. For example, you can use them to count, average, or total values in a field for only those records that meet specified criteria.

Debug To find and fix the error (or bug) in a macro procedure's code.

Declare To define a variable in the Visual Basic for Applications programming language.

Delete A command that removes cell contents from a worksheet.

Delimiter In text files, the tab, space, or other element that separates columns.

Dependent cell In What-if Analysis, a cell, usually containing a formula, whose value depends on the data in the input cells.

Descending order Data organized from Z to A or 9 to 0.

Destination program In a data exchange, the program that receives the data.

Dialog box A window that displays when you choose a command whose name is followed by an ellipsis (...). A dialog box allows you to make selections that determine how the command affects the selected area.

Divide-by-zero error A mistake in the worksheet that occurs when you attempt to divide a value by zero.

Dynamic Information that updates automatically when certain parts of the workbook change.

Edit A change made to the contents of a cell or worksheet.

Embedding In a data exchange, the process of inserting a copy of the original object in the destination document. An embedded object can be edited from within the destination program, using the source program's tools and commands. It retains no connection to the original object.

Export In a data exchange, to send or pass data from the source program to the destination program.

External reference indicator An ! (exclamation point) within a formula indicating that the cell referenced is outside the active sheet.

Extract To place a copy of a filtered list in a range you specify in the Advanced Filter dialog box.

Field A labeled column in a list; it contains the same kind of information for each record, such as a phone number.

Field name A column label that describes the field.

File properties Characteristics of a workbook file such as its name, size, and type.

Fill handle Small square in the lower-right corner of the active cell used to copy cell contents.

Filter To hide data in a list that fails to meet certain criteria.

Find A command used to locate information the user specifies.

Find & Replace A command used to find one set of criteria and replace it with new information.

Font The typeface used to display information in cells.

Footer Information that appears at the bottom of each printed page; for example, the page number and the date.

Form A data entry window used when working with lists. *See also* **Data form** *and* **Criteria form**.

Format The appearance of text and numbers, including color, font, attributes, and worksheet defaults. *See also* **Number format**.

Formula A set of instructions that you enter in a cell to perform numeric calculations (adding, multiplying, averaging, etc.); for example, +A1+B1.

Formula bar The area below the menu bar and above the Excel workspace where you enter and edit data in a worksheet cell. The formula bar becomes active when you start typing or editing cell data. The formula bar includes an Enter button and a Cancel button.

Freeze Lock-in specified columns and/or rows to assist in scrolling through large worksheets.

Function A special predefined formula that provides a shortcut for commonly used calculations; for example, AVERAGE. Also, in the Visual Basic for Applications programming language, a predefined procedure that returns a value.

Graphic object A picture such as a drawing, logo, or photograph.

Header Information that appears at the top of each printed page; for example the report name and the date.

HLOOKUP function An Excel function that helps you locate values in a list. It searches horizontally across the topmost row of a list until the matching value is found, then looks down the number of rows you specify.

HTML The file format for all documents on the World Wide Web. *See also* **HyperText Markup Language**.

Hyperlink An object (filename, word, phrase, or graphic) in a worksheet that you click to access another location in that worksheet, another worksheet, a document created in another program, or information on the World Wide Web.

Hyperlink document A file containing hyperlinks to another location in that file, another file, a file created in another program, or information on the World Wide Web.

Hypertext A system of documents or information linked together with hyperlinks.

HyperText Markup Language The programming language used to format documents for access and display on the World Wide Web. *See also* **HTML**.

Import To bring a file from another program (such as a database or word processing program) into Excel.

Input cells Cells in which data, not formulas, are entered.

Insertion point Blinking I-beam that appears in the formula bar during entry and editing.

Internet A large computer network made up of smaller networks and computers connected electronically.

Internet Assistant Wizard A series of dialog boxes that helps you to save or convert a worksheet file or part of a worksheet into HTML format. *See also* **HTML**.

Intranet site An Internet-like site that exists within a company or organization.

Jump The action of clicking a hyperlink in a document to navigate to another location in that document, or to another hyperlink document.

Keywords Words that are recognized as part of the Visual Basic for Applications programming language.

Label Descriptive text or other information that identify the rows and columns of a worksheet. Labels are not included in calculations.

Landscape orientation Printing on a page whose dimensions are 11" (horizontally) by 8½" (vertically).

Linking In a data exchange, a process in which you insert a copy of the original object in the destination document but retain a connection between the copy and the original. A linked object is updated automatically when the data in the original object changes.

List A collection of information organized by fields and records. A telephone book, a card catalog, and a list of company employees are all lists.

List range A range of a worksheet that organizes information into fields and records.

Locked cells Cells that are protected so that their contents cannot be altered.

Logical test When the condition is a question that can be answered with a true or false response.

Macro A set of recorded instructions that tell the computer to perform a task or series of tasks.

Macro code The Visual Basic for Applications programming language Excel uses to translate your keystrokes and commands into words.

Main procedure In the Visual Basic for Applications programming language, a procedure that runs multiple procedures in sequence.

Manual Calculation An option on the Calculation tab of the Options dialog box that allows you to determine when the formulas in a worksheet are recalculated.

Model A worksheet that is used to produce a what-if analysis and acts as the basis for multiple outcomes.

Module The Visual Basic for Applications equivalent of a worksheet, in which you store a macro procedure.

Name A name assigned to a selected cell or range in a worksheet. *See also* **Range name**.

Name box The leftmost area in the formula bar that shows the cell reference or name of the active cell. For example, A1 refers to cell A1 of the active worksheet. You can also get a list of names in a workbook using the name list arrow.

Network Two or more computers connected together for the purpose of sharing information and resources.

Number format A format applied to values to express numeric concepts, such as currency, date, and percent.

Object Every element of a program, including a cell, a range, a worksheet, and a workbook.

OLE Object linking and embedding. A Windows technology used in data exchanges.

One-input data table A range of cells that show the resulting values when one input value is varied in a formula.

Operators Perform mathematical functions.

Option button A circle in a dialog box that can be clicked when only one option can be chosen.

Order of precedence The order in which Excel calculates parts of a formula: (1) exponents, (2) multiplication and division, and (3) addition and subtraction.

Outline A command that displays buttons that allow you to show only the most important rows and columns in a worksheet. For outlining to work properly, all formulas must point consistently in the same direction.

Page Break Preview Allows you to view and change page breaks manually in the Print Preview window.

Page field A feature that makes the data in a PivotTable appear as if it is stacked in pages, thus adding a third dimension to the analysis.

Pane A column or row that always remains visible.

Paste A command that moves information on the Clipboard to a new location. Excel pastes the formulas rather than the result, unless the Paste Special command is used.

Paste Special A command that enables you to paste formulas as values, styles, or cell contents.

Personal Macro Workbook A file in which to store commonly used macros.

PivotTable A feature that allows you to summarize selected data in a worksheet, then list and display that data in a table.

Plot area The main area of a chart, containing the plotted and formatted chart data and chart axes.

Point A unit of measure used for fonts and row height. One inch equals 72 points.

Precedence The order in which Excel calculates parts of a formula: (1) exponents, (2) multiplication and division, and (3) addition and subtraction.

Presentation graphics program A program used to create slide show presentations.

Print Preview window A window that displays a reduced view of area to be printed.

Print Title The first row of a list (containing the field names) that appears as descriptive information on all worksheet pages.

Procedure The sequence of Visual Basic for Applications statements contained in a macro.

Procedure footer The last line of a Sub procedure.

Procedure header The first line of a procedure.

Project In the Visual Basic for Applications programming language, another term for a workbook. Contains all the workbook's worksheets and modules.

Project Explorer A part of the Visual Basic Editor that displays a list of all open projects (or workbooks) and the worksheets and modules they contain.

Properties window The part of the Visual Basic Editor that displays a list of characteristics (or properties) associated with the selected module.

Property In a Visual Basic for Applications procedure, an attribute of an object that defines one of the object's characteristics (such as size) or an aspect of its behavior (such as whether it is enabled).

Protect An option that lets you prevent cells in a worksheet from being changed.

Range A selected group of adjacent cells.

Range format A format applied to a selected range.

Range name A name applied to a selected range.

Range object An element of Visual Basic for Applications code that represents a cell or range of cells.

Record Horizontal rows in a list that contain related information.

Reference Populate cell data using existing cell content. You do this by typing = (equal sign) and then selecting the desired cell(s).

Refresh To update a PivotTable in order to reflect changes made to the source list.

Relative cell reference Used to indicate a relative position in the worksheet. This allows you to copy and move formulas from one area to another of the same dimensions. Excel automatically changes the column and row numbers to reflect the new position.

Report Manager An add-in program that lets you create reports containing multiple worksheets in a workbook.

Row height The vertical dimension of a cell.

Run To execute a macro.

Scenario A set of values used to forecast worksheet results.

Scenario Summary An Excel table that compiles data from the changing cells and result cells for each scenario.

Sheet A term used for worksheet.

Sheet tab A description at the bottom of each worksheet that identifies it in a workbook. In an open workbook, move to a worksheet by clicking its sheet tab. *See also* **Tab**.

Solver A feature that finds the most appropriate value for a formula by changing the input values in the worksheet.

Sort To rearrange rows of a worksheet, usually rows in a list, in a particular order. *See also* **Ascending order** *and* **Descending order**.

Sort key Any cell in a field by which a list or selected range is being organized.

Source list The list used to create a PivotTable.

Source program In a data exchange, the program in which the data you want to import was created.

Standard chart type A kind of Excel chart (available on the Standard Types tab of the first Chart Wizard dialog box) to which you need to add formatting and other options. Useful when you need to control exactly which elements appear in your chart.

Statement A line of code in a Visual Basic for Applications procedure.

Status bar The bar near the bottom of the screen that provides information about the tasks Excel is performing or about any current selections.

Sub procedure A series of Visual Basic for Applications statements that perform an action but do not return a value.

Summary function In a PivotTable, the function that controls what type of calculation is applied to the table data. By default, Excel applies the SUM function to numeric data and the COUNT function to text.

Syntax The formatting rules of the Visual Basic for Applications programming language.

Tab A description at the bottom of each worksheet that identifies it in a workbook. In an open workbook, move to a worksheet by clicking its tab.

Tab scrolling buttons Enable you to move among sheets within a workbook.

Table An Excel data list that has been converted to Access format.

Target The destination file reached from clicking a hyperlink.

Target cell When using Solver, the cell containing the formula for which you want to find the most appropriate value.

Template A fill-in-the-blank worksheet that can include any text, formatting, formulas, layout, and other workbook elements. You open a template, fill in the missing information, then save the file as a regular workbook, leaving the template intact.

Toggle A button that can be clicked to turn an option on. Clicking again turns the option off.

Tracers When auditing a worksheet, arrows that point to (or from) cells that might have caused an error from (or to) the active cell containing the error.

Two-input data table A range of cells that show the resulting values when two different input values are varied in a formula.

Uniform Resource Locator (URL) The unique address that identifies a Web document's location on the World Wide Web. For example, http://www.course.com is the URL address for Course Technology's Web page.

Validation A command that allows you to specify what data is acceptable for a range of cells.

Values Numbers, formulas, or functions used in calculations.

Variable In the Visual Basic for Applications programming language, a slot in memory in which you can store, temporarily, one item of information.

View A set of display and/or print settings that you can name and save, then access at a later time. *See also* **Custom view**.

Visual Basic for Applications The programming language used to create Excel macros.

Visual Basic Editor A feature that allows you to view and edit Visual Basic for Applications procedures.

VLOOKUP function An Excel function that helps you locate values in a list. It searches vertically down the leftmost column of a list and then reads across the row to find the value in the column you specify.

Web browser A software program that enables users to access, view, and navigate all the documents on the World Wide Web.

Web document A hyperlink document that is part of the World Wide Web. Also referred to as a Web page.

Web form A form that visitors to a Web site can use to submit various types of information. For example, a customer could order products online by filling out a Web form.

Web Form Wizard A series of dialog boxes that helps you create a Web form. *See also* **Web form**.

Web query A request to retrieve information from an external source located on the World Wide Web.

Web servers The computers that are connected to the Internet and store Web documents. Also referred to as Web sites.

What-if analysis The process of manipulating the variables in a worksheet to project outcomes and answer the question "what-if?" There are many ways to perform what-if analysis using Excel, including creating scenarios; creating data tables, using Goal Seek; and using Solver.

Wildcards Special symbols used when defining search criteria in the data form or Find dialog box. The question mark (?) wildcard stands for any single character. The asterisk (*) wildcard stands for any group of characters.

Wizard   A series of dialog boxes that lists and describes all Excel functions and assists the user in function creation.

WordArt   Specially formatted text you can add to your chart or worksheet using the Drawing toolbar. It is considered a drawing object rather than text, which means you cannot sort it, spell-check it, or use its cell reference in a formula.

Workbook   A collection of related worksheets contained within a single file.

Worksheet   An electronic spreadsheet containing 256 columns by 65,536 rows.

Worksheet Menu Bar   Also called the menu bar; a special toolbar that contains commands you use when working with worksheets.

World Wide Web   A structure of hyperlink documents connected electronically over the Internet. Also known as the WWW, or the Web.

***x*-axis**   The horizontal axis in a two- or three-dimensional chart on which categories are plotted.

***y*-axis**   The vertical axis in a two- or three-dimensional chart on which values are plotted.

***z*-axis**   The third axis in a three-dimensional chart on which the scale is plotted.

Zoom   Enables you to focus on a larger or smaller part of the worksheet in print preview.

Zoom box   Option on the Standard toolbar that allows you to change the screen magnification percentage.

Index

Index

Index

Index

Index

The Exam Prep Series

Your Quick, Visual Path to Certification Success!

Each Exam Prep Study Guide comes with an award-winning CD-ROM that provides interactive training.

Exam Prep Series Snapshot

The Exam Prep Series from Certification Insider Press is designed to prepare you for a certification exam. The first four titles in the series prepare you for the Microsoft Office User Specialist exams. Each Exam Prep Series text covers all of the required objectives of the corresponding exam.

The Certification Insider Press strategy is to use Exam Prep study guides in conjunction with Exam Cram books to thoroughly prepare for certification exams.

Exam Prep Features:

- Highly interactive tutorials that feature step-by-step projects and lessons.
- Performance-based quiz feature to help you quickly test your skills.
- Study approach officially endorsed by Microsoft.
- Illustrated in full color to help clarify confusing concepts.
- Explains the most practical techniques readers will need to know to be truly proficient in an application.
- Includes an award-winning CD-ROM that provides interactive training.
- Written by an experienced certification trainer.

Coming in 1998!
Exam Prep for MCSE titles

- hands-on projects reinforce key concepts
- content officially endorsed by certification vendor
- troubleshooting tips for solutions to common problems

See the previous page for a list of available titles.

Titles in the Exam Prep Series include:

Microsoft Office User Specialist, Microsoft Word 97 — Exam Prep
(ISBN 1-57610-234-3)
$29.99 U.S., 41.99 Canada

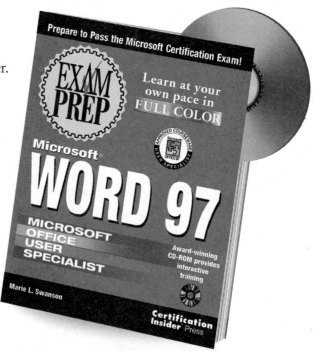

Prepare to Pass the Microsoft Certification Exam!

EXAM PREP

Learn at your own pace in FULL COLOR

Microsoft

WORD 97

MICROSOFT OFFICE USER SPECIALIST

Award-winning CD-ROM provides interactive training

Marie L. Swanson

Certification Insider Press

Exam Cram Series

The First and Last Books You'll Need To Read Before Taking Your Certification Exam

Exam Cram Series Snapshot

The Exam Cram Series from Certification Insider Press is designed to help you study for and pass a specific exam, going right to the core of certification. Each guide is jam-packed with hundreds of test-taking tips, insights, and exam strategies you will not find anywhere else.

Each book in the Exam Cram Series is closely linked to a specific certification exam. The first part of each text reviews and analyzes a specific section of the exam and discusses important exam-taking terminology. The second part contains review questions and thoroughly discusses the wrong and right answers to questions. The third part of each text contains resources, as well as online pointers.

The Certification Insider Press strategy is to use Exam Cram books in conjunction with Exam Prep study guides to thoroughly prepare for certification exams.

Exam Cram Features:

- Includes sections on exam-taking strategies, warnings on trick questions, time-saving study tips, multiple-part question strategies, and shortcuts.
- Features unique editorial content that serves as an ideal complement to any exam study guides and training materials.
- Provides practice exams that feature questions formatted similarly to those found on the actual exam.
- Provides all of the necessary overview, concepts, and associated terminology to help you get up to speed as quickly as possible.
- Includes bonus reference sections at the end of each chapter to help you make use of the best study aids available.
- Exam Cram books are planned for MCSE, Microsoft Office User Specialist, and MCSD certification exams.

MCSE Networking Essentials Exam Cram
(ISBN 1-57610-192-4)
$29.99 U.S., 41.99 Canada

Certification Insider™ Press
International Thomson Publishing I(T)P*

To order any Certification Insider Press title, complete this order form and mail or fax it to us, with payment, for quick shipment.

TITLE	ISBN #	QTY	PRICE	TOTAL

Shipping

For orders shipping within the United States, please add $4.95 for the first book, $1.50 for each additional book. For 2-day air add $7.95 for the first book, $3.00 for each additional book.
e-mail: vorders@kdc.com for exact shipping charges.
Note: Please include your local sales tax.

Subtotal = $
Shipping = $
Tax   = $
Total   = $

Mail To: **ITP Media Group** ▪ 7625 Empire Drive ▪ Florence, KY 41042

US Orders: **800/332-7450** ▪ Fax: **606/283-0718**
Canadian Orders: **800/268-2222**
Europe/Africa/ME/India Orders: **44 126 434 2960** ▪ Fax: **44 126 434 2759**
Asia Orders: **65 336 6411** ▪ Fax: **65 336 7411**
Japan Orders: **81 3 32211380** ▪ Fax: **81 3 323 71459**
Australia/NZ Orders: **61 39 6854111** ▪ Fax: **61 39 6854199**
South/Central America/U.S. Possessions: **606 282 5786** ▪ Fax: **606 282 5700**

Name _____

E-Mail _____ Daytime phone _____

Company _____

Address (No PO Box) _____

City_____ State _____ Zip _____

Payment enclosed _____ ❑ VISA ❑ MC Acc't # _____

Signature _____ Exact name on card _____

Check your local bookstore or software retailer for these and other bestselling titles, or call toll free:

800/332-7450
8:00 am - 6:00 pm EST

Satisfaction Survey

We'd like to hear from you!

First Name:_____ Last Name:_____

Street Address: _____

City: _____ State: _____ Zip: _____

E-Mail Address:_____

Daytime Telephone: (   ) _____

Book title: _____

Date product was purchased: Month _____Day _____Year__ ___Your Occupation:_____

Overall, how would you rate this book?
- ❏ Excellent   ❏ Very Good   ❏ Good
- ❏ Fair   ❏ Below Average   ❏ Poor

What did you like MOST about this book?

What did you like LEAST about this book?

Did you use the CD-ROM? If so, how did you use it to prepare for the exam?

Are you planning to take, or have you taken, the certification exam?

Did you use this book in conjunction with an Exam Cram book?

Would you use another Exam Prep or Exam Cram book to prepare for a Certification Exam?

Is there any subject or program you would like to see an Exam Prep or Exam Cram book for?

What is your level of computer expertise?
- ❏ Beginner   ❏ Intermediate   ❏ Advanced

Please describe your computer hardware:
Computer _____
Hard disk _____
3.5" disk drives_____
Video card _____
Monitor _____
Printer_____
Peripherals _____
Sound Board _____
CD-ROM_____

Where did you buy this book?
- ❏ Bookstore (name):_____
- ❏ Discount Store (name):_____
- ❏ Computer Store (name):_____
- ❏ Catalog (name):_____
- ❏ Other _____

What price did you pay for this book?

What influenced your purchase of this book
- ❏ Recommendation   ❏ Advertisement
- ❏ Magazine review   ❏ Store Display
- ❏ Mailing   ❏ Book's format
- ❏ Other _____

How many computer books do you buy each year?

Please send to:

Certification Insider Press ▪ c/o Course Technology ▪ One Main Street ▪ Cambridge, MA 02142

Certification Insider™ Press

International Thomson Publishing I(T)P®

WWW.CERTIFICATIONINSIDER.COM